THE LAST WORD

THE

LAST

WORD

The New York Times Book of Obituaries and Farewells
A Celebration of Unusual Lives

Edited by Marvin Siegel
Foreword by Russell Baker

WILLIAM MORROW AND COMPANY, INC. *New York*

It is the policy of William Morrow and Company, Inc., and its imprints and affiliates, recognizing the importance of preserving what has been written, to print the books we publish on acid-free paper, and we exert our best efforts to that end.

Library of Congress Cataloging-in-Publication Data

The last word : the New York Times book of obituaries and farewells :
    a celebration of unusual lives / edited by Marvin Siegel.— 1st ed.
        p.   cm.
    ISBN 0-688-15015-2
    1. Obituaries—United States. 2. Biography—20th century.
    3. United States—Biography.   I. Siegel, Marvin.
    CT220.L35   1997
    920.073—dc21   97-11960
                                                                        CIP

Printed in the United States of America

First Edition

    2   3   4   5   6   7   8   9   10

BOOK DESIGN BY LEAH S. CARLSON

Foreword

The obituaries are best left until last, right after the comics, or funny papers as they used to be called when the Katzenjammer Kids bedeviled the Captain while Jiggs humiliated Maggie by passing up the caviar for corned beef and cabbage. Katzenjammers and the Captain, Maggie and Jiggs, they are all gone now, gone with the Yellow Kid, Harold Teen, and Fearless Fosdick, but what lovely funny obituaries could be written about them, if only they had waited to die in the present age when obituaries are no longer required to be solemn as death.

Obituaries these days often provide the only pleasure to be had from the daily newspaper and should be savored slowly, saved for leisurely reading over the last cup of breakfast coffee. To plunge into them first thing, before having endured the rest of the day's news, is like eating the dessert before tackling a fried-liver dinner.

What blessed relief they provide after the front page—people butchering the neighbors' wives and children to serve God, right injustice, and display cultural superiority; science announcing that everything you love to do, eat, or drink will kill you. What calm satisfactions they afford after the hospital fumes of the sports pages with their pulled hamstrings, torn knee cartilage, dislocated shoulders, ripped tendons, broken collarbones, crushed vertebrae, shattered elbows, torn rotator cuffs. There the reader must also suffer muscular hulks whining that at $3 million per year they are shamefully underpaid.

Then, at last, the obituaries. Oases of calm in a world gone mad. Stimulants to sweet memories of better times, to philosophical reflection, to discovery of life's astonishing richness, variety, comedy, sadness, of the diverse infinitude of human imaginations it takes to make this world. What a lovely part of the paper to linger in.

This is not to say that there has been a revolution in obituary literature. It is a fact, however, that the obituary has become a fairly sophisticated journalistic form. Until recently editors treated it as drudge's work, little more than a punishment for reporters who misspelled the mayor's name or published the wrong date of the next Hadassah meeting.

Except for the greatest men—and they were almost always men— obituaries in those days were stitched up on a moment's notice by people who knew little or nothing about the deceased. As a rewrite man, I sometimes paused between six-alarm fires and gas-station stickups to churn out a five-hundred-word life of some freshly departed gentleman whose name until that moment had meant nothing to me.

At *The New York Times* these brief lives are now apt to be written by someone artful at distilling a life in a few paragraphs that try to show how this particular life differed from all others. Sometimes the reporter knows his subject personally, or has covered him, or worked with him. Some subjects are so obviously marked for obituary glory that reporters interview them while they are still peppy enough to laugh at the idea that they may actually die.

Alden Whitman, *The Times*'s famous obituary man who pioneered the advance interview, became so well known that people welcomed his requests to visit. What could it mean when Whitman came to call, except that you were destined to receive a full-dress obituary in *The Times*?

Only the most exalted can be sure of the full treatment. The wisdom of the newsroom has it that if you want a glittering obituary you must be careful in picking your time to die. There are good days for it, and there are bad days. Die on a day when war is breaking out or Presidents being assassinated or earthquakes wiping out the city, and you will be lucky to get an obituary at all. Even the most celebrated stars may end up, much abbreviated, far back in the paper.

Living too long may also damage your prospects. People worth a full column at the peak of their glory should not dawdle about going offstage unless they want their full column to shrivel down to a few skimpy inches. The general rule is that an obituary shrinks in proportion to the number of years its subject outlives the deeds that once made him catnip to editors. Fame has a short shelf life in America. By living too long, people often outlive their obituary appeal.

Not invariably, however. There are many old-timers so fascinating that their stories can never fail to delight. Once such is Wrong Way Corrigan, whose obituary appears in this book. Douglas Corrigan lived fifty-seven years after the single feat that earned him his obit, but what a feat it was! In a tiny overloaded plane held together with little more than baling wire and chewing gum, Corrigan took off from New York one morning for California (he said). Some twenty-eight hours later he landed in Ireland, saying that a faulty compass had betrayed him. Absolutely nobody believed him, and everybody instantly fell in love with him. He was ever after known to all as Wrong Way Corrigan. Doers of such deeds never lose the magic that makes for lovely obits.

This is a book about people who, like Douglas Corrigan, enriched the tale of life in the twentieth century without shaking the earth as, say, Churchill, FDR, Hitler, Stalin, and Mao did. The rule here is: no giants, thank you. Giants may have walked among us, manhandling history, but the nature of twentieth-century life has also been shaped by multitudes of whom most of us have never heard. A few of them appear in this book. Julian Hill is here. His name probably means nothing to you, yet he influenced our world more decisively than many Presidents; he "invented" nylon.

There is a prizefighter who got knocked down so many times he made boxing change its rules. The man who perfected popcorn is here. So are the first Miss America, the man who discovered Kitty Litter, and the fellow who claimed he created the zoot suit.

The zoot suit! Here is one of the serendipitous delights of the obituary page. You probably don't know about the zoot suit unless you are collecting Social Security, but those who are can tell you about it and maybe make you smile when they do.

Imagine trousers so baggy the knees could hide watermelons, imagine those trousers tapering to a cuff so tight that Cinderella could barely have slipped a foot through them. Imagine those trousers rising all the way up to the armpits. Imagine a jacket with shoulders that would have dwarfed Arnold Schwarzenegger. It was pinched in at the waist, then ballooned into a skirt that fell almost to the knees. Imagine lapels that went on forever. Those lapels alone had enough fabric in them to make an entire two-pants suit, complete with vest, in the style men wear today.

Accessories included a fedora wide as a beach umbrella and a key chain that dangled to the shoe tops. Yes, people actually wore zoot suits and wrote songs about wanting one "with a reet pleat, and a reave sleeve, and a drape shape, and a stuff cuff." Enough. I merely seek to demonstrate obituaries' power to set the mind rambling pleasurably back through time.

Aside from their nostalgic value and the pleasant instruction they provide in recent history, moreover, obituaries have a calming effect on the fevers with which Americans fling themselves at daily life. They encourage the long view and raise entertaining questions. For instance, is the world replacing the human resources being lost to death? Approximately 2,300,000 people now die each year in the United States. About 4,000,000 are born. But will the net gain in numbers—1,700,000—produce a net gain in talent, knowledge, initiative, creativity, imagination, skill? No one can know.

Death obviously produces a loss of knowledge. To cite the previous case, notice how death has reduced knowledge of the zoot suit. Consider the multitudes who once knew how to cook in an open fireplace, how to harness a horse to a buggy, how to hand-crank a tin lizzie on a freezing morning, how to butcher a hog, how to bake a cake from scratch, how to bank a coal furnace. Most of those multitudes have left us, and more depart every day.

More alarming is the loss of knowledge of old realities. Each day death takes another batch of people who experienced the time of Hitler and his war. This is a serious loss, for many of their replacements have been encouraged to think of Nazis as sources of entertainment. Sitcoms have portrayed them as comical bunglers. Film has spread a romantic taste for those smashing Nazi uniforms. Those beautiful ankle-length leather coats! Those fantastic red-and-black armbands!

Here is a case where death is robbing us of valuable knowledge. The Nazis were not entertaining, not comical, and not bunglers. They were fine soldiers and dangerous, terrifying, dreadful people. In their enchanting red, black, and leather, they were as romantic as the machine-gunning of a mass grave.

What will the annual crop of four million new people yield? It's a crap shoot. At the moment of birth, each tiny howler is all potential. He may become Socrates; she, Cleopatra. She may become Catherine the Great; he, Al Capone. Anything is possible at the instant these new people greet the world. Each new life begins an exploration to discover what its potential may be and whether this possibility can be fulfilled. When reading an obituary we have turned to the end of the book to see how it comes out. Death is the end of all that awesome potential that the infant brings into the world, and each obituary is a tale about how well someone fulfilled it.

The people celebrated here all fulfilled some kind of potential, though Socrates is, regrettably, absent. For better or worse so are Cleopatra, Catherine, and Capone. The lives that made the subjects of this book obit-worthy will not be told three thousand years from now by some blind Homer. Still, they were lives important to the fabric of American life in the century now passing. Almost all were born in the twentieth century, and a great many lived through a large percentage of it. While their lives may not define the twentieth century, they tell us an awful lot of what it was like to be a citizen of that mythic age.

Mythic? Of course mythic. Who since King Arthur has been more mythic than Babe Ruth, Sultan of Swat, consumer of hot dogs galore, and ladies' man par excellence? All have surely heard the mythic tale: how the Babe, touched at seeing a dying lad in the hospital, promised to hit a home run for him in the World Series. There was such a lad, believe it or not. His obituary is in this book. He died in 1990. Whether it was Babe Ruth who saved him for long life may seem doubtful, but only to prosaic drudges who hate mythology.

There is something mythic too about a woman who can turn chopped liver into a million-dollar business. Such a woman—"Sylvia Weinberger, 89; Built Thriving Business on Chopped Liver"—died in 1995. Her contribution to American cuisine is recorded herein.

So is the contribution of Richard Loo, who died for a living. American mythology is filled with dying. Half the stories we love and a great many of our films exploit the myth of dying. Sylvester Stallone stacks corpses by the cord. In the myth these voluminous deaths are almost always violent, and yet so painless, so harmless in fact, that the dead return to die again and again, and earn pretty good money doing it.

This has probably contributed to the twentieth-century American myth, widely believed by our child gunslingers, that death is not that big a deal. Mr. Loo's deaths, of course, were always welcome in movies in which he subjected decent American soldiers to barbaric cruelty while representing a foreign power which political correctness forbids me to identify in print.

While celebrating the virtues of obituaries, let me not overlook the pleasures of melancholy they stir. The older one becomes, the more aware he grows of his culture collapsing and another culture, increasingly alien to his own, replacing it. An example is the famous generational quarrel about music. People who had come of age when crooners and big-band swing dominated popular music felt angry, then bereft, as rock-and-roll took over the pop universe. Now there are so few left who remember Benny Goodman that they may feel like relics. When young and in charge of musical culture, they used to laugh at old crocks who held out for "Silver Threads Among the Gold." Now they have become the old crocks they used to laugh at.

Deaths of cultural heroes, like death of people one knows, will make even the young feel uncomfortably older. Because they have such slight experience of death, younger people are shaken forcefully by deaths of people their own age. This probably accounts for the passionate displays of youthful mourning for people like James Dean, Janis Joplin, Jimmy Hendrix, John Lennon, and Kurt Cobain, when these heroes of the youth culture were suddenly dead so young.

As youth turns into middle age, and middle age into grayness and failing vision, the cultural collapse accelerates. It becomes routine to arrive at the obituaries and find another part of your past has been moved out during the night. At a certain age the past starts vanishing so fast that it is impossible to keep track any longer of who is dead and who still alive.

Preparing for this essay I consulted the final pages of *The World Almanac*. Every year it publishes the names of many of the notable people who have died since the last edition. My almanac, picked off the shelf at random, listed 151 people who had died between the fall of 1990 and the fall of 1991. Of these, 82 had been, in some degree or other, meaningful to me. I have even known a few.

Gone in a single year were musicians like Aaron Copland, Charlie

Barnet, Claudio Arrau, Miles Davis, Rudolf Serkin, and Stan Getz; ac-
tresses like Eve Arden, Jean Arthur, Peggy Ashcroft, Joan Bennett, Eva
Le Gallienne, Joan Caufield, Colleen Dewhurst, and Lee Remick.

Writers? Angus Wilson, Dr. Seuss, Isaac Bashevis Singer, Howard
Nemerov, Sean O'Faolain, and Graham Greene. All dead in a single year.
Roald Dahl, too, and A. B. Guthrie, Jerzy Kosinski, Lawrence Durrell.

Martha Graham was gone. So was the great ballerina Margot Fonteyn. King Olav V of Norway, gone. Charles Goren, the bridge player.
Philadelphia's former mayor Frank Rizzo.

Going down that list was to see an entire world going, going, leaving
me behind. Red Grange, America's hero when I was in knee pants, died
that year. Old baseball players whose names I had collected way back
when baseball was fun: Luke Appling, Smokey Burgess, Bucky Walters,
Pete Runnels, James (Cool Papa) Bell. And Leo Durocher! The Lip himself. Thrown out of the game for the last time.

Armand Hammer, dead. Senator John Heinz, dead. Former Senators
John Sherman Cooper and John Tower, dead. Marietta Tree was dead;
and Robert Motherwell, who painted; and Arthur Murray, who never
succeeded in teaching me dancing in a hurry; and Edwin Land, the Po-
laroid inventor.

Klaus Barbie, "the Butcher of Lyons," dead at last, along with a
clutch of onetime television stars like Robert Cummings, John Daly, Redd
Foxx, George Gobel, Danny Thomas. Stars no more. Some awfully good
journalists went too: Homer Bigart, Douglas Kiker, Clark Mollenhoff,
Harry Reasoner.

Keye Luke, Charlie Chan's Number One Son, was gone, leaving me
with sticky memories of Saturday afternoons eating Jujubes in the Lord
Baltimore Theater. Gone too was Frank Capra, but not, mercifully, his
masterpiece, *It Happened One Night*.

The list runs on, leaving its residue of melancholy. Lisa Kirk, Happy
Chandler, Mary Martin, Mildred Dunnock. It is not an unpleasant melancholy, though. I am amused to realize that half the present population
of the United States will not recognize a single one of these names that
made up the environment in which my life once was lived. From their
viewpoint I am a creature from another planet.

This is rather a pleasant feeling. I have been to a place the young can never know. It provides a harmlessly spiteful pleasure to realize that, though my culture is vanishing, those creating the new culture can never know the pleasures of chewing Jujubes while Charlie Chan scolds Keye Luke, of falling in love with Margot Fonteyn at Covent Garden, and remembering the time when the Lip taught me the roguish joys of irreverence by preaching that nice guys finish last.

For long thoughts and easy living, it's the obituaries every time.

RUSSELL BAKER

Contents

Introduction

Obituaries tell us not only about who died, but who lived—and how. In reading them we discover that some of the lives that have had the most impact on our own were lived by men and women we have never heard of. Other lives have had an impact that is small or even nil, but seem to suggest something large or telling about what it is to be human in a particular place and time.

Few people had a greater impact on the way we live now than J. Presper Eckert, Jr., and John W. Mauchly, who are regarded as the principal developers of the computer. Their pioneering work changed the world forever, but when they died they were hardly household names, even in the households in which their invention has become a common appliance.

Maggie Kuhn, who had worked twenty-five years for the United Presbyterian Church in New York, commuting daily from her home in Philadelphia, reached the mandatory retirement age of sixty-five and was forced to leave her job in 1970. "They gave me a sewing machine," she recalled, "but I never opened it. I was too busy." Within months of her retirement, she was organizing the Gray Panther movement to campaign against age discrimination.

Anne Scheiber had no close family and no friends. She had no projects, no charities, did no volunteer work. She lived simply and cared nothing about possessions. After she retired a half century ago from the Internal Revenue Service, she devoted herself to the stock market, turning her $5,000 savings into a $22 million portfolio. She lived reclusively until she was 101, and when she died, she left her entire fortune to

Yeshiva University—an institution with which she had no direct contact—to set up scholarships for needy women students.

J. Prosper Eckert, Jr., and John W. Mauchly, Maggie Kuhn and Anne Scheiber, are among the hundred or so men and women you will meet in the pages of this celebratory book. They had little in common except that they were Americans and that when they died their lives were illuminated in obituaries and farewells in *The New York Times*. These brief and elegantly written accounts of their time on earth—however glorious or humble, happy or sad, long or short—evoke laughter or tears or wonder at the astonishing variety of human experience. At least that is what I thought when I chose them from among the thousands of obituaries and farewells that have appeared in *The Times* since the early 1980s.

The selection process was quite personal. I responded largely to storytelling that was lively, that stimulated or moved me or made me smile. I particularly enjoyed reading about the remarkable life of someone I had never encountered before and feeling that with his or her passing, the world had become a duller place. I also rooted for people who sustained hardships and came out all right in the end. I'm sure my reactions matched those of legions of *Times* readers who have discovered that the obit pages are the best read in the newspaper, invariably satisfying and even joyful on occasion. These readers understand that there's nothing morbid about a good obituary because a good obit is about life and not death.

Nowadays *Times* obits are not written under the old *nihil nisi bonum* code. It is no longer the burden of the obituary writer to eulogize "the loved one" with phrases like "Now she belongs to the ages..." and "He was a great humanitarian, a great American, and a great ventriloquist..." That is best left to speakers at funeral and memorial services.

The contemporary *Times* obituarist also seeks to avoid composing articles that are little more than extended lists of schools attended, degrees earned, honors won, jobs held, books published. However detailed and accurate such a list may be, it almost guarantees a certain dullness to a report and makes the reader wonder if the person they are reading about was *ever* alive.

While the obituarist is now permitted to use anecdotes and details that may not always reflect the subject in his best light, he is not issued a license to kill the subject a second time by settling scores, or gossiping, or permitting unnamed sources to assail someone's character. The law says that a dead man can not sue for libel, but a fair-minded obituarist seeks a moderate, reasonable tone anyway, remembering that among his readers will be bereaved family members and friends.

Alden Whitman, who wore a French policeman's cape and a neatly trimmed beard and who became well known in his day for the stylish obituaries he wrote for *The Times,* once tried to define the qualities of a good obit: "It is not a comprehensive biography, not a scholarly essay, not a tribute, not totally a personality sketch. A good obit has all the characteristics of a well-focused snapshot, the fuller the length the better. It does not disclose everything yet it conveys a vivid and accurate impression. If the snapshot is clear, the viewer gets a quick fix on the subject, his attainments, his shortcomings and his times. Composing the snapshot is much easier said than done; it takes time, patience, digging and, finally, a certain skill with words."

An anonymous writer for *The Economist* said in a 1994 article called "The Obituarist's Art" and subtitled "Lives After Death": "In acknowledging for a moment the passage of such lives, we remind ourselves that our world is shaped and colored not only by the actions of great leaders and the interplay of economic forces, but by countless lesser contributors, be they dancers, airmen, inventors, doctors, entertainers, architects, batsmen, thinkers, villains or mere players of walk-on parts in the scenes of history."

It is an objective of this book to introduce the reader to some of these splendid players. Every day *The Times* prepares and publishes obituaries of people of vast, acknowledged accomplishment—heads of state, generals, bishops, center fielders, movie stars. Despite our celebratory intent, you will not find such celebrities here.

Although many worthy deeds were performed by the people you will encounter in this book, not everyone had a strong character. Most were decent, but not all. Some were the life of the party, some never got out of the house. Some lived long enough to have led several lives. A few died before they really had much chance to live, but the manner of their departure compels us to ponder difficult questions about the sort of society we live in and the kind of people we have become.

If the people in this book seem interesting, perhaps that's partly because the men and women who wrote about them for *The Times* did so with great skill, style, and imagination. In some cases, the writers chosen to do the obituaries were specialists in the field and may even have interviewed their subjects over the years. Sometimes they were given time to do a substantial amount of research before they wrote their accounts in advance of their subjects' deaths. Their research may have involved reading the yellowing and brittle clippings in the newspaper's extensive and appropriately named Morgue, zipping through computerized information retrieval systems, leafing through books and periodicals in *The Times*'s library, consulting experts, talking to friends and foes, and even interviewing the subject himself with an obituary specifically in mind. Yes, there are many people of accomplishment who welcome the opportunity to discuss their lives and who are even amused about the prospect of being interviewed for an article they will never read, viewing it as a variant on attending their own funeral. "I have just been visited by the angel of death," Alger Hiss was heard to say after consenting to an interview with Alden Whitman.

After these "advance" obits are written, they are held in reserve until the day when the subject actually dies. Then new material may be added to bring the obituary up to date and fresh details provided about the cause of death, the place where it occurred, and the names of survivors. Marilyn Berger, whose vivid obituaries are one of the pleasures of reading *The Times*, reassures her subjects that the obituaries she prepares in advance remain so long on the shelf that she has become known around the office as "the angel of life."

There are other stories in this book that were written under deadline pressure in a matter of hours by reporters who did not know much if anything about their subjects until an editor approached their desks with folders of clippings and a telephone number or two. The results here are models of what talented and resourceful reporters can achieve.

The reader will also discover other pieces—interviews, columns, tributes, editorials—selected because they serve to illuminate a life. Some of these articles and essays were written for "The Lives They Lived" issues of *The New York Times Magazine*. Since 1994 the magazine has set out to consider notable lives that ended during that year. Often these contributions are by well-known people and take the form of personal reminiscences or ruminations inspired by someone's life or work.

In editing the obituaries and farewells that appear in this book, I have sometimes added or subtracted material here and there from the versions that originally appeared, chiefly to remove redundancies. I have also corrected a mistake or two and provided some amplification, using material that may have been unavailable to the writer when he was working under deadline pressure to prepare the obit. But I have tried to preserve the context and conventions and spirit in which the obituaries and farewells originally appeared.

I have done so in part because obituaries are indicators of social change. From what they will or will not mention it is sometimes possible for the discerning reader to detect shifts in the social landscape.

Before the 1960s, the obituary pages would underscore the importance of Pillars of the Community. An obituary of a minister—a white minister—would surely quote copiously from his sermons because it was likely that an account of his Sunday sermon appeared regularly in the newspaper every Monday over the years until his file in the Morgue bulged with such articles. No obituary of a Titan of Industry would be complete without a full-dress list of his clubs and his charities and his honorary degrees. Earlier in the century, the moral and philosophical pronouncements of a college president might be front-page news, and when his time came columns of obituary space were routinely devoted to him as befitted a man of wisdom and institutional pomp. Certainly there were short obits of wives and mothers, but if there weren't many about professional women, don't blame it on the newspaper, which only was functioning as society's mirror. Accounts of the passing of nonwhite people were rarer still.

There was a time not too long ago when survivors were reluctant to tell reporters that their loved one had died of cancer, convinced that a stigma was attached to the disease. Euphemisms sprang up as a consequence; such people usually died "after a long illness" or "after a short illness." Regular readers of obituaries learned to read between the lines and guessed "cancer."

A similar reluctance was felt more recently by many survivors of people who had died of complications resulting from AIDS. Now, AIDS is routinely cited as a cause of death and the numerous accounts of young people of promise and attainment who have died of the disease is a melancholy fact of today's obituary page.

In 1986, Allan M. Siegal, an assistant managing editor of *The Times* and the guardian of the newspaper's standards and style, issued guidelines on issues raised by AIDS.

"If we know or can reliably learn a specific cause of death, we print it," he instructed staff members. "If we lack the information, we try to learn it through all normal reporting methods. We never harass the bereaved, especially if the deceased was a reasonably private figure. In reporting the death of a well-known figure, we feel freer to press for details, but always within the bounds of compassion.

"If we reasonably suspect we are being given an incorrect cause of death, we omit it. If we suspect we are being given only a partial truth, we print it, with pointed and specific attribution to the source."

The acknowledgment of a relationship not bound by marriage is also a relatively new development in the writing of obituaries. The 1986 guidelines, which sought to align *The Times*'s obituary standards with the diversity of human relationships being experienced more openly in American society, permitted mention of a live-in companion of the same or opposite sex.

If the mention of a companion was to be made in the paragraph devoted to survivors, the companion was to be cited before or after the survivors ("Ms. Smith's longtime companion was John P. Manley. Survivors include Ms. Smith's parents, Mr. and Mrs....").

In that period, *The Times* elected to save the terms "survive" and "survivor" for their narrow technical sense only: relatives by blood or by legal sanction (marriage, adoption). The newspaper considered "companion" a more appropriate word than "lover," which, "when applied to private or semi-private people, suggests an invasion of intimacy. 'Lover' is acceptable in discussion of literary figures and highly public personalities whose relationships were also highly public."

In 1992 *The Times* decided "to embrace widespread usage and apply the terms 'survived' and 'survivor' to unmarried companions of the same sex or the opposite sex. In other words, when we learn that a companion is among the survivors, we list her or him as such, along with family members and without differentiation."

Another chapter may be evolving. There are many gay people who find the term "companion" offensive, maintaining that it is a designation that falls short of the "husband" or "wife" accorded heterosexual survivors and therefore relegates them to a second-class status.

One last observation about companions. Generally, *The Times* mentions an unmarried companion if associates of the deceased request it. If the reporter learns that family and/or friends are divided on the point, senior editors are asked to resolve the issue on a case-by-case basis. It can be a headache.

Although readers love obits and tell surveys the obituary page is a favorite part of the paper, many reporters usually hate to write them. It is a paradox that serious newspapers have always had to face.

Historically, the obit desk is thought to be a kind of Siberia of journalism, a distant and undesirable land occupied by newcomers too inexperienced to be trusted with a story about people who might talk back to them, grizzled old-timers playing out a frayed string, and hard cases exiled for some transgression until they show some signs of discipline or remorse. Even when none of these conditions is at work, the mythology is too ingrained in the newspaper culture to dispel.

In addition, most reporters are proud of their ability to perform under deadline pressure and addicted to the instant gratification of researching and writing a complicated story in hours and seeing that story appear in the newspaper the next day with their byline. Imagine the reaction of such a reporter when asked to write an advance obituary of a figure who might not die for days or weeks or months or even, God forbid, years. Imagine his state of mind when he realizes that if the subject is lucky—and the writer's bad luck continues—he might not even be around to see the obit in print with his byline.

Fortunately, there is a talented pool of reporters who recognize the creative challenges and pleasures of capturing a life in a thousand words, of writing a story with a beginning, middle, and end. For these reporters the joy of writing obits is one of the best-kept secrets in journalism. *The Times* has a rich number of such obituarists and it is good to be able to acknowledge the contributions of a staff that produces quality work day in and day out, often without the recognition it deserves: Marilyn Berger, David Binder, Panny King, Enid Nemy, Holcomb B. Noble, Eric Pace, Wolfgang Saxon, Richard Severo, Norma Sosa, and Robert McG. Thomas, Jr.

I wish to thank some colleagues for their invaluable assistance and encouragement in preparing this book: Allan M. Siegal, an assistant managing editor of *The Times*; Jack Rosenthal, editor of *The New York Times Magazine*; Mitchel Levitas, editorial director, Book Development; Doreen Weisenhaus, editor of "The Lives They Lived" issues of the magazine; David W. Dunlap, reporter; Pam Gubitosi, business manager; Tom Holcomb, staff assistant to the technology editor; Charles Robinson, director of Information Services; Gloria Bell, administrator; Linda Amster, research manager, and Judith Greenfeld and Linda Lake, researchers.

I also wish to express appreciation to Rebecca Goodhart, my editor at William Morrow and Company, for her many helpful suggestions. My thanks also to the novelist Mary Gordon and Berny Horowitz for their rigorous reading of the manuscript and to Josh Siegel for his enthusiasm and encouragement.

And permit me an expression of deep respect for the talents and compassion of the writers of these wonderful pieces.

MARVIN SIEGEL

'Tis an old well-known proverb of mankind,
"You cannot tell men's fortunes till they die,
In any case, if they be good or bad."

Sophocles, Trachiniae

Golden lads and girls all must,
As chimney-sweepers, come to dust.

Shakespeare, Cymbeline

[The] growing good of the world is partly
dependent on unhistoric acts; and that things
are not so ill with you and me as they might
have been is half-owing to the number who lived
faithfully a hidden life, and rest in unvisited tombs.

George Eliot, Middlemarch

So attention must be paid.

Arthur Miller, Death of a Salesman

Life Could Be a Doo-wop Dream

JIMMY KEYES

By David Gonzalez

A hit parade of doo-wop dignitaries streamed up to Jimmy Keyes's coffin, gray-haired but still sharp in their shades, Ban-Lon shirts, and white patent leather shoes. It was time to dedicate a special request. "If we don't sing 'Sh-Boom,' " said Arthur Crier, a onetime member of the Chimes, "he'll come out of there!"

As his friends knew, you could never put anything past Mr. Keyes, who helped write "Sh-Boom," the song that in 1954 made his all-black sextet, the Chords, the first rhythm-and-blues group to crack the pop music Top 10. And as any doo-wop diehard will attest, the success of "Sh-Boom" led some music critics to consider it the first rock-and-roll hit.

With a few finger snaps, the dimly lit Ortiz Funeral Home on Westchester Avenue in the Bronx became a time machine in which the singers embraced their youth with the kind of gusto that carried Mr. Keyes through sixty-five years of life. In a magical moment, as fleeting as the harmonies that once drifted into the night air decades ago, their strong voices accompanied him on his final journey.

"Life could be a dream," they crooned, as mourning gave way to clapping and swaying, *"if I could take you up to paradise up above."*

Before there was Elvis, Jerry Lee, or a dozen others with guitars and pompadours, there was the Chords. Although their tune was the original crossover dream, a musical bridge between black and white worlds, lasting fame and success proved elusive for Mr. Keyes, at least by conventional bottom-line standards. But he took a lasting pride in being first at the gate when black and white musical cultures were beginning to sculpt the sound of rock.

"Sh-Boom," written in the back of a Buick convertible parked on a Bronx street, was a mantra for Mr. Keyes, who died after an operation on an aneurysm. His friends remembered him as elegant and undaunted to the end, rehearsing his latest lineup and taking to the road even as his health declined, confident that there was still room on the charts for just one more hit.

It is a feeling shared by members of the Cadillacs, Harptones, Tokens, Wrens, Chantels, and Vocaleers, who returned to the borough that gave birth to countless doo-wop wonders. It was not about nostalgia. It was about hope. " 'Sh-Boom' was a song about what could possibly be— that if we gave a little effort, life wouldn't be so hard," said Sammy Fain, a childhood friend of Mr. Keyes's who sang with the Limelighters and the Mellows. "That's why we don't want the music to die. If it does, we lose that innocence we had as teenagers before we learned about war, politics, and all that stuff."

Mr. Keyes came to the Bronx in the mid 1940s, a slim, good-looking Kentucky kid who might have been a painter had it not been for the lure of the vocal groups that commanded center stage on the street corners and schoolyards of his Morrisania neighborhood. Gifted with a clear voice, he fell in with Claude and Carl Feaster, two brothers who would form the core of the Chords.

Mr. Crier remembered that when "Sh-Boom" was released, he and Mr. Keyes would go to Crotona Park, where they pumped themselves up with pushups and play boxing, all the while wondering what the future would hold. Within days, he said, he saw the Chords return to the neighborhood smiling triumphantly and sporting new clothes. His group, and others, soon followed, as white disc jockeys and their teenage listeners discovered the meld of jazz and rhythm-and-blues that was doo-wop.

"They opened the door," Mr. Crier said of the Chords.

It would prove to be a revolving door, as record companies took the songs and repackaged them with matinee-idol white singers. For many black musicians, a lifetime of day jobs lay ahead. Mr. Keyes made a living as a handyman and manufacturer of Afro combs until he re-formed the group in the 1980s.

Yet among the doo-wop faithful, race was not an issue. "We respect these artists, because they deserve it and because they did not get respect in the fifties," said Charlie Rocco, a member of Yesterday's News, an a cappella group that recently shared the stage in Washington with the Chords, the Cadillacs, and the Coasters. "Outside, it's like a war, but there is no color line when it comes to doo-wop."

Mr. Keyes wasn't bitter about the money; unlike many other black performers of his day, he and the other members of the group got songwriting credit and continued to receive royalties. But Buddy McRae, an original member of the group who retired from it years ago, said his friend was irked by the lack of recognition. "That's why he kept the group going," Mr. McRae said. "He felt a sense of letdown. He hoped somebody would be wise enough to say these were the guys who helped build the music business to the million-dollar business that it is."

Mickey Collier, for one, vowed never to forget. A member of the group since 1980, he recently re-joined after having an operation for cancer in his leg. The doctors said he would have to use a wheelchair. Mr. Keyes told him to get on crutches and join the group onstage, even if he had to hop instead of dance.

"Nothing changes," he vowed, leaning on his crutches before the coffin. "The group is going to go on and Jimmy Keyes's name is going to go at the top of the group. Nobody in this group is going to let Jimmy down."

Nobody would, at least that night. When the singers belted out the lyrics, the mood transformed itself in seconds, with sobs and laughter mixing with bips, booms, and dingdongs.

"Life could be a dream, if I could spend my whole life loving you."

This was a rock-and-roll revival in every sense.

"Sweetheart hello, hello again."

With a bow to their friend, the chorus dissolved into grins and hugs. "He's loving it!" Mr. Crier said. "He's checking us out!"

If so, he only had to look outside the funeral parlor, where the Westchester Avenue el rumbled overhead, cars sped by, and raindrops fell. A woman cradled her child and sang a tender lyric.

The sounds of the city blended with a serenade from the soul.

Just like 1954.

July 27, 1995

The Calvin Klein of Space

RUSSELL COLLEY

By Robert McG. Thomas, Jr.

Russell Colley, a thwarted women's fashion designer who used his consolation career as a mechanical engineer to become the Calvin Klein of space wear, died at the Ohio Masonic Home in Springfield, Ohio. He was ninety-seven and known to a generation of astronauts as the father of the space suit.

By the time the United States began its efforts at manned space flight in the 1950s, Mr. Colley, a longtime engineer with the B. F. Goodrich Company in Akron, Ohio, was an old hand at outfitting high-altitude aviators. Indeed, he had earned his sobriquet as the father of the space suit in the 1930s when he worked closely with the visionary barnstorming aviator Wiley Post in designing the pressurized man-from-Mars suit that Post used in setting high-altitude flying records. A later modification by Mr. Colley for navy pilots in World War II became the basis for the series of suits he helped design for the Mercury astronauts.

Mr. Colley, whose engineering feats ranged far beyond fashions for outer space, obtained some sixty-five patents during his thirty-four-year Goodrich career, among them one for the rubberized pneumatic de-icer still used to clear ice from airplane wings and one for the Rivnut, a device that allows a single worker to apply rivets to airplane wings, something that would be impossible under traditional riveting methods requiring a second worker positioned on the far side of riveted material.

A native of Stoneham, Massachusetts, where his father operated a pharmacy, Mr. Colley was both artistically and mechanically inclined as a child, but for all the model airplanes he made in his youth, it was not until he got to high school that he figured out what he wanted to do with his life. But when he announced that his dream was to become a designer of women's fashions, his teacher was so aghast at the notion of a boy aspiring to such a career that Mr. Colley was lucky there was no school psychologist to send him to. Instead, he was shooed to a mechanical-drawing class, where he discovered the joys of finding inventive solutions to tough problems, something that would become his specialty at Goodrich.

Mr. Colley, who studied at the Wentworth Institute of Mechanical Engineering in Massachusetts, held a series of jobs in Ohio before joining Goodrich in 1928.

Four years later he invented the de-icer. The test pilot was so skeptical that he thought it advisable to have the inventor put his life on the line during the first test flight, a hop from Cleveland to Buffalo through a severe winter storm. Mr. Colley obliged, even though he had to sit on an orange crate in the cramped mail compartment of the single-seat Martin biplane. "It was a day when even the ducks were walking," Mr. Colley later recalled. "Nobody else was stupid enough to be up in the air." The de-icers worked perfectly, however, and pilot and inventor made it safely through the storm.

It was two years after that, in 1934, that Mr. Colley was assigned to satisfy Post's request for a pressurized rubber suit that would allow him to fly well above the forty-thousand-foot level, where the air pressure becomes so low that an unprotected flier would simply explode. Although pressurized clothing had been used by mountain climbers since the early 1900s and had become a staple of science fiction, Mr. Colley was charting new territory in designing a suit capable of protecting a pilot during extended periods of high-altitude flight.

After several failures, he came up with a design that owed so much to science fiction that when Post was once forced to make an emergency landing, the first person he encountered after he walked away from his stricken aircraft almost passed out from fright thinking the creature wearing an aluminum version of a diver's helmet must surely have arrived from Mars. The specter must have been especially frightening because Mr. Colley's customized head gear featured an off-center viewing port tailored to the one-eyed Post's good eye.

As a fashion designer for outer space, Mr. Colley was a hands-on expert. He ran up part of the Post flight suit at his home using his wife Dorothy's sewing machine, while Post passed his time teaching the Colleys' ten-year-old daughter, Barbara, how to play craps—so well, in fact, that, as she later recalled, when he left he signed an I.O.U. "for 50,000" without specifying 50,000 what.

A year later, before his final, fatal flight, she said, Post called and told her he planned to pay off in kisses.

The development of pressurized cabins made pressurized suits unnecessary until the space program created a new need. Then Mr. Colley came through once again, tackling a series of difficult technological problems with his usual flair, among other things using the movement of a tomato worm to solve a problem of flexibility.

Like the famous designers of the Yale Bowl who were so taken with their engineering feat that it was not until seventy thousand spectators showed up for the first game that they remembered they had not provided rest rooms, Mr. Colley and his colleagues had one famous lapse, much to the embarrassment of the astronaut Alan Shepard, who had to spend so much time testing one suit that—well, later models have included built-in facilities.

Mr. Colley, who designed gloves for John Glenn's first orbital flight containing tiny light bulbs in the fingertips, was given the National Aeronautic and Space Administration's highest honor for civilians in 1994.

By then he had long been living in retirement, such as retirement was for a man who continued to make his own skis and archery equipment in his basement shop and who spent his last years turning out a series of watercolors that gained him recognition as one of northeastern Ohio's most acclaimed artists.

Mr. Colley's wife died several years ago. He is survived by his daughter, Barbara Fuldine of Pinehurst, North Carolina, two grandchildren, and a great-grandchild.

February 8, 1996

She Lit 22 Million Candles

ANNE SCHEIBER

By David Gonzalez

Anne Scheiber lived quietly in her rent-stabilized studio apartment on West Fifty-sixth Street that was bereft of luxuries: Paint was peeling, the furniture was old, and dust covered the bookcases. She walked everywhere, often in the same black coat and matronly hat.

Ben Clark, her lawyer, said she never had a sweetheart and seldom went out, except to visit her broker. She had left the Internal Revenue Service in 1944, investing her five-thousand-dollar savings in the stock market with the same studiousness she had applied to auditing tax returns. "She did nothing but study the market," he said. "When you add it all up, she was the most unusual person I ever knew in my life."

Over the next half century, she parlayed that $5,000 into a portfolio that included holdings in Coca-Cola, Paramount, Schering-Plough, and more than a hundred other stocks that by her death last January at the age of 101 were worth about $22 million.

Living thriftily and anonymously in a city of high rollers, she allowed herself only one final act of big spending. In her will she left that $22 million to Yeshiva University, a school she never attended, to help students she never met.

University officials had never heard of her, and at first they thought her lawyer's request for a meeting was a nuisance call. But their skepticism vanished in a blink when they learned of Ms. Scheiber's bequest, the second largest in their university's history.

Yeshiva officials will announce at their Hanukkah Convocation the establishment of the Anne Scheiber Scholarship and Loan Awards. Her gift will help bright and needy women attending Yeshiva's Stern College for Women and the Albert Einstein College of Medicine.

Her few friends, namely her lawyer and stockbroker, said the endowment was born of her desire to help Jewish women battle the kind of discrimination she felt she had encountered during twenty-three years with the IRS. While she served with distinction, she toiled without promotion. Still, when she retired in 1944 she had audited enough returns to know the big money was in stocks. She invested eagerly and wisely, and as her fortune grew, so did her desire to make sure other women wouldn't be shortchanged.

"The Torah says that he who teaches his friend's son Torah, it is as if he gave birth to him," said Dr. Norman Lamm, the president of Yeshiva University. "Here's a woman who for 101 years was childless and now becomes a mother to a whole community. Not only now, but for generations to come."

Ms. Scheiber had known tough times as a child in turn-of-the-century Brooklyn. Her father died young, after suffering substantial losses on his property holdings. Her mother sold real estate to support the family and Ms. Scheiber went to secretarial school and took a bookkeeping job. She later attended law school in Washington, D.C., and joined the IRS as an estate auditor.

Mr. Clark said that while she led her office in scouring returns for underpayments, she never made more than four thousand dollars a year, and never received a promotion. "She was always on top of production," he said. "Yet in her mind, women always got the short end of the stick."

In retirement, she embarked on her investment career with boundless vigor. Analyzing earnings reports, management philosophy, and product quality, she bought into a variety of industrial companies and other blue chips. Long interested in movie studios, she bought an array of entertainment stocks, devouring the *Variety* box-office results the way others followed celebrity gossip.

Her investment strategies were simple, if not old-fashioned. Forget about market highs and lows on any given day, month or year. Reinvest your dividends. Hang tough and seldom sell. "She was never looking for a quick buck," said William Fay, her broker at Merrill Lynch. "Her whole idea was to get performance on a long-term basis. She felt over the long run the value would grow." Did it ever.

"You think Warren Buffett, you know, that guy, was good at this sort of thing?" said Mr. Clark. "She ran rings around Warren Buffett."

Mr. Clark almost got the runaround earlier in the year when he tried to meet with Yeshiva's president after Ms. Scheiber's death. "My secretary said, 'How do we avoid him?' " Dr. Lamm recalled. "Lawyers usually call for harassment, summonses, or things of that sort." Instead, he was given a handwritten letter from Ms. Scheiber, in which she outlined her life, her belief in helping other women, and her desire to give nearly all her fortune to Yeshiva. Nobody at the university had heard of her.

The gift comes at a time when more women than ever are enrolling at Yeshiva, despite the challenge faced by their families in coming up with tuition.

The $22 million gift also comes at Hanukkah, a time when Jews commemorate another miracle, the burning of the menorah oil for eight days instead of one, as the Maccabees rededicated the temple in Jerusalem after retaking it from the Seleucid Greeks.

This year, Dr. Lamm and others will celebrate enlightenment and illumination.

"She lit many candles for us," said Dr. Lamm. "Twenty-two million instead of eight."

December 2, 1995

Harvard's Mr. Chips

JOHN H. FINLEY, JR.

By Robert McG. Thomas, Jr.

John H. Finley, Jr., the classicist who brought ancient Greece alive and taught a generation of Harvard men how to live, died at Exeter Health Care Center in Exeter, New Hampshire. He was ninety-one and a resident of Tamworth, New Hampshire.

There were close to three hundred years of Harvard before he came along, and the university has continued for more than a decade since he left. But almost from the moment he joined the faculty in 1933 until one thousand students, including the university president, gave him two standing ovations at his final lecture in 1976, John H. Finley, Jr., was the embodiment of Harvard. He wrote the Harvard book. He taught the Harvard course. He lived the Harvard life.

As the principal author of *General Education in a Free Society*, in 1946, Professor Finley laid down the principles—and the handful of required courses—that governed education at Harvard until the 1980s.

None of the courses was more popular than Humanities 103—the Great Age of Athens—in which Professor Finley interpreted Homer, explained Plato, and defended Aristotle with a mesmerizing delivery that took wing on unexpected flights of image and notion. "A single three-by-five card," his son, John III, said, "would last him an entire lecture."

He was born in New York City at a time when his father, a renowned educator who later became the editorial page editor of *The New York Times*, was serving as president of City College, and he came to Greek early. As a child he would carry a Greek New Testament to church every Sunday to check on the adequacy of the King James version.

A 1925 magna cum laude graduate of Harvard, he continued his studies of Greek literature abroad before obtaining his doctorate from Harvard in 1933, becoming an associate professor that fall and a full professor in 1944.

But for all his achievements at the lectern and for all his scholarly accomplishments, including books on Thucydides and other Greek luminaries, it was in the dining hall and sitting rooms of Eliot House, one of Harvard's residential complexes, that Professor Finley put his most lasting imprint on a generation of students.

As master of Eliot House from 1941 to 1968, Professor Finley took far more pains than his fellow housemasters in evaluating the freshmen who applied to live there for their last three years. He not only studied each résumé carefully and interviewed every applicant, he also memorized their names and advised them on life's perils. The purpose of college, he would tell them, was to reduce the time they spent thinking about women from 80 percent to 60 percent. For those who found this a daunting challenge, he would propose a list of other alternative obsessions—football, whiskey, poker, perhaps even reading a book.

His goal, his son recalled, was the well-rounded man, one who combined intelligence with a range of social and other skills, especially those that ran to athletic prowess. "Sports were very important to him," his son said, noting that Eliot House invariably won the most intramural competitions.

The care he took paid off academically, too. During a year Professor Finley spent as a visiting professor at Oxford, his son recalled, he was pleased to note that something like twelve of the eighteen Rhodes scholars in attendance had come from Harvard and that eleven of those twelve had come from Eliot House.

"One of the great pleasures of university life," he once said, "is the cheerful company of the young." As a traditionalist, however, Professor Finley drew the line at admitting women, saying: "I'm not quite sure people want to have crystalline laughter falling like a waterfall down each entryway of the house at all hours. I should think it would be a little disturbing if you were taking advanced organic chemistry."

A short, trim man, Professor Finley said his soul was shaped like a shoehorn, the result of getting so many Harvard men into jobs and academic positions for which they did not immediately seem all that qualified. He once asked, "How should I have known that God as humorist had in store for me the letter of recommendation as an art form?"

In addition to his son, he is survived by a daughter, Corrina Hammond of Exeter, New Hampshire, and five grandchildren.

June 14, 1995

Cat Owners' Best Friend

EDWARD LOWE

By Robert McG. Thomas, Jr.

Edward Lowe, whose accidental discovery of a product he called Kitty Litter made cats more welcome household company and created a half-billion-dollar industry, died at a hospital in Sarasota, Florida. He was seventy-five and had divided his time between homes in Arcadia, Florida, and Cassopolis, Michigan. His son, Tom, said the cause was complications from surgery for cerebral hemorrhage.

Cats have been domesticated since ancient Egypt, but until a fateful January day in 1947, those who kept them indoors full-time paid a heavy price. For all their vaunted obsession with paw-licking cleanliness, cats, whose constitutions were adapted for arid desert climes, make such an efficient use of water that they produce a highly concentrated urine that is one of the most noxious effluences of the animal kingdom. Boxes filled with sand, sawdust, or wood shavings provided a measure of relief from the resulting stench, but not enough to make cats particularly welcome in discriminating homes.

In a story he always relished telling, that began to change in 1947, when Mr. Lowe, a twenty-seven-year-old navy veteran who had been working in his father's sawdust business, received a visit from a cat-loving Cassopolis neighbor named Kaye Draper, whose sandbox had frozen. She asked Mr. Lowe for some sawdust, but on a sudden inspiration he suggested she try something he had in the trunk of his car, a bag of kiln-dried granulated clay, a highly absorbent mineral that his father, who sold sawdust to factories to sop up grease spills, had begun offering as a fireproof alternative.

When Ms. Draper came back a few days later asking for more, Mr.

Lowe thought he might be onto something. To find out for sure, he took ten sacks, carefully wrote the words "Kitty Litter" on the sides and filled them each with five pounds of the granules. When his suggestion that they be sold at a local store to cat owners for sixty-five cents—at a time when sand was selling at a penny a pound—drew a hoot, Mr. Lowe suggested they be given away. When the customers returned asking for "Kitty Litter" by name, a business and a brand were born.

It took a while, but Mr. Lowe, who began by filling his '43 Chevy coupe with hand-filled bags of Kitty Litter and visiting pet stores and cat shows, soon had a booming business.

Adapting clay for use as a cat box litter made Mr. Lowe a millionaire many times over, in part because it has been credited with giving dogs a rival in American homes. Indeed, in 1985 cats passed dogs as the most popular American pets, and according to a survey by the Pet Industry Advisory Council, in 1994 there were 54.2 million pet dogs in the country and 63 million cats, enough to consume $600 million to $700 million worth of clay-based cat box litter, perhaps a third of it Kitty Litter and subsidiary brands created by Mr. Lowe.

He spent lavishly on research to maintain his market position in the highly competitive industry he had created. But Mr. Lowe, who recalled growing up so poor his family burned corncobs for heat and had no indoor toilet, spent even more lavishly as a conspicuous consumer, acquiring among other things, twenty-two homes, a seventy-two-foot yacht, a stable of quarter horses, a private railroad, and an entire Michigan town.

Material success had its personal price, however, as became evident in 1984, when Mr. Lowe dismissed his four children and his three sons-in-law from their company positions, saying they were conspiring to take over the company by having him declared incompetent as an alcoholic. Mr. Lowe, who denied he had a serious drinking problem, said his three daughters had joined Al-Anon, an organization for children of alcoholics, as a ruse. The daughters said they were simply trying to understand what they regarded as his strange behavior.

In part to help other entrepreneurs avoid similar family problems, Mr. Lowe created the Edward Lowe Foundation, which sponsors a variety of programs at his three-thousand-acre estate in southwestern Michigan. He sold his Kitty Litter operation for $200 million plus stock in 1990.

It is now part of the Ralston Purina Company. And after a long, bitter estrangement, Mr. Lowe softened his views toward his family in his last few years, his son said.

In addition to his son, Tom, of Granger, Indiana, Mr. Lowe, who was divorced in 1974, is survived by his second wife, Darlene; three daughters, Marilyn Miller of South Bend, Indiana, Kathy Petersen of Washington, D.C., and Marcia O'Neil of Naples, Florida; a sister, Meredith Murray of Fort Myers, Florida, and twelve grandchildren.

October 6, 1995

A Fighter Pilot's Final Flight

FRANK D. GALLION

By Michael Winerip

Flight Officer Frank D. Gallion was buried in Millersburg, Ohio, near his home in Amish country today, Memorial Day, more than fifty-two years after his P-47 Thunderbolt fighter plane was downed by German machine-gun fire and crashed into the waters of the Zuider Zee.

The twenty-nine-year-old pilot was reported missing on November 3, 1943, his body never found. Then last year the propeller of a Dutch dredging ship hit something, and when a diver went down to investigate, there, in ten feet of water, was the skeleton of Flight Officer Gallion, almost intact, seated in the cockpit of his plane.

At precisely 1:00 P.M. in a pouring rain, an honor guard from Fort Knox, Kentucky, placed a container smaller than a shoe box holding Flight Officer Gallion's ashes in the back of a long silver hearse. Then a procession of twenty cars snaked past the Holmes County Courthouse and war memorial, which look exactly as they did when Frank Gallion and his brother Ottmar were boys swimming in Saps Run Creek, and on past places that those country boys could never have imagined, like the Wal-Mart and Pizza Hut on State Road 83.

As the procession climbed the last hill before Pleasant Grove Cemetery, Maj. David Deckard, the casualty officer who had organized the ceremony, worried that there would be "more press and army than mourners." But then his car reached the hill's crest, and there, parked along the road to the cemetery, were cars and pickups, Suburbans and minivans, as far as the eye could see, and the major was reminded of the strong pull that World War II still holds for Americans.

Of the more than sixteen million Americans who served in the military in World War II, the remains of about 78,700 have never been recovered. Each year 10 to 20, like those of Flight Officer Gallion, are found by farmers in France or the Netherlands or the South Pacific, by workers for water authorities or highway departments. "Sometimes they'll recover a B-17 or B-29 and we'll get back eight or nine in one aircraft," said Harold Campbell, the chief of disposition for army casualty and memorial affairs operations.

Flight Officer Gallion, a member of the 334th Fighter Squadron, had taken off from England that November day in 1943 to escort American B-17 bombers, part of a five hundred-plane attack force that passed over the Netherlands on its way to a military base in Wilhelmshaven, Germany.

Two weeks later his wife, Phyllis, received a seventeen-word cable saying that he was missing in action. Notice that he was MIA appeared in the *Holmes County Farmer-Hub*. In August 1945, his mother placed a headstone for Flight Officer Gallion in Pleasant Grove Cemetery, but his only surviving brother, Ottmar, now seventy-eight, said that for years he had wondered whether Frank had been taken prisoner by the Germans and died in a camp.

As the decades passed, family members would periodically make inquiries to Dutch and American officials, with no luck. In 1990, Phyllis Gallion died. She had never remarried, nor had children, but had worked much of her life as a hairdresser. Until her mother-in-law's death in the late 1960s, Phyllis would visit her once a year. After that, the Gallion family lost track of her.

In early 1995 came word of the Dutch dredging company's find about a quarter of a mile into the Zuider Zee, fifty miles north of Amsterdam. Gary Gallion, a forty-three-year-old nephew, said the Dutch were able to identify his uncle by his dog tags and a serial number on the plane. After a ceremony in the Netherlands attended by family members, the remains were flown to the army's central identification laboratory in Hawaii.

Several weeks ago, Major Deckard, the casualty officer, drove the "artifacts" recovered from the plane to Gary Gallion's home in this village of thirty-two hundred about fifty miles southwest of Akron. "It's not pretty stuff," the major told the nephew and other family members as he spread the muddy items on top of the kitchen table. "But it is the facts of your uncle." There were scraps of fabric, buttons, a rusted Zippo lighter, a brass compass, a fishing lure that may have been part of a survival kit, a pant cuff, and two boot soles marked size 10E. "Frank had thick ankles," Ottmar Gallion said.

Before the funeral began, people asked what Frank had been like, and Ottmar, who had earned a living as a laborer and salesman, seemed to have trouble remembering so far back. Mainly he spoke of their hiking trips, their swimming together in the creek, and their competitiveness. Ottmar Gallion had spent the war guarding German prisoners in Oklahoma, and he was asked if perhaps Frank, who had gone to Canada in 1941 to join up early, had been the more adventurous brother. "Oh, I wouldn't say so," he replied. "I was the only one around here who would dive off the bridge into the river."

At the graveside service in the unrelenting rain there were women and children, Vietnam veterans like Jim Buehler, World War II veterans like Francis Emerick and Ted Anielski, Robert Spahr, a villager, who grew up next door to the Gallions, and Flight Officer Gallion's only surviving sister, Clela Joy Davis, eighty-eight, who lives nearby in the Walnut Creek nursing home. Family members sat in three rows under a tent facing the box of ashes atop a table.

There were several speakers, including an army chaplain, the minister from the family's Seventh Day Adventist Church, and Representative Ralph Regula, the area's congressman. Ottmar Gallion spoke for the family. He said there was relief and closure in finding how his brother died. "It was a clean kill," he said. "He was out of his misery, and from then on, the thing was in God's hands."

Many times in recent weeks, Ottmar Gallion had said he wasn't saddened; it was all so long ago. But by the conclusion of his speech, his voice was barely audible, and when he sat down, he blew his nose.

At the end there was a twenty-one-gun salute and a bugler blowing taps, then 1st Lt. William J. Duggan III presented Ottmar Gallion with an American flag.

Afterward, the whole village was invited to American Legion Post 192 in downtown Millersburg. "They're going to have a nice little spread," Major Deckard said.

May 28, 1996

Eve in the Garden of Aspen

ELIZABETH PAEPCKE

The Chicago philanthropist ELIZABETH NITZE PAEPCKE *(pronounced PEP-key), who died at the age of ninety-one of complications from a head injury she suffered in a fall in June 1994, helped transform Aspen from a largely abandoned nineteenth-century Colorado mining town into a world-famous resort. But her vision was more idealistic than commercial. With her husband, Walter, who headed the Container Corporation of America, she founded the Aspen Institute and the Aspen Music Festival, which attracted legions of writers, composers, scientists, and intellectuals to share their work. But by the end of Mrs. Paepcke's life Aspen had changed and become a Hollywood playground; her next-door neighbor was Jack Nicholson.*

By Ted Conover

Desperate to divert a houseful of guests after a plumbing disaster at her Colorado ranch in 1939, Elizabeth Paepcke acted on a tip and led her friends on a ski outing to the lapsed silver-mining town of Aspen. They hitched a ride partway up Aspen Mountain in the back of a truck filled with the area's last mining crew, pulled sealskins over their skis for traction, and proceeded to herringbone uphill for five hours. "At the top, we halted in frozen admiration," Mrs. Paepcke wrote in a memoir. "In all that landscape of rock, snow, and ice, there was neither print of animal nor track of man. We were alone as though the world had just been created and we its first inhabitants."

Today, the residents of a reborn Aspen cherish a creation story that begins with Elizabeth Paepcke on that frozen peak. Upon returning in

1945 with her husband, Walter, a Chicago industrialist, the two saw in Aspen's superb setting and shuttered Victorian houses the possibility of a new Chautauqua. Assisted by her brother, the arms-control adviser Paul Nitze, and friends like Robert Hutchins, president of the University of Chicago, and the philosopher Mortimer Adler, the Paepckes soon laid the foundation for a ski town with a highbrow cultural life—an "Athens of the West," Mr. Adler liked to call it.

The Aspen idea, in Walter's words, was to create a place "for man's complete life ... where he can profit by healthy, physical recreation, with facilities at hand for his enjoyment of art, music, and education." The purity of their original vision and the continuing despoliation of the garden by developers and pleasure seekers make the Paepckes seem, to present-day Aspenites, a lot like Adam and Eve.

Elizabeth, who had studied painting at the Art Institute of Chicago, was a pillar of that city's cultural life and worked as a decorator and theater designer—and teacher to her husband. When Walter was contemplating an advertising campaign for the Container Corporation, Elizabeth pushed him to use distinguished designers instead of commercial artists. The resulting Great Ideas of Western Man campaign became an advertising milestone. The two combined culture and commerce again in Mortimer Adler's first Great Books group (the Fat Man's Group it was called, for all the prominent business members) and later in the Aspen Institute.

"In Aspen, I met this beautiful lady in her eighties who looked like Katharine Hepburn," Andy Warhol wrote in 1985. Her beauty—she had cobalt blue eyes and a dazzling smile—was the first thing people noticed about Elizabeth Paepcke, but references to it vexed her. "She thought it was shallow," said Merrill Ford, a longtime friend. Instead, Elizabeth Paepcke—or Pussy, as her grandmother and then everyone else called her—loved ideas and art and those who cared about them. And though she was known as the consummate gracious lady, she was equally willful.

"Her style was to hold strong opinions and to raise expectations to her standard," wrote David McLaughlin, the Aspen Institute chairman, in a tribute last summer. Even leisure was held to the highest standard. "It should concern itself with those things we do to replenish the spirit, such as listening to music, watching good films or theater, taking part in discussions of politics and ideas," she wrote. "It is the opposite of killing time."

The Paepckes's high-minded circle followed European intellectual trends and the couple soon became important American promoters of the Bauhaus design movement. Walter engaged as a consultant the architect Walter Gropius, helped bring Laszlo Moholy-Nagy to the Institute of Design in Chicago, and installed the artist and designer Herbert Bayer as Aspen town manager.

Elizabeth's father, William A. Nitze, was for many years chairman of romance languages at the University of Chicago; Walter was the son of a prominent German business family. The couple spoke German at home; their daughter, Antonia, says she was at a disadvantage for not knowing English when she started school. After World War II, the Paepckes tried to revive an appreciation of German culture by staging a bicentennial celebration of the birth of Goethe—in, of all places, Aspen. Working with Mr. Hutchins and Mr. Adler, they attracted such figures as Thornton Wilder, the philosopher José Ortega y Gasset and, on his only visit to the United States, Albert Schweitzer.

As the historian James Sloan Allen has written, the Paepckes believed in moral discipline, social responsibility, hard work, and restraint. Aspen, which they came to regard as their child, thrived on these values during the 1950s, but later rebelled. After Walter's death in 1960, Elizabeth reigned alone during a decade that brought drugs, free love, and Hunter S. Thompson to Aspen. Elizabeth's disenchantment increased in the 1970s during a brouhaha in which the anti-growth-minded city council refused the Aspen Institute's application to build a hotel for its visitors; the institute angrily moved most of its operations to Maryland. In the 1980s, new wealth poured into Aspen, bringing in megamansions and pricing out full-time residents.

Ariane Zurcher, Elizabeth's granddaughter, said, "She hated the display of wealth, the competition." Addressing the opening session of the design conference in 1987, Elizabeth asked: "Are we going to kill the golden goose by feeding the animal until its liver becomes distended and we produce a pâté which is so rich that none of us can digest it anymore?

What price glory?" She told a reporter that Aspen had "become a town of glitz and glamour . . . a nut without a kernel." "My heart," she said, "is broken."

But the town continued to love its queen and conscience. A Harvard-educated land surveyor explained his admiration: Elizabeth Paepcke, blessed with looks, wealth, and intelligence, had somehow resisted the temptations that can wreck similarly advantaged people. Perhaps Aspen admired her so much because, though similarly blessed, it has not likewise succeeded.

Mrs. Paepcke was celebrated for her hospitality, for her ability to listen, for her love of a good bawdy joke, for ascending a ladder every Christmas to light the real candles on her tree. Into her eighties, she still shoveled snow from her walk ("I think she thought she could do it better than anyone else," said a friend) and worked for hours in her garden. On hikes into the surrounding hills, according to her granddaughter, she would pack not only a little sipping whiskey but also gloves that would allow her to pull up thistles. It says much about Paepcke aspirations that she would attempt to weed the mountains.

"When I die," she once told a friend, "just throw me on the compost heap."

January 1, 1995

THE NEW YORK TIMES MAGAZINE

Dying for Work

RICHARD LOO

By Russell Baker

Richard Loo died for the last time in Los Angeles the other day. He was eighty, had acted in some 150 films over a fifty-year career, and had died in a fair proportion of them. Though his roots were Chinese, he was in great demand for roles as Japanese villains during World War II.

"He was always either stabbing himself or committing hara-kiri or kamikaze," his daughter said. "He always played the big honcho who was really going to make life tough for the Americans, the really nasty Japanese general or colonel who ended up killing himself as a point of honor because he never got the best of the Americans."

Forty years ago or thereabouts I saw Mr. Loo die many times and, though it may seem shameful nowadays, cheered each death without the slightest sensation of unseemly behavior. Revisers of history may clutch at this confession as proof that I was besotted with anti-Asian racism cooked up by American propagandists to promote the war effort against Japan. To which I say, "Poppycock!"

American love of all things Chinese was as irrational and deep then as its hatred of all things Japanese. What made Mr. Loo's deaths so easy to cheer was much simpler than racism. First, you always knew he would be back at this devilish business of tormenting American G.I.'s before the month was out at the movie theater. Second, he always died in good taste. Even when committing hara-kiri, he was neat about it. I wish present-day movie actors would study his work. When a movie actor faces a violent end nowadays, the audience has to put up with a mess so gory that only the strongest stomach can go on digesting the popcorn.

When the scene is over, they are not a jot deader than Mr. Loo was after prodding a wooden sword at his entrails and grimacing a few times to indicate a hara-kiri in progress. Even racists in that time didn't want to look at ripped intestines; seeing villainy brought to justice was the point of the show.

I am unable to determine whether Mr. Loo holds the record for dying on film. Dying was not a highly respected skill when Hollywood produced movies like sausages, and those who did it rarely received much attention. To this day there is no Academy Award for the best dying performance. Most of those who died for a living were bit players who had scarcely a line before being plugged by Randolph Scott or John Wayne. These actors were so little valued that the studios rarely even wasted any ketchup on them to suggest that they could bleed.

Bleeding, in fact, rarely seemed to occur after fatal movie shootings, and for this I was always grateful. There was a period of my life when I watched Barton MacLane get shot to death two or three times a month, and deservedly so on each occasion. Never once did I see Barton MacLane bleed. I class him up there close to Mr. Loo as a rat who knew how to die like a gentleman. Stars, of course, hardly ever died. When they did, they certainly didn't bleed or stagger around with pieces of their skulls missing, as actors do nowadays. Edward G. Robinson, pumped lethally full of lead, might roll down a long flight of stone steps, which could make you wince at the thought of the bruises, but he always died intact. Americans who grew up on these old studio movies could hardly escape the impression that a violent end, though undesirable, could nevertheless be achieved with neatness.

It was shocking to encounter the real thing—the work of a razor, a meat cleaver, a shotgun—when I started newspaper work. Present-day movies with their prurient close-ups of ax work, chainsaw applications, and shotgun attacks on the human body are no more accurate at capturing the real thing than the old bloodless Hollywood product. The aim now seems to be to titillate a public appetite for disgust. The notion that they might send the audience out with a healthy repugnance for violence is such transparent baloney that no sensible filmmaker even proposes it.

Audiences may be different, but they are no dumber than they were forty years ago when Richard Loo was playing at dying. They know the actors with the severed heads, spurting arteries, and spilled intestines are already back at work before another camera, or at least hounding their agents for another role. What has changed between Mr. Loo's heyday and *The Texas Chainsaw Massacre* is not the transparent fraudulence of the illusion; it is the aesthetic taste of the audience, which can now be entertained by being revolted.

November 26, 1983

The Queen of Chopped Liver

Sylvia Weinberger

By Robert McG. Thomas, Jr.

Sylvia Weinberger, who used a sprinkling of matzoh meal, a pinch of salt, and a dollop of schmaltzmanship to turn chopped liver into a commercial success, died at a hospital in Fort Lauderdale. She was eighty-nine and had lived in Boca Raton, Florida.

Mrs. Weinberger started making chopped liver for a luncheonette she and her husband, Irving, had opened in 1944 on the Grand Concourse at 169th Street in the Bronx. She ended up presiding over a $2-million-a-year operation as the proprietor of the semi-eponymous Mrs. Weinberg's Chopped Liver. She once explained that her name had been shortened because of typographical necessity when her first labels were printed: "My whole name wouldn't fit."

According to her son Fred, Mrs. Weinberg's had become the leading brand of chopped liver at kosher counters from New York to Chicago by the time she retired in 1989. But when it began, it was all Mrs. Weinberger could do to make it acceptable on the Grand Concourse. At that time, store-bought chopped liver was almost an oxymoron, something to be smuggled home in a plain brown wrapper because no self-respecting Jewish homemaker was likely to admit that she did not have enough bedrock mother love or culinary skills to make it herself.

"I used to give it away," Mrs. Weinberger once said.

Never mind that chopped liver is the metaphorical butt of a Jewish retort ("What am I, chopped liver?"). In many Jewish homes, it is both a staple and a delicacy, one whose proper preparation has been described as the culinary test that divides Jewish moms from Jewish mothers.

Mrs. Weinberger's version apparently passed the test. After much wheedling and cajoling by Mrs. Weinberger to get her luncheonette customers to take it home to their families, her chopped liver caught on—so much so, Mrs. Weinberger once recalled, that when she put up a sign, MRS. WEINBERGER'S CHOPPED LIVER WITH A SMILE, "People used to say, 'Keep the smile, just give me the liver.'"

As the product became more popular, Mr. Weinberger started soliciting supermarkets in the Bronx. But when the first big order came in, for two cases, his wife was somewhat unprepared. "We didn't have any boxes or cases," she said. "We delivered the individual containers in plastic bags."

Mrs. Weinberger, a Hungarian refugee, came to the United States in 1937 with two young sons to join her husband. She helped support the family by working as a seamstress while her husband worked in a laundry until they had saved enough to buy the luncheonette.

They sold it in 1955 to manufacture chopped liver full-time. Other kosher products, all based on Mrs. Weinberger's recipes, were later added to the Mrs. Weinberg's Food Products line. The family sold the manufacturing company, but Mr. Weinberger continues to be the distributor.

In addition to her son, Fred, of Mamaroneck, New York, Mrs. Weinberger is survived by another son, Sidney, of Boca Raton, Florida, and six grandchildren.

August 2, 1995

Mrs. Weinberger's Chopped Liver

1 pound beef liver, broiled	Salt and pepper to taste
1 pound onions, sautéed in oil	1 hard-boiled egg, chopped
Sprinkling of matzoh meal to taste	

Put the liver, onions, matzoh meal, and salt and pepper into a meat grinder and grind once for a coarse consistency. Add the hard-boiled egg to the meat mixture and mix well with a spoon.

Chill for an hour before serving.

Yield: 4 servings

A Bulldog for Justice

HAMILTON E. HOLMES

By Lawrence Van Gelder

Hamilton E. Holmes, who braved the hostility of racists to integrate the University of Georgia with Charlayne Hunter in 1961 and went on to a distinguished career in medicine and ultimate reconciliation with his alma mater, died in his sleep at his home in Atlanta. He was fifty-four. His brother Gary said the cause of death was not immediately known, but Dr. Holmes had undergone quadruple bypass heart surgery two weeks earlier.

"The University of Georgia has lost one of its most distinguished graduates," Charles B. Knapp, president of the university, said.

The atmosphere was distinctly different in the winter of 1961 when Mr. Holmes, then nineteen, and Ms. Hunter, eighteen, who was later to achieve renown as the television journalist Charlayne Hunter-Gault, won a two-and-a-half-year court battle to overturn segregation at the 176-year-old university. On January 9, 1961, after last-ditch efforts led by Gov. S. Ernest Vandiver, including the closing of the campus, had been turned back by the United States Supreme Court, Mr. Holmes and Ms. Hunter were admitted to the university.

At first their arrival on the campus in Athens, Georgia, created little disturbance among the university's seven thousand white students. But within a short time a group of youths, swelled by some fifteen hundred spectators, were jeering Ms. Hunter and shouting, "Go home, nigger, and don't come back!" On January 11, a howling, cursing mob of about six hundred students and a few outsiders laid siege to Ms. Hunter's dormitory. The disturbance raged out of control for nearly an hour before it was ended by the police, using tear gas and fire hoses. There were injuries and arrests, and when the unrest was over the university announced that Mr. Holmes and Ms. Hunter had been suspended for their own safety.

But the next day they were readmitted. Then, largely ignored and friendless among the white students, Mr. Holmes—who came to the University of Georgia after two years at the all-black Moorehouse College in Atlanta—went on to be elected to Phi Beta Kappa when he graduated in 1963.

"He was amazing," Ms. Hunter-Gault said as she recalled an incident in which Mr. Holmes faced down a group of racist fraternity members. "He had quiet dignity, scholarship. He wouldn't let anything stand in the way of his desire to become a doctor."

Mr. Holmes became the first black student admitted to the Emory University Medical School in Atlanta, and received his medical degree from Emory in 1967. At the time of his death he was an orthopedic surgeon in Atlanta, associate dean and a member of the faculty of the Emory University School of Medicine, and chairman of the orthopedic unit at Grady Memorial Hospital in Atlanta, the largest in the Southeast.

For many years after his graduation, Dr. Holmes, admitting to "bitterness," had little to do with the University of Georgia. But in 1983, he was invited to become a trustee of the University of Georgia Foundation, the university's private fund-raising organization. At first he refused. Then he relented, and became the university's first black trustee.

Two years later, as part of its bicentennial, the university established the Holmes-Hunter Lecture, which brings a noted African-American speaker to the campus each year to discuss racial issues.

After the first of the lectures, almost twenty-five years after he and Ms. Hunter integrated the university, they were presented with its bicentennial medallion. In accepting the award, Dr. Holmes said: "I have come to really love this university. People look at me and say, 'You're crazy, man. How can you love that place?' But I will never forget this, and I will cherish it forever."

Seven years later, in 1992, Dr. Holmes and Ms. Hunter-Gault announced that they were creating the Holmes-Hunter Scholarship for African-American students. "I would like to think I would have made it if I had not been one of the first black students here," Dr. Holmes said. "But I think I have been enriched much more because of that experience.

We want to continue this with our young brothers and sisters at the university and enable them to get an education they can be proud of."

On another occasion, he said, "Improving this university—making it the best—will benefit everyone in Georgia, blacks and whites."

Dr. Holmes's son, Hamilton, Jr., graduated from the university in 1990.

Dr. Holmes, the son of Alfred Holmes, a businessman, and Isabella Holmes, a schoolteacher, was born in Atlanta. At the all-black Henry McNeal Turner High School, where Mr. Holmes and Ms. Hunter were classmates, he was co-captain of the football team, captain of the basketball team, and president of his junior and senior classes. He maintained a 3.88 scholastic average and was valedictorian of his class.

Besides his son and his brother Gary, both of Atlanta, Dr. Holmes is survived by his wife of thirty years, the former Marilyn Vincent Holmes of Atlanta; a daughter, Alison, of Charlotte, North Carolina; his mother, Isabella C. Holmes of Atlanta; two other brothers, A. Herbert, of Atlanta, and Michael, of Manhattan, and a sister, E. Lauren Holmes, also of Manhattan.

October 28, 1995

REMEMBERING HAMP

CHARLAYNE HUNTER-GAULT, an anchor for PBS's News Hour With Jim Lehrer *and a former reporter for* The New York Times, *added this reminiscence:*

The year Hamilton Holmes was our high school football co-captain and I was the homecoming queen, we became a team. It was the spring of 1959, and until then, Hamp, the scholar-jock who wanted to be a doctor, and I, the aspiring journalist, had mostly gone our separate ways. But we became the team that was Georgia's entry into the civil rights revolution after we were admitted as the first black students to the 176-year-old University of Georgia—an institution into which the governor had vowed that "no, not one" black student would ever be allowed.

Hamp, a straight A student, was more deeply hurt than I was by the university's year and a half of ruses to keep us out. The officials had rejected him as unqualified during the admissions procedure, and after we were admitted, they refused to let him play football. They said it was too risky. He could be killed. Deliberately. But with his old-fashioned sense of loyalty, commitment, and duty, he blocked and tackled for me, even as he ran the gantlet of insults, including finding the air let out of his tires by some white kid who just didn't get it.

When from time to time I had to go to the infirmary with stomach pains of uncertain origin, the first person to appear at my bedside would be Hamp. "You all right, Char?" he would ask. And whatever was on my mind or in my gut would recede. This must have been the manner he later brought to the bedside of his patients, after he had graduated, Phi Beta Kappa, and then become the first black graduate of Emory University School of Medicine.

Not long before his enormously good heart failed him and he died, Hamp, a prominent orthopedic surgeon and teacher, had been asked to introduce me at a public event. I was in Atlanta for a reading of my book, In My Place, a memoir of our college days. At one point, I heard him say, "Of course, she's a lot nicer now than she was then." As he flashed that big face-filling grin of his, we exchanged knowing glances that took us all the way back to our intense competitions at Turner High, when they eliminated the Best All-Around Student honor because both of us insisted on having it.

Hamp had all but buried the unhappy ghosts of the past; he had even forgiven the university, becoming one of its governing officials and biggest boosters. In fact, at the foot of the blanket of flowers that adorned his coffin lay a red-and-black Georgia Bulldogs cap.

He had told me that his book, were he ever to write it, would probably tell our story a bit differently than mine did, and I allowed that he was probably right, especially given the importance he attached to proving to whites that he was as good as any of their best.

When I finished my reading, I assumed Hamp was gone. As I headed for a table in the lobby, a long line of people were waiting for me to sign their books. At one point, I turned to a page and saw that big, round, curving signature that I used to poke fun at in high school—unmistakably that of Hamilton Earl Holmes. I looked up, and there was Hamp working the line from the back, talking with the people and signing everyone's copy of my book. Our book. About the best team I ever joined.

December 31, 1995
THE NEW YORK TIMES MAGAZINE

In Love with Genes

BARBARA McCLINTOCK

By Gina Kolata

Dr. Barbara McClintock, one of the most influential geneticists of the century, died at Huntington Hospital on Long Island. She was ninety years old and lived nearby at the Cold Spring Harbor Laboratory, where she had conducted research for more than fifty years.

Decades before biologists discovered the molecular tools to dissect genetic material, Dr. McClintock had an uncanny ability to understand the nature of genes and how they interact. Working with corn all her life, she is best known for her discovery that fragments of genetic material move among chromosomes, regulating the way genes control the growth and development of cells.

Modern genetics has known no figure quite like Dr. McClintock, who worked alone and chose not to publish some of her revolutionary observations for years, explaining later that she thought no one would accept the findings. She never gave lectures, as most scientists do to build their careers. Instead, until her last days, she worked in her laboratory. Until 1986, she did not have a telephone, requesting that anyone who wanted to talk to her write a letter instead.

J. R. S. Fincham of Edinburgh, Scotland, writing in *Nature*, the British science journal, said that Dr. McClintock's "solitary style of work, total independence of thought and extraordinary record of getting things right have elevated her to the status of a prophet in the eyes of some."

Dr. McClintock's findings were so profound that she garnered honors and prizes throughout her long career, including membership in the National Academy of Sciences in 1944, presidency of the Genetics Society in 1945, the National Medal of Science in 1970, the first MacArthur

Laureate Award, for sixty thousand dollars a year for life, in 1981, and a Nobel Prize in medicine in 1983. She was the first woman to win an unshared Nobel Prize in medicine and the third woman to win an unshared Nobel science prize. The first was Marie Curie in 1911 and the second was Dorothy C. Hodgkin in 1964, both for chemistry.

"She was a giant figure in the history of genetics," said Dr. James Shapiro of the University of Chicago. "I think she is the most important figure there is in biology in general."

Dr. James Watson, director of the Cold Spring Harbor Laboratory and co-discoverer of the structure of DNA, the chemical that makes up genes, said Dr. McClintock was one of the three most important figures in the history of genetics, one of "the three M's," he said. The other two, Gregor Mendel and Thomas Hunt Morgan, lived in the nineteenth and early twentieth centuries and laid the groundwork for notions of inheritance.

In the 1930s, Dr. McClintock discovered that chromosomes break and recombine to create genetic changes in a process known as crossing over, a discovery that explained puzzling patterns of inheritance. She also discovered a structure called the nucleolar organizer of the chromosome, which seemed to order the genetic material during cell division, a finding that was not explained by molecular biologists for three more decades.

In her work with corn, Dr. McClintock used the telltale patterns of colored kernels to disclose the breaking, joining, and rearranging of genes and chromosomes inside the cells. Because the pigments of the kernels are inherited, Dr. McClintock could trace genes through the changes in the kernels. To the astonishment of molecular geneticists, whose precise tools now allow them to cut and snip submicroscopic genes, Dr. McClintock's discoveries about the nature of genes and inheritance were made at a time when no one even knew what DNA was.

In the 1930s, Dr. McClintock established her reputation by becoming one of the scientists to develop an understanding of chromosomes as the basis of heredity, work that was honored by her National Medal of Science.

Dr. McClintock's Nobel Prize was for her discovery that the genetic material is not fixed, but fluid. Small fragments of DNA, called transposable elements, actually move from place to place and, in doing so, control the expression of genes. She made this discovery nearly forty years before she won the Nobel Prize, at a time when genetics was still so rudimentary that her ideas baffled other scientists and were often dismissed outright or ignored.

In an introduction to a volume of papers about Dr. McClintock, produced in celebration of her ninetieth birthday, Dr. Nina Fedoroff of the Carnegie Institution of Washington and Dr. David Botstein of Stanford University described Dr. McClintock's plight. Her ideas about transposable elements, they wrote, were "ahead of her time and Barbara found herself in an anomalous and unique position," adding, "She was universally respected and admired as one of the leading geneticists of her era, yet the reaction to her latest and perhaps most profound discoveries and insights was often uncomprehending or indifferent and not infrequently dismissive or even hostile."

Concluding that she could never convince the scientific community, Dr. McClintock doggedly carried on with her research, carefully filing her data away and writing them up only in her annual reports to the Carnegie Institution of Washington, which supported her work.

In her biography of Dr. McClintock, *A Feeling for the Organism*, Dr. Evelyn Fox Keller of the Massachusetts Institute of Technology writes that geneticists were baffled by Dr. McClintock's ideas because they seemed too much at odds with the very nature of Darwinian evolution. The theory of evolution holds that changes occur randomly in genes, giving rise to variations that may or may not prove beneficial. Dr. McClintock, however, was saying that purposeful changes occur in genes, that transposable elements jump to specific places to insert themselves into genetic material and alter it.

Another stumbling block, Dr. Keller says, was that Dr. McClintock was working with corn, a species whose complex patterns of development were clear to her, but not to many others. And she had done her work alone without the benefit of long discussions trying to explain her ideas to colleagues.

Finally, in the late 1970s, when molecular biologists isolated transposable elements in bacteria and then discovered that they were universally used by cells to control genes, Dr. McClintock's work was recognized and widely celebrated as prescient. Dr. Shapiro said: "I think the implications of this work are just being realized. The idea that the genome is capable of repairing itself, and that it is capable of reconstructing itself, that there are systems in the cell that can detect damage and do appropriate things to repair it, has tremendous implications for evolution as well as for genetics."

Because Dr. McClintock worked alone, emphatically rejecting reductionism, because she was so often right and saw so clearly when others were muddled, she has gained a reputation as almost a mystic. But Dr. Shapiro said she was more "someone who understands where the mysteries lie than someone who mystifies."

Dr. McClintock "understands the complexity of the genome and the limits to our understanding of it," he said, adding, "She appreciated that the problems we are addressing are enormously deep and complex."

Barbara McClintock was born on June 16, 1902, in Hartford, Connecticut. The daughter of a doctor, she grew up in Brooklyn and learned to love science while attending Erasmus Hall High School there. When she was seventeen, she enrolled in Cornell University's College of Agriculture. When she was a junior she was invited to take the university's graduate course in genetics and became, unofficially, a graduate student.

From the time she received her Ph.D. in 1927 until 1941, she worked at Cornell University and at the University of Missouri, collaborating with some of the country's most eminent geneticists. From 1941 until her death, Dr. McClintock worked at Cold Spring Harbor, following her own course.

Dr. McClintock is survived by a sister, Mignon Crowell, who lives in Florida, and a brother, Thomas N. McClintock of Newtown, Connecticut.

September 4, 1992

A FEELING FOR MAIZE

JOHN NOBLE WILFORD wrote this report when DR. BARBARA McCLINTOCK was awarded her Nobel Prize in Medicine:

When Barbara McClintock learned she had won the Nobel Prize in medicine, she was heard to exclaim, "Oh dear," and then she walked out into the brisk morning air to pick walnuts. She is like that. She is known for baking with black walnuts. She is also known as a very private person, a loner in the laboratory and in life.

So the eighty-one-year-old Dr. McClintock, dressed in dungarees and carrying tongs for grappling the walnuts, left her apartment on the grounds of the Cold Spring Harbor Laboratory and strolled alone along a wooded path down by an inlet of the Long Island Sound. She once confessed that she finds "applause is crushing." It was quiet out there in the woods.

She must have been bracing herself for the applause. For when she returned from her walk, Dr. McClintock told William Udry, the laboratory's administrative director, "I will do what I have to do."

She issued a statement that was characteristic of her. She did not acknowledge the invaluable assistance of co-workers, for when she had made the discovery of "jumping genes" thirty years earlier, she was working alone. No, she wished to share the credit with her subjects, the ordinary maize plants from which, after meticulous observation, she had extracted an important insight into genetics. She is like that too. With good reason, a recent biography of Dr. McClintock is entitled *A Feeling for the Organism.*

In the statement, Dr. McClintock said: "It might seem unfair, however, to reward a person for having so much pleasure over the years, asking the maize plant to solve specific problems and then watching its responses."

Next, she obliged by holding a news conference at the laboratory on Long Island. She is slim and spry, only a little more than five feet tall. Her brown hair, graying slightly now, is cropped short. Dutifully and courteously, she sat on a stool and spoke in a whisper, trying to explain herself and her work. "You don't need the public recognition," she said. "You just need the respect of your colleagues."

Public recognition has come late in life. And though she has long been respected by her colleagues, they did not come to recognize the importance of her research to biological thought until recent years. With her discovery that genetic information was not stationary, that it can transpose from one chromosome to another, Thomas Broker, a senior scientist at Cold Spring Harbor, said that Dr. McClintock "ranks up with Darwin in understanding evolution."

When she enrolled at Cornell University in 1919, she wanted to study plant breeding, but the department would not accept a woman as major, so she majored in botany. She turned to plant genetics as a graduate student at Cornell, where she earned her doctorate in 1927.

For several years she taught and did research at Cornell and other campuses, but was considered too much of a maverick for university life. Out of a job in 1942, she got some timely encouragement from Marcus Rhoades, a colleague from Cornell who was then at Columbia University. He helped her land a research position at the Carnegie Institution's department of genetics, which was at Cold Spring Harbor. It marked the beginning of a long association with Carnegie and the laboratory, which is now an autonomous private institution engaged in basic biological research.

Her early work on anomalies in corn genetics was quickly recognized by her election in 1944 to the National Academy of Sciences, only the third woman to be so honored at that time. In her acceptance message, she said: "I am not a feminist, but I am always gratified when illogical barriers are broken—for Jews, women, Negroes, etc. It helps us all."

When Dr. McClintock first reported her discovery that genes "jump" around, at a symposium in 1951, she was met with stony silence, according to her biographer, Evelyn Fox Keller. The other scientists either did not understand or would not believe this attack on the orthodox view of stationary genes. "No one much believed her or cared," said Stephen Blose of Cold Spring Harbor. "It didn't help that she was a woman."

This cool reception, it seemed, caused her to retreat even further into solitary working and living habits.

Finally, in the past ten years, the revolution in molecular biology brought confirmation of Dr. McClintock's theories. James D. Watson, director of the laboratory and a Nobel laureate for discovering the structure of DNA, the blueprint of life, noted that "it's really that science caught up with Barbara."

Dr. Keller, in her biography, says: "If Barbara McClintock's story illustrates the fallibility of science, it also bears witness to the underlying health of the scientific enterprise. Her eventual vindication demonstrates the capacity of science to overcome its own characteristic kinds of myopia, reminding us that its limitations do not reinforce themselves indefinitely."

Since then, the honors have been many and frequent.

But little has changed Dr. McClintock's ways. She still resists public appearances. She lives quietly alone—she has never married—a short walk from the laboratory building that now bears her name. She is there seven days a week, often from early morning until 8:30 at night.

Once, in an interview with Dr. Keller, Dr. McClintock spoke of the "real affection" one gets for the pieces that "go together." In her experience, she said, "As you look at these things, they become part of you. And you forget yourself. The main thing about it is you forget yourself."

October 11, 1983

Chronicler of the Unsung

JOSEPH MITCHELL
By Richard Severo

Joseph Mitchell, whose stories about ordinary people created extraordinary journalism, died of cancer at Columbia-Presbyterian Medical Center in Manhattan. He was eighty-seven and lived in Manhattan.

At the height of his creative powers, from the 1930s to the mid-1960s, Mr. Mitchell tended to avoid the standard fare of journalists: interviews with moguls, tycoons, movie stars, and captains of industry. Instead, he pursued the generals of nuisance: flops, drunks, con artists, panhandlers, gin-mill owners and their bellicose bartenders, at least one flea-circus operator, a man who sold racing cockroaches, a bearded lady, and a fast talker who claimed to have written nine million words of "An Oral History of Our Times" when, in fact, he had written no words at all.

Joe Mitchell was also the poet of the waterfront, of the limelight of New York's greatness as a seaport, of the Fulton Fish Market, of the clammers on Long Island and the oystermen on Staten Island: people who caught, sold, and ate seafood and talked about it incessantly. He wrote about clams and oysters with sensuousness and passion. On Sunday in August 1937, he placed third in a clam-eating tournament on Block Island after consuming eighty-four cherrystones. He regarded that, he said, as "one of the few worthwhile achievements" of his life.

He liked dreamers and drinkers, and for him, people were always as big as their dreams, as mellow as the ale they nursed in the shadows of McSorley's saloon off Cooper Square in the East Village. He wrote during a time when New Yorkers were mostly convinced that they were of good heart and that they had the best of intentions, whatever the rest of the world thought of their abrasiveness and contentiousness. Mr. Mitchell's articles offered evidence that they were right.

When somebody suggested that he wrote about the "little people," he replied that there were no little people in his work. "They are as big as you are, whoever you are," he said.

When Mr. Mitchell became a staff writer at *The New Yorker* in 1938, the city had come through the Depression and was soon to send its sons and daughters off to fight a war. Even with the hard times and a jaded past, there was still an innocence of sorts, and an interest in the people Mr. Mitchell liked to write about as well as a tolerance for them. His nonfiction had grace and was rich with the sorts of people a reader could find in Joyce or Gogol, two of the writers Mr. Mitchell admired. He was to letters what the Ashcan School had been to painting.

Mr. Mitchell arrived at *The New Yorker* when the magazine's editor, Harold Ross, was giving its top nonfiction writers, among them St. Clair McKelway, A. J. Liebling, and Philip Hamburger, more space and time than was available to reporters of the day. *The New Yorker* writers used their good fortune to advantage. In stories and "Profiles" and "Reporter at Large" articles, Mr. Mitchell helped to pioneer a special kind of journalism, setting standards to which later generations of reporters would aspire.

If his name is not as widely known as it might have been, that is mostly because for the last three decades of his life, he wrote not a word that anybody got to see. For years, he would show up at his tiny office at *The New Yorker* every day and assure his colleagues that he was working on something, but that it was not quite ready. "He told his pals he was writing about his roots in North Carolina," said Charles McGrath, who was then deputy editor of *The New Yorker* and is now the editor of *The New York Times Book Review*. "Then it became a book about his living in New York." Whatever it was, nothing of any substance emerged from his typewriter after 1965 and his friends came to think of it as an exceptionally bad case of writer's block. Mr. Mitchell had always been a perfectionist and Mr. McGrath said he suspected that Mr. Mitchell was raising his standards all the time. The janitor would find reams of copy in his wastepaper basket.

"I'm a ghost; everything's changed now," Mr. Mitchell said when he was in his eighties, adding that he had become used to being obscure.

Although Mr. Mitchell always had an extraordinary reputation among nonfiction writers and his out-of-print books were eagerly sought by collectors, he emerged from his obscurity in 1992 when the body of his work was reissued in a volume entitled *Up in the Old Hotel*. The book was a critical and commercial success, and Mr. Mitchell said he was pleased to learn that younger readers found merit in his prose.

The centerpiece of the book was the series of articles that appeared in *The New Yorker* in the late 1930s and early 1940s, and then was published in 1943 as *McSorley's Wonderful Saloon*. Mr. Mitchell had discovered McSorley's Old Ale House shortly after he joined *The New Yorker*. The saloon opened in 1854 and, as the oldest continuously run institution of its kind in New York, immediately endeared itself to Mr. Mitchell. He loathed most forms of progress and technology and so did the succession of people who drank in McSorley's.

"It is equipped with electricity," he wrote of it, "but the bar is stubbornly illuminated with a pair of gas lamps, which flicker fitfully and throw shadows on the low, cobwebby ceiling each time someone opens the street door. There is no cash register. Coins are dropped in soup bowls—one for nickels, one for dimes, one for quarters, and one for halves—and bills are kept in a rosewood cashbox."

And what of the service?

"It is a drowsy place; the bartenders never make a needless move, the customers nurse their mugs of ale, and the three clocks on the walls have not been in agreement for many years."

Who went to such a place?

"The backbone of the clientele is a rapidly thinning group of crusty old men, predominantly Irish, who have been drinking there since they were youths and now have a proprietary feeling about the place. Some of them have tiny pensions, and are alone in the world; they sleep in Bowery hotels and spend practically all their waking hours in McSorley's."

When Mr. Mitchell started writing such pieces about New York, the people who were then old could remember the draft riots of 1863, the various financial panics, the huzzahs that accompanied the end of the Spanish-American War in 1898, and the sorrow that attended the death of John McSorley, the original owner of the saloon, in 1910. These men, many of them retired mariners, went to McSorley's to avoid conversing with their wives and to spend the afternoon nursing an ale and listening to the clock tick. "Old John believed it was impossible to drink with tranquillity in the presence of women; there is a fine back room in the saloon, but for many years a sign was nailed on the street door, saying NOTICE. NO BACK ROOM IN HERE FOR LADIES.

It is not possible to determine who the most memorable person was in Mr. Mitchell's stories, but there were many who rivaled the regulars of McSorley's.

There was Dick, a Neapolitan who ran a perfectly acceptable gin mill, then made the mistake of trying to transform it into a grand saloon by purchasing furniture made of chromium tubing. He even began to abide by the liquor laws. "He began to cringe and bow and shake hands with the customers, and he would even help them on with their coats," Mr. Mitchell reported, adding that when patrons finished eating, Dick would ask them if their pot roast was okay. "When it was just a gin mill, Dick and his bartenders made you think they were doing you a favor by letting you in the place," Mr. Mitchell wrote. "He would say, 'If you don't like my grub, you don't have to eat in here. I'd just as soon I never saw you again.'" The gin mill survived but the respectability of the newer clientele was such that Mr. Mitchell entitled his piece "Obituary of a Gin Mill." "You never hear any conversation worth listening to in that place," he complained.

There was Commodore Dutch, who somehow convinced rich and unrich alike that they should go to his annual charity ball, which he gave to benefit himself. "I haven't got a whole lot of sense," the commodore told Mr. Mitchell, "but I got too much sense to work."

There was Arthur Samuel Colborne, who announced in 1941 that he had not uttered "a solitary profane word since a Sunday morning in the winter of 1886." He was so pleased with himself that he started the Anti-Profanity League and took to touring bars in Yorkville, preaching against the sin of swearing. "You start out with 'hell,' 'devil take it,' 'Dad burn it,' 'Gee-whiz,' and the like of that, and by and by you won't be able to open your trap without letting loose an awful, awful blasphemous oath," Mr. Colborne told Mr. Mitchell. Mr. Colborne felt he had just about eliminated profanity in the saloons of Yorkville, but not without a price, since Mr. Colborne had to quaff a great deal of beer while spreading the word. His story, entitled "The Don't Swear Man," ran in the magazine in 1941.

There was Cockeye Johnny, King of the Gypsies, at least in Brooklyn, who said there were only two kinds of merchandise—lost and unlost. "Anything that ain't nailed down is lost," he said.

There was a ragged old man who said he was "John S. Smith of Riga, Latvia, Europe," who began hitchhiking around the United States in 1934, virtually penniless. Every time a benefactor gave him a free cup of coffee or a little soup, he would give him a check for hundreds, even thousands of dollars drawn on the Irving National Bank of New York, which had gone out of business in 1923. Mr. Mitchell wrote: "I began to think of the vain hopes he raised in the breasts of the waitresses who had graciously given him hundreds of meals and the truck drivers who had hauled him over a hundred highways, and to feel that about John S. Smith of Riga, Latvia, Europe, there is something a little sinister." This was published as "Santa Claus Smith" in *The New Yorker* in 1940.

There was Mazie P. Gordon, who sold movie tickets at the old Venice Theater, near the start of the Bowery, who made the rounds of the all-night restaurants, giving the bums small change so they could eat. The bums sometimes patronized the Venice and Mazie boasted she kept it clean for them. "Nobody ever got loused up in the Venice," she said. He called her story "Mazie," and it appeared in 1940.

There was Charles Eugene Cassell, who decided that since he appeared to be unemployable, he would launch "Captain Charley's Private Museum for Intelligent People." To those who had the price of admission, Mr. Cassell would let them sit on what Mr. Mitchell said was "a rat-gnawed Egyptian mummy." This story ran in 1938, and was called "Hit on the Head with a Cow."

And there was Joseph Ferdinand Gould, who had graduated from Harvard in 1911 and come to New York, not long after he left an archaeological expedition in which he measured the skulls of the remains of fifteen hundred Chippewa and Mandan Indians in North Dakota. He took to hanging around Greenwich Village coffee shops, where with no provocation he would do an imitation of a sea gull. Indeed, he claimed to have mastered sea gull language and had reached the point where he was about to translate Longfellow into it.

Joe Gould persuaded almost everybody who was anybody that he was writing an "Oral History of Our Times." He carried around paper bags that many believed contained his research but that, in reality, merely contained other paper bags and a few ratty newspaper clips. He lamented that he was the last bohemian and all the others he had known had fallen by the wayside. "Some are in the grave," he said, "some are in the loony bin and some are in the advertising business." Malcolm Cowley admired Joe Gould and so did e. e. cummings. William Saroyan gave him alcohol and Ezra Pound trusted him.

It was not until 1964, twenty-one years since his first *New Yorker* profile of Mr. Gould and seven years after Mr. Gould's death in a psychiatric hospital (he died as he was doing a sea gull imitation), that Mr. Mitchell told his readers the truth: That whatever the "Oral History" was, it reposed only in Mr. Gould's noggin.

Mr. Mitchell's first story about Mr. Gould, entitled "Professor Sea Gull," ran in 1943. The final Joe Gould articles, which appeared in 1964, were Mr. Mitchell's last signed contributions to *The New Yorker*. Two of his books, *The Bottom of the Harbor* and *Joe Gould's Secret*, have been recently published.

Reviewing *Up in the Old Hotel* in *The New York Times Book Review*, Verlyn Klinkenborg wrote: "Mr. Mitchell always mediates the sadness such subjects bring—the loss of time, the life slipping by, the way the old manners fail to hang on—and he lets the reader feel only the pleasure that comes from his own very personal discoveries. He himself remains, in this prose at least, a melancholy man, wandering with a sandwich in his pocket among the wildflowers in abandoned cemeteries, seeking the company of solitary men who are gregarious only in the company of other isolates, sniffing out the odors of the Fulton Fish Market and its old hotels. And in such moments the reader gets a glimpse of Mr. Mitchell himself, even as he seems to disappear into the scene he describes."

Joseph Mitchell was born July 27, 1908, on his Parker grandparents' farm near Iona, North Carolina, the son of Averette Nance and Elizabeth A. Parker Mitchell. His family was in the cotton and tobacco trading business. Mr. Mitchell studied at the University of North Carolina from

1925 to 1929. He sent an article he had written on tobacco to *The New York Herald Tribune,* which liked it so much that it published it and summoned him to New York in 1929. Over the next nine years, he wrote for *The Herald Tribune, The Morning World,* and *The World-Telegram,* the paper that first sent him to the Fulton Fish Market.

Mr. Mitchell married Therese Dagny Jacobsen in 1931. She died in 1980. He is survived by his companion, Sheila McGrath; a sister, Linda Mitchell Lamm of Wilson, North Carolina; a brother, Harry Mitchell of Fairmont, North Carolina; two children from his marriage to Ms. Jacobsen, Nora Sanborn of Eatontown, New Jersey, and Elizabeth Curtis of Atlanta; three granddaughters, two grandsons, and one great-granddaughter.

Mr. Mitchell also wrote some fictional pieces about North Carolina, among them "The Downfall of Fascism in Black Ankle County" (1939), "I Blame It All on Mama" (1940), and "Uncle Dockery and the Independent Bull" (1939). Another fictional character, "Old Mr. Flood," was said to be a composite of several men at the Fulton Fish Market and his stories were told in 1944 and 1945. A work of nonfiction, "The Mohawks in High Steel," about American Indians who worked on steel bridges and skyscrapers, was published in *The New Yorker,* then used as the introduction to Edmund Wilson's *Apologies to the Iroquois.*

In a 1992 interview, Mr. Mitchell reminisced about New York and *The New Yorker* and how both had changed. He wasn't opposed to change, he said, but it was clear that his heart remained with the New York of Fiorello LaGuardia and *The New Yorker* of Harold Ross. "At the old *New Yorker,* the people were wonderful writers," he said. "A lot of us would go to lunch together: Liebling and Perelman and Thurber, who was idiosyncratic and funny. Now, everybody goes in and out. I go to lunch at the Grand Central Oyster Bar and eat by myself."

May 25, 1996

Popcorn Visionary

ORVILLE REDENBACHER

By Robert McG. Thomas, Jr.

Orville Redenbacher, the agricultural visionary who all but single-handedly revolutionized the American popcorn industry, died in his home in Coronado, California. He was found in a bathtub with a whirlpool in his condominium, where he drowned after a heart attack, the medical examiner's office said. He was eighty-eight.

By his own account Orville Redenbacher was just "a funny-looking farmer with a funny-sounding name." But for all his bumpkin appearance, the man with the signature white wavy hair and oversized bow tie was a shrewd agricultural scientist who experimented with hybrids for years before he came up with the first significant genetic improvement in popcorn in more than five thousand years.

Until Mr. Redenbacher and his partner, Charlie Bowman, achieved their breakthrough in 1965, popcorn was essentially the same product the Wampanoag Indians had introduced to the Pilgrims at the first Thanksgiving more than three centuries earlier. And for that matter, the Wampanoag variety was virtually unchanged from popcorn that archeologists have traced back fifty-six hundred years.

In contrast to garden-variety popcorn, whose kernels expand some twenty times their original size when popped, the Redenbacher-Bowman "snowflake" variety expanded as much as forty times, producing a lighter, fluffier popcorn.

It was also far more expensive to produce. When industry officials scoffed at paying two and a half times as much for a product they insisted was a commodity, Mr. Redenbacher packed up his station wagon and started peddling the popcorn, then called Red Bow, from store to store in his native Indiana.

For all the initial success—Mr. Redenbacher said he never failed to make a sale—Red Bow popcorn might have remained a regional fluke if not for the advice of a Chicago marketing firm that Mr. Redenbacher hired. For a thirteen-thousand-dollar fee, the specialists suggested he call the popcorn Orville Redenbacher's Gourmet Popping Corn, the name, he never tired of pointing out, his mother had dreamed up free. The specialists also suggested that Mr. Redenbacher put his picture on the label.

The premium-priced Orville Redenbacher's Gourmet Popping Corn was introduced by Marshall Field's, the Chicago department store, in 1970, and within five years was the leading national product, a somewhat dubious distinction since there had been no dominant American popcorn in a highly fragmented industry.

In 1976 Mr. Redenbacher and Mr. Bowman sold out to Hunt-Wesson, now a Conagra Inc. subsidiary, and Mr. Redenbacher began a career as a company spokesman, making hundreds of personal appearances a year and appearing in scores of television commercials. According to industry estimates, the brand, still the national leader in the $1 billion annual popcorn market, accounts for about 45 percent of the microwave market.

A native of Brazil, Indiana, Mr. Redenbacher grew up on his father's farm, sometimes selling homegrown popcorn from a roadside stand. It was while attending Purdue University that the college's hybrid experiments caught his attention and convinced him he could do better. After his graduation in 1928 he worked as a county agricultural agent and then managed a twelve-thousand-acre farm before he teamed up with Mr. Bowman.

Although popcorn's growing popularity has been attributed in large part to the development of popcorn that can be microwaved, which accounts to 80 percent of annual sales, Mr. Redenbacher remained a popcorn purist. Until the end, a grandson said, he preferred the old-fashioned stove-top variety.

Mr. Redenbacher had been a presence in advertising for the products bearing his name since they were introduced nationally; his face was also an integral part of package logos. But in most recent advertising for newer products in the line, Mr. Redenbacher's presence has been played down.

Mr. Redenbacher is survived by two daughters, Billie Ann Atwood of San Jose, California, and Gail Tuminello of Valparaiso, Indiana; twelve grandchildren, and ten great-grandchildren.

September 20, 1995

Our Inner Nerd

Gail Collins added this assessment:

Orville Redenbacher originally called his popcorn Red Bow, a discreet reference to his own name and that of his partner, Charlie Bowman. A Chicago advertising consultant decreed that the product would sell much better if it was called Orville Redenbacher's Gourmet Popping Corn, and sent the men a thirteen-thousand-dollar bill for the insight. Thus Mr. Redenbacher's name ascended into the pantheon of great American Living Trademarks, while Charlie Bowman's went the way of the fifth Beatle.

Like other immortals—Colonel Sanders, Frank Perdue, Dr. Scholl— Mr. Redenbacher had a negative glamour that inspired trust. He looked like a man who would spend forty years crossbreeding thirty thousand popcorn hybrids in search of "the perfect kernel." Mr. Redenbacher's version, which he didn't perfect until he was sixty-three, popped up twice as fluffy as the competition's. It also had fewer of those unpopped kernels, which Mr. Redenbacher called "the shy fellows."

Hunt-Wesson, which bought the brand in 1976, was canny enough to keep Mr. Redenbacher as company spokesman. He became one of the best-known human logos in American commerce, more sympathetic than the Smith Brothers, less politically correct than Ben & Jerry.

Perhaps his lanky frame reminded people that popcorn is a relatively low-calorie snack (though not when presented, as a Redenbacher cook-book suggests, in the form of Indiana Farms Blue Cheese Balls). Maybe his prewar hair style, bow tie, and spectacles called up a sympathetic response from the inner nerd in all of us.

He began wearing bow ties while in high school in Indiana. He played the Sousaphone in the Purdue marching band. He became the first county agricultural agent to broadcast radio interviews direct from the cornfields. He never bought a sports team, marketed his own merlot, or got caught nightclubbing with Cindy Crawford.

His was an all-American ascendency—the builder of the better mousetrap, the triumphant ninety-pound weakling, the Revenge of the Nerd. But in a bittersweet coda, Orville Redenbacher died at eighty-eight while researchers were still struggling to bring his ultimate goal to frui-tion—the "100 percent pop" for every kernel, including all the shy ones.

December 31, 1995
THE NEW YORK TIMES MAGAZINE

"Coya, Come Home"

COYA KNUTSON

By Robert McG. Thomas, Jr.

Former Representative Coya Knutson of Minnesota, a fierce champion of family farms, medical research, and campaign finance reform and a creator of federal student loans, died at a nursing home in Edina, Minnesota, her legislative achievements all but overshadowed by her vindictive husband's "Coya, Come Home" campaign that led to her defeat after two terms in 1958. She was eighty-two. Her son, Terry, said the cause was kidney failure.

If there had ever been any doubts that a woman's place is in the House, they must surely have been dispelled in 1954 when the former Coya Gjesdal unseated a six-term Republican and swept into Congress like a whirlwind from northern Minnesota. There had been women in Congress continuously for more than thirty years, and Mrs. Knutson, although the first from Minnesota, was one of seven elected in 1954. But it is safe to say that the House had never seen anything quite like her.

A Norwegian immigrant's daughter who grew up on a North Dakota farm, graduated from Concordia College in 1934, and spent a year studying voice and piano at the Juilliard School in New York before returning to North Dakota to teach school, she married in 1940 and settled in the little town of Oklee, Minnesota, just across the state line.

She and her husband operated a small hotel cum café until Mrs. Knutson, a populist inspired by Eleanor Roosevelt, got the political bug and made a successful run for the Minnesota legislature in 1950. A tireless campaigner who accompanied herself on the accordion while singing her own campaign song in a lilting soprano, she stunned the Minnesota political establishment when she won the 1954 congressional election, and when she got to Washington she stunned Congress even more.

Despite her lack of seniority, Mrs. Knutson promptly won a place on the powerful House Agriculture Committee. She subsequently initiated the first federal appropriations for cystic fibrosis research, introduced the first bill calling for the income tax checkoff to finance Presidential election campaigns, and was said to have originated the idea and the legislation that established the federal student loan program.

Mrs. Knutson was an independent-minded woman, and she made her share of political enemies along the way. But despite opposition from some leaders of her own Democratic-Farmer-Labor party, she appeared headed for a long and brilliant career in Congress as her second term drew to a close. Then, in May 1958, when her party declined to formally endorse Mrs. Knutson for a third term, forcing her to run in a primary to seek reelection, Andy Knutson, the farmhand she had married eighteen years earlier, dropped a bombshell. In an open letter to his wife, Mr. Knutson, who had remained in Minnesota, urged her to leave Congress and return to what he described as the "happy home we once enjoyed."

Never mind that Mr. Knutson, a seventh-grade dropout who had once worked on her father's farm in North Dakota, had not shared a bedroom with his wife for years or that he had regularly beaten her so badly during her visits to Minnesota, as their son later recalled it, that she had to wear dark glasses to hide her black eyes from her fellow members of Congress. Once the resulting "COYA, COME HOME" newspaper headline was carried across the country, it created a firestorm of publicity that accepted Mr. Knutson's story as the plaintive truth and portrayed his wife as an uncaring wife who had abandoned her family for political ambition.

Mr. Knutson later stirred the fire by accusing his wife of having an affair with a legislative aide half her age; and although the charge was a blatant fabrication, Mrs. Knutson refused to denounce her husband.

She managed to win the primary, but lost the general election by 1,390 votes to Odin Langen, a Republican who was six feet four inches tall and campaigned on the slogan "A Big Man for a Man-Sized Job." There was never any doubt that the "Coya, Come Home" campaign had cost Mrs. Knutson the election, and as it turned out, her political career.

She failed in a comeback bid in 1960, divorced her husband in 1962, and then spent a dozen years working in the Defense Department in Washington before trying another abortive race in 1977, polling 13 percent of the vote in a primary in which one of her opponents was her former legislative aide.

According to her son, who was adopted when he was eight over the objections of Andy Knutson, Mrs. Knutson, a deeply religious woman who frequently cited the biblical passage "Vengeance is mine, sayeth the Lord," never expressed bitterness toward her husband. But she was also apparently content to leave forgiveness to the Lord. When Mr. Knutson died of acute alcohol poisoning in 1969, she did not attend his funeral.

Besides her son, of Bloomington, Minnesota, Mrs. Knutson is survived by two sisters, Helen Riets of Devil's Lake, North Dakota, and Crystal Greguson of Edina, Minnesota; two grandchildren, and a great-grandchild.

October 12, 1996

"Being Rich Is Being Warm"

MEYER MICHAEL GREENBERG

By Lawrence Van Gelder

Meyer Michael Greenberg, known to the poor and homeless of New York City for a simple act of charity he performed for thirty years on its meanest street, died at Rivington House, a Manhattan nursing home. He was sixty-seven and had lived much of his life in Greenwich Village. The cause was cancer, said a cousin, Russell Aaronson of Manhattan.

In the side of life that obituaries customarily record, Mr. Greenberg worked for many years as a print coordinator on the Revlon account in the media department of Grey Advertising, and later at Bates Advertising, until retiring in 1990. Earlier, he taught English in the public school system.

But Mr. Greenberg's renown rested not on what he accomplished between Monday and Friday, but on what he shared between Thanksgiving and Christmas, when autumn surrendered to winter, and winter intensified the misery of those who had no shelter. It was at that time that Mr. Greenberg, a small, jaunty man, could be found on Skid Row, the Bowery, giving away pairs of gloves from a canvas bag slung over his shoulder, in an annual ritual that memorialized his father and redressed a sense of loss attached to his own hard youth in Brooklyn.

"Who was that guy?" a man on crutches asked one year, rubbing his gloved hands together.

"Gloves" came the reply. "That was Gloves."

He was Gloves Greenberg, and when one man asked what the gloves cost, Mr. Greenberg had a ready reply. "A handshake," he said.

"Say what?" said the man. "You don't want us to join a church or anything?"

Mr. Greenberg smiled, handed the man a pair of red wool gloves, and shook his hand.

Mr. Greenberg knew he could give away his hundreds of pairs of gloves in a few hours if he went to missions, but he said: "I prefer to go looking for the people I want. The ones who avoid eye contact. It is not so much the gloves, but telling people they count."

"Happy Thanksgiving," Mr. Greenberg would say on his rounds, greeting a bare-handed man. "It's cold. You need some gloves. They're yours."

Some snatched the gloves quickly. Others were more cautious. Sometimes, it took him fifteen minutes to persuade someone to accept the gloves.

"These are not my gloves," an old man said once. "I cannot take them. No one has ever given me anything. What do you want from me?"

Finally, the man accepted the gloves. "Happy Thanksgiving," Mr. Greenberg said.

On the Bowery, he once gave gloves to a man who had been one of his teachers at Brooklyn College—an economics teacher.

And he gave gloves to a man whom he recognized from his days as a supernumerary with the Metropolitan Opera. "I was handing out gloves in the Bowery," Mr. Greenberg recalled, "and I saw a man who had been a leading baritone at the Met when I was an extra, a spear carrier. He didn't recognize me, of course. The lead singers at the Met would never have associated with the likes of us. I wanted to say: 'You were so wonderful!'" But Mr. Greenberg feared he would embarrass the man, who silently took the gloves and walked away.

At first, Mr. Greenberg purchased all his gloves. Later, after his mission became well known following the theft of a batch of gloves, Mr. Greenberg began receiving many gloves, some times even singles, in the mail.

Born in the Williamsburg section of Brooklyn, Mr. Greenberg was the eldest of five children of Pinchus Joseph Greenberg, who sold baked goods in a market at Lee Avenue and Wilson Street. As a boy, Mr. Greenberg rose before 5:00 A.M. to help his father wheel the merchandise in a pushcart to the market.

Through his life, after his schooling at a yeshiva and at Brooklyn

College, Mr. Greenberg carried with him the memory of those cold mornings. "One winter, when I was eleven or twelve, I lost my gloves," he said. "I felt very guilty about it; don't ask me why. I never even asked for another pair. I don't think I ever had another pair until I went into the army. Ever since then, for me, being rich is being warm."

When his father died in 1963, Mr. Greenberg decided to honor his memory by giving away gloves. He remembered something his father had told him: "Don't deprive yourself of the joy of giving."

In 1993, his cousin, Mr. Aaronson, said, Mr. Greenberg became too ill to continue to go to the Bowery. Mr. Aaronson said he intended to carry on Mr. Greenberg's charity.

Mr. Greenberg is survived by two brothers, Bernard, of Jerusalem and Martin, of Brooklyn, and two sisters, Toby Loewy of Belmore, Long Island, and Barbara Handler of East Northport, Long Island.

June 21, 1995

What the Roaches Taught Her

Berta Scharrer

By Charles Siebert

On the list of laboratory animals being defended by animal-rights activists, it is safe to say that you will not find the creatures now being kept in Lab Room 011 of the Natural Sciences Building at the State University of New York in Old Westbury, Long Island. There, in a row of six small aluminum pens stocked with wood chips, water dishes, fresh apple chunks, and rat chow, are hundreds of members of the family Blattaria, more commonly known as the cockroach.

It is a particularly unembraceable species of roach that is dwelling in Old Westbury. The Leucophaea maderae, or South American roach, is nearly two inches long, with a walnut coloring, a decidedly musky odor, an annoying habit of loudly clicking when it moves, and, perhaps most upsetting to those who have to work with and around it, the ability to fly. "We had one go right up the front of a student's blouse," a neuroscientist named George Stefano said as he lifted a wriggling specimen with tweezers, brought it over to a dissecting table, and unceremoniously snipped off the head. "She wasn't very pleased."

The roaches in Lab Room 011 (the penned and fed ones, at least) are a little-begrudged bequest to Dr. Stefano from Dr. Berta Scharrer, who until her death at the age of eighty-eight on July 23, 1995 was one of the world's leading authorities on the cockroach—specifically the nerve cells of the cockroach brain, which, Dr. Scharrer discovered, has significant similarities to our own. Nerve cells were previously thought to be merely wirelike conductors of impulses; but as Dr. Scharrer confirmed, they also secrete hormones into the blood. Her findings helped revolutionize our understanding of the nervous system and spawned a new discipline: neuroendocrinology, which explores how the nervous system communicates with the body's endocrine system, affecting our early development and growth.

In recent years, Dr. Scharrer's research on neurosecretion also contributed to the emergence of other disciplines like psychoneuroimmunology, the study of how our psychological and emotional states can chemically affect the immune system. In effect, Dr. Scharrer and her cockroaches helped guide Western scientists toward a modern empirical understanding of the ancient mind-body precepts of Eastern medicine.

"Berta looked at this," Dr. Stefano said, holding up a freshly excavated roach brain, a speck of white fatty tissue no bigger than a pinhead, "and was able to demonstrate that the foundation of the sympathetic nervous system, which took so long to evolve, has been conserved in the DNA of even the most primitive and ancient of animals."

Dr. Scharrer's entire career might best be described as a supremely bold leap of sympathetic imagination. She earned her doctorate in biology from the University of Munich in 1930 when, as she later described it, "prospects for an academic career in Germany were bleak and for a woman, virtually nonexistent."

It was during her studies at Munich that she met and, in 1934, married a fellow student, Ernst Scharrer. In 1928, his discovery of what he called "gland nerve cells" in fish brains—neurons that secrete blood-borne chemical signals—inspired the then-controversial theory of neurosecretion and a lifelong collaboration between the Scharrers to prove it; the collaboration was tragically interrupted when Ernst drowned in a swimming accident in 1965.

The Scharrers decided early on that they could best prove the widespread existence of neurosecretion by divvying up the animal kingdom. Ernst would continue to study vertebrates while Berta, having done her graduate thesis on honeybees under the Nobel Prize-winning zoologist Karl von Frisch, would take on the back-boneless world of insects. "I used to ask Berta why it broke down that way," said Dr. Stefano, who collaborated with her on a number of research projects right up until she died. "I asked her why they didn't both just work on the same tissue types together. She never wanted to answer, but as I got to know her I realized that with all the difficulties she had to face as a woman scientist starting out, she probably decided that if she took the invertebrates, it would give her husband the greater visibility, while giving her the opportunity to do her work alongside him."

From the outset, Berta became accustomed to working in Ernst's shadow. They spent the first three years of their marriage in Munich, then moved to Frankfurt to work at the Edinger Institute of Neurology, where, in a pattern that would be repeated for the next twenty years, Ernst received the faculty appointment and Berta the unsalaried, untitled position of research associate.

In 1937, the Scharrers, unable to countenance Hitler's policies, left Germany, even though as non-Jews they could have easily advanced their careers at a time when an increasing number of positions held by Jewish scientists were being vacated. "Our colleagues said: 'You're crazy. This is the chance of your life academically,'" Dr. Scharrer once recalled. "That was factually correct, but philosophically unacceptable." Taking advantage of a one-year fellowship that the University of Chicago offered to Ernst, the Scharrers came to America with two suitcases and eight dollars.

For Berta, who had little grasp of English, limited lab space, and no money for purchasing lab animals, it was a godsend when a custodian in her lab building directed her to the supply of roaches in the basement.

Ernst's next appointment was in New York, at Rockefeller University—which, if it had any roaches in its basement, was not forthcoming about them. Then a shipment of lab monkeys arrived from South America, and Berta's eyes lit up at the sight of the stowaways scurrying in the bottom of the crates. Bigger and slower than the American roach, the Leucophaea maderae—whose distant descendants now live in Old Westbury—proved to be an ideal lab model, and soon became Berta's traveling companions in the course of her husband's career peregrinations.

After Rockefeller, Ernst was offered a position at Case Western Reserve University in Cleveland in 1940, where Berta was given the title of instructor and fellow in anatomy—again with no salary, and the stipulation that she could attend departmental seminars if she agreed to make tea for the faculty.

In 1947, she followed Ernst to the University of Colorado Medical School. She kept working with her roaches, and by 1950 established such a reputation that when she was invited to organize an international symposium in Paris, which required her to list an academic title, the dean of the University of Colorado had to give her one: assistant professor—still unsalaried. Five years later, when Ernst became the chairman of anatomy at the Albert Einstein College of Medicine in the Bronx, Berta was granted a full professorship in the department, her first paying academic appointment.

After Ernst's death Berta began to receive the recognition and awards she never coveted during her life with him. She was given the National Medal of Science at a White House ceremony in 1985 and was nominated for a Nobel Prize for pioneering research in brain chemicals.

"I believe she was worthy of one," says Peter Satir, the chairman of the department of anatomy and structural biology at Einstein and a longtime associate of Berta's. "Part of the difficulty perhaps was that the original observation about neurosecretion was Ernst's. Had he lived, I think it's very possible they would have shared a Nobel. But for thirty years after his death, Berta had a whole other career. When I arrived here in 1977, she was seventy and had already achieved emeritus status, but she was still in the lab, working. She worked all the time. She really liked what she was doing."

It was only last winter that Dr. Scharrer decided to close up her laboratory in the Mount Morris section of the Bronx so that she could devote more time to writing papers and devising experiments for other researchers. Her roaches were shipped to Old Westbury. "The great exodus," she told Douglas Martin of The New York Times when her roaches, hundreds of them, left the Bronx for the suburbs. "I felt nostalgic. I said good-bye to them."

One of Dr. Scharrer's last projects with Dr. Stefano involved studying the brain's natural opiates. They recently isolated a unique receptor that responds only to the natural morphine secreted by human nerve cells. Dr. Stefano has conducted preliminary studies, based on this research, indicating that when hospital patients are given a substantial dose of morphine before surgery, the drug has the potential to reduce internal inflammation and help patients to recover faster.

"Berta was up on all of this research," Dr. Stefano said, looking down at the headless body of one of her lifelong lab subjects. "She was able to see the larger significance of her findings till the very end. It was one of her greatest attributes. She never lost her enthusiasm. Even when she was sick in bed with heart failure she would be calling me for test results. I came to think of her as a twenty-one-year-old mind trapped in an eighty-eight-year-old body. 'My mind is running,' she'd say, 'but my body is going out from under me.'"

December 31, 1995
THE NEW YORK TIMES MAGAZINE

The Man Who Knew Everything

STEVEN SLEPACK

By Robert McG. Thomas, Jr.

Steven Slepack was as bright as anyone who ever came out of Brooklyn, and when he won a full science scholarship to the University of Hawaii he appeared well on his way to a successful career as a marine biologist. But for all his academic promise, Mr. Slepack wasn't cut out for college, or for Hawaii. He took to strumming his banjo on the beach, reflecting on life, basking in the sun, and soaking up the rebellious spirit of the 1960s.

By the time he dropped out of school two years later and returned to New York, the trajectory of his life—and the shape of his death—had been set. When he died at his home outside Rochester, Vermont, Mr. Slepack was forty-six years old and had been suffering from mela-noma for a year; his wife, Catlin Hill, said his doctors had traced the malignancy to his exposure to the Hawaiian sun.

Although his wife said he later attended Hunter College in New York mainly as a way to avoid the draft, Mr. Slepack pursued education on his own and was uncommonly well read. "He knew everything," she said.

And what *does* a man who knows everything do with his life? For one thing, he keeps convention at bay, becoming a career street performer, first as a banjo player and eventually, when he sought more interaction with his audience, as Professor Bendeasy, one of New York's most visible and colorful street entertainers for two decades.

He was the man in the beribboned tuxedo jacket who delighted a generation of schoolchildren by twisting balloons into animals in Central Park and elsewhere. A strong, powerfully built man who could blow up one of his elongated balloons with a single breath (and never had to pay the hundred dollars he promised to anyone who could match him), Mr. Slepack, who worked to the beat of 1920s jazz playing on his tape deck, could turn a balloon into an exotic bird or animal within seconds.

In the 1970s, he made an extended trip to San Francisco, where he taught his craft to a nightclub comedian named Steve Martin. And although he worked as far away as Paris, Mr. Slepack was always drawn back to New York. On summer weekends, he could be found at the Alice in Wonderland statue in Central Park. During the Christmas season, he would stand in front of F.A.O. Schwarz on Fifth Avenue.

On certain matters, the man who knows everything bides his time, as became apparent on St. Mark's Place one January day in 1990, when Mr. Slepack, an exotic-car buff, was sitting in the side bay of his personal ambulance beneath a hand-printed sign advertising old tapes for sale. When a young woman who had noticed him on her way to do her laundry stopped on her way back and asked what he was doing, he told her he had been on a round-the-world search to find the girl of his dreams. He was forty and she was only twenty, but he sensed her spirit was as free as his. "Ten minutes after we met," Ms. Hill said, "he asked me to be his partner."

By the time they married, she had become Princess Oulala, a name more suggestive than her comparatively demure costume of tuxedo jacket and harlequin tights, and she had learned that for all the pleasure of delighting children, twisting balloons can be hard work. After spending eight hours in front of F.A.O. Schwarz on a cold December day, she said, "my hands would feel like they were ninety."

At a dollar for a balloon, the couple could make enough in a couple of days to last them for weeks.

So what does the man who knows everything do on his days off? "We'd stay at home," his wife said, "and listen to music."

In addition to his wife, Mr. Slepack is survived by his mother, Gloria Sterling, a former belly dancer, and his grandmother, Anna Lapidus, both of Brighton Beach.

February 16, 1996

The Emperor of Ice Cream

Reuben Mattus

Reuben Mattus, who died in the North Broward Medical Center in Deerfield, Florida, in 1994 at the age of eighty-one, was a Polish immigrant who started out as a teenager with a horse and wagon in the Bronx, peddling the family product that would make his fortune. The financial rewards were modest until 1959, when he made up a nonsensical foreign-sounding brand name and stuck an umlaut on it. Eventually he was overseeing a multimillion-dollar company with a coast-to-coast string of hundreds of franchise stores that ultimately spread as far as Tokyo.

By Ruth Reichl

In 1959, Reuben Mattus invented Häagen-Dazs. Most people thought it was ice cream. They were wrong. It was a new way to sell food to a nation convinced that everybody else in the world ate better. Call it the vichyssoise strategy.

Vichyssoise is a native New Yorker. Created at the Ritz-Carlton in 1917, it masqueraded as a French soup and enjoyed enormous success. When Mr. Mattus created his richer, more expensive ice cream, he used the same tactic. He had been selling the family ice cream in the Bronx for thirty years, and he was not the first to think that Americans would be willing to pay more for a better product. But he was the first to understand that they would be more likely to do so if they thought it was foreign. So he made up a ridiculous, impossible-to-pronounce name, printed a map of Scandinavia on the carton, and the rest is history.

The absurdity in this is that in those days America truly was the empire of ice cream. What passed as ice cream in Europe was a sweet, hard, grainy substance that came in crumbling cones best suited for use as packing material. Americans didn't care; they honestly believed that any food from across the ocean had to be better than the home-grown sort. And once they tried the ice cream with the silly name, they were hooked.

The success of Häagen-Dazs spawned imitations with even sillier names, like Frusen Glädjè. But it didn't stop there; before we knew it, all sorts of perfectly wonderful American foods were pretending to be imported. In New York, somebody invented a thicker waffle, dubbed it "Belgian," and watched its popularity soar. Smirnoff vodka, made in Connecticut, enjoyed a sudden vogue. A fish called "Dover sole," which often is neither a sole nor from Dover, became the seafood of choice. Nobody much liked sherbet, but when it changed its name to sorbet it became suddenly chic. Even poor old rocket, a hardy weed, was not taken seriously until somebody thought to call it arugula.

But things may be changing. In 1993, Mr. Mattus, having sold his high-fat ice cream to the Pillsbury Company, decided to reverse course and market a low-fat ice cream. When the king of butterfat cuts the calories, a new day must be dawning. But the medium isn't the message here; the name is. Just look at what Mr. Mattus decided to call his new product. He could have given it a silly name like plickenwohl or mincesse. Instead, he gave it a straightforward American moniker—Mattus' Lowfat Ice Cream—and ushered in a new era in eating.

January 1, 1995
THE NEW YORK TIMES MAGAZINE

The Wrong Way into History

DOUGLAS CORRIGAN

By Robert McG. Thomas, Jr.

Douglas Corrigan, a brash, errant aviator who captured the imagination of a Depression-weary public in 1938 when he took off from Brooklyn on a nonstop solo flight to Los Angeles and landed his improbable airplane in Dublin a day later, died in a hospital in Orange, California. He was eighty-eight and had been lionized for more than half a century as Wrong Way Corrigan.

The few people who were at Floyd Bennett Field when Mr. Corrigan took off at 5:15 on the morning of July 17, 1938, were baffled when the thirty-one-year-old aviator turned into a cloud bank and disappeared to the east. According to his flight plan, he should have been heading west.

As they and the world learned when his overloaded secondhand airplane touched down at Dublin's Baldonnel Airport twenty-eight hours and thirteen minutes later, Mr. Corrigan had not only known what he was doing, he had also flown straight into the hearts of the American people. "I'm Douglas Corrigan," he told a group of startled Irish airport workers who gathered around him when he landed. "Just got in from New York. Where am I? I intended to fly to California."

Although he continued to claim with a more or less straight face that he had simply made a wrong turn and been led astray by a faulty compass, the story was far from convincing, especially to the American aviation authorities who had rejected his repeated requests to make just such a flight because his modified 1929 Curtiss-Robin monoplane was judged unworthy of more than an experimental aircraft certification.

Unmoved by evidence that he had not checked weather reports for the North Atlantic before his flight and had carried charts showing only his supposedly planned route to California, the authorities deemed his plane so unsafe and his flight so illegal that it took a six-hundred-word official telegram to detail all the regulations he had violated. But if Mr. Corrigan had such a twinkle in his eye when he told his story that he appeared to be trying to suppress a wink, the authorities had trouble stifling a wink of their own.

Although his pilot's license was instantly suspended, Mr. Corrigan, who returned to the United States by ship, did not miss a minute of flying time. He served the entire suspension at sea. The license was re-instated as soon as he and his crated-up plane sailed into New York Harbor aboard the liner *Manhattan* on August 4, and received a tumultuous greeting.

There was an even larger welcome the next day when an estimated one-million New Yorkers lined lower Broadway for a ticker-tape parade that some thought eclipsed the one given for Charles A. Lindbergh after his solo flight to Paris in 1927. Mr. Corrigan's 3,150-mile flight was an immediate sensation, pushing depressing economic news and grim inter-national reports aside on the front pages of American newspapers and dominating radio broadcasts across the country.

Although half a dozen well-known pilots, among them Amelia Ear-hart and Wylie Post, had made solo flights across the Atlantic since Lindbergh had blazed the trail in the *Spirit of St. Louis* in 1927, none struck such a chord with the American people as Mr. Corrigan did. That was partly because he was seen as an engaging and impish young pilot who had boldly thumbed his nose at authority, then baldly denied it, and partly because he had made the flight not in a state-of-the-art aircraft with cutting-edge instruments, but in a rickety plane so precariously patched together that it was variously dubbed an airborne crate and a flying jalopy.

Among other things, Mr. Corrigan, who had bought the plane in New York for $310 in 1933, nursed it cow pasture by cow pasture back to California, giving rides to make money. Over the next two years he tinkered with the plane extensively, ripping out the original 90-horsepower Curtiss OX-5 engine and replacing it with a 165-horsepower model cobbled together from two old Wright engines. He had also

installed extra fuel tanks of his own construction, which, like on Lindbergh's *Spirit of St. Louis,* completely cut off all forward vision. Various
parts, including the cabin door, were held together with baling wire. According to Charles V. O'Donnell of Eugene, Oregon, in 1936 Mr. Corrigan undertook trials to find the optimum throttle and fuel mixture
settings for maximum range. This involved flying coast to coast several
times, after which he installed two more fuel tanks and a reserve oil tank.

Mr. Corrigan, who was born in Galveston, Texas, and grew up in
Los Angeles, had been dreaming of a flight across the Atlantic for a long
time. Enchanted with aviation at an early age, he had become a barnstorming pilot, flying instructor, and an aviation mechanic who helped
build Lindbergh's *Spirit of St. Louis* in San Diego. It was Mr. Corrigan, in
fact, who pulled the chocks away from the wheels when Lindbergh took
off from San Diego on his flight to New York in 1927.

Mr. Corrigan, who had speculated openly with friends about making
an unauthorized trans-Atlantic flight, flew his plane to New York on July
10, 1938, setting a solo nonstop record of twenty-seven hours, fifty
minutes for the twenty-seven-hundred-mile flight.

When he took off a week later, ostensibly to return to California
after accepting his failure to win permission for a transatlantic flight, he
carried a few chocolate bars, two boxes of fig crackers, and a quart of
water.

Within months of his feat he had made a triumphant American
tour, endorsed wrong-way products like a watch that ran backward and
signed lucrative contracts for an autobiography and a movie, *The Flying
Irishman,* in which he played himself.

Mr. Corrigan was a test pilot during World War II and later operated an air freight service. In the 1950s, he bought an orange grove in
Santa Ana, California, but was forced to sell most of it in the 1960s.
His wife, Elizabeth, died in 1966. After a son was killed in a plane crash
on Catalina Island in 1972 he became increasingly reclusive. But in 1988
he was lured back into the limelight by an offer to display his plane at
an air show.

Mr. Corrigan, who had taken it apart in 1940 and stored it in his
garage, was so enthusiastic that the show's organizers became alarmed.
Although Mr. Corrigan had not flown since 1972, the organizers found

it prudent to station guards on the plane's wings during his appearance at the exhibition and even discussed anchoring the tail of the plane by rope to a police car.

He is survived by two sons, Douglas, of Santa Ana, California, and Harry, of Apex, North Carolina, and a sister, Evelyn, of Santa Ynez, California.

December 14, 1995

A Landscape for Everybody

JAMES W. ROUSE

By Paul Goldberger

James W. Rouse, the visionary developer who built new towns in the countryside, shopping malls in the suburbs, and "festival marketplaces," like Faneuil Hall in Boston, in older downtowns, and later used the profits from these ventures to help generate housing for the poor, died at his home in Columbia, Maryland. He was eighty-one. The cause was Lou Gehrig's disease, said a spokesman for the Enterprise Foundation, the organization Mr. Rouse set up in 1982 to help community groups build housing.

Mr. Rouse was an anomaly among real-estate developers, a man who sought not just to make profits but to transform the landscape and the quality of civic life. Long before he retired in 1979 as chairman of the Rouse Company, his development concern, to devote full time to his effort to build affordable housing, he had made his mark as a socially conscious developer, determined to rethink the traditional forms of suburban growth and downtown retail organization.

Columbia, a new town Mr. Rouse created in the late 1960s on fourteen thousand acres of farmland outside Baltimore, was intended as an ordered response to chaotic postwar sprawl and as an integrated, self-contained community. Organized around nine small "villages," each with several hundred houses and its own small shopping area, by 1981 Columbia had fifty-six thousand residents, roughly 20 percent of them African American. "It's not an attempt at a perfect city or a utopia, but rather an effort to simply develop a better city, an alternative to the mindlessness, the irrationality, the unnecessity of sprawl and clutter as a way of accommodating the growth of the American city," Mr. Rouse said on the occasion of Columbia's fifteenth birthday in 1982.

Columbia, like a smaller project closer to Baltimore, Cross Keys, which Mr. Rouse completed in the early 1960s, took its shape as a result of Mr. Rouse's nearly obsessive tendency to observe social patterns. He watched people walk on streets, he watched them shop, he watched them socialize in public places, then he sought ways to make his real-estate projects encourage rather than discourage social interaction.

In a notoriously cautious industry that tends to produce nearly identical products, Mr. Rouse's real-estate developments invariably stood out. His most ambitious was Columbia, but his most influential effort was surely the Faneuil Hall Marketplace in Boston, in which a set of 150-year-old abandoned Greek Revival buildings were restored and converted into the first "festival marketplace." Faneuil Hall, designed by Benjamin Thompson, inspired an entire genre of urban malls, including Harborplace in Baltimore, the South Street Seaport in lower Manhattan, and Grand Avenue in Milwaukee.

Before Mr. Rouse had turned his inquiring eye to the center of older downtowns, that turf had been largely written off by most national real-estate developers. He envisioned an intersection of the suburban shopping mall and the more vibrant, intense city street, and if critics sometimes tended to find his festival market-places too self-contained, enclosed, and cut off from the real life of the city, the public had no such doubts. Harborplace was widely credited with bringing about the renewal of Baltimore's waterfront, and Faneuil Hall and the South Street Seaport gave tourists the kind of comfortable town square in the center of unfamiliar cities that they craved.

But it was the capstone of his career, the Enterprise Foundation, that Mr. Rouse pointed to with the greatest pride. Calling it "by far the most important work" of his life, Mr. Rouse and his wife, Patricia, who joined him in forming the foundation, conceived of the nonprofit Enterprise as not only a source of housing money but also as a broad-based advocate for the urban poor. The foundation has worked with several hundred local groups in cities around the country, providing expertise as well as money to assist them in developing affordable housing, and by 1994, it had built more than 42,500 housing units.

In a model project in Baltimore's Sandtown neighborhood, Enterprise expanded its agenda to organize job-training programs, crime-prevention efforts, and school and health-care improvements as well as housing rehabilitation. "It's my conviction that we cannot seriously improve the lives of the people at the bottom of our society today unless we do all these things at one time," Mr. Rouse said in an interview last year, explaining why he had broadened the focus of the foundation. "And it is my conviction that it is far easier to do that all at one time than it is to approach the problems by the single-shot approach."

James Wilson Rouse was born on April 26, 1914, in Easton, Maryland, the son of a prosperous canned-foods broker who was determined that his five children grow up accustomed to hard work. As a child he rose at dawn to tend a family vegetable garden and sold its produce to a local grocer. His family's comfortable times ended in 1930 with the death of his father, who had left so many business debts that the mortgage on the family's house had to be foreclosed.

He attended the University of Virginia, but left in 1933 when the Depression required him to work full-time. He earned a law degree at night at the University of Maryland, and in 1936 persuaded a Baltimore bank to open a mortgage department, which he ran until 1939, when he opened the Moss-Rouse Company, a mortgage concern. In World War II, he was a lieutenant commander in the navy, serving in the Pacific fleet.

After the war, Mr. Rouse expanded from underwriting mortgages for one-family homes to underwriting them for apartment houses and shopping centers. By 1954 he had bought out his partner and reorganized his business into James W. Rouse & Company Inc. He was politically active throughout the 1950s as a liberal Republican supporting urban renewal and helped to organize Baltimore's Charles Center redevelopment project.

Financed by the profits from his mortgage operation, Mr. Rouse began to develop shopping centers himself. He was one of the first developers to create an enclosed mall with Harundale, a suburban mall south of Baltimore, completed in 1958. He had considered enclosing an even earlier mall in 1955, he recalled years later, "but we lost our nerve."

He was rarely to lose his nerve again. In the 1960s, Mr. Rouse came to operate on several tracks: as a builder of relatively conventional and highly profitable suburban malls, as the visionary builder of Columbia, and as an increasingly prominent urban advocate.

Although his projects were generally considered well designed and Mr. Rouse liked to think of himself as supportive of architecture, he made clear that aesthetics were never the driving force in his projects, or in his thinking. Columbia, designed by a team of architects and planners under William E. Finley and Morton Hoppenfeld, has always been viewed as more successful as a social effort than as an architectural one. Most of its buildings are comfortable and unexceptional, and the overall look of Columbia is more like a conventional suburb than the real city Mr. Rouse had hoped it would be. It is the strength of the overall concept, and the consistency with which Mr. Rouse's vision of a cluster of villages of manageable size was realized, that is considered Columbia's great achievement.

Mr. Rouse, an easygoing man with a rumpled, casual appearance, lived in a house overlooking Lake Wilde, one of Columbia's man-made lakes. In his later years he came more and more to take on the manner of an urban evangelist, preaching a gospel of self-help urban rescue. Helping neighborhoods build was not only the right thing to do morally, Mr. Rouse argued, it was cheaper for the country in the long run than letting them deteriorate.

Donna E. Shalala, Secretary of Health and Human Services, called Mr. Rouse "a creative and passionate advocate who did more to revitalize American cities than anyone this century."

Mr. Rouse was awarded the Presidential Medal of Freedom, the nation's highest civilian honor, by President Clinton in September 1995.

In addition to his wife, whom he married in 1974 after his divorce from the former Elizabeth J. Winstead, he is survived by three children, Lydia Robinson Rouse, James W. Rouse, Jr., and Winstead Rouse.

April 10, 1996

Keeper of the Literary Kingdom's Keys

STANLEY ADELMAN

By James Barron

Stanley Adelman, whose typewriter repair shop on the Upper West Side served as an intensive-care unit for the malfunctioning margin releases and cantankerous carriage returns of well-known writers, died at the Washington Adventist Hospital in Takoma Park, Maryland. He was seventy-two and lived in Manhattan. The cause was heart failure, his family said. He had had health problems since a bicycle accident in Putnam Valley, New York, in 1984 left him unable to speak.

Mr. Adelman's customers lionized him for keeping their old-fashioned, mostly manual machines tapping along in the computer age. Over the years, he tended the typewriters of everyone from Isaac Bashevis Singer to David Mamet. Alfred Kazin, Erich Maria Remarque, Roger Kahn, Philip Roth, and Murray Schisgal turned out books, articles, and plays on machines that he cleaned, oiled, and fixed when keys stuck or carriages jammed. And at least one customer wrote him into a book.

"Mr. Adelman had nearly wept when I had shown up at his shop on Amsterdam with my hammered, ruined Olympia," David Handler wrote in his 1991 novel *The Man Who Would Be F. Scott Fitzgerald*. "It was he who had sold it to me and lovingly maintained it through the years. I begged him to save it. He'd said he was a typewriter man, not a magician."

Mr. Handler continued: "He was a magician. It shone like new there, now on his counter, straining for action. He shone, too, a proud craftsman of the old, old school. Before he would let me take it home, he made me swear I'd never run over it again with the Jeep or whatever I had done to it."

Mr. Adelman filled a bookshelf with volumes by authors whose carriages he helped keep moving smoothly from left to right, except on right-to-left Yiddish machines. It helped that Mr. Adelman was fluent in Yiddish and Polish—he had been born in Dąbrowa Górnicza, Poland—as well as in German and Russian. But he could figure out typewriters in languages he did not read, like Arabic, from keyboard diagrams.

Whether they were casual hunters and peckers or machine-gun touch typists, Mr. Adelman's customers valued his over-the-counter advice. One client was Howard Fast, the author of more than seventy novels. "When I got married in 1937, my wife and I spent our last thirty-five dollars on an Underwood upright," Mr. Fast said in 1994. "The 1937 Underwood was one of the great machines of the twentieth century. But about twelve, fourteen years ago, the Adelmans couldn't find any more parts for it."

Choosing a replacement raised an emotional issue when Mr. Adelman suggested a 1949 Olympia. "I felt as a Jew I could not write on a German typewriter," Mr. Fast said, recalling his conversation. "He said: 'I was in a concentration camp. If I can sell that typewriter, you can write on it.' That sold me."

Mr. Adelman, who had been held in five camps in World War II, learned to repair typewriters in Munich after he was freed. Before the war, he had planned on a career as a marine engineer. But the clackety machines he toiled over were a bridge to literature and politics.

Arriving in New York in 1949, he mastered English by reading *The Red Badge of Courage* by Stephen Crane, but typewriter repair jobs were hard to come by. He did construction work, lugging steel beams. In 1951, he met Karl Osner, who owned a typewriter shop on Amsterdam Avenue. Mr. Osner had spent much of World War II in an internment camp in France. His one employee wanted to be a painter, and one day, Mr. Osner called Mr. Adelman and said: "You have a job." Mr. Osner made him a partner in 1961 and sold him the shop when he retired in 1968.

Mr. Adelman is survived by his wife, Mary; two daughters, Frederica Adelman Gulezian of Takoma Park, Maryland, and Anne Adelman Taswell of New Haven, Connecticut, and a grandson.

December 1, 1995

Our First Ideal

MARGARET G. CAHILL

By Robert McG. Thomas, Jr.

Margaret Gorman Cahill, who became the first Miss America in 1921 and spent the better part of the next seven decades trying to live down the bathing beauty image, died at a nursing home in Bowie, Maryland. She was ninety and had lived her entire life in Washington, D.C.

Unlike latter-day Miss Americas, who can assert that it was really their talent or their poise that made the difference, Mrs. Cahill could make no such claim. In September 1921, when she beat out seven other contestants, including a New York show girl, the pageant was an unabashed beauty contest. Lest there be any misunderstanding, the organizers billed it both as the Inter-City Beauty Contest and the Atlantic City Bathing Beauty Contest and conducted it on the beach.

To be sure, the swimsuits of the era were demure by modern standards, none more so than Mrs. Cahill's. While some of her rivals violated a local modesty ordinance by appearing bare-legged on the beach, she wore dark, knee-high stockings and a chiffon bathing costume with a tiered skirt that came almost to her knees.

A petite, blue-eyed beauty whose long blonde ringlets made her a Mary Pickford look-alike, Mrs. Cahill was not only the first Miss America, but also set two pageant records that still stand. At 5 feet 1 inch and 108 pounds, she remains the smallest Miss America, and with a 30-25-32 figure that was close to the flapper era ideal, the slimmest.

But Mrs. Cahill had a certain advantage. When she won in 1921, she was only sixteen years old, and by some accounts, only fifteen. When she defended her title in 1922, a year older and more mature, she lost to Miss Ohio, Mary Campbell, who beat her again the next year to become the only two-time winner.

Whatever her age was at the time—Mrs. Cahill would never discuss the matter—when reporters from *The Washington Herald* came to her Georgetown home in the summer of 1921 to notify Margee Gorman that on the basis of a photograph submitted by her parents she had been selected to represent the newspaper in the Atlantic City contest, they found her in a nearby park shooting marbles in the dirt. Mrs. Cahill later took great pains to correct what she saw as the implications of the activity. "I was not a tomboy," she said. "I loved all the boys."

In later years, as the contest grew into a major annual event, Mrs. Cahill, who in 1925 married Vincent Cahill, a real-estate broker, sought to distance herself from her role in the pageant, especially the beauty queen label. "My husband hated it," she said. "I did, too."

Even so, three years after her husband's death, she was persuaded to attend the 1960 contest, but she later called the organizers cheap for not reimbursing her for fifteen hundred dollars in expenses.

She is survived by a brother, William L. Gorman of Fort Myers, Florida.

October 5, 1995

Marathon Man

Fred Lebow

By Michael Janofsky

Fred Lebow, who created the New York City Marathon and developed it into not only the largest such race in the world but also a citywide celebration, died at his home on the Upper East Side. He was sixty-two. The cause of death was brain cancer. He was admitted to Memorial Sloan-Kettering Cancer Center on February 17 after a magnetic resonance imaging revealed a recurrence of lymphoma of the brain, which had first been diagnosed in 1990. He had also undergone surgery in 1991 to have a malignant tumor removed from his thyroid gland.

Because of his failing health, he was inducted into the National Track Hall of Fame on August 23 in a special ceremony in Manhattan, more than three months before other inductees would be so honored in St. Louis. "I'm flattered and honored, and I don't deserve it," he said in a whisper at the ceremony in Central Park. "I'm just a peon. I'm awed and embarrassed."

While his cancer was in remission, Mr. Lebow (pronounced LEE-boh) decided in 1992 to run in his own marathon for the first time since it expanded into all five boroughs in 1976. His doctors tried to tell him that it was not necessary for him to finish the race, but he never considered stopping short of his objective and completed the 26 miles 385 yards in 5 hours 32 minutes 34 seconds. At the finish line in Central Park, he and Grete Waitz of Norway, the nine-time women's winner of the event and his running partner every step of the way, fell into a tearful embrace. After keeping a promise to kiss the finish line, he captured the spirit of the race by saying, "I never believed so many people would watch a miserable runner two hours behind."

For all the growth of the New York Road Runners Club under his leadership, including twenty years as president, Mr. Lebow will be remembered as the creator and promoter of the marathon, which has always seemed to celebrate the city as much as the runners. The race on November 6 marked the twenty-fifth New York City Marathon.

In 1970, the first year it was held, bankrolled by three hundred dollars of Mr. Lebow's own money, 127 runners started and 55 finished. The runners never left Central Park and few beyond their friends and families even knew such an event existed. As the years passed, the race grew in number and profile, playing a large role in the expanding popularity of long-distance road racing in the United States and elsewhere. Within six years of the marathon's inaugural, the New York course was changed to include all five boroughs, and by 1989, the race set records for the number of starters (24,996), finishers (24,314), and percentage of finishers (97.3), even though recently the number of runners has been slightly reduced to unclog the start. Among the participants have been runners of world-class caliber from scores of nations, whose presence each year increased in number and drew enormous worldwide attention to both the race and Mr. Lebow, the race director.

On race day, Mr. Lebow was always ahead of the pack, riding in the pace car, making sure everything was just so along the course. And if the crowds lining the route cheered for him, too, well, he could bear it. How many others of his job description had brought a foot race to such universal renown?

And there were also unique events he helped develop into annual staples on the running calendar, like the Fifth Avenue Mile; the L'eggs mini-marathon, the first distance race for women only; the Empire State Building Run-Up, a quarter-mile race up 1,550 steps; and the New York Games, an international outdoor track-and-field meet that became a fixture on the world calendar.

But on a daily basis, the New York City Marathon, more than any other event, was his prime concern. He was principally interested in signing the world's best runners for the race. To do so, he traveled extensively to attend other marathons, to introduce himself, to preach the joys of New York City in November. Over the years, his guest list included many of the best distance runners in history, including Waitz, Ingrid

Kristiansen of Norway, Rob de Castella of Australia, Juma Ikangaa of Tanzania, Ibrahim Hussein of Kenya, and leading American runners like Alberto Salazar and Bill Rodgers.

"People devoted to a single cause are usually a little crazy," Henry Stern, the former Commissioner of Parks and Recreation, once said of Mr. Lebow. "That's what you expect and you don't judge them by normal standards. I'd call him a combination of Joseph Papp and Truman Capote—Papp, in his single-minded promotion and development of an institution, and Capote in some of his odd behavior. But Lebow delivers and Lebow performs. If you're asking me if New York City is better off because Fred Lebow is around, the answer is yes."

Fischl Lebowitz was born in Arad, a town in the Transylvania region of Romania, on June 3, 1932. After surviving Nazi occupation in World War II, he and his Orthodox Jewish family, which included four brothers and two sisters, escaped the country in different directions before the Soviet takeover at the end of the war. Mr. Lebow, then a teenager, made his way through Czechoslovakia, the Netherlands, and Ireland before reaching the United States in the early 1960s. Other members of his family settled in Israel and the United States.

In Manhattan, he attended the Fashion Institute of Technology. After brief periods in Cleveland and Kansas City, he returned to New York and worked in the garment district through the 1970s, marketing knockoffs.

At the time, tennis was his avocation. But he found that losing a match nullified many of the benefits. To build his stamina, he tried distance running, and it changed his life. In 1970, he ran thirteen marathons, including the first in New York. In 1973, he became president of the Road Runners. He was in love with running, and it showed: The only difference between his participating in a race and making a deal was his clothes. Racing, he wore shorts with his running shoes. Negotiating, he wore a suit with his running shoes.

"When I worked, I was a very hard worker," he said in an interview in 1980. "One beautiful spring day, I was in my office early in the afternoon, and on sudden impulse, I left, went up to Ninetieth Street, and started running. It was wonderful, and I told myself that if it was so important to me, it would be immoral not to deliver the message to others."

He is survived by three brothers, Michael Lebov of Chicago, Simcha Lebowitz of Brooklyn, and Schlomo Lebowitz of Tel Aviv; two sisters, Sarah Katz of Monsey, New York, and Esther Greenfeld of Haifa, Israel, and many nieces and nephews.

October 10, 1994

THE CHARMER FROM TRANSYLVANIA

GEORGE VECSEY, *a sports columnist of* The New York Times, *added this:*

The best way to remember Fred Lebow is smack in the middle of his own race.

I could tell you about the fraternal warmth I always felt whenever Fred Lebow would sidle up to me at somebody else's party, probably wearing a jogging suit and running shoes, witty and perceptive in his lush Transylvanian accent, even when he wasn't pushing his own event or explaining away some problem, which was always, you understand, extremely minor.

Charming hustler that he was, he brought in big-time appearance and prize money at the front end of the New York City Marathon, which has become the most delightful sporting day in New York, every year. But the reason so many of us enjoyed him was that he turned this giant city into a playland one Sunday every November. He arranged for thousands and thousands of people, fat and skinny, young and old, from dozens and dozens of countries, to romp through the five boroughs, a celebration of human will.

I could give a private or historical view of a man I liked very much. But better, I should tell you about Fred and the New York City Marathon. There were two marathons I will remember more than all the others. One in 1981, when Fred was still totally Fred, the master of nuance and detail, controlling that marathon from an open Jeep. The other was in 1992, when Fred was acting on sheer nerve after coming through surgery for brain cancer, when he controlled that marathon on his own two feet, in the company of his dear friend Grete Waitz.

The marathon was already a big deal by 1981, the time I rode in the pace car with Fred. He was hardly inhibited by my presence. At the staging area in Staten Island, he pushed and pulled and cajoled and threatened everybody, from hard-bitten city cops to timid volunteers. "Allan, I have just heard a rumor," he gritted into a walkie-talkie, at Allan Steinfeld, the longtime backbone of the New York Road Runners, who became the thirty-one-thousand-member club's leader after Fred died. "The rumor says the race will start at 10:45 instead of 10:38. It will start at 10:38."

A man with a movie camera asked him for "a little time" and as he moved on he snapped, "I am Fred Lebow and I do not have any time."

As the cannon erupted to start the race, Lebow spotted a few runners who had infiltrated the elite front ranks. "You hot-doggers, get back, you won't last to the other side of the bridge," Fred roared through a bullhorn. "I know who you are, you hot-doggers."

I still hear that word, "hot-doggers," as the ultimate insult for interlopers.

He was as tough on the volunteers as on the hot-doggers. As the parade entered Bay Ridge, somebody in the crowd shouted, "Nice race, Fred," but Lebow was more concerned with cautioning: "Move those water tables back. They're too close to the runners."

When the driver of the time-clock car refused to speed up, gesturing that the runners had to see the split times, Lebow shouted into the bullhorn, "Leave the course!"

Of all the people Fred fired that day, none left, and none displayed hard feelings afterward. That was just Fred.

Coming into the strongly Hasidic neighborhood in the Williamsburg section of Brooklyn, Lebow called out in Yiddish, *"Lama heren,"* which he translated as "Let me hear it," but few of the black-frocked Hasids applauded. It took me years to even sense Fred's tangled feelings about his religion. His family had barely escaped Europe ahead of the Holocaust; most of the others kept the name Lebowitz and the Orthodox rituals, but Lebow had become worldly, a bachelor who dated many "vimmen," a runner who trained on the Sabbath, a man who did business in the polyglot world. Yet I came to think that Fred was spooked by the impassive stares of the Hasids, almost as if they were judging him.

Somebody told me that at the end, Fred was speaking only Yiddish and Hungarian to one of his sisters; it reminds me that he always knew who he was and where he came from.

The last thing I remember about that 1981 marathon was the way he leapt off his Jeep to embrace Alberto Salazar and murmur "thank you" for the world record, and how he waited to embrace and thank Allison Roe a few minutes later. He was a good leader. In my column that day, I compared him with Patton racing through the French countryside to liberate Paris.

In 1992, when he was recovering from brain cancer, a ghastly assassin, there was the indomitable Fred, coming back from an operation, not only running the marathon but running the marathon. Both ways. Waitz volunteered to run with him, willing her superb runner's body to run slowly while Fred willed his stricken body to run at all. I could see the changes in Fred. He was thinner, older, more gaunt, more preoccupied. He used to have an extra awareness of other people's personalities, even if just to flatter or criticize them for his own purposes. But now he was more introverted. He had become a case, his own life a desperate struggle, and he didn't have as much attention for other people. I mourned that part of him, but good grief, look how far he had come. I sat with them on a sunny morning in October as they planned their race in November. I described them as Hepburn and Tracy preparing for one more movie together.

"In my wildest dream, I would like to finish half the race before the winner crosses the finish line," Lebow told her.

"It's better to be conservative," Waitz said softly. "I always say, 'Take the first eighteen miles as transportation. Without wasting too much energy.' Then you can run. If we can get to First Avenue...."

He got to First Avenue. He got to where he and Waitz could hear the announcements: "Fred is on the twenty-first mile. Fred is approaching the park." Later Waitz would say, "When we came into the park, I got goose bumps."

We all got goose bumps when the two of them crossed the line together in 5 hours 32 minutes 34 seconds, and they fell into a clinch, better than Hepburn and Tracy, both of them crying, surrounded by friends and family.

That day I wrote: "There have been many beautiful moments in the stadiums and arenas of New York, but this moment, on a roadway in Central Park, between a Romanian émigré and a Norwegian champion, could stand for all of them." Later, of course, Fred wanted to know who had messed up at the starting line.

The New York City Marathon will go on. The city should name something after him, maybe one street in each of the five boroughs he united one Sunday every November.* But definitely the final stretch in Central Park should be named Fred Lebow Boulevard. I like the word "boulevard." It has such a grandiose ring to it, and Fred Lebow was a grandiose man who just happened to pull off all his dreams. Fate handed him a short race. With his gall, with his love of life, Fred Lebow turned it into a marathon.

October 10, 1994

---

*Runners intending to use the track surrounding the Central Park reservoir will pass close to Fred Lebow Place, a part of East Eighty-ninth Street that also boasts Frank Lloyd Wright's Solomon R. Guggenheim Museum and the headquarters of the New York Road Runners Club.

Lost Boundaries

THYRA JOHNSTON

By Robert McG. Thomas, Jr.

Thyra Johnston, a blue-eyed fair-skinned New Hampshire homemaker who became a symbol of the silliness of racial distinctions when she and her husband announced that they were black, died at her home in Honolulu. She was ninety-one.

Mrs. Johnston was the real-life heroine of *Lost Boundaries*, a motion picture that stunned the nation in 1949.

It is doubtful that Norman Rockwell could have dreamed up a family that better epitomized the small-town Depression-era American ideal than Albert and Thyra Johnston and their four children.

Dr. Johnston, who was born in Chicago, graduated with honors from the University of Chicago Medical School, and studied radiology at Harvard. He was such a respected figure that in the ten years that he practiced in Gorham, New Hampshire, he headed the school board, served as a selectman, was president of the county medical society, and became chairman of the local Republican party.

Mrs. Johnston, who was born in New Orleans, grew up in Boston and married her husband when he was a medical student. She was at once a model homemaker and mother and a civic and social leader whose well-appointed home in exclusive Prospect Hill was the scene of the annual Christmas social of the Congregational Church.

But Mrs. Johnston, described by her son Albert Jr. as looking as Irish as any of her neighbors, had a secret. In a society of such perverse attitudes that black "blood" was simultaneously scorned and regarded as so powerful that the tiniest trace was considered the defining racial characteristic, she was born one-eighth black, enough to qualify her as "Negro" on her birth certificate.

Although he was listed on his birth certificate as white, according to his son, Dr. Johnston was also part black, as well as part Indian. He was black enough to be one of two "black" students admitted to his medical class under a racial quota established to assure a supply of black doctors to treat black patients. But after graduation he could not find a job at one of the few hospitals that accepted black interns.

When Maine General Hospital in Portland accepted his application without inquiring about his race, a deception of sorts began. "We never once intended to pass over as white," Mrs. Johnston said years later. "It just happened accidentally." So, too, did the denouement.

It began in 1940, when the navy recruited Dr. Johnston and then withdrew his commission after the naval intelligence authorities had questioned him about reports that he had "colored blood." Stung by the rejection, Dr. Johnston, who moved his family to Keene in southern New Hampshire in 1939, told his children about their background.

A few years later Albert Jr. related the story to a neighbor, Louis De Rochemont, the movie producer, who immediately grasped its implications. As a result, the family's story was told, first in a widely read article in the *Reader's Digest* in 1947 by William L. White, then in a book, and, lastly, in *Lost Boundaries,* which starred Mel Ferrer and Beatrice Pearson as Albert and Thyra Johnston. The theme was considered so controversial in the 1940s that Mr. De Rochemont, who had won an Academy Award in 1936 for his *March of Time* documentaries, was denied studio backing and had to finance the film himself.

When the lights came up at the world premiere of *Lost Boundaries* in New York, the audience sat in stunned silence. No wonder. The movie, which went on to receive a series of major awards, undermined the very foundation of social attitudes that link race and personal characteristics. Its message to white America was unmistakable. Because if you did not know that a person is black, and he would be the very one you would want to examine your X rays and run your school system, and she would be the one you would want to play bridge with and work with on civic projects, what possible difference could it make if you did know?

In Keene the answer was essentially none. The Johnstons' friends seemed to realize that the family had not been passing as white, but as Americans.

Their children, who had, after all, grown up in a society that re-garded race as defining, had to make some psychological adjustments. But there was virtually no social backlash, and Dr. Johnston's practice actually grew until he accepted a lucrative offer to move to Hawaii in 1966.

In 1989, a year after her husband's death, when she attended a movie reunion in Keene, Mrs. Johnston offered her own prism for looking at her palette of grandchildren and great-grandchildren. "I just call them flowers in a garden," she said.

In addition to Albert Jr., of Honolulu, surviving are two other sons, Donald, of Thornton, Colorado, and Paul, of Buzzards Bay, Massachu-setts; a daughter, Anne Breen of North Granby, Connecticut; a sister, Antoinette Reed of Tuskegee, Alabama; six grandchildren, and eight great-grandchildren.

November 29, 1995

Witness to the Plague, Victim of the Plague

Jeffrey Schmalz

By Richard J. Meislin

Jeffrey Schmalz, a journalist who wrote with passion and insight about the determination and despair of AIDS sufferers, died of complications of the disease at his home in Manhattan. He was thirty-nine.

When his illness was discovered three years ago, Mr. Schmalz, who spent his entire two-decade career as a reporter and editor at *The New York Times*, saw his situation not only as a patient but also as a journalist.

Returning to work after a year of battling AIDS-related illnesses, he persuaded his editors to allow him to report about AIDS and gay issues. His writing gained him national attention as he brought readers into the world of gay politics and of people with AIDS in a blunt and sometimes startling way. "To have AIDS is to be alone, no matter the number of friends and family members around," Mr. Schmalz wrote in a searingly personal article in Week in Review section of *The Times* on December 20, 1992. "Then, to be with someone who has HIV—be it interviewer or interviewee—is to find kinship."

Colleagues credited Mr. Schmalz with a finely honed news sense, a devotion to accuracy, a sharp-edged writing style, and an innate sense of politics, both of the government and of *The Times*, that helped him to rise quickly at the newspaper.

Born in Abington, Pennsylvania, Mr. Schmalz began his career as a night copy boy in January 1973 while a student at Columbia University, where he studied economics. He was a regional editor and a metropolitan news reporter before being named chief of *The Times*'s bureau in Albany in 1986, where he covered the early years of the administration of Governor Mario Cuomo. Then he joined the national staff in 1988, working as bureau chief in Miami before returning to New York two years later as deputy national editor.

"The healthy Jeff was an outstanding correspondent and editor with a great future in American journalism," Max Frankel, executive editor of *The Times*, said. "Jeff in illness plumbed the depth of his experience and applied it brilliantly to his coverage of the plague, producing a remarkable bequest to American journalism."

Mr. Schmalz was deputy national editor in December, 1990 when he suffered a brain seizure at his desk that led to the discovery he had AIDS.

Part of the price of his ascent at *The Times*, Mr. Schmalz long believed, was that he hide his homosexuality from at least some of his superiors. But after his illness became known, and with his sexual orientation no longer a secret, he became an eloquent spokesman for the frustrations of people with AIDS and an outspoken supporter of equal rights for gay people. In public speeches, he frequently apologized for coming late to the cause.

At the same time, he was careful to limit how much his own feelings got into print. The potential conflict in having this "by-the-book *Times*-man, no personal involvement allowed," as he put it, covering the disease that was killing him, was one of which he was acutely aware, and he addressed it head-on in his Week in Review article. "Now I see the world through the prism of AIDS," he wrote. "I feel an obligation to those with AIDS to write about it and an obligation to the newspaper to write what just about no other reporter in America can cover in quite the same way." He spoke of his situation as a reporter in the context of women who cover women's issues, or blacks who cover issues of importance to blacks, calling it "the cutting edge of journalism."

"Some people think that it is the journalism that suffers, that objectivity is abandoned," he wrote. "But they are wrong. If the reporters have any integrity at all, it is they who suffer, caught between two allegiances."

Mr. Schmalz's life centered on his association with *The Times*. But with his career ambitions blunted by his illness, he became more contemplative and more philosophical. In a talk to students at the Dalton School earlier this year, he marveled at the idea that, after a year of fighting a usually fast-killing brain infection, blood clots, and pneumonia, he had been given "time to get my life in order; my life is more together now than it ever was."

His sense of humor, always acid, took on a fatalistic edge. Told by a doctor in April 1992 that he would have to give himself blood-thinning injections each day for the rest of his life, he cracked, "Well, at least it won't have to be for too long." When the count of his T cells, an indicator of the strength of his immune system, dropped into single digits, he joked about giving them names.

He was acutely aware of the "looking-glass world" in which he lived, seeing his disease as "a good story" as well as a reporter's tool as he sought to give a human face to the AIDS epidemic.

Mr. Schmalz is survived by a sister, Wendy Wilde of Manhattan, a literary agent.

November 7, 1993

THE GUY FROM *THE TIMES* WITH AIDS

Someone once poked a microphone into JEFFREY SCHMALZ's face and asked him, challengingly, "Are you here as a reporter or as a gay man with AIDS?"
Here is Mr. Schmalz's reply:

Two years ago tomorrow, I collapsed at my desk in the newsroom of *The New York Times*, writhed on the floor in a seizure, and entered the world of AIDS. I had been, as far as I knew, absolutely healthy, and it took the doctors a few weeks to reach their diagnosis: full-blown AIDS, with a brain infection often fatal within four months. That I have lived these two years is a miracle. How long my luck will hold, no one knows. But for now, I am back working, a reporter with AIDS who covers AIDS.

I've thought a lot about my dual identity since the death last Sunday of Ricky Ray. I wrote about him and his family in 1988, about their new life in Sarasota, Florida. It was a year after their home was destroyed by arson in Arcadia, Florida, a town where many people hated Ricky and his two younger brothers because they were infected with HIV, a town where pickup trucks bore the bumper sticker "This vehicle protected by a pit bull with AIDS."

I recall my late-summer evening with the Rays vividly: Three barefoot boys in jeans and T-shirts, scrambling on the floor with their hamster. A sooty Garfield the Cat, himself a survivor of the fire, looking down from the china cabinet. "I'm only human," Garfield said when his string was pulled, and the Ray boys would turn giggly.

How proud I was of myself. How noble of me to write about these people nobody wanted to touch. How smug I was that I, a gay man, had escaped AIDS. (I know now that I was already infected. But I had not been tested; I felt great.) And how ambivalent I was about the Rays, these people who had parlayed personal tragedy into celebrity—they seemed just a little too available for interviews—and who talked so glibly of death.

Now, four years later, at the age of thirty-nine, it is I who talk matter-of-factly of life and death and who have used my affliction to advantage, to obtain interviews and force intimacy. Does that make me feel guilty? You bet. But to have AIDS is to live with guilt and shame. So many tensions are at work on those of us with AIDS that it's hard to chronicle them. My mother, seemingly healthy, died last year at seventy-three, a few months after my sister told her of my AIDS. A coronary? A stroke? Who knows? In my mind, it will always be a broken heart.

I make sure everyone with AIDS whom I interview knows that I have it, too. To be sure, that is an interview ploy; I'm hoping the camaraderie will open them up. But there is more to it than that: I want them to take a good look at me, to see that someone with full-blown AIDS can carry on for a while, can even function as a reporter. Much of the time, it works. Their faces light up. There is hope.

But sometimes it fails, and I am the one changed by our chat, overcome by guilt that I have lived these two years when so many of my friends and hospital roommates and people I've interviewed have died. At times, I think my fellow AIDS sufferers are laughing at me, looking up from their beds with eyes that say, "You'll be here soon enough."

Endlessly, I fret about my interviews. I know the buttons to push with people with AIDS and I push them well. Do I cross the line, pressing too hard for the sake of a good quote?

"I wish it wasn't true," Bob Hattoy said of having AIDS just before he addressed the Democratic National Convention. "But it isn't overwhelming me. Really. I don't know why."

I knew from my own experience the nightmares of waking up in a coffin, of wondering whether every cold was the big one that would do me in. I challenged him for not being honest, and he broke down. I wanted to hold him. I wanted to apologize. Then he hit me as hard as I had hit him.

"I think I will probably die of AIDS," he blurted out. "Won't you?"

Yes, I expect so. In my gut, I know it. Yet in the back of my mind, I just can't believe it: Maybe, just maybe, I'll live to see a treatment breakthrough.

How different these AIDS interviews now are from the one four years ago with the Rays, when all was well and I was just a spectator to the train wreck, not riding in one of the cars. It was simple then: A quick good-bye. A shake of the hand. A perfunctory wish for the future. Then off into the night. Now, it's embraces and tears and whispers from me and for me: "Stay well," "Don't give up," "God bless." And always there is that one futile question: Have you found the magic cure?

To have AIDS is to be alone, no matter the number of friends and family members around. Then, to be with someone who has HIV—be it interviewer or interviewee—is to find kinship. "I'm so glad they picked you to do this," Mary Fisher said in an interview just before she spoke at the Republican National Convention as a woman with HIV. With her, as with Magic Johnson and Bob Hattoy and Larry Kramer and Elizabeth Glaser, who spoke at the Democratic convention, the talk was the same: of anger and courage and politics. We talked of that deep nausea in the pit of your stomach when even cancer patients pity you and when a doctor, who should know better, puts on latex gloves just to shake your hand.

There are time-outs in each of the interviews for both of us to get tissues, for both to pop our AZT, for both to laugh and always to hug.

"I will see you again," Magic Johnson said pointedly, in what was not a social nicety but an affirmation of life between two people with HIV. Like each of the other interviews, ours was therapy for him. It was therapy for me.

"Who are you?" a TV reporter asked me at a funeral march in Greenwich Village for an Act-Up leader dead of AIDS. The reporter knew full well who I was: the guy from *The Times* with AIDS.

The lid of the coffin had been removed, the open box carried on shoulders in the rain, led in the dusk by mourners with torches, the dirge of a single drumbeat setting the pace of this, a funeral turned protest against President Bush's handling of AIDS. "Are you here as a reporter or as a gay man with AIDS?" the TV correspondent persisted, shoving a microphone in my face. His camera spotlight went on.

I didn't respond. People in the crowd moved closer; they wanted to know the answer. I wanted to know it, too. Finally, it came out: "Reporter." Some shook their heads in disgust, all but shouting "Uncle Tom!" They wanted an advocate, not a reporter. So there I stood, a gay man with AIDS out of place at an AIDS funeral, an outsider in my own world.

I walked back to the office in the rain, thinking along the thirty blocks about how tough it must be for blacks to report about blacks, for women to report about women. Yet that kind of reporting is the cutting edge of journalism. Some people think it is the journalism that suffers, that objectivity is abandoned. But they are wrong. If the reporters have any integrity at all, it is they who suffer, caught between two allegiances.

Don't misunderstand; it was I, not my editors, who pressed for me to write about AIDS. For twenty years, I had been a by-the-book *Times*-man, no personal involvement allowed. But now I see the world through the prism of AIDS. I feel an obligation to those with AIDS to write about it and an obligation to the newspaper to write what just about no other reporter in America can cover in quite the same way. And I feel an obligation to myself. This is the place—reporting—where I am at home. This is the place where I must come to terms with AIDS.

I didn't write an article about the funeral march, judging it worth only a picture and a caption. I passed the journalism test that afternoon in the rain by failing the activism test. To turn activist would mean that

AIDS, not reporting, would define me. It would be to surrender totally to the disease. But no matter how neatly it works out in the mind, that doesn't make it any easier, even when I'm reporting on issues besides AIDS.

Traveling the country to interview voters about the Presidential election, I dropped by an Iowa café where, as a reporter from New York, I was hailed as a mini-celebrity. Asked to say a few words at a breakfast of thirty leading citizens, I wanted to tell them I had AIDS, to watch the stunned look on their faces. But I didn't. That would have crossed the line between reporter and activist. Yet I do tell some politicians I interview. In my mind, that's okay. I can't explain why. I left the breakfast in Iowa feeling hypocritical, a disciple who professes to carry the message of AIDS but is most comfortable preaching to the converted.

"Why are you here with me?" Jerry Brown asked when, while I was covering his Presidential campaign for a few days, the conversation turned to AIDS and I told him that I had it. "I'm here," I said, "because it is what I do." He leaned closer to me, asking quietly, "Don't you want to be off getting in touch with your spirituality?"

Religion. How I have wrestled with that one. I had wanted to stop in church the day before brain surgery. But to me it would have been the height of hypocrisy to turn to God in desperation after years of turning away. Yet I *have* become more spiritual. I think often of the dozen friends who have died of AIDS, and I feel them with me. It's not that I am writing editorials, avenging their deaths. It's that I feel their strength, their soothing me on. They are my conscience, their shadows with me everywhere: In the torchlight of the march. Over my shoulder. By my desk. In my sleep.

On its surface, life is much the same as before: I walk into the newsroom, sit at my desk, work the phone. But it is a through-the-looking-glass world. Sitting in my doctor's office, listening to the latest update, I can't help thinking, "This is a good story."

An interview with Bill Clinton on gay issues and AIDS was the oddest I've ever had. He had been briefed that I had the virus, but we never discussed it. It seemed self-centered for me to bring it up, and I guess he thought it rude for him to do it. So there we were, talking about AIDS. I knew that he knew that I knew that he knew.

Before me on the desk are the letters—a hundred of them this year, some from people who read that I had AIDS, others from people who figured it out between the lines of my pieces. Those are the ones that I am proudest of. "Consider this letter a giant hug," wrote a man from Philadelphia. I have killed the message on my phone tape from a man dying of AIDS who had called begging me to save his life, to give him some nugget of information that would keep him alive. "Please!" he cried. I called him back to say there was nothing I could do except recommend doctors. I kept that tape for weeks, playing it over and over. "Please!"

I wonder if he is dead now.

Oh, I have come to understand the Rays—those people who seemed so glib. Now, I see that they are like all of us with AIDS, trying to go on about their lives but caught up in this nightmare. They do what they have to do. We all do. I think about them. I am one with them. And I think about Ricky, the newest shadow looking over my shoulder.

My editors keep an eye on me, I am sure, to make certain that AIDS has not yet weakened my reporting. But I suspect I will be the first to say when it is time to call it quits. As I write this, I feel tired but sharp. The AZT is holding for now. The brain infection, though diminished, is still present, making the fingers of my right hand stiff and clumsy on the keyboard. I use a tape recorder; my short-term memory isn't what it was.

I hold a different job—one that is supposed to be less stressful. But I am sitting in my old spot in the newsroom to finish this, the same spot where I suffered the seizure. As I look up, I can see the wall clock clearly. I couldn't that December 21, 1990, when failing vision was the first sign of trouble. Now, two years later, I see things more clearly than ever. And I am alive.

December 20, 1992

WEEK IN REVIEW

A Life in Three Chords

RICHARD BERRY

By Jon Pareles

Richard Berry, who wrote the legendary three-chord rock song "Louie Louie" died at his home in Los Angeles. He was sixty-one. The cause was possible complications from an aneurysm, said John Kim, who was working with Mr. Berry on a film biography, the Associated Press reported.

"Louie Louie," written and recorded in 1956, is a cornerstone of rock. It has a simple but indelible beat, three basic chords and a melody that encourages even the tone-deaf to sing along. Its lyrics are the lament of a Jamaican sailor telling a bartender named Louie how much he misses his girlfriend.

Yet ever since the words were famously slurred by the Kingsmen in their hit version of the song in 1963, they have been a subject of speculation by generations of listeners, many of them convinced that the lyrics are lewd. There are hundreds of recordings of the song, by surf, punk, hard-rock, soft-rock, rap, reggae, and high-school marching bands; it has probably been performed millions of times. Frank Zappa called it "an archetypal American musical icon."

"Louie Louie" was by no means Richard Berry's only song. During the 1950s, he wrote and recorded dozens of songs with the Flairs, the Crowns, and other groups. He provided the menacing bass voice, a possible precursor of gangsta rap, in the Robins' 1954 "Riot in Cell Block No. 9," and he was the eager voice of Henry in Etta James's 1955 hit, "Roll With Me, Henry." But the improbable ubiquity of "Louie Louie" sets him apart from many other journeyman songwriters of rock's early years.

Mr. Berry was born in Extension, Louisiana, near New Orleans, in 1935. He was sent to Los Angeles a year later to live with an aunt; his parents followed. While in elementary school, he taught himself to play his aunt's piano. A childhood hip injury left him with a lifelong limp, and at a camp for handicapped children he learned to play the ukulele.

In Los Angeles, he attended Jefferson High School and sang in its choir, which had nurtured many doo-wop singers. He also found a mentor, Jesse Belvin, a Jefferson alumnus who had national hits like "Goodnight My Love," and who collaborated on the Penguins' "Earth Angel." Mr. Berry once recalled, "If you could sing like Jesse, you had the girls."

Mr. Berry and fellow choir members formed doo-wop groups—the Flamingos, the Turks, the Debonairs—and in 1953, the Debonairs began auditioning. Signed to Modern Records, the sixteen-year-old doo-woppers changed their name to the Flairs and had a modest regional hit with "I Had a Love" and Mr. Berry's "She Wants to Rock," an early production by Jerry Lieber and Mike Stoller. For the next two years, the Flairs released a single every two months. They also recorded as the Chimes, the Rams, the Howlers, and the 5 Hearts, and Mr. Berry released songs under his own name and in a duo, Ricky and Jennell. He worked long hours at sessions, writing songs, playing instruments, and singing parts from bass up to falsetto.

In 1954, Mr. Lieber and Mr. Stoller were working with the Robins on "Riot in Cell Block No. 9," and called on Mr. Berry to sing the bass part. The next year, he appeared on Ms. James's "Roll With Me, Henry." He left the Flairs and continued writing and recording. He also sang in the clubs of Los Angeles, including a regular Sunday-night engagement with the Rhythm Rockers, a Latin group led by two Filipino-American brothers, Barry and Bobby Rillera.

In the summer of 1956, Mr. Berry was backstage when he heard the Rhythm Rockers play the dance tune "El Loco Cha-Cha," by Rene Touzet. Mr. Berry borrowed its distinctive opening riff: the five-note pattern that became the basis of "Louie Louie." In *Louie Louie* (1993), his book about the song, Dave Marsh describes the beat as: "Dud duh duh. Duh duh." For the lyrics, Mr. Berry borrowed the concept of talking to the bartender from the Frank Sinatra hit, "One for My Baby" and the idea of a lovelorn Caribbean sailor from Chuck Berry's "Havana Moon," and came up with his own terse song in an invented pidgin. He wanted Latin percussion in his version, but his record company vetoed the idea.

Flip Records first released Mr. Berry's "Louie Louie" as the B side of his version of "You Are My Sunshine." But "Louie Louie" became the hit; for one week, the Los Angeles disc jockey Hunter Hancock played the song every hour on the hour on KGFJ. It sold tens of thousands of copies on the West Coast, but Mr. Berry's attempts at a follow-up hit were unsuccessful.

In 1959, he needed money to get married, and he sold the publishing rights to "Louie Louie" to Max Feirtag, the owner of Flip, for $750. He did, however, retain the rights to royalties for radio play.

Meanwhile, "Louie Louie" had made its way to the Pacific Northwest, where it became a staple of local bands. A version by a Seattle band, Rockin' Robin Roberts with the Wailers, released in 1961, turned the song into a bar-band rocker. And in 1963, two bands from Portland, the Kingsmen and Paul Revere and the Raiders, both recorded "Louie Louie" in the same week. The Kingsmen's version—sloppy and energetic with slurred vocals—became the much bigger hit after Arnie (Woo-Woo) Ginsberg, a Boston disc jockey, played it twice while declaring it the worst record of the week; it went on to sell millions of copies.

Rumors spread that the words were obscene, and the FBI began a thirty-month inquiry into the song. Mr. Berry was questioned twice, although the Kingsmen's lead singer, Jack Ely, was never called. Eventually, the investigation was closed without prosecution.

Mr. Berry was still playing the clubs and lounges of Southern California, often in after-midnight sessions. He recorded in the early 1960s for small local labels, with meager success. A song he wrote, "Moments to Remember," recorded by Jennell Hawkins, reached number 50 on the pop chart in 1961.

But until 1980, his regular job was playing versions of Top 40 songs. The work wore him down, and by 1981 he was on welfare. He became a keypunch operator and studied computer programming. In 1984, he was attacked by a pit bull and laid up with spinal injuries; his doctor encouraged him to return to performing.

Meanwhile, "Louie Louie" was enjoying a new revival as an anthem of all-American amateurism. A San Francisco radio station, KFJC, ran marathons of the song, playing all the versions it could find and soliciting new ones from listeners. In 1983, Mr. Berry and Mr. Ely of the Kingsmen performed the song together for the first time at the station. In Philadelphia, there were "Louie Louie" parades, with marchers wielding kazoos, through the late 1980s. In Washington, a resolution was introduced in 1985 to make "Louie Louie" the state song, with new lyrics; it was not adopted.

Publishing royalties for the ever-increasing number of versions of "Louie Louie" went to Max Feirtag until 1986, when Mr. Berry finally recovered three quarters of the publishing rights to his song, although he did not receive back royalties. The song continues to be played at fraternity parties, football games, parades and anywhere else that its three chords and basic beat draw a smile of recognition.

Mr. Berry is survived by his mother, Bertha Harris, and six children, Pamela, Richard Marcel, Stephani, Karen, Linda, and Christy, who all use their father's surname. Richard Marcel and Christy Berry are also musicians.

January 25, 1997

Settling the Suburban Frontier

MARTIN BUCKSBAUM &
MAX H. KARL

By Paul Goldberger

Architects like to think they control the future of the landscape. Martin Bucksbaum and Max H. Karl knew better. Each had an impact on the American landscape that was more transforming, in its way, than that of nearly any architect or city planner practicing today. Focusing on the aspirations of the middle class, Mr. Bucksbaum and Mr. Karl helped to shape the world of suburbia—changing the nature of the American town and proving that the physical form communities take does not just happen but is brought into being by conscious decisions.

It's not quite right to say that Martin Bucksbaum invented suburban sprawl, either in his native Iowa or anywhere else. But when Martin and his brothers, Matthew and Maurice, decided in the early 1950s that, instead of putting their family's fourth supermarket in someone else's building, they would become landlords themselves, it marked a turning point in the growth and development of the Midwest. The Bucksbaums' first shopping center, the Town and Country, built with $1.2 million in borrowed money, opened in Cedar Rapids in 1956, and they went on from there to become one of the largest builders of shopping malls in the United States. They shed their family's grocery business before the Cedar Rapids center even opened, decisively staking their future on erecting what Matthew Bucksbaum would later call "the new downtowns."

The Bucksbaums built dozens of shopping centers all around the Midwest, believing that, as Matthew Bucksbaum recalled, "people did not want to go downtown and fight traffic and parking ramps." About the alternative he and his brothers provided—the open "strip center" with its parking lot and entrance on the two-lane—he commented: "We sometimes had some misgivings—you felt sorry for the downtown merchants and the downtown landlords. But they had had their way for many years, and many of them didn't reinvest in their properties. They just didn't keep up with the times."

Martin Bucksbaum proceeded with no kind of all-encompassing vision of the city. What he had was a sense of pragmatic goodwill: He saw himself as providing an innovative service, which was convenient shopping for an increasingly automobile-oriented society. The times were making the old-fashioned pedestrian city obsolete, and he had no more desire to stand in the way of this kind of progress than he would have wanted his family's grocery business to stay small. To him, change was a given; it was not his role to question it, to ponder whether it was good or bad for society, but only to ask how he could build a successful business within this new world.

By all accounts, he was a thoughtful man and a fair-minded one; he was definitely modest, operating out of a small, messy office in Des Moines. He had neither the bearing nor the accoutrements of a real-estate pasha: He had the sensibility of the middle-class consumers for whom he built.

Not a single Bucksbaum shopping center could be called an event of architectural distinction. Mr. Bucksbaum talked to his architects about things like square footage and the optimum distance between parking and store entrances. These are not the sorts of ingredients from which aesthetic statements are made.

In the 1960s, when the trend moved toward large, enclosed shopping malls, the Bucksbaums didn't miss a beat. They gave up building strip centers and picked up on the new style as easily as they had moved on from the grocery store. Thus was the American postwar landscape created: not as part of a grand, utopian plan, but bit by bit, town by town, as Martin Bucksbaum moved across the plains, a Pied Piper of ease and convenience.

Max Karl had more of a vision. He knew that this country was full of people who wanted to buy houses in the suburbs and couldn't quite afford them, largely because banks, wary of too much risk, generally refused to lend more than 75 to 80 percent of the cost of a house. Buyers who couldn't come up with 20 or 25 percent down payments—and there were plenty of them in the 1950s, as postwar prosperity spread its promise and expectations soared faster than the economy could deliver—were frozen out of the market. Subsidized loans from the Federal Housing Administration helped some, but many were ineligible for the FHA's favorable rates and, even with steady jobs and modest incomes, couldn't make the threshold for conventional borrowing.

Then, in 1957, Mr. Karl, a real-estate attorney in Milwaukee, had what *Forbes* magazine described as "one of those elegantly simple ideas that make businessmen rich"—to create an insurance company that would insure 20 to 25 percent of private mortgages, thus reducing the risk banks would have to take and making them willing to lend home buyers more money.

The rest, as they say in the mortgage business, is history. He used $250,000 raised from friends and other investors to start his own company in Milwaukee. Mr. Karl's Mortgage Guaranty Insurance Corporation burst upon America like a revelation; suddenly the suburban dream truly was open to all, not just to veterans or people with large savings accounts. It is not for nothing that M.G.I.C., as the company was known, was soon given the nickname "magic," for it appeared to have worked some kind of financial wizardry, expanding the universe of home buyers by leaps and bounds, bringing the purchase of a house within reach of people who had as little as 5 percent to offer as a down payment.

It was not Mr. Karl's irritation with the inherent conservatism of 1950s bankers that was original, but the way in which he figured out how to do an end run around them. Like Martin Bucksbaum, Max Karl took reality as it came; instead of denouncing the bankers, he devised a system that let them have their aversion to risk but still justified lending money to the new, growing middle class. The impact was tremendous and led eventually to such things as mortgage-backed securities—the packages of mortgages sold to investors, which have made the private-home mortgage in effect a commodity, not a simple contract between a borrower and a local bank.

Of course, the most profound impact of Mr. Karl's invention was not in the financial vehicles it created but in the landscape itself. As home buying became accessible to more people, more and more suburban tract developments were built, taking away more and more fields and farms and meadows. A nation that had once consisted primarily of cities, separate villages and towns, and open countryside began to amalgamate. City emptied into suburb, suburb sprawled into country, village was eaten up by the spread of the whole thing.

Max Karl died in his sleep at the Baptist Hospital in Miami on April 19, 1995. He was eighty-five and had retired to Florida.

Martin Bucksbaum died of a heart attack at his home in Des Moines on July 10, 1995. He was seventy-four.

Neither Mr. Bucksbaum nor Mr. Karl was a flashy type; they were both, as real-estate people go, on the earnest side of the ledger. Each in his own way saw himself as creating a device, a system, for making life easier for the nation's rapidly growing middle class. Max Karl gave them a house and Martin Bucksbaum, a Main Street. That the system they were doing so much to create would have the unintended consequence of fostering an exodus of both jobs and people from the city is something neither man, it would seem, was much troubled by. Both men were ardent philanthropists and would have been aghast at any thought that their hard work might eventually contribute to the decline of urban America. Their real social consciences simply did not make a connection between the development of their commercial and financial innovations and the changes in the postwar American landscape. Men whose outlooks were shaped by Depression childhoods were not likely to challenge the larger forces of the Zeitgeist.

December 31, 1995

The Invention of Minnesota Fats

RUDOLF WALTER WANDERONE

By Robert McG. Thomas, Jr.

Rudolf Walter Wanderone, the charming, slick-talking pool hustler who labored largely in obscurity until he reinvented himself in the 1960s by claiming to be Minnesota Fats, died at his home in Nashville. He was eighty-two, or perhaps ninety-five.

With Fats, who insisted he was the prototype of the fictional character portrayed by Jackie Gleason in the movie *The Hustler*, the only certainty was that you could never know for sure.

His wife, Theresa, said the cause of death was congestive heart failure.

Both she and his first wife, Evaline, insisted that he would have been eighty-three today, although Fats, who long claimed to have been born in 1900, had taken to calling the 1913 birth date that appeared in a 1966 biography his "baseball age." In a career in which he may or may not have sailed around the world six times, survived two shipwrecks, and hobnobbed, as he claimed, with the likes of Clark Gable, Arnold Rothstein, Damon Runyon, and Al Capone, his age was as slippery as his moves around a pool table.

Although he had made his living since the 1920s criss-crossing the country taking on all comers, until *The Hustler* came out in 1961, nobody beyond the small coterie of pool hustlers and their eager marks had heard of him. But Mr. Wanderone, a New York native whose various nicknames had in fact included New York Fats, knew an opportunity when he saw one. He simply adopted the name Minnesota Fats, claiming that the character portrayed by Gleason in the 1961 movie had been based on his life.

Walter Tevis, the author of the original novel, consistently denied the claim, but it was a measure of Mr. Wanderone's mesmerizing ways that his widow insisted that before the author's death Mr. Tevis had made a hefty settlement to her husband to avoid a lawsuit, a claim the former Mrs. Wanderone scoffed at.

"Fats never got a quarter," she said.

It was an index of Mr. Wanderone's grasp of human psychology and his own impish appeal that he realized that it didn't make any difference whether he had been Minnesota Fats before the 1960s. Within months after he decided to cash in on his borrowed fame, Mr. Wanderone, or Minnesota Fats, was a celebrity, appearing on television, making nationwide tours, and passing out stamped autograph cards proclaiming himself the greatest pool player ever.

He certainly looked like a Minnesota Fats, or at least some Fats. At five feet ten inches, he had weighed as much as three hundred pounds.

Mr. Wanderone, who did not drink but was famous for his love of ice cream, pies, and anything sweet, never apologized for his appetite. As he told it in his 1966 biography, *The Bank Shot and Other Great Robberies*, by Tom Fox, "I've been eating like a sultan since I was 2 days old. I had a mother and three sisters who worshiped me, and when I was 2 years old they used to plop me in a bed with a jillion satin pillows and spray me with exotic perfumes and lilac water and then they would shoot me the grapes."

The early pampering perhaps explains why Mr. Wanderone, who once said he never picked up anything heavier than a silver dollar, grew up with a fierce aversion to physical labor, so much so that on their cross-country trips his wife was expected to do all the driving, carry all the luggage, and even change the flat tires. "Change a tire?" Mr. Wanderone once exclaimed. "I'd rather change cars!"

Although his frequent claim that he had never lost a game "when the cheese was on the table" was more fabrication than exaggeration, according to his first wife, Mr. Wanderone was in fact a master hustler who tended to be just as good as he needed to be when he needed to be.

"He knew how to manage money," she said, insisting that while Willie Mosconi, the perennial professional champion, may have been correct in claiming to have won the vast majority of their games, "Fats always left with the money." During their years together, she said, "We lived like kings."

Mr. Wanderone, who had a weakness for Cadillacs and other expensive cars, was also known as an easy touch, one who never said no to a loan and who was so fond of animals he adopted dozens of them. He also had an acknowledged weakness for women, or "the tomatoes," as he called them.

According to both of his wives, Mr. Wanderone was a courtly man of the old school, one who, for example, would inevitably remind his opponents to watch their language whenever he would escort either of them into some dingy pool hall.

He also knew how to take care of himself, the first Mrs. Wanderone said, recalling how she would sometimes be waiting in a convertible outside a back street pool room when her husband, having cleaned out the customers inside, would be forced to fight his way out. "In his hands a pool cue was as good a weapon as a knife," she said.

Mr. Wanderone, whose father was a seagoing Swiss immigrant, was born in the Washington Heights section of Manhattan on January 19, apparently in 1913 (although he once claimed to have been hustling as early as 1910).

He traced his interest in the sport to an uncle who used to take him to saloons and plop him down on the pool table when he was two. "The pool table was my crib," he said.

Dropping out of school in the eighth grade, he accompanied his father to Europe on several trips, once studying with a Swiss pool champion.

No matter how he learned the game, he learned it well enough to support himself without having to take an actual job, although he would have been far better off, his first wife said, had he been able to stay away from gambling at the dice tables.

Curiously, after he became Minnesota Fats, his new persona led to an actual job, something he had studiously avoided. He went to work for a pool equipment company, spending so much time making personal appearances across the country and coming home so grumpy, his first wife said, that she finally divorced him in 1985.

Mr. Wanderone then moved to Nashville, settling in a subsidized celebrity suite at the Hermitage Hotel, where he spent his days feeding bread crumbs to the pigeons in a nearby park and his evenings stamping autographs in Music City honky-tonks. Mr. Wanderone, whose nonstop braggadocio banter had made generations of pool hall denizens laugh, was as charming as ever.

In 1992, when he expressed fear of being declared incompetent and becoming a ward of the state, he married twenty-seven-year-old Theresa Bell. She nursed him around the clock except, she said, when she would stay at home while her husband and her boyfriend went barhopping.

She is his only survivor.

January 19, 1996

THE FAT MAN HIMSELF

DAVID MCCUMBER, *the author of* Playing Off the Rail: A Pool Hustler's Journey, *added this assessment:*

"The pool game is not over until Minnesota Fats says it's over." Paul Newman as Fast Eddie in the film *The Hustler*.

For Rudolf Wanderone, aka Minnesota Fats, the game is finally over. The passing of the most famous pool hustler in history—even more than that of the magnificent Willie Mosconi a couple of years ago—signals the end of an era, and it comes at a particularly hectic time for the game Fatty came to symbolize.

There has always been a good deal of conversation about just how good a player Fatty really was. Many poolroom mavens, many of whom are perhaps understandably jealous, maintain that his talent did not warrant the public notice he received. After all, they point out correctly, Mosconi was a better player. There were other top players of the era who also had more pure talent, including Jimmy Caras and Luther Lassiter.

But nobody was a better showman than Fats, and nobody was a better gambler. His biggest talent was redistributing cash, from others' wallets to his own bankroll, which usually bulged noticeably. (He called it his "carbuncle.") A master at "matching up," or negotiating the bet before play began, Wanderone was a canny student of human nature, and he knew when to play and when to quit—which was most often when he had the cash. In *The Bank Shot and Other Great Robberies*, Fats opined, "Shooting a game of pool without some serious money riding on the outcome is like Rudolph Valentino being chased by 400 gorgeous tomatoes: only he runs to his hotel room . . . and reads *Playboy* magazine."

Fats was a hustler in the sense of being a great promoter, but the hustle came in the conversation, not in any effort to disguise his level of play. "I never hung out in small rooms near the bus station, trying to beat the tourists and working men out of a quick deuce," he wrote. "I always walked into the biggest and best poolroom in town, the one where all the top sharks hung out, and I'd pick up a cue and say, 'Here I am, boys, come and get me,' and they all died trying."

Fats's best games were one-pocket and bank pool, classic gambling propositions, and therefore he didn't play in many tournaments, which in those days, were usually straight-pool contests. He referred to tournament players, somewhat unfairly, as "fun players" more interested in trophies than in money. Of course, there was precious little money in tournament pool then—and, with a few exceptions, the same is true today. Players and several competing pro tour organizations are struggling with the eternal problem: how to get prize money to the level where the best players in the game can afford to compete.

Pool is taking itself quite seriously these days, and it should. Fats presided over the renaissance the game enjoyed after *The Hustler*, but the sport slipped into decline again in the 1970s and early 1980s. Then in 1986, *The Color of Money*, the movie sequel to *The Hustler*, rekindled the public's interest, and never in the game's five-hundred-year history has it been so popular worldwide as it is today. Not surprisingly, given the number of people playing pool, there are more great and near-great players now than ever before.

Certainly purses are getting a little bigger. Two of the competing tour organizations held events in mid-January 1996. Efren Reyes of the

Philippines, who is probably the best pool player on the planet, won the Professional Billiards Tour's Legends of Nine Ball in Los Angeles, and C. J. Wiley won an unusual made-for-television tournament in Santa Rosa, California. Reyes won ten thousand dollars at his event. Wiley won an unprecedented eighty-eight thousand dollars in his, but the tournament's payout dropped off sharply from there; the second-place finisher, José Parica, won only six thousand dollars.

Twelve of the top twenty money winners in 1995 were women, which is encouraging for their growing tour, but casts serious doubt on the health of men's tournaments. At the same time, the pool establishment seems desperate to erase any hint of gambling. Promoters want players' images to be clean-cut, like those in the Professional Golfers' Association. That attitude seems both short-sighted and hypocritical. These promoters prefer to ignore the fact that Wiley and Reyes, for example, are among the highest-stakes match players—read gamblers—in the game, having recently played for a twenty-thousand-dollar stake in a private game in Seattle.

As in Fats's day, there is a significant distinction between hustling—playing beneath your true speed to trick an unsuspecting innocent—and simply playing a match for money. Players betting money on their talents do not make the game evil. Rather, such matches have much to do with pool's unique role in the subculture of American sport.

It is ill-advised—and probably impossible—to remove gambling from pool. Instead of fretting about its image, the game's ruling authorities would do well to promote high-stakes match play, similar to boxing or to the skins game in golf. Spectators would love it, and match play could only increase interest in the game.

Pool has always been blessed with colorful characters, from Cornbread Red and Boston Shorty to the Fat Man himself. What it doesn't need now is colorless, cookie-cutter players.

January 21, 1996

WILLIE MOSCONI

MINNESOTA FATS's great nemesis was WILLIE MOSCONI. Here is what The New York Times *had to say about Mosconi when he died in 1993:*

Willie Mosconi, acknowledged as one of the greatest pocket billiards players in the history of the sport, died at his home in Haddon Heights, New Jersey. He was eighty. Mr. Mosconi died of a heart attack, said members of his immediate family.

Mr. Mosconi, whose name is synonymous with billiards in the way that Babe Ruth's is synonymous with baseball, won the world pocket billiards championship thirteen times in fifteen years from 1941 through 1956, the year he retired from the professional circuit. "There will never be another one like him," said his wife, Flora. "He reminded me of a ballet dancer going around the table. He was so quick, so smooth. He did everything so effortlessly. No one was more graceful or had more finesse."

His most heralded records include a high run of 526 straight balls in exhibition play, set in Springfield, Ohio, in 1954; a high grand average of 18.34 in a world tournament in Chicago in 1950, and a best game in which he sank 150 balls in a row in one inning (a perfect game) against a disbelieving Jimmy Moore in Kinston, North Carolina, in 1956.

Born on June 27, 1913, in Philadelphia, Mr. Mosconi learned the game in his father's Philadelphia pool hall. Although his father locked up the cues, Willie, at the age of six, would assemble potatoes on pool tables and shoot them with broomsticks into the pockets.

As he grew older and honed his skills, Mr. Mosconi was able to combine his great talents with movie star good looks and tasteful attire. He was able to almost single-handedly establish billiards as a reputable pastime in the minds of the general public. His efforts to disassociate billiards from the images of smoky basements, bars, and parlors crawling with drunks and hustlers was the reason for his feuds over the years with his chief rival, Minnesota Fats, a quick-witted, flashy hustler whose real name was Rudolf Walter Wanderone and who always taunted Mr. Mosconi but continually denied invitations to compete against him. "My husband hated Minnesota Fats because he felt that he was always hurting the image of the game instead of helping it," said Flora Mosconi. "Willie thought so highly of the game that he never referred to it as 'pool.' He insisted on calling it billiards."

During the filming of *The Hustler* in 1961, which starred Jackie Gleason and Paul Newman as pool players who seek matches for money, Mr. Mosconi served as technical director and made several cameo appearances.

"At that time, Minnesota Fats, who grew up in New York, was actually called Broadway Fats," said Mr. Mosconi's biographer Stanley Cohen. "But after the movie, Broadway Fats changed his name to Minnesota Fats, the character played by Jackie Gleason. This really got Willie upset. He would ask Minnesota Fats if he had ever been to Minnesota."

After years of feuding, Minnesota Fats accepted an invitation to play Mr. Mosconi. The match received considerable attention, and was telecast live on ABC's *Wide World of Sports* in 1978, with Howard Cosell serving as emcee. Both Mosconi and Minnesota Fats were sixty-five years old, but still in command of their skills. Mosconi, dressed in his trademark sports jacket and slacks, his black shoes shining as always, easily defeated the talkative, disheveled Minnesota Fats. Mosconi's rapid-fire, extremely accurate shooting captured the imagination of those who were watching. For Mosconi, it was more than Willie defeats Minnesota. It was billiards defeats pool.

Along with his work on *The Hustler*, Mr. Mosconi was featured in a 1948 documentary called *The Willie Mosconi Story*. He later wrote *Willie Mosconi on Pocket Billiards* and in 1993 his autobiography, *Willie's Game*, with Mr. Cohen.

Besides his wife, Mr. Mosconi is survived by two daughters, Gloria Dickson and Candace Fritch; a son, William Mosconi, and five grandchildren.

September 18, 1993

An Orderly Mind

ARNOLD NEUSTADTER

By Laurence Zuckerman

Arnold Neustadter, whose invention of the Rolodex card file helped so many millions of people organize their professional and private lives that it became a lasting symbol of the art of networking, died at New York University Hospital in Manhattan. He was eighty-five and lived in Palm Beach, Florida.

Mr. Neustadter was born in Brooklyn and attended Erasmus Hall High School and New York University before joining his father's box-manufacturing business in 1931. But he soon struck out on his own.

His first successful invention was a spring-mounted personal phone directory that popped up at a given letter of the alphabet. Mr. Neustadter named the product the Autodex. His Zephyr American Corporation followed up with a series of lesser-known products, including the Swivodex, a spill-proof inkwell, and the Clipodex, a device secretaries could clip to the knee as an aid in taking dictation.

"He was a very organized man," his wife, Dorothy, said. "He was always one for advancing things that he thought were done in a clumsy way."

In the 1940s Mr. Neustadter and an engineer developed the cylindrical rotating alphabetical card file that he called the Rolodex. It quickly made its way into offices throughout the country, ultimately reaching the status of a cultural icon. Hollywood moguls and national politicians, with their far-reaching contacts, came to be described in terms of their bulging Rolodexes. A 1986 episode of the television series *Moonlighting* revolved around a purloined Rolodex.

Mr. Neustadter ran Zephyr American practically single-handedly until 1961, when he sold the company to the Insilco Corporation of Dublin, Ohio, which later decided to rename the division after its most famous product. Despite the advent of computers and electronic pocket diaries, the Rolodex remains popular, said Don Gels, president of the Rolodex division. He said nearly ten million were sold around the world each year. "A lot of secretaries still keep it on the desk because they don't want to interrupt their software programs," he said.

Made wealthy by the sale of the company, Mr. Neustadter retained the European rights to Rolodex and spent seven years in London managing the business. But he began turning more of his attention to philanthropy and art. He amassed collections of antique paperweights and modern art, including works by Chagall, Picasso, and Henry Moore.

He was also a strong supporter of Israeli and Jewish causes, and made large contributions to the United Jewish Appeal, the Anti-Defamation League, and the Israel Museum.

Besides his wife, Mr. Neustadter is survived by a son, Richard, of Tel Aviv; two daughters, Martha Mendelsohn and Jane Revasch, both of New York; a brother, Morton, of West Palm Beach, Florida; a sister, Ruth Reiss, also of Florida, and four grandchildren.

April 19, 1996

The Power Broker

WILLIAM A. SHEA

By David Margolick

William A. Shea, the politically powerful lawyer whose efforts to bring National League baseball back to New York culminated in both the Mets and in the stadium bearing his name, died at his home in Manhattan. He was eighty-four years old and also lived in Sands Point, New York. He died of complications from a stroke he suffered two years ago, his family said.

Mr. Shea, a burly and affable man with a firm handshake for messengers and moguls alike, never held elective office. Nor, he bragged, had he ever really practiced law in the conventional sense. Around his office, people jokingly speculated whether he even knew where the courthouse was. But for five decades Mr. Shea was a confidant of governors, mayors, and corporate chieftains. His ties helped him build one of New York's largest and most influential law firms, Shea & Gould, whose clients include Toys "R" Us, the Apple, Crossland and Marine Midland banks, and the Yankees and the Mets.

For most of his career, Mr. Shea maneuvered around the crepuscular world of back rooms, board rooms, and banquet halls. By far his most public role began in 1957, when Mayor Robert F. Wagner enlisted him to help the city fill the void left when the Brooklyn Dodgers and New York Giants headed to California. Mr. Shea's efforts helped produce the Mets, who began play in the Polo Grounds in 1962. Two years later they moved into a new home in Flushing Meadows, Queens, named William A. Shea Stadium in his honor.

Mr. Shea's longtime law partner, Milton S. Gould, said the idea of naming the stadium for Mr. Shea was Mayor Wagner's. "There never would have been a stadium if it hadn't been for Bill," the Mayor said at the time. "It would probably still be a parking lot."

The task of obtaining a new baseball franchise for New York, which Mr. Shea accomplished through a combination of charm, street smarts, bluffs, and threats, was one for which he was peculiarly well suited, and not just because he was a passionate sports fan. Though his résumé was heavy with official appointments, affiliations, encomiums, and awards, it omitted his most vital attribute: his knack for bringing people and interests together.

"He is the city's most experienced power broker, its premier matchmaker," Nicholas Pileggi declared in a 1974 profile in *New York* magazine, "a man who has spent 40 years turning the orgies of politicians, bankers, realtors, union chiefs, underwriters, corporate heads, utility combines, cement barons, merchant princes and sports impresarios into profitable marriages." Mr. Pileggi described Mr. Shea as "the unofficial chairman of the state's unofficial permanent government," and as someone who throughout his career had "labored quietly in a political twilight somewhere between the private interest and the public good."

Just as Mr. Shea survived various regimes at Shea Stadium—whoever was in charge, from Casey Stengel to Bud Harrelson, each Opening Day Mr. Shea presented a floral horseshoe to the Mets manager—he survived decades of political vicissitudes at City Hall. He was a close confidant of Mayors Wagner, John V. Lindsay, and Abraham D. Beame. He was also a trusted adviser to Governor Hugh L. Carey.

Shea Stadium is the only major league ballpark named after a lawyer, and Mr. Shea once jokingly predicted that it would be renamed fifteen minutes after he died. But when two city councilmen proposed a decade ago that the stadium be renamed after Jackie Robinson, the man who broke baseball's color barrier, Mr. Shea mounted a quiet campaign to quash the idea.

William Alfred Shea was born in the Washington Heights section of Manhattan on June 21, 1907. After attending public schools, Mr. Shea studied at New York University on a basketball scholarship before transferring, on another athletic scholarship, to Georgetown University. He received his law degree from Georgetown in 1931, and was admitted to the District of Columbia bar that year. He joined the New York bar the following year.

At the beginning of his legal career Mr. Shea became closely associated with George V. McLaughlin, the head of Brooklyn's Democratic party, and held several posts in the state's insurance regulatory apparatus. In 1941 he entered private practice. In the late 1950s, largely under the auspices of William J. Casey, later the director of the Central Intelligence Agency, Mr. Shea became reacquainted with Mr. Gould, a classmate at George Washington High School who had become a prominent trial lawyer. The two formed the twenty-two-lawyer firm of Shea, Gallop, Climenko & Gould in 1964. The firm changed its name several times after that until, in 1979, it became known simply as Shea & Gould. "It's no great secret that this firm is run by Mr. Shea and myself," Mr. Gould said then. "For the first time, the name of the firm is accurate."

The two were an odd match—a strange combination of "blarney and chutzpah," an observer once said. But their firm grew exponentially— by 1990 it had nearly three hundred lawyers—stocking itself not just with the usual corporate lawyers and litigators, but also with politically connected understudies. "If you had to count the five law firms in New York with the most political clout and connections, Shea & Gould would arguably be one, two and three," said Wendeen H. Eolis, a law practice consultant in New York.

Far from hiding his unconventional practice, Mr. Shea prided himself on the fact that he and his partners played hardball just as surely as his boys at Shea Stadium—for most of the time, a good bit better. "We're not statesmen," he told Mr. Pileggi. "We ain't white shoe." What he saw as savvy, others considered unsavory. In their 1983 book *The Permanent Government,* Jack Newfield and Paul DuBrul called Shea & Gould "a factory of legal graft" whose specialty was helping clients in "getting around the law without breaking the law."

Mr. Shea's lifelong interest in sports was fueled in part by his high school Spanish teacher, whose nephew, Herb Pennock, was a star pitcher for the Yankees. Mr. Shea did some legal work for the Brooklyn Dodgers and owned a minor league professional football team on Long Island before World War II.

In December 1957, with New Yorkers still smarting over the loss of the Giants and Dodgers and Mr. Wagner facing reelection, the mayor named Mr. Shea to lead a four-member committee of "prominent citizens" to "corral a National League team." Mr. Shea, the sportswriter Leonard Koppett wrote in his 1970 history of the Mets, "went to work with remarkable effectiveness." First, he tried enticing three existing National League clubs—Pittsburgh, Cincinnati, and Philadelphia—into moving to New York. When that failed—and when he grew convinced that the National League, which had had eight teams since 1900, was unwilling to expand—Mr. Shea set about creating a third professional baseball league, which he called the Continental League. The new league was to have eight teams, including Toronto, Atlanta, Denver, Houston, and Minneapolis as well as New York, and be headed by Branch Rickey, the legendary former president, part owner, and general manager of the Dodgers.

It was, in some ways, an elaborate bluff; few actually expected the new teams ever to take the field. But the major league owners, unwilling to risk their treasured exemption from federal antitrust laws, gave in anyway. In August 1960, Mr. Shea and Mr. Rickey were summoned to a meeting of baseball owners in Chicago, and the major leagues agreed to absorb four new teams from the stillborn new league, including what would become the New York Mets. Four years later they moved into Shea Stadium.

For the christening ceremony, Mr. Shea filled two empty champagne bottles with water—one from the Harlem River, near the old Polo Grounds, and the other from the Gowanus Canal in Brooklyn. Though you could not see the canal from Ebbets Field, he explained, you could always smell it.

Mr. Shea retained his interest in sports and was considered in 1965 to succeed Ford Frick as the baseball commissioner. He helped the city fight to keep the Jets in Shea Stadium—a fight the city eventually lost—and maintained his interest in the Mets.

In addition to politics, law, and sports, Mr. Shea was active in many charities, including Fordham, Georgetown, and Yeshiva universities, and a spate of other philanthropic activities. Each year he provided free Mets tickets—along with five dollars each for hot dogs and snacks—to hundreds of New York children.

Mr. Shea is survived by his wife, the former May Nora Shaw; a son, William Jr., of Manhattan; two daughters, Kathy Anfuso of Portland, Oregon, and Patricia Ryan of Manhattan; a sister, Gloria S. Stroh of Jacksonville, Florida, and eight grandchildren.

October 4, 1991

The End of Blarney & Chutzpah

WILLIAM A. SHEA was once asked how long his name would grace the home of the Mets. "About fifteen minutes after I'm dead," he said, or words to that effect. Mr. Shea's name endures at the ballpark but no one can say for sure how much longer it will remain. Rechristenings have occurred all over the country as cash-strapped municipalities sell the names of their sports arenas to the highest corporate bidders. In San Francisco, Candlestick Park was renamed 3Com Stadium after a Santa Clara computer company paid $4 million for it; similar name sales have occurred in Cincinnati, Chicago, Los Angeles, Boston, San Diego, and Maryland.

If the tide is running against the Shea name in Queens it already has swept away what was thought to be an unassailable monument to Bill Shea. Early in 1994, the shingle of Gould & Shea was removed and the law firm closed. No one could quite believe it.

By Jan Hoffman

For a change, Milton S. Gould, the eighty-four-year-old paterfamilias of the law firm Shea & Gould, decided to wait out the winter in a nice pastel house with a pool and a dock in Naples, Florida. And that is where he was last week, reeling from a recent bitter blast from New York: While he was on vacation, the partners in the scrappy law firm that bore his name voted it out of existence.

"I've been at the same firm since 1933—until I lost my job last week," said Mr. Gould, the legendary litigator who represented Ariel

Sharon, the former Israeli Defense Minister, in his 1985 libel suit against *Time* magazine.

His sense of the betrayal of the legacy built by himself and his deceased partner, the power broker William A. Shea, had a King Lear dimension. "We turned our clients over to these kids!" he said. "We made them big shots! But they got drunk on their own liquor: They looked in the mirror and thought they saw Shea & Gould. And they were deluding themselves."

In its rise, its heyday, and perhaps even its fall, Shea & Gould was widely regarded as the quintessential New York law firm, with a spit-in-your-eye brashness that defied the gentlemanly traditions of the white-shoe Wall Street firms. Mr. Gould ruled the courtroom and Mr. Shea the back room, with Mr. Gould bringing his potent skills in litigation and corporate restructuring to the merger in 1964 with Mr. Shea, who brought his vast political influence with New York State and New York City Democrats and Republicans.

Shea & Gould was run as a benevolent dictatorship. That worked well enough as long as its personable founders were in control, but by the mid-1980s, when age and illness had forced them to step back, they handed the reins to an executive committee that never stopped quarreling about money and the direction of the firm. In recent years, searching for institutional clients as well as a more subdued image, Shea & Gould expanded in a costly frenzy. In the end, which came on January 27 when partners voted to dissolve the firm by March 31, Shea & Gould imploded from greed and factionalism. Referring to the efforts made by Bradford W. Hildebrandt, a legal consultant hired to rescue the firm, one partner on the executive committee said, "There was nothing that man could have done to save us from ourselves."

Within a few days after that January meeting, the carpeted, cavernous offices on five floors at 1251 Avenue of the Americas, where some 240 lawyers and nearly 400 support personnel used to work, were all but silent. Workers wheeled out cartons of files. Doors were shut, lights out; young associates and secretaries stood about, chatting idly. Tucked behind the door of Mr. Gould's corner office was the mahogany and brass-lettered Shea & Gould shingle from the old offices at 330 Madison Avenue. It was inscribed: "With thanks from the partners."

In 1933, when Mr. Gould graduated from Cornell Law School, he was offered an entry-level position at the elite firm of White & Case. But, he said, he was sent to a small back office informally set aside for Jewish lawyers. Anti-Semitism was common among major firms in those days; the lawyers said they were allowed only to write memos and forbidden contact with clients. "My heart sank," Mr. Gould recalled, his plumed eyebrows working like semaphores as he recounted tales in the study of his Florida house, wearing a golf sweater and a Cornell Law School baseball cap.

He quickly signed on at an energetic new firm, Kaufman, Weitzner & Celler, whose founding partners included a future federal judge and a Brooklyn congressman. Except for the few years he spent as a prosecutor of immigration corruption cases, Mr. Gould remained with the firm for the rest of his career: He was named a partner there and eventually joined its forces with Mr. Shea, a classmate at George Washington High School in the Washington Heights section of Manhattan.

In the 1950s and 1960s, he became known as the consummate litigator. Lawyers and judges describe him in the courtroom as wily, charming, eloquent, and erudite, with a light but deft touch at cross-examination. He was a jack of all cases, including white-collar crime, libel, real estate, and admiralty matters. "There's no one like him now," said federal judge Stanley Sporkin. "We have become so specialized in the practice of law that you don't find broad-gauged people like Milton Gould anymore."

And Mr. Gould pulled off coups in the corporate world as well, representing parties in major upheavals at 20th Century–Fox, Columbia Pictures, Curtis Publishing, and at various utilities, including Texas Oil and Gas and Coastal States Gas. "I didn't just become a legend overnight, you know," said Mr. Gould. "I had to work at it."

"Shea had belly-button instincts," Mr. Gould said. "He could predict the direction of events and he had an incredible talent for inspiring talent and confidence in people." He paused, then added, "Shea was incapable of parsing a sentence, of course, but he got his message across."

While Mr. Shea flexed the political muscle of the firm, Mr. Gould groomed young litigators and continued to amass a glossy client roster that included Aristotle Onassis, Donald Trump, William J. Casey, Jack Kent Cooke, Aldo Gucci, and Leona Helmsley. He was famous in legal circles for his many friendships on the bench, and his conversation in his interview was peppered with references like, "And then we made him a judge." (He served on a judicial appointment panel for Mayor Beame.) But when asked what those illustrious friendships amounted to in a courtroom, he looked aghast. "Do you think Willie Mays had to bribe the pitcher?" he said.

The firm was emphatically unpolished and wore its Irish-Jewish ethnicity like a badge. "I don't think Shea and Gould thought of themselves as outcasts," said Wendeen H. Eolis, a legal consultant, "but they were tough, competitive and broke a lot of rules of social grace that the old-line blueblood firms used to play by."

Present and former employees have vividly fond memories of the early years. When Steven E. Levitsky joined as an associate in 1975, he recalled: "There used to be a lot of running up and down the halls, screaming and yelling. The firm hired some people who were visibly crazy but were brilliant, hardworking, and got results. We were team players."

Mr. Shea and Mr. Gould were absolutely in charge. "There was one boss," Mr. Gould said. "Shea and I." Every morning Mr. Gould would pick up Mr. Shea and they would arrive at the office at 8:15; they also drove home together in the evenings. When it came time to determine the partners' salaries, the two would draw up a list, squint at it, then jot down a figure by each name. They divided the leftovers and became millionaires.

They did not loosen their control gladly. In 1979 they set up a five-man executive committee, but until 1984 they retained veto power. In that year, Mr. Gould, then seventy-four, had a triple-bypass operation, and both he and Mr. Shea relinquished their veto power. He was still active in court, however, planning from his hospital room the Sharon libel suit, which vindicated Mr. Sharon's reputation but denied him damages.

The upheaval of the 1980s, with prosperity followed by recession, rocked Shea & Gould as violently as other law firms. But other firms survived by acknowledging the deep secret of lawyers—they are generally weak at managing their own affairs—and hired business managers, created budgets, and established clear lines of decision-making authority. Not so at Shea & Gould. Though leaders came and went, a dynamic dauphin was never officially crowned; instead, rule by a tightfisted committee and revolt by cadres of partners would become the way business was undone.

By 1985, the firm started taking on more partners and offices: a real-estate group came over and an ailing Los Angeles firm became Shea & Gould's new California base. A year later, a Miami branch opened. By decade's end, Shea & Gould had swelled to more than 350 lawyers. In 1988, it had gross revenue of $100 million, netting $44 million, according to *The American Lawyer*. In the magazine's survey of top-grossing firms that year, Shea & Gould ranked twenty-eighth nationally.

But how that rich pie was to be sliced became a never-ending battle. While partners averaged $315,000 in that flush year, *The American Lawyer* reported that members of the executive committee—by then there were nine—drew between $900,000 and $1 million each. One former partner characterized the tone of the fights over money as: "What can I grab today? And if it's from you, so much the better."

In 1989, Mr. Shea had an incapacitating stroke. The seventy-lawyer Los Angeles office collapsed, and the Miami office was losing money. Even so, Shea & Gould moved into stadium-sized offices on the Avenue of the Americas at Fiftieth Street, at a rent of nearly $60 a square foot; the move cost some $25 million. Meanwhile, the firm still paid about $1 million a year on its lease at its old address. A respected group of five partners in their early forties left to form their own firm, reportedly fed up with the intransigence of the executive committee.

In 1991, Mr. Shea died, and the partners called in Mr. Hildebrandt, the legal consultant, to renegotiate their lease and patch up their troubles. And they overwhelmingly elected Thomas E. Constance, a member of the executive committee, as chairman of the firm. Mr. Constance, a corporate lawyer, was unquestionably its biggest rainmaker, bringing in clients like Bear, Stearns & Company and recruiting lawyers with lucrative intellectual property practices. Under pressure, the executive committee agreed to an election, and new, younger members were added.

But with a swelled committee, tensions simmered. Lauren J. Wachtler, a partner who left in 1993, recalled, "We became a firm of solo practitioners."

By October 1993, cash flow was severely strained, and the office missed its monthly payout to partners. A Washington office, favored by Mr. Constance, was also a sore point; it paid high-six-figure salaries to Roderick M. Hills to handle international business, and his wife, Carla Hills, the former United States Trade Representative, to refer international clients. Links were announced with offices throughout Asia and Europe. By then, the climate in the executive committee was so acrimonious that factions met separately, releasing contradictory memos. Even so, the 1993 gross revenues inched up to $85 million. But the overhead was so high that net income amounted to $19 million, a return lower than many law firms expect.

Mr. Hildebrandt was called back in October. He suggested strict reductions in staff and expenses in all offices to make the firm stable on its own, or ripe for a merger. By Christmas, many believed that the firm had turned the corner. And so when reports surfaced in early January that Mr. Constance had been negotiating with the Miami firm of Greenberg, Traurig, Hoffman, Lipoff, Rosen & Quentel to expand its New York office, all hell broke loose. Whether Mr. Constance was discussing a merger for the bulk of Shea & Gould or a deal for himself and the firm's prized teams remains in contention; Mr. Constance did not respond to requests for comment. "I have no reason to believe that Tom was doing anything other than negotiating for the firm or at least a very substantial portion of it," said Peter C. Neger, an executive committee member.

But it was widely seen as the ultimate act of treachery.

The week before the final meeting, Mr. Hildebrandt sat down with a small group of partners late at night, according to someone who was there. He pleaded with them to stop looking for new jobs and to make a commitment to the firm, which was spinning out of control. But at the January 27 meeting, seventy-eight of the eighty partners voted to dissolve the firm. One partner there was heard to remark, "The silence of the leaders of this firm is deafening."

The firm will be nominally open for a year to collect bills and pay off liabilities, but Mr. Hildebrandt said, "The partners won't get anything."

Meanwhile, in Florida, Mr. Gould says he is heartbroken. "I was reared in the tradition where a law firm was a family—we supported each other from a motive of general benefit," he said. "But I have suffered a betrayal by people who owed a lot to me: They didn't discuss it with me, and they used bad judgment to further objectives that were selfish and unjust.

"But I can't escape responsibility for the fact that I gave them the power to do what has been done."

Throughout the long morning, though, the telephone kept ringing. Anxious friends from the firm called, and so did partners from other firms to discuss plans for him and a few stalwarts. Jack Kent Cooke checked in for legal advice.

Mr. Gould shook his head. "I don't know if I'll ever try a case again," he said. "But I would if they asked me."

February 7, 1994

Eat, Drink, and Especially Be Merry

SAM LOPATA

By Molly O'Neill

Sam Lopata, whose whimsical and exuberant restaurant designs set the standard for grand cafés in New York City, died at Lenox Hill Hospital in Manhattan. He was fifty-four. The cause was complications of brain cancer, said his wife, Gayle.

Mr. Lopata's early life contained little of the laughter that eventually became his trademark. He was born in occupied Paris three months after his father, a milliner, was arrested by the Germans during a roundup of Jews; he would die in Auschwitz. After Mr. Lopata's birth, he, his mother, and his two older sisters were taken into custody, but later freed. He grew up, he said, poor and carefree on the streets of Paris. Because the worst had already happened, he said, there was nothing left to worry about except having fun.

Mr. Lopata studied art and architecture at the École Nationale Supérieure des Beaux-Arts, where he organized parades and marches, parties and theatrical installations. His first professional project was designing a topless bar in St. Tropez. He moved to New York shortly after its completion in 1971.

His English at the time consisted of the words "great idea" (always pronounced "eye-dee") and "yes," but he had boundless energy, style, and a capacity for fun. Mr. Lopata was also resourceful. In the five years it took to persuade a restaurateur to allow him to design Chez Pascal, his first dining room in Manhattan, Mr. Lopata supported himself by sculpting prosthetic breasts in a friend's garage in Westchester County. The breasts, said one well-known reconstructive surgeon who commissioned Mr. Lopata, had remarkable personality and grace.

According to the designer, the leap from intimate anatomy to public space was not as great as it would seem. The restaurant craze in New York was all about sex and exhibitionism, and "I was lucky to be in the right place at the right time, no?"

Joanna, the sprawling café he designed in the Flatiron District, was a quirky breath of fresh air when it opened in 1980 and quickly became the place for the young, the hip, and the beautiful. Lopata designs seemed to attract people like himself: dreamers with artsy ambitions. The scene in Lopata-designed restaurants was always one-part Greenwich Village Halloween Parade, one-part Seventh Avenue runway, one-part Wall Street trading floor.

After Joanna, Mr. Lopata designed Cafe Seiyoken, Baton's, Pig Heaven, Cafe Marimba, Safari Grill, La Bohème, Lox Around the Clock, Coastal, Extra! Extra!, Home on the Range, Anabelle, and the Pipeline, all in Manhattan, as well as dozens of restaurants and clubs throughout the United States, Europe, Japan, and Thailand. Analyzing his success, he recently echoed the movie *Field of Dreams:* People are either living in a fantasy or looking for a fantasy. Build it and they will come.

Although he received dozens of design awards, he was proudest of being named Restaurant Designer of the Year by *Time* magazine in 1986. "That means the country is ready to laugh," he said.

Although he was regularly referred to in print as a guru of style, Mr. Lopata was damned as the man who turned up the volume in restaurants; *The New York Times* once described Pipeline as loud and louder. He was occasionally scorned for what appeared to be a theme-park approach to dining rooms.

But Mr Lopata was the indisputed Impresario of Fun. In 1990, *Esquire* magazine wrote that nobody was better at cooking up a highly seasoned ambiance than Sam Lopata.

Shortly thereafter, as the market for cavernous cafés weakened, Mr. Lopata designed more intimate dining rooms, including Vince & Eddie's and Le Select in Manhattan. He was also called to breathe life into such staid and venerable dining rooms as Lutèce and Sardi's. The mood had shifted, he said: Food had moved to center stage and people wanted to be fascinated by the contents of their plates, not by the walls.

Beneath Mr. Lopata's raucous laugh, said André Soltner, the former owner of Lutèce, lurked a serious, driven, indefatigable perfectionist who approached walls and floors, tables and chairs, as an artist approaches a canvas.

Mr. Lopata always worked alone, and at times, his methodology shocked his clients. Deciding, for instance, that he wanted what he called a disheveled, love-in-the-ruins look for Lox Around the Clock, he built a perfectly finished dining room and then hired a wrecking crew to destroy it. The subsequent crumble, replete with dangling electrical wires and occasional glimpses of plumbing pipes and metal supports, remained his favorite dining room.

Life goes on, he said. You go into this wreck of a place and you have fun. Get it?

When he was told in 1994 that he had cancer, Mr. Lopata closed his firm, Sam Lopata Inc., in Manhattan, sold his West Side co-op, and moved to Remsenburg, New York, to enjoy the remainder of his life with his wife and Maxie, the Jack Russell terrier that was as much a part of Mr. Lopata's image as his Missoni sweaters and lizard cowboy boots.

Besides his wife, Mr. Lopata is survived by his sisters, Adele Infeld and Suzanne Kreienbuhl, of Paris.

May 18, 1996

Seeker of the New Paradigm

THOMAS S. KUHN

By Lawrence Van Gelder

Thomas S. Kuhn, whose theory of scientific revolution became a profoundly influential landmark of twentieth-century intellectual history, died at his home in Cambridge, Massachusetts. He was seventy-three. Robert DiIorio, associate director of the news office at the Massachusetts Institute of Technology, said Professor Kuhn, who held the title of professor emeritus at MIT, had been ill with cancer in recent years.

Dr. Kuhn, a professor of philosophy and history of science at MIT from 1979 to 1983 and the Laurence S. Rockefeller Professor of Philosophy there from 1983 until 1991, was the author or co-author of five books and scores of articles on the philosophy and history of science. But Dr. Kuhn remains best known for *The Structure of Scientific Revolutions*.

The Structure of Scientific Revolutions was conceived while Professor Kuhn was a graduate student in theoretical physics and published as a monograph in the *International Encyclopedia of Unified Science* before the University of Chicago Press issued it as a book in 1962. The work punctured the widely held notion that scientific change was a strictly rational process.

His thesis was that science was not a steady, cumulative acquisition of knowledge. Instead, he wrote, it is "a series of peaceful interludes punctuated by intellectually violent revolutions." And in those revolutions, "one conceptual world view is replaced by another." Thus, Einstein's theory of relativity could challenge Newton's concepts of physics. Lavoisier's discovery of oxygen could sweep away earlier ideas about phlogiston, the imaginary element believed to cause combustion. Galileo's supposed experiments with wood and lead balls dropped from the Leaning Tower of Pisa could banish the Aristotelian theory that bodies fell at a speed proportional to their weight. And Darwin's theory of natural selection could overthrow theories of a world governed by design.

Professor Kuhn argued in his book that the typical scientist was not an objective, free thinker and skeptic. Rather, he was a somewhat conservative individual who accepted what he was taught and applied his knowledge to solving the problems that came before him. In so doing, Professor Kuhn maintained, scientists like this accepted a paradigm, an archetypal solution to a problem, like Ptolemy's theory that the Sun revolves around the Earth. Generally conservative, scientists would tend to solve problems in ways that extended the scope of the paradigm. In such peaceful periods, he maintained, scientists tend to resist research that might signal the development of a new paradigm, like the work of the astronomer Aristarchus, who theorized in the third century B.C. that the planets revolve around the Sun.

But, Professor Kuhn said, situations arose that the paradigm could not account for or that contradicted it. And then, he said, a revolutionary would appear, a Lavoisier or an Einstein, often a young scientist not indoctrinated in the accepted theories, and sweep the old paradigm away.

These revolutions, he said, came only after long periods of tradition-bound normal science. "Frameworks must be lived with and explored before they can be broken," Professor Kuhn said. The new paradigm cannot build on the one that precedes it, he maintained. It can only supplant it. The two, he said, were "incommensurable."

Some critics said Professor Kuhn was arguing that science was little more than mob rule. He replied, "Look, I think that's nonsense, and I'm prepared to argue that."

The word "paradigm" appeared so frequently in Professor Kuhn's *Structures* and with so many possible meanings prompting debate that he was credited with popularizing the word and inspiring a 1974 cartoon in *The New Yorker*. In it, a woman tells a man: "Dynamite, Mr. Gerston! You're the first person I ever heard use 'paradigm' in real life."

Professor Kuhn traced the origin of his thesis to a moment in 1947 when he was working toward his doctorate at Harvard. James B. Conant, the chemist who was the president of the university, had asked him to teach a class in science for undergraduates majoring in the humanities. The focus was to be on historical case studies. Until then, Professor Kuhn said later, "I'd never read an old document in science." As he looked through Aristotle's *Physics* and realized how astonishingly unlike Newton's were its concepts of motion and matter, he concluded that Aristotle's physics were not "bad Newton" but simply different.

Not long after Professor Kuhn received a doctorate in physics, he switched to the history of science, exploring the mechanisms that lead to scientific change. "I sweated blood and blood and blood, and finally I had a breakthrough," he said.

The Structure of Scientific Revolutions has influenced not only scientists but also economists, historians, sociologists, and philosophers, touching off considerable debate. It has sold about one million copies in sixteen languages and remains required reading in many basic courses in the history and philosophy of science.

Thomas Samuel Kuhn, the son of Samuel L. Kuhn, an industrial engineer, and the former Annette Stroock, was born on July 18, 1922, in Cincinnati.

In 1943, he graduated summa cum laude from Harvard. During World War II, he served as a civilian employee at Harvard and in Europe with the Office of Scientific Research and Development. He received master's and doctoral degrees in physics from Harvard in 1946 and 1949. From 1948 to 1956, he held various posts there, rising to an assistant professorship in general education and the history of science.

He then joined the faculty of the University of California at Berkeley, where he was named a professor of history of science in 1961. In 1964, he joined the faculty at Princeton, where he was the M. Taylor Pyne Professor of Philosophy and History of Science until 1979, when he joined the faculty of MIT.

Professor Kuhn was a Guggenheim Fellow in 1954–1955, the winner of the George Sarton Medal in the History of Science in 1982, and the holder of honorary degrees from many institutions, among them the University of Notre Dame, Columbia University, the University of Chicago, the University of Padua, and the University of Athens.

He is survived by his wife, Jehane, and three children, Sarah Kuhn

of Framingham, Massachusetts, Elizabeth Kuhn of Los Angeles, and Na-
thaniel Kuhn of Arlington, Massachusetts.

June 19, 1996

THE BROTHER WHO COULD PARADIGM

JAMES GLEICK, the Fast Forward columnist of The New York Times
Magazine *and the author of* Chaos: Making a New Science, *measured*
THOMAS S. KUHN's contribution.

Weightier than the critical mass, sharper than the cutting edge, bigger
even than the quantum leap—the great intellectual cliché of our age is
"paradigm shift." This was Thomas S. Kuhn's contribution to our culture,
and he was not altogether happy about it.

Dr. Kuhn was a physicist turned historian of science, a philosopher
of knowledge, and, in his spare time (what can we read into this?), an
avid rider of roller coasters. His 172-page masterpiece, *The Structure of
Scientific Revolutions,* published in 1962, arguably became the most influential
work of philosophy in the latter half of the twentieth century. It introduced paradigms, new paradigms, pre- and post-paradigms, and, of course,
paradigm shifts. He once said that he had not bothered with an index
because its main entry would be "paradigm, 1–172, passim." "Unfortunately," he said, "paradigms took on a life of their own."

If you yourself have used the word without being exactly sure what
it means, you are in good company. One of Dr. Kuhn's critics (he had
many) claimed to have isolated twenty-two distinct meanings for paradigm in the book, and Dr. Kuhn confessed to a certain elasticity in his
use of the term. Nonetheless, it is a genuine and powerful notion, its
presence in our language well deserved.

Dr. Kuhn saw that science does not always make smooth and gradual
progress, with researchers calmly adding their bricks to the edifice. Some-

times, science changes by means of revolutions. Its practitioners undergo a transformation of vision, like people who stare at that optical-illusion silhouette of a candlestick until they suddenly see it flip into a pair of human faces. The paradigm shift, in contrast to "normal science," means crisis. It means tearing down an established framework and reassembling the pieces into something quite new.

This is a romantic idea, and practitioners of just about every branch of science now claim paradigm shifts almost yearly. Real paradigm shifts are not as common as all that, but they do occur. When I met Dr. Kuhn, a decade ago, I was researching a book on chaos and complexity, the most sweeping transformation of scientific vision in our own time. His words applied perfectly: "It is rather as if the professional community had been suddenly transported to another planet where familiar objects are seen in a different light and are joined by unfamiliar ones as well."

Dr. Kuhn's approach did not altogether flatter scientists. It implied that their enterprise was not a purely rational search for truth but rather an act of construction bound to social forces and constrained by habits and biases. Deconstructionists have seen Dr. Kuhn as an ally. But they have often gone too far, suggesting that Dr. Kuhn thought of science as a kind of "mob psychology," arbitrary and detached from what old-fashioned types used to call "reality." It is true that Dr. Kuhn tried to understand the mechanics of Aristotle, say, on its own terms rather than as a silly and inferior version of Newton. He sought to appreciate its logic as a worldview. "When reading the works of an important thinker," he advised, "look first for the apparent absurdities in the text and ask yourself how a sensible person could have written them."

But he did not mean to suggest that Aristotelian mechanics would come in handy for aerospace engineers. Newton does describe nature better than Aristotle, and Einstein better than Newton. Dr. Kuhn noted that the crises leading to paradigm shifts often begin with new discoveries, experimental discrepancies that cannot be squeezed into the established framework. New data force scientists to see the world differently—and afterward the data themselves look different. He held a complicated picture of knowledge building in balance.

So, thanks to Dr. Kuhn, we've lived through paradigm shifts in child rearing, sports psychology, and stock market analysis. All too many academics have published essays entitled "Brother, Can You Paradigm?" When Dr. Kuhn died, it was inevitable that at least one waggish obituarist would say he had now undergone the ultimate paradigm shift—himself.

December 29, 1996

THE NEW YORK TIMES MAGAZINE

The Matriarch

IMMACULATA CUOMO

By Kevin Sack

It is not unusual, of course, for American politicians to weave folklore out of the threads of their personal heritage. But rarely has any leader been as effective at that particular craft of image making than former Gov. Mario M. Cuomo of New York when recounting the wit and wisdom of his mother, Immaculata Cuomo.

Mrs. Cuomo, who died at North Shore Extended Care Facility in Manhasset, Long Island, at age ninety-two, left an anthology of anecdotes that gave uncommon life and humor to her youngest son's speeches. His stories about her, usually told with a thick Italian accent, were always intended to amuse. But they also had a deeper purpose.

They helped remind Mr. Cuomo's listeners that he was a direct descendant of the immigrant struggle, that he was only one generation removed from the mountainside house in Tramonti, Italy, where she grew up without running water or electricity. As he grappled with unanswerable questions posed by modern plagues and moral decay, his Immaculataisms spoke to the reassuring Old Country values of hard work, frugality, and family.

On January 1, 1983, when Mr. Cuomo was sworn in for the first of three terms as Governor, he spoke of his father, Andrea, and his mother, the former Immaculata Giordano, as "the magnificent immigrant couple who came here with nothing but aspirations and a willingness to work hard." Mrs. Cuomo came to the United States in 1927 to join her husband, who had arrived a year earlier. For three years, the couple lived in Jersey City with their three children, Frank, Marie, and Mario. That Mario died there. The family then moved to South Jamaica, Queens, where they ran a small grocery store. They had another child, also named Mario, who grew up to become Governor.

Andrea Cuomo died in 1981.

Mrs. Cuomo clearly had a profound influence on her son's sensibilities and view of the world. If his ambition, and ultimately his lack of it, grew from his ethnicity, Mrs. Cuomo's life story played a formative role. Few speeches by Mr. Cuomo about the evils of discrimination were complete without his telling the story of the welcome she received after the family moved from heavily ethnic South Jamaica to the more upscale Queens neighborhood of Hollis.

"You must be the Italian woman," said one of the three women who approached her as she swept the sidewalk. "We want you to know you are welcome here, but please remember to keep the tops on your garbage pails."

Mr. Cuomo's stories about his mother often provided a convenient vehicle for self-deprecation, particularly about his choice of profession. "I beat Lew Lehrman," Mr. Cuomo would recall, "and I'm standing on the stage next to Momma and someone at the mike said, 'Mario Cuomo is the first Italian American ever to be elected to a full term as Governor.' So I turned to her and said to her in Italian, 'Ma, what do you think of your son now?' She looked at me and said, 'Itsa no bad, but when are you going to be judge?'"

In a similar story, Mr. Cuomo tells of the day his mother saw him reading *Fortune* magazine with Lee Iacocca's picture on the cover.

"She said, 'Why's he on the magazine?'

"I said, 'It says he made $15 million last year.'

"She said, 'What does he do?'

"I said, 'He's the head of Chrysler.'

"She said, 'You mean Chrysler, the car?'

"I said, 'Yeah, he makes the cars.'

"'So what's the matter,' she said, 'you can't make a car?'"

Mrs. Cuomo sometimes campaigned with her son, and Mr. Cuomo was fond of quoting her. But once, in a light vein, he told a reporter that he had attributed a quotation to Aristotle rather than Immaculata Cuomo because people would pay more attention to Aristotle.

Mrs. Cuomo also taught her son lessons about the realities of politics, whether advising him to change his opposition to the death penalty for the sake of expedience or explaining Ronald Reagan's popularity.

"Momma's watching television and it's in the early days of Reagan," Mr. Cuomo said.

"She says, 'Is that his hair?'

"I said, 'Yeah, that's his hair.'

"She says, 'How old is he?'

"I said, 'Seventy-five.'

"She says, 'Does he color it?'

"I said: 'No, they say he doesn't. That's the way it is naturally.'

"Then she says, in Italian, 'Ahh, God must love him.'"

April 30, 1995

Babe Ruth's Sick Little Pal

JOHNNY SYLVESTER

By Robert McG. Thomas, Jr.

There are those who will tell you that little Johnny Sylvester was never that sick and certainly not dying. They will tell you that Babe Ruth never promised to hit a home run for him in Game 4 of the 1926 World Series, and that the three home runs the Babe did hit in that game in no way saved the eleven-year-old youngster's life.

Any representations to the contrary, these people will tell you, were simply embellishments of a trivial incident by an oversentimental press in a hypersentimental age.

Such people are known as cynics. While their skepticism is understandable in view of the myriad of fulsome and contradictory contemporary accounts of the famous promise and its even more famous fulfillment, such doubt is mere chaff beneath the grindstone of a mighty legend, and, as it turns out, against the hard kernel of fact.

As the record makes clear enough, Johnny Sylvester *was* severely ill in October 1926. And Babe Ruth *did* promise him a home run. And if the three homers Ruth hit against the Cardinals in St. Louis on October 6 did not bring about an instant cure, they most certainly did no harm.

For little Johnny Sylvester not only lived to tell the tale, he also spent the next six decades doing just that. And when John Dale Sylvester died at the age of seventy-four, it seemed occasion enough to tell it once more.

Mr. Sylvester, who lived in Garden City, Long Island, and died at Winthrop University Hospital in Mineola, was a 1937 graduate of Princeton University who served as a lieutenant in the navy in World

War II and later as president of Amscomatic Inc., a manufacturer of packing machinery, in Long Island City, Queens.

There was nothing Mr. Sylvester could have done to match the pinnacle he reached in 1926 when he became the most famous little boy in America.

One reason the skeptics have had a field day debunking the incident is that a range of ailments were ascribed to Mr. Sylvester, among them blood poisoning, a sinus condition, a spinal fusion, a spinal infection, and a back problem. However, according to his son, John D. Sylvester, Jr., and at least one contemporary account, the ailment was an infection of the forehead caused by a kick from a horse after the youngster fell while riding in Essex Fells, New Jersey. His father, Horace C. Sylvester, Jr., a vice president of the National City Bank in New York, maintained an estate there.

Most accounts indicate the youngster was dying. One had his doctors giving him thirty minutes to live before he rallied after his father vowed to fulfill his last request for a baseball autographed by Babe Ruth. It is still unclear whether the youngster initiated the request for an autographed ball, or whether his father or an uncle decided such a present might cheer him up.

What seems clear enough, however, is that urgent telegrams went out from the family to the Yankees in St. Louis and back came an airmail package containing two balls, one autographed by the Cardinals team and the other with the signatures of several Yankees and a special message from Ruth: "I'll knock a homer for you on Wednesday."

A Hollywood version, the version of the incident in the 1948 movie *The Babe Ruth Story*, showing William Bendix as the Babe delivering the promise at the youngster's hospital bed, seems to have been wrong on at least two counts. The promise was not made in person and the youngster was apparently never in a hospital.

The Babe did better than that, of course, but even he was not invincible. A follow-up note from Ruth "to my sick little pal" dated October 9, the day of Game 6, said "I will try to knock you another homer, maybe two today."

Alas, Ruth went without a homer and the Yankees lost, as they did the next day when an unpromised Ruth home run was not enough to save the game or the Series for the Yankees. Or as a consoling Johnny Sylvester told the Babe when Ruth made a well-publicized visit to the youngster after the Series, "I'm sorry the Yanks lost."

In addition to his son, John Jr. of Huntington Station, Long Island, Mr. Sylvester is survived by a sister, Ruth Elliot of Barrington, Rhode Island; a brother, Horace C. Sylvester, Jr., of Osterville, Massachusetts, and two granddaughters.

January 11, 1990

America's Roadside Poet

ALLAN G. ODELL

By Richard D. Lyons

Allan G. Odell, who developed the roadside advertising campaign of rhyming jingles for Burma-Shave that became a fixture of rural America for almost forty years, died at his home in Edina, Minnesota. He was ninety.

Fresh out of college in 1925, Mr. Odell joined a patent medicine company, Burma-Vita Inc., which was operated by his father, Clinton. The elder Mr. Odell had just come up with a new formula for a brushless shaving cream in a jar, but the company wasn't having much luck until Allan won his father's approval to spend two hundred dollars on an innovative advertising campaign for the new product.

He devised a series of six sequential small wooden signs (eighteen by forty inches) spaced one hundred feet apart along two-lane highways. Five of the six signs each carried one line of a rhyme. The rhymes were by turns genial, flippant, cynical, or absurd and loaded with puns, and each pointed toward a snappy payoff line that usually ended on the fifth sign. The last sign carried the name Burma-Shave in the script that was the product's distinctive logo.

The first signs were erected in Minnesota along US 61 near Red Wing and along US 65 near Albert Lea. Mr. Odell's wife, Grace, recalled that "within a year, repeat orders were coming in for Burma-Shave from druggists serving people who traveled those roads."

Drivers tooling along at thirty-five miles an hour on the narrow black-top roads in the 1930s and 1940s had three seconds to read each one of the signs. The signs were strategically placed so it was impossible for anyone to look ahead and read the punch line. Travelers were delighted with the Burma-Shave signs, which they found a bright spot in the monotony of driving. They would memorize the jingles and the advertising campaign quickly became a commercial success. At the peak of the campaign, in the early 1950s, there were seven thousand sets of signs in forty-five states.

Farmers whose property bordered the road were paid rent for the use of their space. Trucks, in teams of two, with the words "Cheer Up, Face" on their sides, would canvass the countryside. The first truck scouted for locations, the second either installed or repaired signs.

Allan Odell, his father, and a younger brother, Leonard (who died in 1991 at the age of eighty-three), wrote the jingles for the signs for the first three years. But when their muse began to falter they held a nationwide contest, paying a one-hundred-dollar award for each of the twenty-five best jingles and promptly giving the prizewinners a place in the sun. In the subsequent contests that the company held, it received an average of fifty thousand entries from amateur versifiers.

Mrs. Odell said this was her husband's favorite jingle:

Within This Vale
Of Toil
And Sin
Your Head Grows Bald
But Not Your Chin—Use
Burma-Shave

Among other jingles popular with the public were these:

Beneath This Stone
Lies Elmer Gush
Tickled to Death
By His
Shaving Brush
Burma-Shave

Henry the Eighth
Sure Had
Trouble
Short-Term Wives
Long-Term Stubble
Burma-Shave

No Lady Likes
To Dance
Or Dine
Accompanied by
A Porcupine
Burma-Shave

With Glamour Girls
You'll Never Click
Bewhiskered
Like a
Bolshevik
Burma-Shave

Mr. Odell became president of Burma-Vita in 1948, but his signs gradually disappeared, a victim of high-speed travel and billboard prohibitions on interstate highways. He retired when the company was sold to the Philip Morris Company in 1963. The signs were discontinued the next year.

Besides his wife and son George, of Tulsa, Oklahoma, Mr. Odell is survived by two other sons, Clinton, of Edina, Minnesota, and Allan, of Redding, California.

January 22, 1994

A LAMENT

RUSSELL BAKER, in a lament for a vanishing America, once fretted:

Brushless shaving cream in a jar, one of the great American inventions that should survive forever, can no longer be found. One thousand miles of American highway can you drive without once sighting a Burma-Shave roadside verse like

Pity all
The mighty Caesars

They pulled
Each whisker out
With tweezers
Burma-Shave

What will become of a nation that has quit providing motorists with roadside poetry? Mr. Baker wondered.

April 5, 1994

POSITIVELY NABOKOVIAN

Vladimir Nabokov had a weakness for jingles and his Collected Letters *are sprinkled with light verse. Here is his unsuccessful try at a Burma-Shave roadside sign, submitted under his wife's name.*

To the Burma-Vita Company
Aug. 22, 1953
    I am writing to offer you the following jingle for your entertaining collection:

He passed two cars
then five
then seven
and then he beat
them all to Heaven.

If you think you can use it, please send cheque to address given above.

September 17, 1989
THE NEW YORK TIMES BOOK REVIEW

At Home in a Random Universe

Amos Tversky

By Karen Freeman

Dr. Amos Tversky, a cognitive psychologist who changed the way experts in many fields think about how people make decisions about risks, benefits, and probabilities, died at his home in California. He was fifty-nine. The cause was metastatic melanoma, said officials at Stanford University, where he was the Davis-Brack Professor of Behavioral Sciences.

Dr. Tversky (pronounced TUH-VER-skee) once said he merely examined in a scientific way aspects of behavior that were already known to "advertisers and used-car salesmen," and indeed much of his work had an economic slant, shaping the way economists look at decision making by consumers and business executives. It also influenced statisticians and other researchers interested in how decisions involving risk are made in fields like medicine or public policy.

Dr. Tversky's research confirmed that people do not always behave rationally when they make decisions, that they generally put more emphasis on risk than benefits, and that there are many more quirks in the human reasoning process than many earlier economic and psychological theories had contended.

Dr. Tversky's work on decision making began in Israel with Dr. Daniel Kahneman, later of Princeton University. When they were instructors at Hebrew University in 1968, Dr. Kahneman said, they became fascinated by how fighter-pilot trainers, taking classes at the university, decided whether to use rewards or punishments to motivate their student pilots.

Even though the pilot trainers were told that rewards were more effective, they argued against that idea. The trainers said that when a student was praised for a good flight, he was more likely to do less well the next time. Conversely, they said, when a student was berated for a poor flight, he tended to do better the next time. Dr. Tversky and Dr. Kahneman understood that the trainers were being misled because they did not recognize that the law of averages would predict that an unusual performance, good or bad, would most likely be followed by a performance closer to average.

That led them to experiments in the early 1970s showing that people would depend on things other than logic to make decisions, said Dr. Frank Yates, a psychologist at the University of Michigan. In these experiments, for example, two book bags would be filled with the same number of poker chips; in one bag, two thirds of the chips would be red and the rest white, with the opposite proportion in the other bag. A sample of chips was drawn from each bag, and the task would be to determine, based on the samples drawn, whether a bag was more likely to have mostly red chips or white chips.

If five chips were pulled from one bag and four were red, while thirty chips were taken out of the other and twenty were red, most people would say that the first bag was more likely to have mostly red chips because 80 percent of the five chips were red—even though the larger sample size meant that the results for the second bag would be more reliable.

Dr. Barbara Tversky, Amos Tversky's wife and colleague in the Stanford psychology department, said the researchers showed that people tended to see patterns and make connections that were not really there and to base their decisions on that.

Dr. Tversky got a lot of attention in 1988 when he published a study during the National Basketball Association playoffs showing that contrary to popular belief, a basketball player who had just made a shot was no more likely, and even a little less likely, to make the next one he attempted. There is no "hot hands" in basketball, he concluded, and backed up his argument by providing an analysis of every shot taken by the Philadelphia 76ers in a year and a half.

One part of Dr. Tversky's work with particular application to economics and policy making looked at how much importance people place on risks and benefits. If people were asked to choose between a public health program that might save six hundred lives or might lose them all and a program that would be guaranteed to save four hundred of the six hundred lives, they would choose the second program. But if the choice was framed as between a program with a 50 percent chance of saving six hundred lives against one that would definitely lose two hundred lives while saving four hundred, the tendency was to choose the first program.

Dr. Tversky was not averse to taking personal risks himself, Dr. Kahneman said. Dr. Tversky was born on March 16, 1937, in Haifa in what was then the British protectorate of Palestine. He fought in three Middle East wars, in 1956, 1967, and 1973, winning Israel's highest honor for bravery in a 1956 border skirmish. Dr. Kahneman said Dr. Tversky rescued a soldier who had gone forward with an explosive charge to blow up some barbed wire and became frozen with fear, lying down on top of the explosive after lighting the fuse. He said Dr. Tversky reached the man and threw him to safety but was wounded himself.

Dr. Tversky received his bachelor's degree from Hebrew University in 1961 and his doctorate from the University of Michigan in 1965. He won many awards, including a MacArthur Foundation fellowship in 1984.

In addition to his wife, he is survived by two sons, Oren, of San Francisco, and Tal, of Stanford; a daughter, Dona, of Stanford, and a sister, Ruth Ariel, of Jerusalem.

June 6, 1996

THE CASE OF THE HOT HAND

"It's what I do for a living: debugging human intuition," DR. AMOS TVERSKY *once said. "If you take the broader view and look at people as intuitive scientists, you find that we are very good at pattern generation, we are very good at generating hypotheses. It's just that we are not very good at all at actually testing hypotheses." It is easy for humans to guess that an association exists. But testing and, if necessary, rejecting such associations tends to go against all our intuitions, he explained.*

Dr. Tversky knew from experience that his explanations often fell on deaf ears. As fascinated as he was to find that the hot hand in basketball was a myth, he discovered that no one wanted to hear it and that most people still believed in the phenomenon.

"I've lost many good friends over it," Dr. Tversky said

Here is JAMES GLEICK's account of Dr. Tversky's hot-hands study.

The gulf between science and sports may never loom wider than in the case of the hot hands.

Those who play, coach, or otherwise follow basketball believe almost universally that a player who has successfully made his last shot or last few shots—a player with a hot hand—is more likely to make his next shot. An exhaustive statistical analysis led by a Stanford University psychologist, examining thousands of shots in actual games, found otherwise: The probability of a successful shot depends not at all on the shots that come before.

To the psychologist Amos Tversky, the discrepancy between reality and belief highlights the extraordinary differences between events that are random and events that people perceive as random. When events come in clusters and streaks, people look for explanations; they refuse to believe they are random, even though clusters and streaks do occur in random data. "Very often the search for explanation in human affairs is a rejection of randomness," Dr. Tversky said.

To understand attitudes about streakiness in basketball, Dr. Tversky and his researchers interviewed many "real mavens" of the sport, as well as players and basketball statisticians. The more intimately their subjects knew the game, the more firmly they believed in hot hands.

To test the theory, the researchers got the records of every shot taken from the field by the Philadelphia 76ers over a full season and a half. When they looked at every sequence of two shots by the same player—hit-hit, hit-miss, miss-hit, or miss-miss—they found that a hit followed by a miss was actually a tiny bit likelier than a hit followed by a hit.

They also looked at sequences of more than two shots. Again, the number of long streaks was no greater than would have been expected in a random set of data, with every event independent of its predecessor.

Do their results contradict the universal belief that players have good days and bad days? Can they be reconciled with the subjective feeling, experienced by everyone who has played any sport, that one's ability can soar or plunge depending on the occasion? Is it possible that hot shooters hurt their percentages by attempting harder shots—and, alternatively, take fewer risks when they are shooting poorly?

In a way, such questions are beside the point, Dr. Tversky believes.

"Could there be, kind of inside their bodies, a hot-hands tendency that isn't reflected in the data?" he asked. "That may well be an epiphenomenon: You feel hot because you're scoring, it's not that you're scoring because you're hot."

It doesn't matter. And no one is claiming that basketball, or any one basketball shot, is somehow a random process. The point is that an observer who bets on any one shot, based on the shooter's last few shots, will do no better than an observer making random guesses.

Indeed, in separate research with men's and women's basketball teams at Cornell University, players took shots from a fixed distance. Both the shooter and an observer were allowed either to bet a nickel on the next shot or to raise the bet to a dime. Both players and observers tended to raise their bets after successful shots, hoping to take advantage of their sense of when a shooter was hot. But there proved to be no correlation between the dime bets and the shots that followed.

Still, facts are facts and belief is belief. Dr. Tversky found that no quantity of data is enough to change mavens' minds about streaks in random-seeming sequences—a phenomenon that may apply to gambling psychology and stock market analysis as well. "It may be that the only way you can learn about randomness is to toss coins on the side while you play," he said.

April 19, 1988

Angel on the High Wire

ANGEL WALLENDA

By Lawrence Van Gelder

Angel Wallenda, who defied cancer by walking the high wire on an artificial limb after her right leg was amputated just below the knee, died at Robert Packer Hospital in Sayre, Pennsylvania. Ms. Wallenda was twenty-eight, and lived in Mansfield, Pennsylvania, about twenty-five miles southwest of Elmira, New York. The hospital would not disclose the cause of death.

Ms. Wallenda, who was seventeen and an utter novice on the high wire in 1985 when she married into the Wallenda family, famous for its aerialists and acrobats, gave her final performance on March 4, 1990, at Mansfield University. She had already lost her leg and was facing cancer surgery for the third time in four years when a roaring crowd responded to her courage and skill at the event, sponsored by the university to help defray her medical expenses.

"When I'm way up in the sky, walking on a thin line with a fake leg, people look up at me and really pay attention," Ms. Wallenda said. "They see that I'm using everything I've got to live my life the best I can. When people think about that, it makes them think about themselves, and some of them see how much better they can live their own lives. That's why I do what I do. Maybe that's my main purpose for being here."

The sixth of seven children, she was born into a family of Hungarian refugees who had fled communism and settled in the suburbs north of New York City. She was named Elizabeth Pintye (pronounced PEN-tya), and because her dour father beat his children frequently, Elizabeth grew up being shuttled between foster homes and her parents' home, being deprived of food, being beaten again, sometimes running away, knowing bleak Christmases and using alcohol and marijuana. But she maintained a cheery exterior that disguised her resolve not to be controlled by others.

In "Angel on High," a biographical article that appeared in the March 1991 issue of the *Reader's Digest*, she attributed her strength and courage to her difficult childhood. "I'm so much stronger because of it," she said. "If I'd had a sheltered life with people looking after me, I know I couldn't handle what's happened to me."

As Lizzie Pintye, she had sworn off drugs and alcohol and was working at the Dipper Dan Ice Cream Shoppe in Mohegan Lake, New York, when she and Mr. Wallenda first noticed each other. Later that day, she was attracted by music and a crowd to a shopping center parking lot, where she realized that Steven Wallenda, the man walking a high wire, was the man who had been staring at her in the ice cream store.

When he invited her to join him on the wire in his next show, she accepted. "She was a natural," Mr. Wallenda said.

She said, "If I could learn the wire and become a performer, I knew it could be the greatest adventure of my life."

From the beginning, he called her Angel.

Not long after they were married in New York City in August 1985, Ms. Wallenda began her training, but after a while she began spitting up blood and noticed a painful lump on her ankle, where she had suffered an injury when she was eleven. Her right leg was amputated in 1987, and surgery removed parts of both her lungs in 1988. Nevertheless, she was determined to walk the wire again. Her success was recorded later that year on the ABC television show *Incredible Saturday*, and she appeared at benefits for the American Cancer Society and the City of Hope Medical Center.

But her cancer recurred. She knew she would die, but she didn't want to know how long doctors thought she might live. "I'm going to live my life to the fullest as long as I can," she said.

She and Mr. Wallenda, the parents of a son, Steven II, now nine, divorced. Ms. Wallenda remarried. She is survived by her husband, Adil Shaikh, of Mansfield, and an infant daughter.

May 4, 1996

The Life and Hard Times of Superman

JERRY SIEGEL

By Robert McG. Thomas, Jr.

Jerry Siegel, whose teenage yearning for girls gave the world Superman, died in Los Angeles. He was eighty-one but was remembered less as the Cleveland visionary who dreamed up the greatest superhero of all time than as the naïve young man who sold the rights to a $1 billion cultural and commercial juggernaut for $130.

It was Mr. Siegel's partner and childhood friend, Joe Shuster, who eventually gave Superman his familiar skintight costume and accompanying cape, but it was Mr. Siegel who had imagined Superman whole, from his birth on the doomed planet Krypton and his rocket arrival on Earth to his superhuman powers and his mild-mannered alter ego, Clark Kent. The vision, as he later told it, came to him in a jumble all at once, during a sleepless summer night in Cleveland in 1934 after his graduation from Glenville High School, where he and Mr. Shuster had already teamed up to produce a stream of comic strip characters, including an earlier Superman, whom Mr. Siegel had imagined as a bald mad scientist.

But for all of the instant-imagined detail of the second Superman's extraterrestrial origins, his upbringing by doting foster parents, and his decision to dedicate his awesome powers "to assist humanity," Mr. Siegel made no secret that the focus of his creative vision, the real creature of his dreams, was Lois Lane, Kent's fellow reporter on *The Daily Planet*. She was the woman who would yearn for Superman even as she shunned the bespectacled Kent, not knowing that beneath that mild-mannered exterior was in fact the very man of steel, not to mention the longing heart of Jerry Siegel.

Even discussing Superman's origins forty years later, Mr. Siegel, who said he had thought of becoming a reporter, seemed still to feel the stings he had suffered as a scrawny, bespectacled high school student: "I had crushes on several attractive girls who either didn't know I existed or didn't care I existed," he said. "It occurred to me: What if I had something going for me, like jumping over buildings or throwing cars around or something like that?"

After Mr. Shuster had rendered Mr. Siegel's fantasy in ink, it still took the partners several years to find a publisher willing to accept their creation. And when they did, in New York, where they had been hired to produce other comic book characters, their dream of cashing in was quickly shattered. In March 1938, in exchange for $130 in cash, they signed away all rights to Superman to DC Comics, the company that brought Superman to commercial life that June—in the very first issue of Action Comics. "We were young kids," Mr. Siegel said. "What did we know?"

When the character proved an immediate sensation and the partners sought a share of the profits, they were dismissed and lived the rest of their lives near the poverty line. Mr. Siegel and Mr. Shuster tried inventing new superheroes but Slam Bradley and Funnyman (who fought evil with weapons attached to his clown costume) and half a dozen other attempts ended in failure. Eventually Mr. Siegel had to sell his treasured early copies of Action Comics, today worth thousands of dollars each, in order to buy food and pay the rent.

After "twenty-four years of frustration and hell," as Mr. Siegel described it, they lost a series of lawsuits to recover their creative property. Mr. Shuster was eventually reduced to becoming a messenger in Manhattan and Mr. Siegel worked as a clerk typist in Los Angeles for seven thousand dollars a year.

But in 1978, after the first Superman movie made more than $80 million, DC, which over the years has received more than $250 million of the more than $1 billion that Superman has earned from movies, television, and an incredible array of commercial products, bowed to public opinion, restored their bylines, and gave each man a $20,000-a-year annuity, later raised to $30,000.

In their final years, the two men lived within a few blocks of each other in Los Angeles, where Mr. Shuster, blind in the last years of his life, died in 1992.

Mr. Siegel may have been the man who created Superman, but his failure to safeguard his rights soured him on the man from another planet. "I can't stand to look at a Superman comic book," he said in 1975. "It makes me physically ill. I love Superman, and yet to me he has become an alien thing."

He is survived by his wife, Joanne; their daughter, Laura Carter Larson of Los Angeles; a son, Michael, by a previous marriage; and two grandchildren.

January 31, 1996

THE MINSK THEORY OF KRYPTON

JULES FEIFFER, the former cartoonist for The Village Voice, *playwright, and author, offered his own theory for the origins of Superman.*

> *"Up in the sky! It's a bird!*
> *"It's a plane! It's . . . Superman!"*

Oh, he was a giant back then. And he may have been a touch innocent, even primitive, but he was unique. One of a kind. And he was like an early New Dealer; he fought on behalf of the helpless and oppressed. This was over a half century and four wars ago.

Hard to imagine today, when we suffer a glut of outlandishly costumed, steroidally muscled superheroes, whose blood lust and paranoia differ only in degree from that of the militia movement. In 1935, life was simpler, more idealistic. There were merely the Depression and Hitler to contend with. The times were pre-angst, pre-noir, pre-self-awareness.

Horatio Alger still lived, very much so in the heart of Jerry Siegel, grown up poor and Jewish in the American heartland. Mr. Siegel felt destined to make it, and make it big. His medium was the funny papers.

His first collaboration with Joe Shuster, his lifelong partner, was a comic strip for their school paper at Glenville High, just outside of Cleveland; *Goober, The Mighty,* a crude mix of *Popeye* and *Tarzan.* E. C. Segar's *Popeye* was, at that time, the strongest man in newsprint, and although cartoony and not exactly super, bullets had bounced off his chest. Tarzan, on the other hand, was a realistically rendered adventure strip, with blocks of text set below the illustrations. The artist was the excellent Harold Foster, who later was to give us *Prince Valiant.* Tarzan's origin, you notice, bears striking parallels to Superman's. A shipwrecked son of an English lord, the baby Tarzan is washed up on African shores to be rescued and raised by nurturing apes who teach him their ways, inspiring him to protect the helpless by fighting lions, tigers, white hunters, and savage tribesmen with scary headdresses.

Jerry Siegel's earliest approach to a super-character was in a high school fanzine, run off on a mimeograph. It was called *The Reign of the Superman,* but this fellow had nothing to do with the Man of Steel. He was a villain, honoring the tradition, still intact, that presents Evil as smarter, cleverer, and stronger than Good. Good prevails only at the last moment, through tenacity and dumb luck. Your local Cineplex is, no doubt, showing recent examples of the genre.

But one summer night in 1934, tossing and turning in bed, Jerry Siegel conjured up a switcheroo. What if his superman was not a villain but a hero? In a world sick with the Depression, violent crime, the threat of fascism and war, Americans seemed in dire need of a neo-Nietzschean hero who used his power to rescue, not subjugate.

The bare bones of plot came in a rush. In a far-off galaxy, a planet (call it Krypton) explodes. The single survivor is an infant, shot aloft in a space capsule by his scientist father. The baby Superman crash-lands, not on African shores like Tarzan but in the American Midwest, where he is rescued and raised not by nurturing apes like Tarzan but by the kindly Kents. They teach him the American way and inspire him to go off, not in a leopard skin like Tarzan, but in cape and leotard, to protect the helpless against not lions and tigers but crooks, mad scientists, dictators, and natural disasters.

Mr. Siegel wrote and revised and handed the scripts to Mr. Shuster, who illustrated the initial comic strip episode, intended for newspaper syndication. Syndicated adventure strips were in their heyday: *Flash Gordon, Terry and the Pirates, Dick Tracy, Wash Tubbs* . . . an odd American art form, trapping the reader's eye with its blatant immediacy, vulgar and elegant at the same time. Daily strips ran large on the comics pages, five or six columns, a visual and narrative treat. Today's minimally drawn, miniaturized strips don't begin to suggest their charm and influence.

The Superman was rejected, revised, rejected again. Mr. Siegel flirted with another, more experienced illustrator, but after more than a year of frustration returned to the neophyte Joe Shuster. With little training as an artist, Mr. Shuster sought models, got the agile Mr. Siegel to leap about as the Man of Steel and was looking for a model for the girl reporter. He hired a pretty girl to pose as Lois Lane and she later became Mrs. Jerry Siegel.

Comic books finally gave Superman a home. By 1937, Mr. Siegel and Mr. Shuster were writing and drawing a batch of features for the Detective Comics line of National Allied Publishing (which later became known as DC Comics): *Slam Bradley, Federal Men, Radio Squad, Spy,* all freely borrowed from successful newspaper strips. The Action Comics line was looking for a lead feature for its first issue. *The Superman,* rejected for syndication, was cut up, reframed, and laid out into the comic-book format. One look and it was clear that it was in the right place. The rest is history.

Comic books, until then a small-time enterprise, took off like a space shot from Krypton, with Superman carrying most of the weight on his shoulders. For their efforts, Mr. Siegel and Mr. Shuster got less, far less, than was due them. To make it into print, they were forced to sign over their copyright to the publisher. Instead of royalties, they were put on page rates of approximately ten dollars a page, the size of which turned into a bad joke. Money arguments led to fights, led to lawyers, led to lawsuits that Mr. Siegel and Mr. Shuster lost. By the time the game was played out in 1948, the creators were fired from their creation.

Their fate constitutes the dark side of the Superman legend. Years later, after the Man of Steel came under new ownership, a gaggle of pugnacious cartoonists prevailed upon management to make amends. By that time in 1975, it was all but too late for Mr. Siegel and Mr. Shuster, but not for their families who at long last have become Superman's heirs.

Sixty years on, why do we care? In the mid-fifties, in *Seduction of the Innocent*, the noted psychiatrist Frederick Wertham wrote: "I have known many adults who have treasured ... the books they read as children. I have never come across any adult or adolescent ... who would ever dream of keeping ... '[comic] books' for any sentimental or other reason." Today, Dr. Wertham is forgotten while Superman still reigns. Original art of the thirties, forties, and fifties sells for tens of thousands of dollars.

A high price for nostalgia, or is something else at work here? What is the significance of it all? You need to look back on that hot summer night in Cleveland when Jerry Siegel, unable to sleep, hit upon a vision. There he was, a first-generation Jewish boy of Russian stock, planted in the Midwest during the birth of native American fascism, the rise of anti-Semitism, the radio broadcasts of Father Coughlin. Mr. Siegel, an uncertain young man of ambition and drive, was not like the kids he went to school with.

If he was at all like me (another Jewish boy in a different place at roughly the same time), he sensed the difference, his otherness. We were aliens. We didn't choose to be mild-mannered, bespectacled, and self-effacing. We chose to be bigger, stronger, blue-eyed, and sought-after by blond cheerleaders. *Their* cheerleaders. We chose to be *them*.

Superman was the ultimate assimilationist fantasy. The mild manners and glasses that signified a class of nerdy Clark Kents was, in no way, our real truth. Underneath the schmucky façade there lived Men of Steel! Jerry Siegel's accomplishment was to chronicle the smart Jewish boy's American dream. Acknowledge that, and you can better understand the symbolic meaning of the planet Krypton. It wasn't Krypton that Superman came from; it was the planet Minsk or Lodz or Vilna or Warsaw.

And when the Depression ended, and the war as well, when the United States rocketed into a cold-war world of affluence and paranoia, the otherness and alienation of Mr. Siegel's poetic construct spread outward, beyond Jews and other minorities, to the blond, blue-eyed hunks that we envied and wished to be. America cloned itself into a country made up of millions of Clark Kents. And day after day, you could hear them muttering to themselves: "I'm not really like this. If they only knew my real identity."

Siegel Man knew.

December 29, 1996
THE NEW YORK TIMES MAGAZINE

The Man with Perfect Pitch

NICOLAS SLONIMSKY

By Allan Kozinn

Nicolas Slonimsky, a formidably gifted musicologist and lexicographer who also made his mark as a conductor, pianist, and composer, died at the UCLA Medical Center in Los Angeles. He was 101.

Mr. Slonimsky's many reference works, among them *Music Since 1900, A Lexicon of Musical Invective,* and the last several editions of *Baker's Biographical Dictionary of Musicians,* are considered indispensable by musicians, critics, and music lovers. A compendium drawn from his writings, *Nicolas Slonimsky: The First Hundred Years,* edited by Richard Kostelanetz, was published in 1996.

Mr. Slonimsky was no mere purveyor of facts. He challenged accepted lore and debunked myths that had found their way into biographies and reference works. Rather than repeat the Romantic depiction of a blizzard at Mozart's funeral, for example, he consulted Austrian weather bureaus and discovered that the story was untrue. He was also fascinated by unusual details. Readers in search of basic information might in the process learn, for example, that Stravinsky had a toothache the day he completed *Le Sacre du printemps,* or that Schoenberg and Rossini had triskaidekaphobia, an irrational fear of the number 13.

He also enlivened his dictionary entries with astute, witty, and sometimes waspish observations, and in the later editions of *Baker's,* he introduced some musicians with lavish evaluations. Where *The New Grove Dictionary of Music and Musicians* soberly describes Mozart, for example, as "one of the composers who brought the Viennese Classical style to its height," Mr. Slonimsky's identifying sentence reads: "Supreme Austrian genius of music whose works in every genre are unsurpassed in lyric beauty, rhythmic variety and effortless melodic invention."

For Mr. Slonimsky, mechanics and detail were inspiration. He was a performer, adviser, chronicler, raconteur, a television quiz show champion in the 1950s, and a lover of multisyllabic words like sempiternal. His playful love of trivia is evident all through the 2,115-page *Baker's*, in which he called Bach "the supreme arbiter and lawgiver of music," described himself as a "failed Wunderkind," chastised Paul McCartney for his involvement with meditation, praised John Cage for being "ultramodern," and noted that Arthur Rubinstein was a "fluent, though not always grammatical, speaker in most European languages."

Mr. Slonimsky's entertaining style was reflected in his other activities. A favorite party trick—one he performed at an Alice Tully Hall tribute to him in 1987 and also on *The Tonight Show* on television—was to play the melody line of the Chopin "Black Key" étude by rolling an orange across the keys. Seemingly open to musical experiences of all kinds, he performed some of his own music at a Frank Zappa concert in Santa Monica, California, in 1981 and maintained a friendship with the iconoclastic rock composer. He named his cat Grody to the Max after learning the expression from Zappa's daughter, Moon Unit.

But he had a thoroughly serious side as well. He was a vigorous champion of new music all his life. In the 1920s he founded the Chamber Orchestra of Boston, and he gave premieres of Ives's *Three Places in New England* in 1931 and Varèse's *Ionisation* in 1933 (Varèse dedicated the work to him). He also championed Henry Cowell and Carlos Chávez, and conducted Bartók's First Piano Concerto with the composer as soloist.

He later said his conducting career had foundered because of his insistence on programming new music. In 1933, when he programmed contemporary music at the Hollywood Bowl to the chagrin of fleeing audiences, he comforted himself that he was ahead of his time.

His severe modernist taste, though, accompanied a love of all music; each sound had its virtues. "All manifestos," he said, "are fakes."

Nicolas Slonimsky was born in St. Petersburg, Russia, on April 27, 1894. In his autobiographical entry in *Baker's*, he wrote: "Possessed by inordinate ambition, aggravated by the endemic intellectuality of his family of both maternal and paternal branches (novelists, revolutionary poets, literary critics, mathematicians, inventors of useless artificial languages,

Hebrew scholars, speculative philosophers), he became determined to excel beyond common decency in all these doctrines." He excelled in several
of them, but music—though absent from the list of family achievements—was his primary interest from the age of six, when he began
studying piano with Isabelle Vengerova, his aunt (and later a teacher of
Samuel Barber and Leonard Bernstein). He studied at the St. Petersburg
Conservatory until 1914. He was drafted into the Russian army just
before the Revolution. In 1918 he began touring as a vocal accompanist,
then worked his way through Turkey and Bulgaria as a pianist in theaters
and silent movie houses, arriving in Paris in 1921. There he became a
rehearsal pianist for the conductor Serge Koussevitzky.

He came to the United States in 1923 to work as an accompanist
in the newly created opera department at the Eastman School of Music
in Rochester, where he continued his composition and conducting studies.
After two years there, he moved to Boston to resume his position as
Koussevitzky's assistant. He also taught music theory at the Boston Conservatory and the Malkin Conservatory, and he began to contribute articles on music to *The Boston Evening Transcript, The Christian Science Monitor*,
and *Etude* magazine. In 1927, he started his Chamber Orchestra of Boston
and began to solicit music from composers he admired.

Ives, thrilled with Mr. Slonimsky's performance of *Three Places*, spon-
sored a European tour that allowed Mr. Slonimsky to present recent
American works. In Paris, during that 1931 tour, he married Dorothy
Adlow, an art critic for *The Christian Science Monitor*. Mr. Slonimsky became
an American citizen the same year and became the father of a daughter,
Electra, with whom he soon conversed in Latin.

His conducting career flourished briefly, but by the mid-1940s he
had returned to academia. He headed the Slavonic languages and literature
department at Harvard from 1945 to 1947, and toured Europe and the
Middle East as a lecturer for the State Department. After his wife died
in 1964, he moved to Los Angeles and taught for three years at the
University of California.

His first book, *Music Since 1900*, appeared in 1937. A day-by-day
chronology of important as well as amusing trivial events in twentieth-
century music, the work has been revised several times, most recently in
1987. In his *Thesaurus of Scales and Melodic Patterns* (1947), he ingeniously

catalogued combinations of notes that could be used as musical themes. Jazz musicians found the book particularly useful; John Coltrane reportedly required his band members to play through it.

Mr. Slonimsky edited *Thompson's International Cyclopedia of Music and Musicians* from 1946 to 1958 and in 1958 became editor of *Baker's*, beginning with the fifth edition. He completely revamped the book for the sixth edition, published in 1978, and oversaw two more editions as well as abridged versions. Taking a break from biography, he turned his attention to musical terms in his *Lectionary of Music* (1989).

His books also include the *Lexicon of Musical Invective* (1953), a collection of scathing reviews of musical masterpieces; *Music of Latin America* (1945), *The Road to Music* (1947), and *A Thing or Two About Music* (1948). His lexicon, in which Mr. Slonimsky hypothesized that music has always required a generation to be accepted, is actually a mockery of less omniscient judges than he, an anthology of music critics' dismissals of their contemporaries, a compilation capable of humbling the most hardened artistic arbiter: Beethoven's music was called "a raw and undigested mass"; hearing Ravel's was likened to "watching some midget or pygmy doing clever but very small things"; Wagner's was termed the "music of a demented eunuch."

Mr. Slonimsky's autobiography (which he wanted to call "Failed Wunderkind") was published as *Perfect Pitch* in 1988. Reviewing the memoir in *The New York Times Book Review*, Helen Epstein had this to say: "This chronicle of a musical life in the twentieth century is about as fast-paced and charming as one can imagine. It is filled with cameos of the famous and the obscure, illustrated by details that only an insider sitting very close up has the privilege to view. We see Koussevitzky struggling with metrical changes in Stravinsky's *Sacre du printemps* and catch a rare glimpse of the music philanthropist George Eastman (He admittedly had no knowledge of music, and could well emulate President Ulysses S. Grant in his famous, if possibly apocryphal pronouncement, 'I know only two tunes: one is 'Yankee Doodle,' and the other isn't')."

As a composer, Mr. Slonimsky wrote (in his own *Baker's* entry) that he "cultivated miniature forms, usually with a gimmick." These include a set of "Advertising Songs" (settings of advertising copy that had appeared in *The Saturday Evening Post*, 1925), "Gravestones at Hancock" (settings of epitaphs, 1945), "Studies in Black and White" (a piano work in which one hand played black keys, the other white keys, 1928), "My Toy Balloon" (which he described as his "only decent orchestral work," 1945), and "51 Minitudes for Piano" (1972–76).

He is survived by a daughter, Electra Yourke of Manhattan, and two grandchildren.

December 27, 1995

Everybody Goes to Mollie's

MOLLIE PARNIS

By Marilyn Berger

Mollie Parnis, the fashion designer, whose Park Avenue living room was as well known to actors, journalists, and Democrats as her Seventh Avenue showroom was to the women who bought her dresses, died at New York University Hospital. She was in her early nineties but had long refused to disclose her exact age. She died of congestive heart failure, said a close friend, the writer Richard Clurman.

Born to a poor immigrant family in New York City before the turn of the century, she started working at odd jobs when she was eight years old, and eventually built a multimillion-dollar dress business. But her interests ranged well beyond her Garment District cutting rooms. She became a skilled collector of art and of people and contributed some of her fortune to the beautification of New York and Jerusalem.

Dresses she designed were worn by First Ladies from Mamie Eisenhower to Betty Ford. Lady Bird Johnson became a a close friend and one year, one of Miss Parnis's designs was bought by four Kennedys in four separate cities. In her office, Miss Parnis kept photographs of the First Ladies wearing her designs posed with their husbands, as well as a signed photograph of Lyndon B. Johnson in a shirt she had made for him. To four Presidents, she was Mollie, but as often as she was invited to the White House, she said she could never get over the thrill of being in what she called "the President's house."

But Seventh Avenue held no interest for her after working hours. "The last thing I want to talk about is what people are wearing," she once told an interviewer. She began to gather the most interesting people she knew at the Park Avenue duplex she moved into with her husband,

Leon J. Livingston, in 1941. First she took up with movie stars, who were as eager to have her come to Hollywood as they were to visit her in New York. Kirk Douglas and his wife, Anne, remained lifelong friends, but when the Hollywood crowd started to lose interest for her, she began a more lasting relationship with writers around the city. With the journalists came the politicians, and Mollie Parnis's salon was born.

Partly because of the company she kept, Miss Parnis keenly felt the absence of a college education. "My greatest regret is my lack of a formal education," she once told *Life* magazine. "I admire people who are able to express themselves well and who grasp facts fast. I read very slowly and have no background in literature or history or anything. When I'm reading, I often stop to look up a word that should be part of my vocabulary."

Even when she was in her eighties, she would sometimes wake in the wee morning hours to read books and newspapers so she could comment on the columns with the best of them. "What did you think of Scotty Reston's piece about Nixon and Kissinger?" she asked one day, and then began a crisp summary of her own very strong opinion. Although she tended to socialize mainly with Democrats, she made an exception for Henry Kissinger and his wife, Nancy, Republicans who were among the New York social lions who liked to go to "Mollie's."

A sharp judge of character, she had a rapier tongue and a distinctive, commanding voice that she used to prick pretension. For her, impatience became a virtue as she cut off the long-winded and went on to someone or something she found more interesting.

Through the Mollie Parnis Livingston Foundation of New York, Miss Parnis gave away at least a million and a half dollars. An early project was giving "Dress Up Your Neighborhood" prizes that helped create vest-pocket parks and green areas in decaying New York neighborhoods. It was patterned on a similar prize she had contributed to the city of Jerusalem.

After the death in 1979 of her only son, Robert Livingston, who for a time had been the publisher of *More* magazine, she established the Livingston Awards for newspaper, magazine, and television journalists under thirty-five years old. Each year, five-thousand-dollar prizes are given to three journalists. Charles Eisendrath, a professor at the University of

Michigan, who oversaw the journalism prize, said the award grew out of her admiration for members of the press. "She collected journalists all her life," he said. "She collected them in the best sense: She loved them, she mothered them, she hectored them and she fed them. And they genuinely loved her."

Mollie Parnis was born on the Lower East Side of Manhattan on March 18. The year was noted in her official biography as 1905, but even Miss Parnis admitted that the date was "close" but certainly not precise. Throughout her life she was militantly unspecific about her age. Some of her friends believed she turned ninety in 1987. She liked to say she was of a certain age, with "a life expectancy of five minutes."

She was the eldest of five children of Abraham and Sara Parnis, who she said had emigrated from Austria before the turn of the century. Miss Parnis grew up on the Upper West Side. She said she attended Wadleigh High School and later Julia Richman. She remembered that when she was eight, she tutored foreigners in English for twenty-five cents an hour.

She said she got some notion that she might want to go into fashion when she was in high school. A beau had invited her to a football game, and she badgered her mother to buy her a new outfit. "She took me down to Division Street and got me a navy dress," she said some seven decades later. "I still remember it. Blue serge." After the football game, she said, her date offered to take her dancing and suggested she go home and change. But she was wearing the only dress she had, so she cut the neckline, took a lace collar from a blouse of her mother's, and added an artificial flower. It was her first design.

In 1923, she became an assistant saleswoman in the showroom of a blouse manufacturer. Occasionally, she made suggestions to the designers—a change of neckline, a jabot, a frill, a different sleeve. One summer, when she made a twenty-thousand-dollar sale to one customer, she asked for a raise. Her boss made a counterproposal—her name in the lobby directory. "Well," Miss Parnis said, "you don't know what that did for me. I got so excited over it I had all my friends come over to Seventh Avenue to look at 'Mollie Parnis, fourth floor.' It was like an actress having her name up in lights the first time."

Meanwhile, the fellow who had taken her to the football game was in the silk business and she figured that if she worked in a dress house where they used silk she might see him more often. It worked out just as she had hoped. She and Leon Livingston were married in 1930, and in 1933, in the midst of the Great Depression, they went into business together. Miss Parnis, who could neither sketch nor cut nor drape, became the designer. Mr. Livingston handled the business aspects. They were successful from the start.

As their business prospered, Miss Parnis hired other designers, but she remained the fashion editor. "Over the years," she once said, "as many designers as we've had, the clothes always looked like Mollie Parnis." That meant versatile, comfortable dresses in good fabrics. They were fashionable but not trendy. She counseled women to avoid fads. "I've always had a theory," she told an interviewer, "that good designing doesn't mean dresses you have to throw away every year. Things shouldn't go out of date overnight."

When Miss Parnis's husband died in 1962, she went out of business. But only for three months. "Then," she said, "I went out to dinner one night with a gentleman who asked when I was going to open my showroom again. I said, 'Maybe never.' And he said, 'Oh, my God! The only thing that made you a little different was that you worked. Don't you know that widows in this town with a little money are a dime a dozen?' Well, I got back into business so fast, I can't tell you."

Miss Parnis said when she was growing up she had no notion of the world "out there"—the world of wealth and society. But as her business prospered, she quickly learned how to design her life as well as she designed dresses. In time, Mollie Parnis became her own best creation.

There was the apartment on Park Avenue ("When we first walked in there to look I could hardly believe I was there—'Park Avenue' I kept marveling to myself"). Then there was the country house in Katonah, in Westchester County. ("We had a tennis court and one of the first swimming pools in the East. Swimming pools in those days were for Hollywood.")

There was the collection of fine china, the decorator (Billy Baldwin), and finally, the paintings—by Picasso, Vuillard, Roualt, Utrillo, Cézanne, Soutine, and her most prized possession, a Matisse painting named *Asia*, a brightly colored 1946 image of a seated woman. When Miss Parnis heard that a friend was selling the Matisse she had admired she immediately agreed to buy it. She remembered that she went into her husband's office and said she had just bought a Matisse. "Well, unbuy it," he told her. Moments later a friend came by and saw her crying. "Why don't you go down to the bank and borrow the money?" he suggested. She said that it had never occurred to her that she could go to the bank herself, without her husband, and get a loan. But she did it—she borrowed twenty-five thousand dollars and got her Matisse.

It was the same Matisse she pledged to the Israel Museum in honor of Jerusalem's mayor, Teddy Kollek, on his seventieth birthday. Years later, she had misgivings and decided it should go into her estate.*

In 1984, when her dresses were selling for $350 to $1,500, she closed her Seventh Avenue showroom. Within weeks, she went back to work once again, designing Mollie Parnis At-Home fashions in a company that had been started by her sister Peggy and was then owned by her nephew, Neal Hochman.

Mr. Hochman, her closest relative, survives her.

July 19, 1992

---

*In 1992 the Kimbell Art Museum in Fort Worth, Texas, bought Matisse's *Asia* from Mollie Parnis's estate at an auction at Sotheby's. The museum paid $11 million for it; the painting had been expected to sell for $7 million to $8 million.

The Green Guerrilla

FRED ROSENSTIEL

By Robert McG. Thomas, Jr.

Fred Rosenstiel, who spent his life planting gardens to brighten the lives of his fellow New Yorkers, and to alleviate an abiding sadness in his heart, died at the Western Queens Community Hospital in Astoria. He was eighty-three.

In a city where corps of volunteer gardeners seem to spring up like wildflowers, Mr. Rosenstiel was a volunteer gardener with a difference, a man so driven that for four decades he did little else. After his arrival in New York in 1951, Mr. Rosenstiel, the son of a prosperous Dutch businessman who left him enough money to live on, spent his time making gardens, coaxing green shoots of life from the New York soil.

"He was a master plantsman," said Barbara Earnest, the director of the New York Horticultural Society, recalling Mr. Rosenstiel as the city's most dedicated and prolific volunteer gardener, one who lent his expertise and his brawn to community gardening groups and worked on his own to plant flowers on virtually any patch of unpaved earth in the city. "He was an inspiration," she said.

Whether part of a group or working alone, Mr. Rosenstiel (whose name means "rose stalk" in German) planted gardens in parks and vacant lots and around schools, housing projects, hospitals, and homeless shelters.

A founder of the Green Guerrillas, a group that has organized and tended hundreds of community gardens since 1973, he was also an unpaid consultant to the New York City Council on the Environment among many other organizations.

A longtime resident of the Upper West Side, he would leave his apartment on West 113th Street at 8:00 A.M. and rarely be home before midnight, sometimes visiting three or more community gardens in a day, checking, perhaps, on the morning glories he had planted next to the ivy or on the moon vine whose white flowers open at evening as the morning glories close. When he was not on his knees, digging his hands into the earth to root out Japanese knotweed threatening a garden in Riverside Park or planting the yellow flowering lamium he knew would thrive in the ubiquitous New York shade, Mr. Rosenstiel, a tall, powerfully built man with granite features, could often be found immersed in a newspaper at an upper Broadway coffee shop.

Known as a sad man who found an elusive joy in gardening and music, Mr. Rosenstiel became a familiar figure on the Upper West Side, a neighborhood character in a beret and tweed jacket who carried a shopping bag crammed with gardening equipment and made it a point of honor never to travel anywhere except by subway. He tended to keep people at a certain distance, but he opened up at community meetings, and he often held court at the old Mill Luncheonette on Broadway near 113th Street, where he would harangue Columbia University students, often urging them to adopt surprisingly radical positions. They called him "the Professor."

"Perhaps I would have had a more interesting career had I been forced to make a living," he once told a friend, before adding, "These are the ironies of life."

Mr. Rosenstiel was on intimate terms with such ironies. In his family the ironies twisted back on themselves. His parents were German Jews who immigrated to England, where they suffered such anti-German prejudice during World War I that they moved to the Netherlands. Mr. Rosenstiel, who was born in London and grew up there and in Rotterdam before going to school in Switzerland, was the only member of his family who survived the Nazis in World War II and the Holocaust. His only brother was killed fighting as a soldier with the Dutch Army. His parents and several aunts, uncles, and cousins died in Auschwitz.

Mr. Rosenstiel, who was in England at the outbreak of the war and who later served four years as a seaman with the Britain-based Dutch navy, seemed to find it hard to forgive himself for surviving the Holocaust, friends said. He felt such guilt, he once told a friend, that he felt he was not entitled to any happiness. That, he explained, is why he never married, never pursued a career. He simply planted gardens, a delight he had stumbled on at a cooperative London youth hostel when he volunteered to tend its garden as a way of getting out of doing the dishes.

In his later years he found a measure of comfort with Esther Lazarson, a woman who had loved him since the day they met in 1969 and who took him in when he became too sick to care for himself. Ms. Lazarson, an Englishwoman who has lived in New York off and on since 1951, recalled that Mr. Rosenstiel had once offered her a white begonia if she would stay in New York, but she wanted more than he was prepared to give at the time. He had learned from the Holocaust, she said, how much you can lose and how quickly when you love too much.

"He gave me a white begonia when I came back," she added.

June 16, 1995

Fueling a Legend

ZORA ARKUS-DUNTOV

By Keith Bradsher

Zora Arkus-Duntov, the Russian engineer and race car driver who turned the Chevrolet Corvette into one of the most popular muscle cars in the United States, died at St. John Hospital in Detroit. He was eighty-six. Mr. Arkus-Duntov, who lived in Grosse Pointe Woods, Michigan, died of kidney failure caused by cancer, said Daniel Gale, a friend of the family and the founder of the National Corvette Museum in Bowling Green, Kentucky.

When Chevrolet introduced the Corvette in 1953, it was a powerful-looking car, but it had only a modest 150-horsepower engine. Mr. Arkus-Duntov was working at the time for a British racing car company and saw a prototype of the vehicle at a General Motors show at the Waldorf-Astoria Hotel in Manhattan. Immediately struck by the vehicle's appearance, he applied to Chevrolet for a job as an engineer. Once hired, he pushed through the decision to turn the Corvette into a high-performance sports car with a succession of more powerful engines. Chevrolet offered a 195-horsepower engine on the 1955 Corvette, a 240-horsepower engine on the 1956 Corvette, and a 283-horsepower engine on the 1957 model.

"The Corvette is a legendary car, and in many ways Zora was the legend behind the legend," J. Michael Losh, GM's chief financial officer, said.

His changes turned a slow-selling two-seater into a symbol of power and ostentation in the late 1950s. GM's total sales of Corvettes crossed the one million mark in 1992. Annual production of the gas-guzzling sports car peaked at 53,807 in 1979 and has been slowly slipping since then as more foreign companies have entered the sports car market.

Mr. Arkus-Duntov came up with a fuel-injection system for the 1957 Corvette that has since become standard on many mass-production vehicles. Several years later, he designed the first four-wheel disc brakes to be included on a mass-produced American car.

The son of a Russian engineer, Mr. Arkus-Duntov was born in Belgium, grew up in St. Petersburg, and led a flamboyant life from his youth on. At age sixteen, he smuggled gold for profit from France into Belgium in the hollowed-out frame of a Mercedes. "He did it until his mother caught him—he was still a young man," Mr. Gale said.

Mr. Arkus-Duntov graduated in 1934 from the Institute of Charlottenburg in Berlin with a degree in mechanical engineering. He soon fled Nazi Germany for France, where he flew in the French air force at the beginning of World War II. When Paris fell, Mr. Arkus-Duntov fled to Britain, and in 1941 he emigrated to the United States, where he became an American citizen.

Although he made his reputation with the Corvette, Mr. Arkus-Duntov was also a successful race car driver and aircraft engineer. Driving a Porsche, he won its engine-size category at LeMans in 1953 and 1954.

Mr. Arkus-Duntov retired from GM in 1975. He spent the last months of his life remodeling a BD5 short-wing stunt plane in hopes of flying it and personally breaking the world speed record for a small aircraft without a jet engine. "He had a very high-performance engine that he was trying to stick in the thing," said Mr. Gale, adding that Mr. Arkus-Duntov, in his last days, "was devastated that he wasn't going to be able to finish it."

Mr. Arkus-Duntov is survived by his wife of fifty-seven years, Elfi Arkus-Duntov.

At the request of Mr. Arkus-Duntov, his body will be cremated and the ashes entombed in a display at the National Corvette Museum, Mr. Gale said.

April 24, 1996

The Cult of the Corvette

If you seek Zora Arkus-Duntov's monument, George F. Will said in appreciation, look around at that 'vette coming on in the passing lane. This is an account of the cult of the Corvette by N. R. Kleinfield.

It was an oppressively hot day in White Plains, and Guy Zani, Jr., was driving one of his Corvettes with the roof down. "I'm a little low now," he said. "I've only got six Corvettes. Usually, I've got eight or ten. This one's a 1957. Some great-looking car, right?" Streets and cars became a blur. Mr. Zani kept up his Corvette monologue. "I have to warn you, I'm not normal," he said, not without pride. "I'm really gone on this car. It's hard for me to explain it. After you've owned one for a while, you get what I call the fever. When I'm behind the wheel of a Corvette, I feel like a new me."

Mr. Zani got into Corvettes early. In 1958, when he was fifteen, a Corvette used to be parked across the street from his grandfather's garage. When nobody was looking, Mr. Zani would climb into it, shut his eyes, and dream that he was piloting it at three hundred miles an hour. The best night of the week was when the television series *Route 66* came on, because he could watch Martin Milner and George Maharis barrel down the highway in a shiny Corvette.

A chatty, weathered-looking man with a tidy beard, Mr. Zani today owns his grandfather's garage. Over the years, he has bought and restored dozens of Corvettes. He can talk Corvettes about seven or eight hours longer than most people are willing to listen. Whenever he learns of an old Corvette for sale, he will hop into one of his Corvettes and roar off for a look. One time, acting on a tip, he drove three hours and found a Thunderbird. He was depressed all night.

Mr. Zani belongs to a peculiar, possessed, mysterious cult. He is a certifiable Corvette nut. The Chevrolet division of General Motors, which makes the Corvette, does not object to these eccentrics. Year after year, it sells about $1 billion worth of Corvettes.

There are hundreds of thousands of people like Guy Zani, who, defying normalcy, are obsessed by Corvettes. Some people love Jaguars and others think nothing equals a vintage Plymouth Duster, but in the hierarchy of car freaks none ranks above the Corvette nut. *Vette Vues*, a monthly magazine devoted to the Corvette, attempted to summarize the phenomenon: "The Corvette carries a very strange, almost unexplainable mystique; one that can turn perfectly rational, sane, mature human beings into incoherent, delirious blabbering idiots!"

There are people like Les Bieri, a former nuclear engineer whose idea of retirement is to dismantle and reassemble the seventeen Corvettes he keeps near his home in Poquoson, Virginia. "I have dedicated my life to my Corvettes," he said. There is a man in Illinois who keeps two Corvettes in his playroom. The doors have been removed and he uses the cars as large armchairs.

Then there are people like Robert Barnette, a car show promotor in Greenville, South Carolina. He married Susie Stephens last year in a Corvette extravaganza: The ceremony took place at a Corvette show in Greenville (there is a Corvette show some place virtually every weekend). His wedding gift to his bride was a Venetian red 1957 Corvette. The wedding cake featured a little plastic Corvette on the top. To take their vows, the couple stood inside a Corvette roadster while the priest arranged himself just beyond the hood. "Somebody once said that a Corvette is an attitude," Mr. Barnette remarked. "I guess that's about how it is with me. I don't know why I love the thing so much. I just do."

Years ago, to promote its latest line of cars, General Motors used to put on an annual traveling show known as Motorama. As added spice, it always created a futuristic "dream" car to spotlight at the event. For the 1953 Motorama, the company decided to build the first American sports car. It was white, with a low-slung, swooping body fashioned out of Fiberglas. It looked like it could go, and it could. GM named it for a World War II escort ship called the corvette. People liked the Corvette so much that GM decided to put it into production. Hurriedly, Chevrolet built three hundred Corvettes by the end of the year. They were priced at $3,498, and all of them sold. John Wayne bought one, but then found that he was too tall to fit into it. He gave it away.

In 1954, production rose to 3,644 cars. Flaws began to show up, though. For one thing, the car leaked. Because the body parts didn't fit together properly, a heavy rainstorm left passengers drenched. The convertible top was designed so poorly that it required two people to put it up or down. Worst of all, there was no security. The car had no exterior door handles or door locks. (To get in, you reached through the window and opened the door from the inside.) You couldn't leave anything of value in the car. For that matter, someone could make off with the whole car.

In 1955, only seven hundred Corvettes were produced and the car seemed destined for oblivion. That year, Zora Arkus-Duntov, a Belgian development engineer who worked for GM, was asked to redo the Corvette. His design solved most of the car's problems, and he is known to this day as the "Father of the Corvette."

The redesign, coupled with publicity from the car's increasing success in motor racing, sparked new sales. Production rose to a peak of 53,807 in 1979. There have been three more redesigns. In 1963, Chevrolet came out with the Stingray body. The Mako Shark arrived in 1968, followed in 1984 by the more aerodynamic design that continues to be marketed today at a cost of about thirty-thousand to thirty-five thousand dollars. While old Corvettes are still regularly bought by shaggy-haired hot-rodders who like to drag them down barren streets at all hours, the new cars have upper-crust appeal. Buyers are customarily white-collar professionals in their late thirties, and boast a median income of seventy thousand dollars.

The car has inspired some five hundred fan clubs across the country. Big Corvette shows draw thousands of people; a recent one in Bloomington, Illinois, pulled more than forty thousand enthusiasts. In 1983, Prince had a big hit with the song, "Little Red Corvette," even though he has never owned one.

Chevy executives are no better than anyone else at articulating the Corvette's mystique. They mention its brute speed, its singular look, its status as the only American-built sports car and then they too start fumbling for words. "There's an association that here's a person who enjoys the art of driving," said David McLellan, the chief engineer for the Corvette.

There's a story making the rounds in Corvette circles. Richard Sampson, a man who built grocery stores, bought himself a new Corvette in 1954. He drove it for a while, but decided to secure his daughter's financial future by leaving the car to her. He didn't want it to get banged

up, so when he was building a store in Brunswick, Maine, in 1959, he
carved out a brick vault in the foundation, drove the Corvette in, and
sealed the chamber. The only opening was a tiny window, which enabled
him to gaze at his prize.

The car sat in that room for twenty-seven years. When Mr. Sampson died last year, his will specified that the car be dug out for his
daughter. Workmen unearthed the car, and his daughter, Cynthia, said
she would bring it home to Florida. It was in good shape, except the
white paint had turned yellow.

The definition of a good life for a Corvette addict is not only being
able to own a Corvette or two, but also being able to transform the
rapture into a living. Mike Yager, for instance, was a toolmaker in Illinois
who caught Corvette fever. In 1974, he thought he would try selling
Corvette patches and T-shirts at Corvette shows. He didn't have room
to pile all that stuff into his Corvette, so he borrowed a friend's Oldsmobile and sold out of the trunk. "Back then, I didn't know what I was
doing," he admitted. "Now I see that I was brilliant."

Corvette fans, it turned out, wanted those extras. Mr. Yager now
has a full-fledged mail-order business called Mid America Corvette Sup-
plies in Effingham, Illinois, that sells $10 million worth of Corvette ac-
cessories a year. You can get Corvette bikini underwear, Corvette beach
towels, Corvette shoes, Corvette wall clocks, Corvette gas pump lights,
and Corvette shower curtains.

There are other good Corvette professions. For fifteen years, Jim
Prather worked as a mailman, mostly along a route in Sandy Springs,
Georgia. In 1972, it occurred to him that Corvette owners probably
needed a magazine. He began with a newsletter called *Vette Vues* that he
ran off on an ancient mimeograph machine. It grew into a glossy magazine
with a circulation of twenty-five thousand that earns significantly more
for Mr. Prather than he ever made lugging letters.

Among other features, the magazine contains a column that sum-
marizes the plots of old *Route 66* episodes. It also covers major Corvette
shows; Mr. Prather personally takes in about two dozen of them a
year. The main appeal of these events is you get to look at a lot of
Corvettes. Ego is also involved, because trophies are awarded for the best
Corvette in various classes. Sometimes the difference between first and

second place is how clean the element is in the car's cigarette lighter.

"This Corvette mystique is a peculiar thing," Mr. Prather said. "I just got a clipping about a young man in Wisconsin who was killed in a car accident in a 1959 Corvette. They brought the car out to the cemetery with him laid out on a platform balanced across the car. I'm not sure that was in good taste, but there you go. The clipping didn't say, but I sure hope he wasn't buried in the '59. It's a beautiful car."

Anytime someone doubts that Corvette nuts redefine the bounds of sanity, aficionados bring up Tony Kleiber.

There's a famous picture among Corvette lovers. It shows the first three Corvettes ever built coming off the production line in Flint, Michigan. The first car was driven off that line by Tony Kleiber. He was a body assembler in the plant. Every now and then, he would pitch in and help get some of the new cars out. Among the Corvette fraternity Mr. Kleiber is revered. After all, the man sat behind the wheel of the first Corvette ever made. When Mr. Kleiber became ill a few years ago, Corvette magazines documented his travail, complete with in-hospital photographs. He died not long afterward, prompting lengthy obituaries in the magazines. Corvette owners throughout the country mourned.

Where are Corvettes No. 1 and No. 2?

A lot of people would love to know. They could be wrapped around telephone poles, or decaying at the bottom of a ditch. Despite tireless sleuthing by Corvette owners, no one has been able to find the first two cars built. Rumors persisted years ago that No. 1 was in South Euclid, Ohio, and that No. 2 was either in Sacramento, California, or perhaps rural Wisconsin. No such luck.

One reason Corvette devotees are curious is that Corvettes can appreciate substantially in value. A twenty-year-old in tiptop condition may command as much as a brand-new model.

Because of the disappearance of No. 1 and No. 2, Corvette No. 3 has necessarily become a most valuable car. Its location is known—sort of. Ed Thiebaud is a California turkey farmer. Though it is unclear exactly when and how he acquired the car, he has demonstrated that his 1953 Corvette is the third one ever made. A lot of people have seen the vehicle identification number on the body—"E53F001003." Pictures of his car have appeared in many magazines.

A few years ago, however, something mysterious happened. In the late 1970s, Phil Havens, an attorney in Lansing, Michigan, bought a 1955 Corvette. In the process of restoring it, he removed the body from the chassis and discovered a stamping on the frame that indicated that it was in fact a 1953 frame. The identification number was "E53F001003." Does that mean that Ed Thiebaud has the No. 3 body but a newer chassis? Nobody knows. Mr. Thiebaud has not commented about his frame. If he's looked at it, he's keeping mum.

"Any time I go out in my Corvette, I attract attention," Guy Zani was saying. He swung down Maple Avenue, up West Post, a left on Soundview, another left on Prospect. "You'll see," he said. "Girls ask for rides. Guys want to know if the car's for sale. We'll just drive for fifteen minutes and something will happen. Bound to happen."

Mr. Zani talked about his show. Next Memorial Day weekend, he plans to stage a Corvette show in Atlantic City. He's working on it with a partner, Paul Green, a promotor who says he would be retired if people like Mr. Zani didn't keep bugging him. He owns a Corvette too. Trump Plaza is the show's co-sponsor. The prizes in the show will be the highest ever, with the owner of the top car walking away with fifteen thousand dollars.

Mr. Zani took a left on South Lexington and got back on Maple. "See that fish market," he said. "The guy who owns it has three Corvettes. The deli owner over there has one. He used to be a gym teacher and couldn't afford the Vette. He went into the deli business, made some money. People change their jobs to get a Corvette."

Mr. Zani braked at a red light. The Corvette sputtered. Mr. Zani gunned it. It died. "I don't believe this," he said. A van with two men in it pulled up alongside. "Man, that car's too pretty to just sit there," the driver said. "Wait a sec while I park this and we'll push you out of the way."

"See that," Mr. Zani said. "What did I tell you. If I were in a Buick, I'd probably sit here all day. I told you something would happen."

July 19, 1987

They Called Him Lucky

BRIAN LOCKHART

By John Tierney

Brian Lockhart was buried the other day and it is probably safe to say that thousands of people in Greenwich Village miss him. They knew him as Lucky, an extraordinary beggar. He wrote poetry about sleeping in the subway and published an essay on homelessness in a newspaper at Princeton University. A comic strip in *The Village Voice* featured him telling his life story while sitting on his milk crate by the subway entrance on the northeast corner of Twelfth Street and Seventh Avenue, across from the hospital where he died at age forty-two.

Neighbors posted a memorial sign at his spot, and a half-dozen bouquets were left there. A woman in a suit reacted to the news by sitting on the sidewalk for two hours and crying. Neighbors, merchants, and commuters stopped throughout the day to reminisce about his smile, his easy wit, his kindness to all, his small gifts to some of his countless friends.

Some neighbors went up to Harlem to a memorial service and met Mr. Lockhart's relatives, who had not known until his death that he was homeless. They were stunned by his downtown reputation. They were intrigued to hear of the street-corner humanitarian who had published an essay castigating Americans who "turned their backs on the ones that need them the most." The Brian Lockhart they knew was a man who stole the rent money from his pregnant wife and did not return to see their son until the boy was ten years old.

"It's like we're talking about two different people," said his former wife, Adrienne Lockhart. "To hear that he was such a good, caring person, wishing everyone a safe trip home, giving presents—and he never gave his own children anything. Maybe he really did change. Or maybe it's just easier to be nice to strangers. You're not obligated."

Their son, Daryle, now nineteen, looked uneasy when he spoke to the people from Greenwich Village about his father, whom he had met three times. He said he had tried repeatedly to find his father since their last encounter in 1986. "I guess he's free now," the son said. "He doesn't have to be anything for anyone, and I'm happy if he's happy. I liked him when I saw him. I appreciate the people from downtown being so nice to him and coming up to the service. But don't romanticize him."

Brian Lockhart did many things before he ended up as a beggar. According to friends, family, official records, and his own accounts, he was a soldier in Vietnam, a college graduate who made the dean's list, a telephone installer, a chauffeur, a broker in the diamond district, a pimp, and a bank robber. His longest-running role was as a drug dealer who, as he put it, used his own product.

He was an only child raised in a middle-class section of Flushing, Queens, by his widowed mother, Devera, a secretary who was active in the African Methodist Episcopal Zion Church. After high school, he married a member of the church and served in Vietnam. He came home in 1969 with a heroin habit.

He soon parted from his pregnant wife, who went on to raise their son in Bedford-Stuyvesant, get a college degree at night, and become a social worker. He went off, had a daughter with another woman, and left them as well. There were scrapes with the law. At age thirty, he made a new start with his mother's help by enrolling at Livingstone College in Salisbury, North Carolina.

"He was a very bright and likable guy, a big fraternity man," said a spokesman for the college, Wilson Cherry. "He was older than most other students, and he dressed a little differently. He wore suits and slicked back his hair."

After he graduated in 1981 with a degree in accounting, he held jobs, but never for long. He often stayed at his mother's three-bedroom house in Flushing, which she bequeathed to him on her death in 1986. She also asked a minister and friend, the Rev. Dr. Harold E. Jones, to look after her son. "She said she knew he was going to lose the house, and he did," Dr. Jones said. "He couldn't make the mortgage payments. He got some money when it was sold, and he went through that. He bought some cars, and he always had his little tramps and his drugs. He would go clean every now and then—he would go to a rehabilitation program or go cold turkey—but it never lasted."

Mr. Lockhart's last home was an apartment that Dr. Jones provided above his church at 229 Lenox Avenue in Harlem. There are two versions of what drove him out, last year.

One is Mr. Lockhart's account in *The Village Voice*'s comic strip *Stan Mack's Real Life Funnies (All Dialogue Guaranteed Overheard)*. In one of the three strips chronicling his life, Mr. Lockhart tells how he took up crack after his mother's death, kicked the habit and then was mugged. "Five kids hit me in an alley, shot me under the heart, and took everything," he says. "While I was in the hospital, my apartment and all my valuables went up in flames. I've been living in a subway tunnel."

The other version is from Dr. Jones. The minister said that Mr. Lockhart was mugged and shot, but that the apartment was intact when he got out of the hospital. Dr. Jones said that the fire occurred later, and that it was started by Mr. Lockhart. "Lucky told me he'd fallen asleep smoking a cigarette," Dr. Jones said. A spokesman for the fire department said firefighters found vials and other items indicating the apartment was being used as a crack den.

"I told Lucky to come and see me so I could get him another apartment, but he never did," Dr. Jones said. "He may have been afraid people were looking for him here. He had kept cashing his mother's pension checks for two years after her death, and they found out. He owed eighteen thousand dollars, I think."

Mr. Lockhart started sleeping on subway plaforms and train stations, and for his last eight months began begging all day and evening on Twelfth Street. He took to writing in a notebook as he sat there. A friend in the neighborhood typed the poems, which had titles like "Walking Alone," "Winter Chill," and "Lonely Man."

In his essay "The United States of Homelessness," published in *The Nassau Weekly*, a student newspaper at Princeton, he asked the reader to imagine that "your family and friends have all turned their back on you and it is the middle of November." He described homeless drug addicts:

"Somewhere something in their life snapped and went to hopelessness, failure and self-destruction."

For him, that somewhere was apparently Vietnam. Dr. Jones, who knew Mr. Lockhart all his life, said he had been a model youth who came home a directionless man. Mr. Mack drew a similar conclusion and entitled one comic strip "Born on the Fourth of July, Too."

"He talked a lot about the awful things he saw there," Mr. Mack said. "I'd say his problems were Vietnam, drugs, being black, and his personality, in that order. It was puzzling to see him without a job, because he was intelligent, he looked strong, and he had an amazing ability to connect with people. It was a certain laid-back charisma. If he'd been white, he probably would have been a successful salesman who did co-caine."

Dr. Jones saw that charm, too. "I was very fond of him," the minister said. "That was why I put up with him. For all the things he did, he was always courteous, and he always promised he'd do better the next time. His problem was that he was not stouthearted."

Mr. Lockhart listed Dr. Jones as his next of kin when he went to St. Vincent's Hospital. He still had a wound in his head, which he attributed to an attack some nights earlier by a man with a stick in Pennsylvania Station. His immediate complaint was asthma. He was treated that morning, according to the hospital, and remained all day, until he died at 7:19 P.M. Dr. Jones said he was told the death was due to cardiac arrest.

Dr. Jones presided at the memorial service in Walters Memorial African Methodist Episcopal Zion Church, in the same building where Mr. Lockhart's last home had burned. Dr. Jones called Mr. Lockhart "a beautiful, respectful person" and reminded the listeners, "God tells us we are not to judge one another."

A eulogy was delivered by Sandy Stillman, a writer and computer consultant in Greenwich Village. He recalled Mr. Lockhart joking about having the city's most expensive alarm clock, costing one hundred and eighty thousand dollars: "It takes six transit cops to wake me up." He told how Mr. Lockhart, after nagging him to wear a hat on cold days, bought him a wool cap. "His ability to be so considerate and to have such good manners, when his own situation was so difficult, was amazing," Mr. Stillman said. "He was an easy guy to respect. Despite the fact that he was homeless, he was able to make the people he spoke to feel like he cared about them."

After the service, several relatives stood on Lenox Avenue and muttered about Vietnam veterans being in vogue downtown. They said the truly moving aspect of Mr. Lockhart's death was his children's initial reaction, before the Veterans Administration agreed to pay the fourteen hundred dollars in burial costs. The two college students had been trying to borrow the money to keep him out of a potter's field.

The son and the daughter, Tara Lockhart, stood on the sidewalk and said they did not know what had gone wrong in their father's life. What puzzled and hurt them the most, they said, was the thought of him begging from strangers and sleeping in a subway station when they and other relatives would have been willing to give him a bed.

"He could have called," his son said.

June 18, 1990

A Man Who Could Be Counted On

WILLIAM H. NATCHER

By Michael Wines

Representative William Huston Natcher, a Kentucky Democrat whose political longevity and spotless reputation won him the most powerful committee post in the House, died of heart failure. He was eighty-four.

Outside of Congress, Mr. Natcher was best known for his streak of 18,401 uninterrupted roll-call votes in the House of Representatives, a feat that ended twenty-eight days ago, on March 3, 1994, when failing health forced him to miss a vote (on a minor procedural matter) for the first time since he took office in 1954.

But on Capitol Hill, Mr. Natcher was an icon, a lawmaker who educated himself on the issues rather than relied on his staff, who took no campaign contributions, who was visibly offended by hints of corruption, and who honored legislative procedures and courtesies to their last jot. He once said that he wanted his epitaph to read, "He tried to do it right."

Those qualities, and his seniority, landed Mr. Natcher the chairmanship of the House Appropriations Committee in 1992, but only after Jamie L. Whitten of Mississippi surrendered the job. The chairman, who effectively controls House action on much of the federal budget, is one of the most powerful figures in Congress. House Democratic leaders had beseeched Mr. Natcher to take the job from Mr. Whitten months earlier, after Mr. Whitten suffered a stroke, but Mr. Natcher refused to overthrow his colleague.

That sense of fairness also led House colleagues to make him chairman of the body's internal gymnasium committee, where they could be assured that he would allot court time and other amenities without regard to politics or personal favors.

Mr. Natcher was said to take more pride in his voting record, his daily entries in a diary, and the weekly essays on history that he sent to his seven grandchildren than in his eminence in the House.

In his district, in central and western Kentucky, he generally campaigned by placing a few newspaper advertisements and driving from town to town in his own automobile. And in contrast to many House members, who operate publicity machines of Wurlitzer proportions, Mr. Natcher issued one press release each year, summarizing his voting record. In 1990 he spent $6,768 of his own money to rack up 66 percent of the vote against an opponent who had spent $144,315. One Republican who tried to unseat him in the 1980s likened the race to running against God.

Mr. Natcher was born in 1909 in Bowling Green, a middle-sized town in Kentucky's rolling limestone cave country. He was awarded a law degree from Ohio State University in 1933. After navy service in World War II and a string of private and public legal jobs, he won a special election to the House in August 1953.

Mr. Natcher's record of not missing a single vote in more than forty years, believed to be the longest in congressional history, became a burden to him in later life. He regularly urged newly elected members to miss a vote early in their careers to avoid his fate.

As his wife, Virginia, lay dying in Kentucky in 1991, Mr. Natcher shuttled almost continuously between her bedside and the House floor to avoid missing votes.

He was visibly weak in January, when the House returned to business after its winter recess. After he entered Bethesda Naval Hospital, the House suspended voting business on March 1 for one day to allow him to keep his voting stream intact, something the House had never done before for a member. On March 2, Mr. Natcher left his hospital bed and had navy aides wheel him onto the House floor on a gurney. There, studded with intravenous tubes but clad in a dark suit, he cast several votes on routine issues.

The next day he was unable to leave his bed, and both his streak and his tenure on the Appropriations panel effectively ended. Mr. Natcher had far surpassed the previous known record for consecutive votes, 16,555, held by Charles Bennett of Florida. But while House Democrats voted to place Representative David R. Obey of Wisconsin in command of the panel, they allowed Mr. Natcher to keep the title of chairman until his death.

Besides his grandchildren, Mr. Natcher is survived by two daughters, Celeste Jirles of Cambridge, Ohio, and Louise Murphy of Berkeley, California, and two great-grandchildren.

Those who eulogized Representative Natcher at his funeral in Bowling Green spoke more often of his simplicity and Kentucky roots than of his record voting streak. Starting with his first election as county prosecutor, Mr. Natcher had held public office since the age of twenty-seven.

President Bill Clinton said: "He found a way to live in Washington and work in politics and still found a way to be exactly the way he would have been if he'd been living here in Bowling Green running a hardware store."

His pastor, the Rev. Richard W. Bridges of the First Baptist Church, said, "Most of us in the second district would rather vote for a dead Bill Natcher than for a living someone else."

March 31, 1994

Zoot Suiter

Harold C. Fox

By Robert McG. Thomas, Jr.

Harold C. Fox, the Chicago clothier and sometime big-band trumpeter who claimed credit for creating and naming the zoot suit with the reet pleat, the reave sleeve, the ripe stripe, the stuff cuff, and the drape shape that was the stage rage during the boogie-woogie rhyme time of the early 1940s, died at his home in Siesta Key, Florida. He was eighty-six.

From the wide, padded shoulders and broad lapels of the long, billowing jacket to the ballooning high-waisted pants with the tourniquet-tight pegged cuffs and the inevitable long, looping watch chain, the zoot suit was an exaggerated fashion fad that not so much defined as defied an era of wartime conformity.

Never mind that the zoot suit has been variously attributed to a Beale Street tailor named Louis Lettes and a Detroit retailer known as Nathan (Toddy) Elkus. Anyone who doubts that a fashion that became widely associated with black and Hispanic swells, World War II drugstore cowboys, and Harvest Moon jitterbuggers was actually created by one man, even a trumpet-playing Chicago clothier who once took his own integrated band to the Apollo Theater in Harlem, wouldn't get much of an argument from Mr. Fox.

For although the Fox version of the zoot suit gained fame as the eye-popping garb of choice of big-band musicians like Dizzy Gillespie, Louis Armstrong, Woody Herman, Stan Kenton, and other customers of the Fox Brothers shop on Roosevelt Avenue, Mr. Fox graciously gave inspirational credit to slum-dwelling teenagers. "The zoot was not a costume or uniform from the world of entertainment," he once said. "It came right off the street and out of the ghetto."

At the Henry Ford museum in Dearborn, Michigan, where one of Mr. Fox's zoots is on display, the clothing curator Nancy Bryk said yesterday that the museum not only has hundreds of photographs of big-name entertainers wearing Fox creations but also old black-and-white photos showing youngsters—some as young as eight—proudly showing off their Fox zoots in front of the store.

As he later told and retold the story, Mr. Fox, whose father operated a piece-goods woolen business in Chicago, had begun his life as a sort of itinerant musician and traveling salesman, occasionally making band uniforms from the bolts of cloth his father would send him.

It was while working in New York in the late 1930s that he first got the idea for the zoot suit, he said. But it was not until he was summoned home to take over the family business after his father's death in 1941 that he put the idea into practice, dreaming up and sketching the designs and farming out the manufacturing to a couple known as Bill and Peanuts Fuchs. Mr. Fox began soliciting business from musician friends visiting Chicago and got his first big break when he received an emergency order for the Bill (Bojangles) Robinson dance troupe and filled it in three days.

As word of his speed and the flamboyance of his designs spread, Mr. Fox was besieged with orders. Even so, he managed to make a brief return to music, playing with a local band led by Jimmy Dale and then, after Mr. Dale was drafted, taking over the band and the name.

The zoot suit era was short-lived, its demise hastened by the Los Angeles zoot suit riots of 1942, which prompted the city council to consider an out-and-out ban on the suits the next year. So Mr. Fox simply reversed course and started turning out what he called the icicle, a shape-less garment he later claimed was the model for the actually much older Brooks Brothers suit.

Whatever the origins of the zoot suit, even the Merriam-Webster company accepted Mr. Fox's claim to the name.

Mr. Fox, who said the name "zoot suit" was chosen as a tribute to the rhyming slang used by many of his black customers, had a convincing explanation for why it did not become, say, "doot suit," or "loot suit," or "moot suit." At a time when the ultimate jive superlative was "the end to all ends," he said, he simply went to the end of the alphabet and found the Z.

Mr. Fox is survived by his wife, Marie; a son, Leo, of Orlando, Florida; three daughters, Arlette Katz of Sherman Oaks, California, Sandra Monzo of Agoura Hills, California, and Audrey Gregory of San Bernadino, California; a sister, Beatrice Gore of Chicago; eight grandchildren, and seven great-grandchildren.

August 1, 1996

Nerves of Diamonds

LAZARE KAPLAN

By Murray Schumach

Lazare Kaplan, one of the world's best-known diamond merchants and the artisan who cut one of the largest and most beautiful diamonds ever found, the 726-carat Jonker, died at his farm just outside Lew Beach in Sullivan County, New York. He was 102. Mr. Kaplan, who founded the diamond concern Lazare Kaplan & Sons, lived on his farm and also maintained an apartment in New York until a few years ago.

Mr. Kaplan's life traced the pattern by which New York City became the diamond capital of the world. From his boyhood in Russia to the diamond business in Antwerp and then to Manhattan, he survived reverses that obliterated other companies and merchants as he attained international respect, not only as a businessman, but also as one of the great diamond artisans of the century.

Thanks to his vision, Puerto Rico, which had no prior association with diamonds, now bustles with diamond-cutting factories. For his achievement, he was cited by the Puerto Rican Government in 1977 on his ninety-fourth birthday.

Because Mr. Kaplan was so expert in judging diamonds, his company became a supplier for many of the elite jewelry stores, such as Tiffany & Company, Cartier, and Van Cleef & Arpels. With such outlets, it was inevitable that the oval-cut diamond that he developed would become popular.

When a hall of fame for the diamond business was started in 1979 by the Retail Jewelers of America, this genial—but very competitive—authority on diamonds, whose burly presence was familiar in the world diamond centers of London, Antwerp, Tel Aviv, and Johannesburg, was the first person selected. And he was one of the few Fifth Avenue diamond men who was highly regarded on Forty-seventh Street, the heart of New York's jewelry district, whose diamond dealers tend to disparage their Fifth Avenue colleagues.

When he was well into his nineties, Mr. Kaplan would still go to his office two or three times a week, though the business was being run mainly by his two sons, Leo—who died last November—and George. "I'm still working hard" studying diamonds and planning how to cleave, or split, them, Mr. Kaplan said. "A diamond is the only gem where the cutting determines the quality."

His company was restructured in 1972, and a holding company, Lazare Kaplan International, became the first diamond-cutting company to go public; it was listed on the American Stock Exchange. A majority of the shares in the holding company was purchased in 1984 by Maurice and Leon Tempelsman, with the Kaplan family retaining a substantial interest.

For all his monetary success, Mr. Kaplan was probably proudest of his supreme achievement as a craftsman—his cleaving of the Jonker diamond, one of the most famous strikes in history, for Harry Winston in 1936. The diamond was found in 1934 on a farm near Pretoria, South Africa, by Jacobus Jonker. It was registered as "extra blue white and pure" and immediately took a place of great importance in the gem world because of its excellence. Fourth among the great diamond finds of history, the Jonker was on display at the American Museum of Natural History before Mr. Kaplan was chosen by Mr. Winston to cleave it. His fee was said to be thirty thousand dollars, enormous for a Depression year but not exorbitant considering the delicacy of the procedure and because the Jonker was to be only the second of the great diamonds of the world to be cleaved. (In 1908 the fabulous Cullinen diamond was split.)

In 1936, Mr. Kaplan described the cleaving process to reporters. Cleaving, he said, was the first step in cutting up a large stone. The exact grain of the gem is found and a groove is cut along it with the sharp edges of other diamonds. A hard steel wedge is inserted into the groove and with the tap of a weight the diamond is split along the grain—if the job is properly done. A slight mistake, a false move, and the stone may splinter into many pieces, largely destroying its value.

Recalling the task in an interview in 1979, Mr. Kaplan said the main reason he had agreed to do the job for Mr. Winston—who, after all, was a competitor—was not so much for the money as for the fact that he wanted his older son, Leo, to gain the experience of participating in the cleaving of a huge diamond. "I did not think it would be a very difficult job," he said, "because when it came to this country it had already been studied for Mr. Winston by foreign diamond experts and they had told him how it should be cleaved."

As Mr. Kaplan studied the diamond, however, he became convinced that the European experts were mistaken and that if he followed their suggestions the stone would be shattered. Although the diamond had been insured for $1 million, the policy did not cover the cleaving operation. No one, not even Lloyd's, would insure that. Mr. Kaplan told Harry Winston of his fears, and Mr. Winston, famous even among the daring diamond dealers for his nerve, told him to use his own judgment.

For more than a year, with his son beside him a good deal of the time, Mr. Kaplan studied the Jonker diamond, making models and marking them with India ink as he discussed his calculations with his son. He made more than 1,000 plaster models of the stone and 161 lead models as part of his calculations.

At one point he thought he had arrived at the solution and scratched a wedged incision into the gem with diamonds, placed his knife into the wedge and was about to bring down a mallet on the knife, when he thought he saw a bend in the Jonker's surface. He restudied the stone and made a different line.

Then twenty-three-year-old Leo Kaplan placed the wedge in the groove and Lazare Kaplan tapped. He used a specially counterbalanced weight that made his tap short and precise. As Leo watched, the great stone split. "It's perfect, father!" he exclaimed.

Lazare Kaplan's subsequent cleavings resulted in a total of twelve diamonds, the largest of which, the Jonker, was 126.65 carats. It was sold to King Farouk of Egypt for a reported $1 million. It has been resold several times since then, and its last owner is said to be a man from Japan who paid about $4 million for it. The eleven other diamonds he cleaved ranged in weight from 40.6 carats to 5.30 carats.

Like most master diamond cutters Mr. Kaplan served an arduous apprenticeship that began at the age of thirteen in Antwerp, after his family left Russia, where he was born on July 17, 1883, in the small town of Zabludova. He was one of thirteen children of Rachel and Simon Kaplan. His father was a watchmaker and jeweler by day and a rabbinical scholar by night.

At the age of twenty Lazare Kaplan opened his own shop and within a decade was doing so well that in 1914, with his wife and infant son, he decided to visit his mother in New York. While he was there World War I broke out. The Germans overran Belgium and his business was ruined. "I had nothing to go back to," he recalled.

He started at the bottom again in the New World with a little shop in lower Manhattan, which then contained the district for the small-diamond trade. But he was dissatisfied with the quality of the diamond cutters he engaged. A cousin who was an engineer in Puerto Rico told him that the people there seemed very skillful with their hands. So Mr. Kaplan went to Ponce and rented a building where he started a diamond-cutting business.

With the cutters in Puerto Rico and his business in New York, Mr. Kaplan prospered once more. But in 1929, after the crash of the stock market, the value of diamonds plummeted and he was once more down to nothing. This time, his son Leo, who was working with him during the day and going to school at night, withdrew his savings of three hundred dollars and turned them over to his father to help him get started again. That canceled savings book was to remain a family treasure.

The Kaplans, unlike many of their competitors, survived the Depression and moved up to mid-Manhattan, preparing the way for the thousands of Jewish diamond workers who fled Amsterdam and Antwerp as the Nazis swept into the Low Countries.

Toward the end of his life, looking back on his success, Mr. Kaplan gave enormous credit to his wife, the former Charlotte Kittower, whom he married in 1911. "She was a real Jewish mother," he said after her death in 1972. "She never asked about finances. Never complained, whatever happened to us, whatever I had to do. She just gave love. The whole family was shaped by it."

Mr. Kaplan started an educational foundation in his and his wife's name, to which his two sons also contributed. It has sent more than a thousand young people from Lew Beach and other communities in the Catskills to college.

Mr. Kaplan is survived by his son, George, of Rye Brook, New York; six grandchildren, and six great-grandchildren.

February 14, 1986

He Stretched the World

Julian W. Hill

By David Stout

Julian W. Hill, a research chemist whose accidental discovery of a tough, taffylike compound revolutionized everyday life after it proved its worth in warfare and courtship, died in Hockessin, Delaware. He was ninety-one. Dr. Hill died at the Cokesbury Village retirement community, where he had lived in recent years with his wife of sixty-two years, Polly.

In the late 1920s, Dr. Hill was a member of a Du Pont Company team studying the behavior of certain molecules that chain together to form larger ones, called polymers. The chemists were engaged in pure research, though finding a substitute for silk was in the back of their minds.

In 1930, while trying to create ever-larger structures by adjusting the amount of water in a batch of carbon- and alcohol-based molecules, the team came up with a concoction that Du Pont's research head, Wallace H. Carothers, thought useless. But Dr. Hill was intrigued after sticking a heated glass rod into a beaker containing the material and finding that it stretched and pulled, like taffy, and that it became silky when stretched at room temperature. Soon, Dr. Hill and his colleagues were playing with the material in the corridor, and finding that it could be shaped into strands that were remarkably long and strong. The substance, of course, was nylon, although it would not be so named until it was introduced at the 1939 World's Fair in New York. "I tell my wife I was something better than a good scientist," Dr. Hill recalled in an interview years later. "I was lucky."

Because Du Pont held the patents to nylon, Dr. Hill made no great fortune from the discovery, but his wife said that the company had treated him well over the years.

A sad footnote is the fate of Dr. Carothers. Beset by personal problems that fueled depression, thinking himself a failure despite a brilliant career, he committed suicide in 1937 at the age of forty-one.

If the development of nylon was in part serendipity, it was not a total surprise. Almost a decade earlier, at an American Chemical Society conference in Buffalo, Dr. Hill and Dr. Carothers reported progress in developing "artificial silks" like rayon, which was then coming into use.

But rayon is derived from cellulose, and in that sense is not strictly synthetic, as is nylon. Nylon was used initially for toothbrush bristles, fishing line, and surgical sutures. Nylon stockings were first sold in 1939. They cost twice what silk stockings did, but women were happy to pay. Nylon stockings were sheer and strong.

The material was deemed so essential that its use was restricted to the military after the United States entered World War II. Nylon was used to make rope, tents, aircraft tires, and parachutes. Young American soldiers stationed in Britain made good impressions on their dates by giving them nylon stockings, available from the military's post exchanges when they could not be bought elsewhere. British soldiers did not appreciate that very much.

The reintroduction of nylon to civilian life after the war caused a sensation, and at least one stampede. A crowd of ten thousand people jammed a San Francisco department store in 1945, causing the sale of nylon stockings to be called off.

In the decades since, nylon has become ubiquitous in carpeting and clothing. And about two thirds of all the luggage manufactured in the world is made from it.

Scientists consider nylon a benign product of technology because it has not been found to have any deadly side effects. But Dr. Hill, who loved wildlife and was a dedicated bird-watcher, said in a 1988 interview that he thought "the human race is going to perish by being smothered in plastic."

Julian Werner Hill was born in St. Louis, graduated from Washington University there in 1924, and earned a doctorate in organic chemistry from the Massachusetts Institute of Technology in 1928. He played the violin and was an accomplished squash player and figure skater until his early forties, when an attack of polio weakened one leg, his wife said.

Before his retirement from Du Pont in 1964, Dr. Hill supervised the company's program of aid to universities for research in physics and chemistry.

Surviving besides his wife are a daughter, Louisa Spottswood of Philadelphia; two sons, Joseph, of Villanova, Pennsylvania, and Jefferson, of Washington, D.C., and five grandchildren.

February 1, 1996

Coming Home

LEWIS B. PULLER, JR.

By Catherine S. Manegold

Tens of thousands of obituaries have been written for the men who fought and died in Vietnam. More will follow as veterans age and die. But some deaths seem larger than others, as if they could serve as obituaries for the war itself.

Lewis B. Puller, Jr.'s was one such death. It happened when Mr. Puller, who was forty-eight, shot himself in the head at his home in suburban Virginia. A veterans' advocate and Pulitzer Prize winner whose hands were disfigured and whose legs were torn from his body by a booby trap in Vietnam, he had finally surrendered in his twenty-six-year battle against depression, drug and alcohol addiction, despair, and perhaps, at the end, sheer fatigue.

His suicide came at a time of physical and emotional pain but professional success, a conundrum that his colleagues and friends confronted with deep sadness and, for some, profound confusion. The lessons of the suicide of Mr. Puller must be as much about his successes as his final failure to hang on, his friends said.

"Lewis Puller never stopped fighting the war of healing," said Kieu Chinh, a Vietnamese actress who worked with him on his last project, an effort to build a school in what once was the no-man's land of Quang Tri. He fought, she said, "to heal not only his own wounds but the common wounds of the two nations."

His legacy, friends said, was not the image of his shrunken body perched on a wheelchair in front of the Vietnam War Memorial, but his book, a difficult and graphic description of his trauma and pain-filled struggles against addiction; his fight for veterans to win fair representation in the Clinton administration; his son and daughter; his friends; and his will to live. It was typical of him, they said, that his last great passion would be the construction of a school in a battered area that was once the demilitarized zone. "We were going to build a monument in Vietnam," said Terry Anderson, the former hostage in Lebanon who worked with Mr. Puller on the Vietnam Memorial Association. "But he was quite strong about his feeling that we should build something more than a pile of stone."

For not quite three months in 1968, Mr. Puller, the marine son of the most decorated marine in American history, the late Gen. Lewis B. (Chesty) Puller, fought an enemy he rarely saw on the shores of the South China Sea. His injury came suddenly. His recovery never ended.

For the next two decades, he worked not only on what physical rehabilitation he could muster but also within the ranks of the veterans' movement to push for the construction of the Vietnam memorial in Washington, D.C., the eventual lifting of the embargo on trade with Hanoi, and the school project. His account of his war experiences and efforts to heal, *Fortunate Son: The Healing of a Vietnam Vet* (1991), won the Pulitzer Prize for biography in 1992.

Early last year, he was approached by the Clinton administration with several offers of work. Instead, he used his computer to trace how many veterans the administration had placed in important positions and concluded that the numbers were too low. Rather than join the government, he chose to work as a writer in residence at George Mason University in Fairfax, Virginia, and on veterans projects.

But in the midst of those public achievements he carried on a private battle. He was still in combat when he died, friends said, battling to save a marriage traumatized by his addictions and trying to help the country with a healing process after a war that in one way or another shadows a generation. "He was fighting 'stump pain' at his two amputations," said his friend John Wheeler. He was also fighting to rebound from addictions to painkilling drugs and alcohol. Last winter, after a fall in which he broke his hip, he entered Bethesda Naval Hospital. "We closed ranks and continued to get the work done," Mr. Wheeler said.

His friends thought his political work would be his salvation. And after he suddenly ended his life, Mr. Wheeler said, "I felt like I let my guard down in helping him heal and keeping a watch over him."

Though he stopped taking painkillers and had stayed away from alcohol since acknowledging his many battles with addiction, Mr. Puller could not shake a sense of bleakness, said Mame Reiley, a friend of the family's. His wife, Linda T. Puller, a member of the Virginia House of Delegates, finally despaired, Ms. Reiley said. "They were going through a very rough time."

Other friends said Mr. Puller had spoken with sadness of his marital troubles and said the couple were planning a divorce. His book, a brutally honest account of his struggles and their toll upon his friends and family, touches on the cost of the addictions to the people he loved. "Lewis, in his book, described how abusive and difficult he became during those times," said Senator Bob Kerrey of Nebraska, a fellow veteran who became a close friend while the two were recovering from wounds at the Philadelphia Naval Hospital in 1969.

Mr. Kerrey said bitterly that laxness on the part of doctors in one of Mr. Puller's more recent hospitalizations may have aggravated his problems just as his life had come to seem more whole. "They put him on narcotics without asking him if he was an alcoholic," Mr. Kerrey said. "Here is a man who won a Pulitzer Prize writing about his addiction in these areas and the hospital didn't even pay attention. I just don't get it."

The physical pain that followed when he stopped taking the drugs mixed with his anguish over the war, over his family's troubles, and over his own future, said Mr. Kerrey. "He inspired so many people," he said. "The tragedy in the end is that he was not able to inspire himself."

Those whom he did inspire, though, stretched well beyond the broad population of war veterans. Marcia Landau, who worked with him on the school project, said his honesty and courage changed her own life. "I am so shaken," she said. "I woke up this morning thinking of a phrase from my childhood. I hadn't thought of it in years: The stronger the light you stand in when you tell the truth, the larger the shadow of the devil becomes." That quality of spirituality both lifted and haunted him, she said. "If you are willing to go to the light, you have to be willing to face the darkness," Ms. Landau added.

The two, perhaps, finally came together for him in a return trip to Vietnam last fall. Several friends said the trip seemed to both exalt and depress him. When he returned, his friend and colleague, Ms. Chinh, asked if he had taken photographs. He said he had not. "Everything," he told her, "is here in my heart."

Ms. Chinh had planned to go back to Vietnam with him. Instead, the last time she saw him was at a recent gathering at the National Press Club in Washington, D.C., before a speech about the school project. She arrived early, after a flight east from California. He was already there. As the elevator doors opened, her eyes were drawn across the room, to a bank of windows. "Here was this man sitting in his wheelchair, looking at the sky," she said. "He was looking at the sky and he was alone."

She stole up behind him and placed her hand softly on his shoulder. He did not turn, but put the gnarled remains of his own hand gently across hers. They stood silently together for a moment, then went to face the public, to talk of Vietnam's sinking literacy rate and the importance of the school.

He was, she said, the kindest soldier that she ever knew.

In addition to his wife, Mr. Puller is survived by a son, Lewis III of Arizona; a daughter, Margaret, of Alaska, and two sisters, Martha Downs of Alexandria, Virginia, and Virginia Dabney of Lexington, Virginia.

May 14, 1994

WRECKAGE OF AN AMERICAN WAR

LEWIS PULLER's 1991 book, Fortunate Son: The Healing of a Vietnam Vet, *was written as a tribute to his father, the late Gen. Lewis B. (Chesty) Puller, the most decorated marine in the history of the corps. The book won the Pulitzer Prize for biography in 1992 and will endure as a testimony to a nightmarish episode in American history.*

When the book appeared, it was reviewed in The New York Times Book Review *by* WILLIAM STYRON, *the distinguished novelist who served in the marines in World War II and the Korean War, and who is the author of his own encounter with demons,* Darkness Visible: A Memoir of Madness. *Mr. Styron's review follows:*

The marines who fought in the Pacific during World War II had much to fear, for the fighting was often lethal and barbaric. Yet because they were marines, with an intense feeling of identity, and were caught up in that mysterious group trance known as esprit de corps, they really did assume that they were invincible. Some of this hubris came from their brutal and very efficient training, but a great deal of their deepest confidence flowed from their leaders. Their officers, both commissioned and noncommissioned, were arguably the best in the world, and of these leaders no marine commanded more admiration than a colonel with a beguilingly menacing countenance and a pouter-pigeon strut named Lewis Burwell Puller.

Puller—the father of the author of *Fortunate Son,* a dark and corrosive autobiography—was nicknamed Chesty for the aggressive thrust of his carriage; he was and still is a legend, an embodiment of the marines in the same way that Babe Ruth embodies baseball or that Yeats stands for Irish poetry. A native of the Virginia Tidewater, Puller was born at the end of the last century, close enough to the Civil War to be haunted by it and to be mesmerized by its Confederate heroes and victims. Like many of the high-level marine officers, disproportionately Southern by origin, who helped defeat the Japanese, Puller learned his infantry tactics while chasing and being chased by the guerrilla forces of Augusto Sandino in the Nicaraguan jungles; his spectacular exploits there won him two Navy Crosses.

During World War II, the last truly just war fought by Americans, Puller was awarded the Navy Cross two more times for gallantry under fire, at Guadalcanal and at Cape Gloucester, and his legend blossomed. Stories about him abounded. Respected extravagantly, he was also greatly feared, especially by very junior officers. It was rumored that he literally devoured second lieutenants; after all, at the gruesome battle of Peleliu, a derelict shavetail was summoned into Chesty Puller's tent and never a shred of him was seen again—he plainly had been eaten.

Puller exhibited little tact, especially with the press. In the aftermath of the deadly Guadalcanal campaign, an asinine journalist inquired, "Colonel, could you tell the American people what it is you're fighting for?" Puller replied, "Six hundred and forty-nine dollars a month."

His fairness and concern for his troops were celebrated and were never so evident as during the retreat from Chosin Reservoir, during the Korean War, when as a regimental commander he led a rear-guard action of such tactical mastery that it manifestly saved countless American lives; this feat won him a fifth Navy Cross and promotion to brigadier general.

As Burke Davis portrays him in his fine 1962 biography, *Marine!*, Chesty Puller, despite the glory he gained in the mechanized setting of modern warfare, was a God-fearing fighting man of the old school, cast in the mold of Lee and Jackson, both of whom he idolized. Amid the most foulmouthed body of men in Christendom he was, if not prudish, restrained in speech. Some of the letters he wrote to his wife from various exotic hellholes are poignant, old-fashioned utterances that touch on the horrors of war but speak of a longing for repose in tones of spiritual anguish reminiscent of Stonewall Jackson.

After he retired to his Tidewater village, nearly two decades before his death in 1971, he was proud when his only son, born when he was nearing fifty, went off as a second lieutenant to combat duty in Vietnam. That twenty-year-old man, his namesake—the "fortunate son" of this bitter though redemptive narrative—became one of the most grievously mutilated combatants to survive the ordeal of Vietnam.

The catastrophe happened on a blazing October day in 1968, when Lewis Puller, Jr., was leading his platoon on a routine patrol through an especially sinister area of the countryside nicknamed the Riviera, a strip of rice paddies and wooded hills bordering the South China Sea. Mr. Puller had served in the combat zone for less than three months, but his activity had been intensely concentrated and appallingly violent. He had seen marines wounded and killed, had engaged in fierce firefights, had been exposed to booby traps; during an attack on a local village one of his men had inadvertently blown off the arm of an eight-year-old girl.

Mr. Puller is a gripping writer when he describes the heat and exhaustion, the physical brutalization, the incessant anxiety and danger suffered by young men engaged in that demented strife nearly a quarter of a century ago. Not without good reason he may be at his most vivid when he tells what happened to him.

That October day he stepped on a booby-trapped howitzer round and was rocketed sky-high. He "had no idea that the pink mist that engulfed me had been caused by the vaporization of most of my right and left legs. As shock began to numb my body, I could see through a haze of pain that my right thumb and little finger were missing, as was most of my left hand." In addition, the explosion destroyed massive parts of both buttocks, ruptured an eardrum, split his scrotum, and sent slivers of shrapnel through most of the rest of his body.

Hovering near death for many days, Mr. Puller developed a stress ulcer that required the removal of two thirds of his stomach, augmenting the already intolerable pain. Transported stateside, he remained for nearly two years at the Philadelphia Naval Hospital, where, through the early phases of his stay, he was utterly helpless and so dependent on morphine that when he was briefly taken off it he was, as he says, "quickly reduced to the level of a snarling animal." When his weight dropped to less than sixty pounds and his stomach resisted food, he was given nourishment through a nasal tube.

These pages exude the whiff of authentic hell and are, accordingly, sometimes difficult to read. But because Mr. Puller writes with simplicity and candor, with touches of spontaneous humor, his outcry of agony and isolation, while harrowing, leaves one primarily overwhelmed with wonder at the torture a human being can absorb this side of madness.

Slowly the worst of the torment receded and slowly the recuperative process began: skin grafts, reconstructive surgery, endless hours on the operating table, all enacted in a continuum of diabolical pain. He regained some extremely limited use of his mangled hands, but the efforts to restore mobility to his legs through prostheses, while tireless, were in vain; he would have to spend the rest of life in a wheelchair. There were compensations, however, for his sacrifice: His face was unscathed and his basic senses, including his eyesight, remained intact. So did his sexual functioning. His young wife, who was pregnant when he went off to Vietnam,

presented him with a son. Escaped like Ishmael from the vortex of oblivion, he had a future and also, clearly, a tale to tell.

Fortunate Son is an amazing tale but in many ways an artless one,
with great cumulative power yet more compelling as a raw chronicle than
a work offering literary surprises. If its prose does not resonate as does
Philip Caputo's eloquent *Rumor of War,* if the book lacks the surreal
wackiness and scathing insights that made Michael Herr's *Dispatches* such
an original tour de force, its act of bearing such passionate witness to a
desecrated moment in history has its own importance and gives it a place
among the meaningful works on the Vietnam nightmare.

As for Mr. Puller's future, it seemed in certain respects almost as
calamitous as the experience of war. He acquired a law degree and an
ambition to run (as a Democrat) for a congressional seat in Virginia. By
this time he had undergone the same traumatic insult as numberless veterans whose brother and sister Americans detested them for an event they
conceived to be the handiwork of the warriors themselves. Smarting at
this mad response but in a rage at the war and its real instigators in
Washington, he made his feelings public, proclaiming that if he were
called up again he would refuse to go.

Such statements, coming especially from the son of Chesty Puller,
did not go down well in a state as profoundly hidebound as Virginia,
where Mr. Puller also was rash enough to choose to run in a district
bordering Hampton Roads—the very marrow of the military-industrial
complex and a busy hive of patriots ill disposed to contemplate any such
paradigm of the monstrousness of war. His image as a horribly maimed
veteran, rather than inspiring compassion and patriotic rapport, aroused
resentment and guilt among the voters and plainly contributed heavily to
his defeat. Then he slid into perhaps his deepest peril yet. He had always
been an enthusiastic drinker, but shortly after his political loss his de-
pendency became overpowering; he subsided into the near-madness of
alcoholism, becoming so deranged and incapacitated that he came close
to killing himself. With the help of Alcoholics Anonymous he recovered,
and his wretchedly difficult but successful climb out of still another abyss
makes up the rest of *Fortunate Son,* the coda of which culminates in a
revealing irony: Apparently at peace with himself and the world, Mr.

Puller is currently a senior attorney in the office of the general counsel of the Department of Defense.

Or the irony may not be so striking after all. Throughout the book one senses in Mr. Puller a hesitation, an ambivalence about the marines that he seems unable to resolve. About the marine corps, he wonders at one point how "I could love and despise it with such equal ardor." This tells much about the powerful hold that military life, at its most idealistic, can have upon thoroughly decent men, quite a few of whom are capable of complex quandaries and apprehensions about what they are called upon to do.

What Mr. Puller was called upon to do was to fight in a war that never should have begun, but once begun tainted the souls of all those connected with it. Yet the quality of devotion sometimes inexplicably and maddeningly remains. Just before the famous gathering of 1971, when protesting Vietnam veterans planned to discard their medals on the steps of the Capitol, the author debated agonizingly with himself before putting his medals back in the closet. "They had cost me too dearly," he writes, "and though I now saw clearly that the war in which they had been earned was a wasted cause, the medals still represented the dignity and the caliber of my service and of those with whom I had served."

It would be wrong for flag-wavers to misinterpret these words and cheer Mr. Puller's nobility, and just as wrong for those who reflexively condemn all wars to read them as the sentiments of the enslaved military mind. Like his father, who served heroically in several just wars—or at least understandable ones—Mr. Puller was a professional engaged in what many men of goodwill still regard as an honorable calling, and one likely to remain so until wars are made extinct; yet he was too young and too unaware, at least at the beginning, to realize the nature of his involvement in a national dishonor.

His father, Mr. Puller notes, came home twice from the Far East in triumph, while his own reception was one of scorn and jeers. The old man, he writes, almost never gave vent to his deepest emotions. But no wonder Chesty Puller finally wept, looking down at his legless and hand-less son, wreckage of an American war in which random atrocities would serve as the compelling historical memory, instead of the suffering and sacrifice, and for which there would be no Guadalcanal or Iwo Jima, no Belleau Wood, no Shiloh or Chickamauga.

June 16, 1991

THE NEW YORK TIMES BOOK REVIEW

A Wise Woman Fished Here

FRANCES STELOFF

By Herbert Mitgang

Frances (Fanny) Steloff, one of America's most distinguished independent booksellers, died of pneumonia at Mount Sinai Medical Center. She was 101 years old and lived in Manhattan.

Miss Steloff founded the Gotham Book Mart in 1920 and, over the years, turned it into an international literary haven. It is still thriving at 41 West Forty-seventh Street in Manhattan, an anachronism in a time of failing independent bookstores.

Soon after the Gotham opened, it attracted authors, dramatists, poets, and artists. Among those who came to chat, to browse, and to see if their books and plays were on the shelves were Theodore Dreiser, John Dos Passos, H. L. Mencken, and Eugene O'Neill. Miss Steloff's customers also included George and Ira Gershwin, Ina Claire, and Charlie Chaplin, and, more recently, Alexander Calder, Stephen Spender, Woody Allen, Saul Bellow, John Guare, and Garson Kanin. J. D. Salinger—who left the store if people gave signs of recognition—headed for the philosophy and religion section.

Miss Steloff championed the experimental and challenged the censors. Her courage in purchasing shipments of the banned *Lady Chatterley's Lover* directly from D. H. Lawrence in Italy in the late 1920s and in ordering smuggled copies of *Tropic of Cancer* from Henry Miller in Paris during the 1930s led to lawsuits and landmark decisions on censorship.

Although she sold the Gotham in 1967 to Andreas Brown, another book lover, she continued to live in an apartment on the third floor, above the store, and remained as a working consultant. Miss Steloff, a diminutive woman with pale blue eyes and gray hair knotted in a bun, ignored her age and her semi-retirement, descending every afternoon to sit at a desk in her own corner, occasionally jumping up to press books on browsers, and then to direct them to the cash register.

Essentially a person of no literary pretensions, Miss Steloff made her bookstore a place cherished as the habitat for the new and the avant-garde in literature, where small magazines and forgotten books of poetry, out-of-print books on belles-lettres, and works on film and the theater could be found in an atmosphere congenial to browsers.

Under her guidance the Gotham became a meeting place for the literati and a bibliophile's paradise. The number of well-known writers, dancers, artists, and theater people who were her customers, clients, and friends made up an encyclopedia of twentieth-century culture. Above the cozy bookstore, where the literate still browse, in the hall on the second floor hang oversized photographs of Miss Steloff with Dylan Thomas in 1952, Anaïs Nin in 1966, Jean Cocteau in 1948, Salvador Dalí in 1963, and Marianne Moore in 1967.

At her one hundredth birthday celebration, on December 31, 1987, greetings arrived from all over the world.

From the critic Alfred Kazin: "No one around has your history of service to literature and no one has fought so gallantly for the freedom of literary expression. You have inspired me and so many others dedicated to writing, to intellectual freedom itself, in our embattled world."

From Mayor Teddy Kollek in Jerusalem: "I remember my very first visit to New York, in the harried and pressured days before the creation of the State of Israel. There was rarely a free minute, but when one did emerge, I knew that the Gotham Book Mart was not far away. It was the opportunity to enter a rare world presided over by a rare person."

And a cable from Sommières, in southern France: "A 100-gun salute from Lawrence Durrell."

Miss Steloff was one of the founders of the James Joyce Society, which still meets at the Gotham, although she never met the author. "Sylvia Beach took care of his book wants at Shakespeare & Company in Paris," she said. "But sometimes Joyce ordered books from the Gotham directly by mail—he ordered books during the last year of his life."

After working in several bookstores, she opened her own on West Forty-fifth Street in 1920. The store moved twice to larger quarters. "It was a struggle at the beginning," she recalled. "There were some days during the Depression when we didn't sell a single book."

"I am not the great brilliant person to decide about how good a book is," she said once. "I judge books by my customers who buy them and spark others to read them." She was greatly interested in Oriental teachings, mystical experiences, and philosophers not connected with established Western churches. Books in these fields were represented in her corner of the store.

Along with its fame and reputation, the Gotham was also a very carefully operated book business. As the owner and the person who paid the salaries, Miss Steloff was demanding, irascible, unwearying, and unable to understand why no one else was willing to put as many hours or as much concentration into the store as she did.

Miss Steloff recalled some of the clerks who had worked for the Gotham over the years. "There was Allen Ginsberg and LeRoi Jones and many poets in their youth," she said. "Tennessee Williams lasted less than a day—he couldn't get here on time in the morning and, also, he wasn't very good at wrapping packages."

Miss Steloff and Mr. Brown maintained "security" when they received requests for books from award jurors—including the committee in Stockholm that awards the Nobel Prize in literature. "When they order a half-dozen copies of a book, we suspect that something's up and that a particular author is under consideration," Mr. Brown said. "Of course, that's confidential and we would never give out the author's name."

A more mundane form of security is maintained at the Gotham to prevent shoplifting. A sign put up by Miss Steloff reads: "ATTENTION SHOPLIFTERS—REMEMBER YOUR KARMA." Mr. Brown added: "Of course, the occasional shoplifter here is a rather special person. He might try to walk off with a two-dollar paperback of Rimbaud's poems. Nothing major."

Ida Frances Steloff was born December 31, 1887, in Saratoga Springs, New York, a town full of gaiety in the summer and a bleak, wintry place for the rest of the year, especially for the poor. The Steloffs, who lived year-round in Saratoga Springs, were among the very poor. When Miss Steloff was little, she sold flowers on the verandas of the big hotels. The early death of her mother increased her misery, especially when her stepmother expressed her frustrations with poverty in the harshness she showed the children.

At twelve, Miss Steloff was taken in by a couple who offered her a home. But she soon found herself a menial in the household and was forced to drop out of the seventh grade—her last formal schooling. Once in desperation she ran away to New York City. It was not until she was nineteen, though, that she made a final move to New York. She landed a job at Loeser's, a Brooklyn department store, "working in 'corsets.'" But during the Christmas rush, she was transferred to the book department. It was like giving a copy of Euclid to Isaac Newton: She had found herself and a way of life.

For the next twelve years she worked in various bookstores: Schulte, Brentano's, and McDevitt-Wilson, where she developed what one friend called "an instinctive taste for the best in modern literature," a taste that she was willing to gamble on when she had her own shop. She never referred to Gotham as a store; it was always a "shop."

Her stature concealed her stamina. She ran the place, but she also opened the correspondence, wrapped and mailed packages, climbed up and down ladders, and argued with publishers. Bookstore people were continually helping her down from ladders when she was in her eighties. "She felt," Mr. Brown said, "as if she still had to stock the store."

Miss Steloff was awarded a prize by the National Institute of Arts and Letters for distinguished service to the arts, was listed in *Who's Who in the Theater*, and received an honorary doctorate from Skidmore College— an award that stood in sharp contrast to one of her remarks: "I used to feel bitter and cheated about not having a formal education. But why should I? How could I, no matter what my education, ever have had the wonderful chance to have Thornton Wilder and other people talk to me personally, and right here in my shop! As if they were in their classrooms! I couldn't ask for anything more."

A battle to save the bookstore ended in February 1988, when Mr. Brown bought the building that houses the store from the American Friends of the Hebrew University Foundation. With the $1 million proceeds, the foundation has established a scholarship at the Hebrew University in Jerusalem in the name of Miss Steloff's parents.

Mr. Brown said that Miss Steloff would be buried in the family plot in the Jewish Cemetery in Saratoga Springs. The Gotham will be closed on that day in her memory. Mr. Brown said he would post a sign and pictures of Miss Steloff in the bookstore window.

Miss Steloff was married to David Moss in 1923. They were divorced in 1930. Surviving are a half sister, Belle Sidoroff of Wilmington, Delaware, and a half brother, Al Steloff of Saratoga Springs, New York.

A sign familiar to New Yorkers swings over the outside of the Gotham. It reads: "WISE MEN FISH HERE." Miss Steloff once said, "The sign was done for me by John Held, Jr., the artist. I hope it—and the Gotham—go on forever."

April 16, 1989

Sweetener of Lives

BENJAMIN EISENSTADT

By Robert McG. Thomas, Jr.

Benjamin Eisenstadt, the innovative Brooklyn businessman who set Americans to shaking their sugar before sweetening their coffee and then shook up the entire sweetener industry as the developer of Sweet'n Low, died at New York Hospital–Cornell Medical Center. He was eighty-nine and a major benefactor of Maimonides Medical Center in Brooklyn. The cause was complications of bypass surgery, his son Marvin said.

Considering the scope of his eventual philanthropy, Mr. Eisenstadt, a Brooklyn resident who gave millions to Maimonides, followed a circuitous path to business success. The son of an ironworker who died when he was seven, Mr. Eisenstadt, who was born on the Lower East Side of Manhattan, seemed headed for a brilliant career as a lawyer, but his timing was off. He graduated first in his class from St. John's University law school in 1929—just in time for the Depression.

Taking a job at a cafeteria his father-in-law operated in Brooklyn, Mr. Eisenstadt later ran a couple of cafeterias of his own, eventually finding a measure of success by opening one in 1940 on Cumberland Street, in the Fort Greene section, just across from the Brooklyn Navy Yard, which became a boomtown in World War II. When the end of the war turned the Navy Yard into a ghost town and left him bereft of customers, Mr. Eisenstadt, recalling that his uncle had once operated a company that filled tea bags, turned the Cumberland Cafeteria into the Cumberland Packing Company, transforming it into a tea bag factory, one that was never a threat to Tetley or Lipton and that limped toward oblivion in 1947.

Faced with yet another business failure, Mr. Eisenstadt had the brainstorm that changed the way Americans dispense sugar. The same equipment that injected tea into tea bags, he realized, could be used to put sugar into little paper packets.

At a time when restaurants had never used anything but open sugar bowls or heavy glass dispensers, the idea of individual sanitary sugar packets was so revolutionary—and Mr. Eisenstadt was so naïve—that when he proudly showed his operation to executives of giant sugar companies, his son said, they simply set up their own sugar-packet operations. A contract with the little Jack Frost sugar company kept Cumberland alive, but without a branded line of its own it was little more than a marginal operation.

That changed in 1957 when Mr. Eisenstadt and his son Marvin, who had studied chemistry at the University of Vermont, began fooling around with saccharin. The low-calorie sweetener had been around since the nineteenth century (Teddy Roosevelt used it), but until then it had been available only as a liquid or in pill form, and its use was restricted to diabetics and the obese. When the Eisenstadts mixed saccharin with dextrose and other ingredients to make a granulated low-calorie sugar substitute, another coffee revolution was at hand. Taking care to obtain a patent for the use of saccharin as a sugar substitute, Mr. Eisenstadt, recalling a Tennyson poem that had been made into a song, came up with the name Sweet'n Low. The treble-clef musical logo on a pink packet set Sweet'n Low apart from the white sugar packets on restaurant tables.

In what turned out to be a savvy marketing strategy, Mr. Eisenstadt sold Sweet'n Low initially to restaurants (Cookies in Brooklyn was his first client) and as the number of restaurant clients increased, their customers began asking for the product in stores and the line expanded, initially with a big order from the A & P. This time, his timing was perfect. The man who had made spooning sugar obsolete and created millions of sugar-pack shakers rode the crest of the health craze of the 1960s.

In time, an even lower-calorie sugar substitute, aspartame, marketed in blue packets under the brand name Equal, would challenge Sweet'n Low. Even so, the company, which also makes a butter substitute, Butter Buds, and a salt substitute, Nu-Salt, still derives the bulk of its revenues from Sweet'n Low.

With sales of about $100 million a year, the company, which employs four hundred people, turns out fifty million Sweet'n Low packets a day in what used to be a cafeteria.

You just can't buy a cup of coffee there anymore.

In addition to his son, who lives in Neponsit, Queens, Mr. Eisenstadt is survived by his wife, Betty; another son, Ira, of Manhattan; two daughters, Ellen Cohen of Washington, D.C., and Gladys Eisenstadt of Brooklyn, seven grandchildren, and six great-grandchildren.

April 10, 1996

Computers

WHO INVENTED THE COMPUTER ANYWAY?

By Steve Lohr

The electric light bulb, we all know, was invented by Thomas Edison. The telephone was the work of Alexander Graham Bell. And the computer...

"If you took a hundred people off the street and asked them who invented the computer, ninety-nine would have no idea, and one would say Von Neumann," observed Joel Shurkin, author of *Engines of the Mind*, a history of computing. It is true that John von Neumann, the eminent mathematician and pioneer of game theory, became involved in computing and even did some programming himself—but in the late 1940s he was a relative latecomer to the field.

The strongest claim to invention of the computer—though the matter remains a subject of some debate—rests with two researchers, John Presper Eckert and John W. Mauchly, who worked at the University of Pennsylvania during World War II. They first demonstrated their general-purpose electronic computer on February 14, 1946. It was given an ungainly name, the Electronic Numerical Integrator and Computer. But no matter, it would be known forever after by its catchy acronym, Eniac.

In February 1996, Vice President Al Gore joined scientists, politicians, and university officials in Philadelphia to celebrate the fiftieth anniversary of the Eniac, hailing its development as the birth of the information age.

Back in the 1940s, no one could have foreseen the transforming nature of the technology. The Eniac pioneers were awarded a military contract in 1943 to accomplish a specific task—quickly calculate firing trajectories for artillery shells. To the army, the Eniac was simply a promising tool.

The machine itself was a thirty-ton black behemoth housing eighteen thousand vacuum tubes and miles of wire—working at a hundred times the speed of the calculating machines of its time, but merely an amusing artifact by modern standards. A desktop personal computer today has a thousand times the Eniac's processing power, and several million times the capacity to store data. Yet the story of the Eniac, and its aftermath, shares much with today's computer technology, its development and commercialization. The Eniac was a case of sharing—or "open," in modern jargon—technology standards. The machine employed a primitive type of parallel processing, an approach now used in advanced supercomputers.

The Eniac team succeeded as much because of organization and discipline as technological prowess. They actually made a working machine, unlike some who later claimed to have invented the computer. And establishing a tradition in the industry, they shipped the product late.

Herman H. Goldstine is the highest-ranking member of the Eniac team still alive. (Mr. Eckert died in 1995, and Mr. Mauchly died in 1980.) As a young lieutenant, Mr. Goldstine was sent to Philadelphia as the officer in charge of the Eniac project, making sure the army got its money's worth. Mr. Goldstine understood both the technology and the escalating set of requests he could expect from his army overseers. That led to a crucial decision to make sure the Eniac could tackle all manner of calculating chores, which helped ensure its place in computer history. "I certainly wasn't going to build a special-purpose machine," Mr. Goldstine recalled, "because I knew the army's demands would be greater than single purpose. And Mauchly totally agreed."

The Eniac was a versatile general-purpose machine, and that was central to its claim to being the first modern computer. Its rivals were also electronic machines that operated according to the on-off signals of electrical impulses—the ones and zeros of the digital language. The pretender with the greatest claim as the first computer—the Colossus, developed by the British mathematician Alan Turing—was designed for the single purpose of cracking Germany's coded military messages. John V. Atanasoff, a professor at Iowa State University, did early work with another computer using vacuum tubes, but it could solve only one kind of mathematical equations. In Germany, Konrad Zuse, an engineer, was also building computers, but all his machines were bombed in 1944.

In a sense, the accomplishment of Mr. Eckert and Mr. Mauchly was much like that of Wilbur and Orville Wright. In the early days of computing, as with airplanes, many people were making contributions to the field. But the Eniac team got the real thing up and running first. "The stored-program computer would have been developed without the Eniac," said Gwen Bell, director of collections for the Computer Museum in Boston. "But the Eniac was the catalyst for a lot of things. It certainly has a legitimate claim for being the starting point for the computer age."

The design of the Eniac, and its immediate successor the Edvac (Electronic Discrete Variable Automatic Computer), which added stored memory, became widespread after a Philadelphia conference in the summer of 1946. "It was an example of sharing the technology standards," Ms. Bell said. "They were pioneers of open systems."

Mr. Goldstine, now eighty-two, recalls those pioneering days vividly. Mr. Mauchly, a physicist, had thought about computers for years, and he conceived the idea for the Eniac. Mr. Eckert, the younger of the pair, an engineer, was the one who then took over and made the machine. "Early on, it became Eckert's project," Mr. Goldstine said. "This is not to run down Mauchly, but he was not the kind of person to get the machine finished and built. And getting the machine built was what the Eniac project was about."

Mr. Eckert and Mr. Mauchly declined an offer from Thomas J. Watson, Sr., to join IBM. Instead, they founded their own company, sold it to Sperry Rand, and developed the Univac computer. For years, the Univac technology was considered superior to any of IBM's offerings. But IBM won the battle in the marketplace. Neither Mr. Eckert nor Mr. Mauchly got rich from their pioneering work.

For his part, Mr. Goldstine did join IBM, helped set up its famed Watson laboratory, and became an IBM Fellow, a title that bestows recipients wide freedom in research and funding. Asked if he ever imagined what might come in the Eniac's wake, Mr. Goldstine replied: "Oh no, it's just amazing. But I'm also amazed that I made it to eighty-two. I never thought I'd live that long."

A Brief History of the Computer

1642 • Blaise Pascal invented an adding machine. It was the first example of a true adding machine where tens were carried to the next column.

1822 • Charles Babbage completed a model of the "difference engine," which linked adding and subtracting mechanisms to calculate the values of more complex mathematical equations.

1936 • Alan Turing, a British mathematician, published *On Computable Numbers,* a description of a machine that could, in principle, solve any mathematical problem.

1939 • At Iowa State University, John V. Atanasoff began work on an electronic computer that used vacuum tubes like the Eniac computer. But the Atanasoff computer was designed to solve only one type of algebraic problem.

1941 • Within a few days of America's entry into World War II, Konrad Zuse demonstrated a working, programmable calculator to German military authorities.

1942 • At the University of Pennsylvania, John Presper Eckert and John W. Mauchly proposed an electronic version of a differential analyzer for the army that would be digital instead of analog. The proposal led to the creation of Eniac.

1945 • The Eniac was completed and tested at the University of Pennsylvania's Moore School of Electrical Engineering.

1946 • On February 14, the Eniac was demonstrated to the public. In the summer, a series of lectures at a conference in Philadelphia led to widespread adoption of stored program.

February 19, 1996

J. Presper Eckert, Jr.

By Walter R. Baranger

J. Presper Eckert, Jr., co-inventor of the mammoth Eniac computer in 1945, believed by many computer experts and historians to be the first electronic digital computer, died in Bryn Mawr, Pennsylvania. He was seventy-six and lived in Gladwyn, Pennsylvania. The cause was complications from leukemia, a family friend, Thomas Miller, said.

Working under an army contract in World War II to automate artillery calculations, Mr. Eckert and Dr. John W. Mauchly, who died in 1980, designed a computer with more than eighteen thousand vacuum tubes that received instructions through hundreds of cables resembling an old-time telephone switchboard. The thirty-ton Electronic Numerical Integrator and Computer, or Eniac, was assembled in late 1945 and could complete in thirty seconds a trajectory calculation that took a clerk twenty hours. Stacks of punched cards provided the data, which at times included work for the Manhattan Project.

Mr. Eckert and Dr. Mauchly founded a company that became a predecessor of the Unisys Corporation, and Mr. Eckert obtained eighty-seven patents.

Controversy dogged the inventors. In a case in 1973 a federal court canceled a crucial patent. The court ruled that the root of the Eniac design was the pioneering work of Dr. John V. Atanasoff, who had invented a computing device called ABC in the 1930s.

Critics said that Dr. Atanasoff had never used his computer for solving practical problems and that it could solve only a class of problems called simultaneous linear equations. In a letter to a group of students in 1990, Mr. Eckert called Dr. Atanasoff's work at Iowa State University a joke. "He never really got anything to work," Mr. Eckert wrote. "He had no programming system. Mauchly and I achieved a complete workable computer system. Others had not."

In any case, only Eniac could confirm design calculations for the atomic bomb.

Although Eniac resembled a scene from a 1950s science-fiction movie, its flashing pink lights, clicking switches, and miles of cables hid a design remarkably similar—in concept, at least—to modern personal computers. Computers today execute instructions more than a thousand times faster than Eniac, and their sophisticated software and desktop designs make them many times more efficient and easy to use. But the basic process of breaking a number into a series of ones and zeros and sending the resulting stream of data through a series of switches called logical "and" and "or" elements, is shared with Eniac's design.

Mr. Eckert is also credited with having solved the thorny problem of reliability by running the delicate vacuum tubes, which failed often, at low voltage and avoiding brittle solder connections by relying on hundreds of old-fashioned plugs. By rearranging the plugs and their cables, the computer could be reprogrammed to solve a wide variety of problems.

John Presper Eckert, Jr., was born in Philadelphia. He earned a bachelor's degree at the Moore School of Electrical Engineering at the University of Pennsylvania and joined the faculty shortly after graduation. In 1943 he earned his master's degree and began collaborating with Dr. Mauchly on solving the problem of compiling the ballistics tables that artillery officers use to aim their guns.

For centuries artillery officers labored over those calculations, and a small error could be disastrous. Many variables, including wind, humidity, target elevation, distance, and shell weight, made the calculations extremely complicated and caused the army to issue volumes of hand-compiled tables. Mechanical calculators helped. But the army spent much of World War II looking for a way to avoid recalculating thousands of tables whenever even small changes were made to the artillery.

In addition, the Manhattan Project severely strained even the most accurate mechanical calculators, which were Rube Goldberg devices that used motors, generators, photoelectric cells, and vacuum tubes.

Eniac was the answer to both problems, and it was not unplugged until 1955.

In 1946, Mr. Eckert and Dr. Mauchly founded the Electronic Control Company and were co-developers of the Binac and Univac computers. Their successor business, the Eckert-Mauchly Computer Corporation, was sold to the Rand Corporation, which merged with the Sperry Corporation and, after a series of changes, became Unisys.

Mr. Eckert received an honorary doctorate from the University of Pennsylvania in 1964. In 1968, President Lyndon B. Johnson awarded him a medal for his work as co-inventor of the computer. Mr. Eckert retired from Unisys in 1989, but continued to be a consultant.

Surviving are his wife, Judith, of Gladwyn, Pennsylvania; a daughter, Laura E. Phinney, and three sons, John P. Eckert III, Gregory A. Eckert, and Chris C. Eckert.

June 7, 1995

JOHN W. MAUCHLY

By Jill Smolowe

Dr. John W. Mauchly, co-inventor of the world's first electronic computer, died while undergoing heart surgery at the Abington Hospital near his home in Ambler, Pennsylvania. He was seventy-two.

Dr. Mauchly and his co-inventor, J. Presper Eckert, Jr., made front-page news February 14, 1946, when the War Department announced their invention of a machine that applied electronic speed for the first time to mathematical tasks. Dubbed the Eniac (Electronic Numerical Integrator and Computer), the machine covered the entire fifteen thousand square feet of the basement of the Moore School of Electronic Engineering at the University of Pennsylvania in Philadelphia.

In later years, the team of inventors would perfect the computer, scaling it down in size and up in its number of functions.

Dr. Mauchly was born in Cincinnati. He received a bachelor's degree and Ph.D. in physics by the age of twenty-four from Johns Hopkins University. In 1941, he joined the staff of the Moore School.

The next year he wrote a proposal for an electronic computer for which the United States Army later contracted. The Eniac was completed in 1946, and in 1947 Dr. Mauchly and Mr. Eckert established their own company in Philadelphia.

In 1949, they made public their Binac computer, which was one tenth the size of the Eniac but had an electrical memory twenty-five times that of its parent. They also directed the development of the Univac I, which was first used by the Bureau of the Census in 1951 to handle the alphabet and simple written material as well as offer a good game of chess.

The inventors' company in 1950 was bought by Remington Rand, which merged with the Sperry Corporation. Dr. Mauchly remained with the company for ten years as director of Univac applications research.

In 1959, he formed Mauchly Associates, which in 1962 introduced a "critical path" computer that was designed to permit the scheduling of complicated projects. That year, at a meeting of industrial engineers, he announced that he was working on a pocket-size computer to replace another of his inventions, the suitcase-size one.

After founding Dynatrend, a computer-consulting company, in 1967, Dr. Mauchly returned in 1973 to the Sperry Corporation, where he remained as a consultant.

At the annual conference of the Association for Computer Machinery in Chicago in 1971, the twenty-fifth anniversary of the invention of the Eniac was commemorated. *The New York Times* said in an editorial that it was "gross injustice" that the names of the co-inventors were "not likely ever to become household words on a par with the Wright Brothers or Thomas A. Edison, let alone the Beatles."

While his name has not become a household word, Dr. Mauchly has received many science honors, including the Scott Award in 1961, the Franklin Medal in 1949, and the Howard N. Potts Medal in 1950. Both the University of Pennsylvania and Ursinus College awarded Dr.

Mauchly honorary doctorates, and he was the recipient of the Pennsylvania Award for Excellence in 1948.

Dr. Mauchly is survived by his wife, the former Kathleen McNulty, who was a programmer at the University of Pennsylvania; two sons, five daughters, seventeen grandchildren, and two great-grandchildren.

January 9, 1980

John V. Atanasoff

By Walter R. Baranger

John Vincent Atanasoff, a physicist whose pioneering computer research in the 1930s was overshadowed by the successes of wartime computers, died in Frederick, Maryland, where he lived. He was ninety-one. The cause was a stroke, said Steve Jones, a spokesman for Iowa State University.

Working at Iowa State in the late 1930s and early 1940s, Dr. Atanasoff and a graduate student, Clifford Berry, invented a digital computing device called the Atanasoff-Berry Computer, or ABC, that could solve a certain type of algebraic problem. In the 1970s, a federal court ruled that the device was a predecessor of the successful Eniac computer, voiding a crucial patent filed by Eniac's inventors and casting doubt on previous accounts of the early days of computing.

There is no doubt, however, that Dr. Atanasoff's device was unlike the mechanical calculators of the era. It had a distinctive look, with two knobby rotating drums that contained capacitors. Electrical charges held by the capacitors served as ABC's memory, and data was entered using punch cards. To print out the results, an electric spark was passed through other cards; the arrangement of burned spots represented answers, which could be fed into the computer again for further analysis.

Despite its strange appearance, ABC used the latest 1930s technology, including vacuum tube switches that processed binary numbers, and it cost just a thousand dollars. But ABC suffered from serious shortcomings: It could not be reprogrammed and it was unreliable when dealing with large problems. Critics later pointed to ABC's flaws when arguing that it was actually an electronic calculator, not a computer. Still, many computer historians recognize ABC as the first electronic digital computer of any kind.

The history of digital electronic computing is complicated because several major projects—including Eniac, several Harvard University machines and a British computer called Colossus—were built in various levels of secrecy during the war years. The two scientists who received earliest credit for inventing electronic digital computers were Dr. John W. Mauchly, who died in 1980, and J. Presper Eckert, Jr., who died in 1995. They developed Eniac to compute artillery trajectories and were later honored by President Lyndon B. Johnson as co-inventors of the modern computer.

Fame eluded Dr. Atanasoff until Honeywell, a computer maker, successfully sued to cancel Eniac's patent. In 1990, President George Bush presented the National Medal of Technology to Dr. Atanasoff for his early work in computers.

John Vincent Atanasoff was born in 1903 in Hamilton, New York, and received a bachelor's degree in electrical engineering from the University of Florida in 1925. In 1926, he received a master's degree in mathematics from Iowa State, where he was teaching. He earned a doctorate in physics from the University of Wisconsin in 1930.

He left Iowa State in 1941 and joined the staff of the Naval Ordnance Laboratory in Washington, and in 1946 he participated in atomic bomb tests at Bikini Atoll in the Pacific. In 1952, he established the Ordnance Engineering Company, which he later sold to the Aerojet Engineering Corporation. In 1961 he retired from Aerojet Engineering but continued to work on computers. He developed a phonetic alphabet for computers and in 1981 was awarded the Computer Pioneer Medal from the Institute of Electrical and Electronic Engineers.

Dr. Atanasoff fought hard to receive the credit he believed he deserved. "I haven't been given my due, but I might be partially to blame," Dr. Atanasoff, who was then eighty, said in an interview with William J.

Broad of *The New York Times* in March 1983. "To get ahead in the world you have to make a lot of noise, and maybe I didn't make enough."

Dr. Atanasoff's rivals. Dr. Mauchly and Mr. Eckert, like any good inventors, had applied for a patent. It was granted in 1964 after much delay. By that time the rights had been purchased by Sperry Rand, which hoped to reap huge profits from royalties over the seventeen-year life of the patent. But as Mr. Broad related it, Honeywell, another company that made computers, decided to search for a way to avoid payment. They attacked the validity of the patent in court. Honeywell filed a lawsuit in 1971 claiming that Mr. Eckert and Dr. Mauchly had "pirated" their ideas from a visionary who had built a vacuum-tube computer at Iowa State in the 1930s. That unsung inventor was Dr. Atanasoff.

Dr. Atanasoff showed his invention to anyone who displayed interest. Indeed, during the 1940s Dr. Mauchly traveled to Iowa to see Dr. Atanasoff's computer and the two men subsequently exchanged letters. "Is there any objection," Dr. Mauchly asked in one piece of correspondence, "to my building some sort of computer which incorporates some of the features of your machine?"

That letter, along with other items, helped sway the judge. In 1973 the court found that "Eckert and Mauchly did not themselves first invent the automatic electronic digital computer, but instead derived the subject matter from one Dr. John Vincent Atanasoff." The patent, which would have expired in 1983 after generating billions of dollars in revenue, was ruled invalid.

The court may have been convinced, but many computer scholars continue to insist that the true fathers of the computer are Mr. Eckert and Dr. Mauchly. "Just because you have a pile of tubes and that kind of stuff doesn't mean you have a working computer," said Dr. Nancy Stern, a historian and computer expert at Hofstra University. Dr. Stern, who wrote a book on the controversy, *From Eniac to Univac*, told Mr. Broad that the court ignored critical facts.

Dr. Atanasoff never really used the machine in a practical way, she said. It was a prototype and merely solved demonstration problems. Moreover, it was specifically aimed to solve only one group of problems—simultaneous linear equations—whereas the Eniac could be programmed to solve myriad problems, as it did successfully for nearly nine years.

Other defenders of the originality of the Eniac maintain that the court was wrong in saying Dr. Atanasoff influenced the work because Dr. Mauchly was hard at work on vacuum-tube devices long before he visited Dr. Atanasoff in Iowa.

Dr. Atanasoff acknowledged some of the limits of his invention. "It's true that my machine wasn't used much, but that's not the point," he told Mr. Broad. "I introduced seven or eight fundamental things for which other people have taken credit." Those fundamentals, he contended are the foundation for every computer in the world today.

He scoffed at the efforts to diminish his invention because it was small and limited. Of course it was, he said, after all, he didn't have the resources to build a big machine. He put his device together for less than a thousand dollars, whereas the military built the Eniac for half a million.

Stepping back from the rounds of charge and countercharge in the debate, Mr. Broad said some historians note that credit for an invention can be more a matter of timing than of accomplishment. The acknowledged birth of the computer had to wait until the time was ripe. When Dr. Atanasoff started his work, the country was mired in the Depression and vacuum-tube technology was primitive. His invention was a curiosity that was quickly shelved. In contrast, the Eniac was financed in the 1940s as a crash project for the military. "It was the influence of the war that matured the field of electronics," said Dr. Herman H. Goldstine, the military officer who oversaw the construction of the Eniac. "The tremendous advances in radar and fire control work changed electronics from a hobby into a great industry. That was the watershed. Atanasoff had some ideas, but not the technology."

Dr. Atanasoff's first marriage, to Lura Meeks, ended in divorce. He is survived by his second wife, Alice Crosby Atanasoff; two daughters, Elsie A. Whistler of Rockville, Maryland, and Joanne A. Gathers of Mission Viejo, California; a son, John V. III, of Boulder, Colorado, and ten grandchildren.

June 17, 1995

The Little King of Torts

HARRY LIPSIG

By Robert McG. Thomas, Jr.

Harry Lipsig, the New York lawyer who won millions of dollars in damage awards for clients who had been widowed, orphaned, crippled, maimed, or merely inconvenienced through someone else's negligence, died at his home in Manhattan. He was ninety-three.

In a career that spanned six decades, Mr. Lipsig became famous for his heart-wrenching courtroom depictions of the plight of accident victims and the huge jury awards his eloquence often elicited. The total amount of the awards he won is not known, partly because many of them were sealed out-of-court settlements agreed to by rival lawyers eager to avoid the open-ended uncertainty of a Lipsig-coaxed jury verdict. As they knew, once Mr. Lipsig got wound up and started vividly describing the years, even decades, of hour-by-hour agony and day-by-day suffering endured by his clients, there was no telling how unhinged a jury might become.

In one celebrated case, Mr. Lipsig outdid himself. Seeking a staggering $4 million for a man whose legs had been crushed by a runaway car with a defective accelerator, he was so eloquent in describing the grim future his client faced that the jury awarded the victim $8 million. (The startled judge cut the award in half, on the ground that state law prohibited juries from awarding a plaintiff more than he had sought.)

Mr. Lipsig, who could bring tears to his own eyes describing the work he did on behalf of the little people of the world, tended to see his courtroom battles as David and Goliath struggles, and he took pains to make sure juries saw them that way, too. On one side of the courtroom in the typical Lipsig case, the jury would see a phalanx of high-powered lawyers jumbled several deep behind the defendant's table. They were representing one or more large insurance companies. On the other side, jurors would see Mr. Lipsig, all five feet three inches of him, sitting alone.

While his forte was his ability to wrest huge jury awards or settlements for his client victims, he was equally adept at establishing that the inevitably wealthy defendant was responsible for the injury. He won a case for the estate of a man killed by a shark in Acapulco by convincing the jury that the shark was attracted by garbage thrown into the ocean by workers at the man's hotel. ("Although we did not have the testimony of the particular shark," he recalled, "that is what brought him here.")

And when a child darted out into the street between parked cars and ran into the rear wheels of a passing car, Mr. Lipsig successfully argued that the motorist really should have been more careful.

Mr. Lipsig, who was born in the Ukraine and brought to New York when he was six, laid the groundwork for his success as soon as he graduated from Brooklyn Law School in 1926. As he once recalled, "I went to every lawyer I knew and asked him for all the cases he couldn't win. I think I won my first twenty."

Mr. Lipsig, who was never accused of immodesty, made sure that the word of his triumphs got around. In time the resulting headlines made him so famous as the "King of Torts" that he had more business than he could handle.

He was associated with several law firms over the years and had been involved recently in litigation with two sets of previous law partners.

In 1989 he and his wife, Miriam, adopted his former secretary, Mary Lou Castillo, who later married Mark Manus, a partner in his law firm, Harry Lipsig & Partners.

Since 1982, Mr. Lipsig had done most of his work outside of court, but he made a special appearance in 1988 on behalf of the estate of a man who had been struck and killed by a car driven by a drunken New York City police officer. While recognizing that the city could hardly avoid responsibility in the wrongful-death suit, lawyers representing the city confidently figured that they would be able to limit the damage award, which in such cases is based on loss of earnings, by arguing that the victim, a seventy-one-year-old psychiatrist, was at the end of his earning curve.

Their confidence vanished when Mr. Lipsig got up to make his opening argument and cited himself as an exhibit, pointing out that he was an eighty-seven-year-old practicing lawyer and suggesting that the psychiatrist, too, could have looked forward to many more years of practice. Whether the jury would have bought that argument will never be known. Shortly after Mr. Lipsig finished his opening remarks, the city's lawyers, mindful of Mr. Lipsig's mesmerizing reputation, decided it would be best to settle.

In addition to his daughter and his wife, Mr. Lipsig is survived by two grandchildren.

August 13, 1995

TRAGEDY'S CLEARINGHOUSE

JOHN TIERNEY added:

To appreciate Harry Lipsig's skills, suppose for one horrible moment that he is cross-examining you. You're on the witness stand, being sued for hitting a child with your car. You were driving below the speed limit when the child dashed from between two parked cars. You know it wasn't your fault. But try answering this question from Mr. Lipsig: "As you were driving, were you aware that little children frequently played on that street?"

Say no, and Mr. Lipsig will sadly tell the jury that you should have known better. Say yes, and he'll sadly explain that you should have used that knowledge and driven more carefully. Either way, Mr. Lipsig would be moving jurors to tears, and your lawyer would be quickly calculating how much to settle for. Mr. Lipsig used to say, "Anyone who loses a pedestrian-knockdown case involving an infant is guilty of legal malpractice."

He was appalled by tort-reform proposals to limit damages: "It makes my blood boil. Men who walk the world in full health talk in selfishness about large verdicts while tightening the stitches on their pocketbooks."

Much of his work was routine—sidewalk falls were a lucrative perennial—but he also loved to push back the frontiers of negligence. By collecting a settlement on behalf of a murdered eyewitness, he established the precedent that police departments must protect witnesses in criminal trials. He is the reason concessionaires at arenas no longer sell drinks in bottles. Representing a man injured by a hurled bottle, Mr. Lipsig intrigued the jury by keeping a sealed bag at the defense table throughout the trial. He finally opened it to pull out his closing argument: a paper cup.

A trailblazer outside the courtroom as well, he became famous in the era before lawyers advertised. He knew how to get quoted by saying things like "My door is tragedy's clearinghouse."

Mr. Lipsig pioneered direct-mail marketing by compiling index cards containing the names and addresses of just about anyone he ever met. The cards were pulled out annually for a mass mailing of "season's greetings." His partners continued the tradition after he died by sending cards to tens of thousands of Mr. Lipsig's closest friends. Harry Lipsig's data base lives on.

December 31, 1995
THE NEW YORK TIMES MAGAZINE

ADVOCATE FOR THE AFFLICTED

"I try to give jurors a feeling of royalty," HARRY LIPSIG once told ALAN RICHMAN, "so they can feel royal in their disposition of the amounts in the case. It boils down to telling them they have the ancient power of the kings of yore."

Here is Mr. Richman's account of a visit to Mr. Lipsig.

Harry Lipsig, who has done more for the lame and the afflicted than the Statue of Liberty has done for the tired and the poor, is asked this question: Are juries not being extravagant when they award millions of dollars to his clients?

Hearing this, he stands to his full height, not in itself an awesome act when a man is five foot three. But height is not to be confused with stature, and Harry Lipsig—perhaps the preeminent negligence lawyer in the country—rises far above his field.

As he straightens in moral outrage, he seems above even the law. Mr. Lipsig is speaking, as always, for the plaintiff. "Jurors," he begins in a voice as soft as a subpoena slipped under a door, "have all too slowly reached the stage of sophistication where they are thinking in proper amounts that can compensate people."

Intensity starts to build, the glycerin disappears from his throat. "You people who have not been paralyzed," he says, speaking of the majority who hoard their wholeness, "don't understand the terrible cost of medical, institutional, servant, and nursing care that a person needs. They lie there in misery, at the mercy of a nurse or attendant."

Here he thrusts himself away from the desk in his office as he might push away from the railing of a jury box. Stiffly, he walks away, a good and righteous man wounded by the narrowness, the inhumanity, of people. The impulse is to call him back, to apologize, but the gesture is unnecessary. The lawyer wheels around, back at the listener's throat, reciting a roll call of afflictions and distress. "Ulcers of the body ... cannot turn over ... messiness of excrement ..." He is whispering again, his face inches from yours but turned away, sparing you the contempt in his eyes. Again the voice is soft and you are carried with him, on a roller coaster you never intended to board.

"I never get more vicious than when I talk to people who criticize large verdicts when they have never spent a day with a cripple who is imprisoned for life in his living, but dead, body." He is almost shouting now. "How often we rise with indignation for a person imprisoned falsely for one year, two years," he says. "We give him the sky, yet he is able to walk. We are talking now about a man who is in the worst prison in the world. The prison of the quadraplegic"—he begins rocking with intensity, swaying on the balls of his feet, his finger sharply tapping the polished desk with each word—"who is looking out upon the world with live eyes while tied to a bed or a chair by the worst bonds in the world, motionlessness."

He takes one backward step, his head nodding hypnotically, his eyes demanding acquiescence. Suddenly motionless, he continues. "Do you know what I would pay to such a person?" he says. "Not $2 million, but $20 million. Do not talk to me of large verdicts. It makes my blood boil. Men who walk the world in full health talk in selfishness about large verdicts while tightening the stitches on their pocketbooks. A lawyer once said of a man who lost both his hands, 'He ate like a dog.' I never forgot that. They never get enough."

Breathing heavily, his passion expended, he returns to his seat. It has truly been a vintage performance, for Mr. Lipsig is seventy-seven years old.

For almost all of those years he has practiced in the negligence field, a branch of civil law in which juries award damages both as compensation to those who have been harmed and to deter those who might do harm.

For the successful lawyer—and Mr. Lipsig has endured only three jury verdicts in the last twenty years in which his client was awarded nothing—it can be lucrative. The payoff in a negligence case is not a restraining order, declaration, recision, or retraction. It is cash, one third going to the attorney. It may be safely assumed that Mr. Lipsig has made more money practicing the law than all but a few men have made breaking it.

He is not as flamboyant as F. Lee Bailey, as controversial as Roy M. Cohn, as powerful as Clark Clifford, as scholarly as Arthur J. Goldberg, as imposing as Edward Bennett Williams. Yet none of these men has done so much for the nameless and the powerless, the fireman fallen through a rotted roof, the child struck by a thoughtless driver.

And while Mr. Lipsig's triumphs appear less grand, they are often more pervasive. His dogged pursuit of damages for a client who suffered for years with a surgical clamp sewn inside her led to a new statute of limitations in malpractice cases. Under the present law, the period in which a person may sue begins with the time malpractice is discovered, not the time it occurred.

He took on the New York City Police Department in the early

1960s representing Max Schuster in a negligence suit against the city. Mr. Schuster's son Arnold was murdered after helping the police capture Willie Sutton, the bank robber.

He represented a seaman bitten by a mosquito off the coast of Africa, the issue being that the company knew about and ignored the threat of malaria.

He sued for the estate of a man who was looking out his window and dropped dead from fright as an automobile rolled up on his lawn. He went to trial for a man with "Born to Die" tattooed on his arm who was killed after wandering into a dark railroad tunnel.

He won all the cases, either by settlement or by jury verdict.

"Trial preparation," he says, "has nothing to do with what you learn at law school. Just because you've read all the plays doesn't mean you can direct a play. Staging a trial is like staging an important drama. It's up to you to be in control."

In the office his attire is conventionally dapper, gray suit with gold watch chain, tie tucked into beltless slacks, lavender handkerchief with burgundy border. In court the handkerchief becomes his battle flag, pure white until the enemy is in chaos. Then Mr. Lipsig shows his true colors.

"The trial of a case is pure psychology," he says. "When it has gotten to the point where I feel the jury is in the palm of my hand, then I take liberties with my clothes." At the start of a trial he speaks so softly the jury must strain to understand him. By the conclusion, he expects them to be quietly cheering as he comes from behind.

There are virtually only two kinds of defense lawyers in Manhattan—those who have lost to Mr. Lipsig and those who have not faced him. "The only thing that ever worried me was my lawsuit, not my adversary," Mr. Lipsig says. "I'm not impressed with the opposition." Even though he has battered three generations of Manhattan lawyers, none will say worse of him than that he preens a bit much.

"Fifteen or twenty years ago, when I was a young lawyer, I watched him try a case in the Supreme Court in Bronx County," recalls Thomas Costello of Diamond Rutman & Costello. "I remember the lawyer for the defense in his summation saying, 'I apologize if I've said anything to offend you.' In his summation, Harry Lipsig said, 'Well might the attorney for the defendant apologize.' It was a very difficult case and I'm certain that spontaneous remark, which had nothing to do with the case, got the verdict for him."

"What he can do like few others is create that dramatic moment," says Norman Landau, a lawyer who worked for Mr. Lipsig in the late 1950s. "Once or twice a jury is sucked up into a trial. If a lawyer doesn't come out of that moment a winner, he is in trouble. Time after time, Harry Lipsig is in control at those moments."

Mr. Lipsig's office is laden with strange artifacts, many of them hundreds of years old and none of them, if you believe Mr. Lipsig, older than he. His desk, about twenty-five square feet, is lighted by an antique Spanish chandelier. His washroom door is decorated with the ivory tusk of a narwhale.

Earlier this year, a small but threatening electrical fire broke out on the same floor as his office. Tenants of the Church Street building cried out for a general evacuation. Smoke hovered over his desk. Mr. Lipsig sat stubbornly in his deep leather chair, refusing to abandon his practice.

This, you should know, is a man who courted his wife of fifty-four years by reciting real-property and inheritance-tax case histories. Mary Lou Castillo, his executive secretary, finally prevailed, dragging him out and standing guard at the ground-floor elevator to prevent him from sneaking back upstairs.

"My practice," he says, "is my breath and my life."

In 1979 he took a case to court seeking a total of $6.5 million from the chain that owns the Plaza Hotel, the people who operate Trader Vic's restaurant, and the company that sells them spareribs. Mr. Lipsig's suit contended that his clients, who included Yul Brynner and Joan Diener, contracted trichinosis at the restaurant in 1974. When he opened to the jury, there was one woman in it who had been so charmed during the selection process that she shyly waved to him while entering the box.

In his opening remarks, he referred with great irony to the specialty of the house, which he continually called "tasty spareribs." He related dramatically how Mr. Brynner and Miss Diener, then performing in a show on Broadway, "had had to steel themselves from this nightmare into which they were plunged." But he did not hurry to get to those points.

First, he sat unblinking through the friendly wave. Then he rose slowly to his feet, pulling from his breast pocket a pure white handkerchief, and prepared to discuss his clients' parasitic affliction. Finally, he spoke. Turning away with loathing on his face, he hissed, "Worms."

April 25, 1979

PICKING A JURY

Here is Harry Lipsig's guide to jury selection:

LIPSIG ON WOMEN: "Where my client is a good-looking woman, get rid of women jurors . . . if she's dashing, women jurors would burn her at the stake . . . young ladies with small mouths are a nightmare. The pursed mouth is a tight pursestring."

LIPSIG ON MEN: "A jovial man is a good juror. A skinny man has to be analyzed . . . the neatly and carefully dressed man is a man who equally neatly and carefully appraises money."

LIPSIG ON OCCUPATIONS

POSTAL WORKERS: "Prefer them for an accident case, because they are very generous-hearted despite being so poorly paid . . . also prefer them in defense of a criminal case, because they have the feeling postal inspectors are looking over their shoulder and thus resent prosecuting authority."

BANK CLERKS: "Accustomed to proving at the end of each day to the penny and are generally conservative."

SALESMEN: "Love them, because of their worldly experience and general need to be hail fellows well met."

ADVERTISING AND PUBLIC-RELATIONS PEOPLE: "Good, unless the public relations is creating the fraudulent, poisonous ads of the insurance companies that talk about premiums and try to bury justice."

BUSINESSMEN: "Worried about the costs of insurance, yet have a decent sense of fairness."

ENTERTAINERS AND ARTISTS: "A dream... money is something they find easy to part with."

JOURNALISTS: "Taboo... too cynical and consider themselves worldly wise."

April 25, 1979

Gentle Man in the Dhoti

RAMCHANDRA V. PATWARDHAN

By Robert McG. Thomas, Jr.

Ramchandra V. Patwardhan, who long provided the cultural and religious thread that knitted New York's Indian community together as the city's only Hindu priest, died at St. Vincent's Hospital in Greenwich Village. He was seventy-nine. His wife, Tara, said the cause was congestive heart failure.

For the better part of three decades, Mr. Patwardhan was an indispensible figure in New York's Hindu community, the man in the dhoti and turban who by virtue of his priestly birth and his religious training could do what no other Hindu in New York could do, officiate at the elaborate wedding and other ceremonies that have been the hallmark of Hinduism for twenty-five hundred years.

It may seem surprising now, but for all New York City's reputation as an international melting pot, when Mr. Patwardhan arrived in the city from India in 1947 to study international law at New York University, the entire Indian presence in the city largely consisted of a handful of journalists, diplomats, and students on temporary visas. The race-based immigration laws of the time simply precluded significant migration from the Asian subcontinent. Mr. Patwardhan, himself, a native of Pandharpur who had studied law and practiced with his father, had fully expected to return to India, but when the country won independence from Britain in 1947, he accepted a job at the Indian Consulate, summoned his wife, who also worked at the consulate, and took an apartment on Perry Street that became their home for almost fifty years.

Mr. Patwardhan, who took daily five-mile walks exploring and savoring his adopted city, quickly realized there were drawbacks to being a member of a tiny minority in an alien culture, among them the inability to practice his religion in a city where the few Hindu residents included no priests. As a Brahmin, a member of the priestly caste, and one who had also mastered Sanskrit and Hinduism's Vedic texts, Mr. Patwardhan needed no other qualifications to become a priest, so he decided to fill the void.

The first wedding ceremony he performed, in 1956, was considered such a novelty that it was broadcast live on television. Indeed, a Hindu priest was such a rarity in the United States that Mr. Patwardhan was soon traveling all over the country to perform weddings, eventually for the children of those he had married earlier.

For a while there were so few Hindus in New York that he per-formed only the occasional wedding, but after the immigration laws were liberalized in the 1960s, touching off a wave of migration from India, Mr. Patwardhan was in such demand that he quit his job in 1968. By 1972 he had performed more than five hundred ceremonies.

In time, the wave of immigration brought other Hindu priests to the city, but Mr. Patwardhan remained a favorite, partly because the man known as Nana, Panditji, or simply Pat had become a venerated figure and partly because he had virtually patented the New York–style Hindu wedding ceremony. In India, weddings sometimes last for days, but Mr. Patwardhan, mindful of the peculiar pace of life in New York, streamlined the ceremony, distilling it to its essence, and, in an innovation that would have shocked the sometimes austere and rigid priests in India, he inter-laced the service with simple English explanations that kept the children in attendance enthralled and provided many young Hindu Americans with their only training in their ancestral religion.

Mr. Patwardhan sometimes had to provide similar instruction to their elders. After a couple had set a date, it was not uncommon for a grandmother, armed with astrological tables, to protest that the time was not auspicious. After Mr. Patwardhan would pay the good woman a visit and gently explain that the eternal truths of the Veda certainly did not depend on the coincidental alignment of the stars, the wedding would usually proceed on schedule.

Perhaps his most inspired New York innovation concerned the heart of the Hindu wedding ceremony, fire, the sacred witness to whom the priestly hymns and chants and the couples' vows are addressed. In India, the intricate arrangement of mighty logs precisely specified by the Veda can sometimes produce quite a conflagration, which is why the ceremonies are often performed outdoors or in large pavilions. Mr. Patwardhan, who conducted most of his ceremonies in small apartments and was respectful of the city's fire laws, simply created a symbolic wedding fire by arranging tiny strips of wood in a small brazier and setting them alight.

After all, like Hinduism, itself, the priest who had planted the small seed of his religion in New York, knew that fire was fire.

His wife is his only survivor.

June 23, 1996

Opera's Conscience

CHRISTOPHER KEENE

By James R. Oestreich

Christopher Keene, an energetic conductor and arts administrator and the enterprising general director of the New York City Opera, died at New York Hospital in Manhattan. He was forty-eight.

The cause was lymphoma arising from AIDS, said Susan Woelzl, a spokeswoman for the City Opera. His lymphoma was discovered early in the year, along with a tumor on a vocal cord. The tumor was removed surgically and the lymphoma treated with radiation and chemotherapy. Mr. Keene meanwhile fulfilled almost all of his conducting engagements until last month, when he was hospitalized for anemia and forced to withdraw from the City Opera production of Hindemith's *Mathis der Maler* after two performances.

In a recent conversation, he revealed that he had tested positive for HIV, the virus that causes AIDS, more than a decade ago. Yet he insisted that his illness was not related to AIDS, and he spoke avidly of his plans for the coming years. "At no time have I been symptomatic in any way," he said. "In a very real sense, survivors like myself should give hope to people, because it is absolutely possible to live very many years without any problems whatsoever."

In his six years as director of the City Opera, Mr. Keene strove to wean the company from a steady diet of classic delicacies and frothy desserts to sterner, more contemporary fare rich in nutritive challenges. The current season, just a month old at his death, was to be his most adventuresome yet. It began with *Mathis der Maler*, a famously unwieldy work, which Mr. Keene said he had dreamed of presenting all his life. The season also includes the American premieres of Toshiro Mayuzumi's

Kinkakuji (The Temple of the Golden Pavilion) and Jost Meier's *Dreyfus Affair.* Mr. Keene had planned to conduct them all.

"Keene is one of the few authentic cultural heroes New York has left, thanks to his many recent acts of courage, personal as well as artistic," the critic Peter G. Davis wrote in his review of *Mathis* in *New York* magazine.

Mr. Keene was born in 1946 in Berkeley, California, and took to music and drama early. He studied piano and cello and organized neighborhood productions of operas and plays, initiating a pattern of self-study and spontaneous performance that carried into his adulthood. Although firmly wedded to music, he majored in history at the University of California at Berkeley to avoid having to restudy what he had already learned on his own. There, too, he organized and conducted opera performances.

He worked briefly at the San Francisco Opera as a conducting assistant to Kurt Herbert Adler, who recommended him to Gian Carlo Menotti and the Spoleto Festival in Italy, where he conducted in 1968. He became music director of the festival from 1972 to 1976 and of the Spoleto Festival U.S.A., in Charleston, South Carolina, from 1977 to 1980. On a further recommendation from Mr. Menotti, Mr. Keene became music director of Eliot Feld's American Ballet Company from 1969 to 1971.

Mr. Keene returned to the Charleston Festival in June 1995 in the frailest of health to make what would be his last concert appearance. *The Charleston Post and Courier* called his performance "a magnificent tribute to the human spirit."

He made his City Opera debut in 1970, having received the company's first Julius Rudel Award the year before, and his Metropolitan Opera debut in 1971. He became music director of the Artpark Festival in Buffalo from 1974 to 1989 and of the Syracuse Symphony Orchestra from 1975 to 1984. He founded the Long Island Philharmonic in 1979 and directed it until 1990.

All the while, he continued to conduct at the City Opera, during the regimes of Julius Rudel and Beverly Sills. Ms. Sills appointed him music director of the company from 1982 to 1986 and was instrumental in his appointment to succeed her as general director in 1989.

Mr. Keene's first season as head of the company was aborted by a musicians' strike, and later seasons were troubled by financial deficits, with the shortfall amounting in 1992 to $2.9 million of a $26 million budget. The company managed to put its house back in order in time for its fiftieth-anniversary celebration in 1993. But as the celebration approached its climax, with a week of premiere performances, Mr. Keene was admitted to the Betty Ford Center in Rancho Mirage, California, to be treated for alcoholism.

"I had a real nervous breakdown, and the heavy drinking I was doing at the time was certainly a component," Mr. Keene said of that period. "It was a time we lost so many friends and colleagues, close and professional, and the company seemed to be going under. My health was in doubt, and it was a time when I couldn't go on." Mr. Keene was referring in part to the ravages of AIDS within arts institutions, with the City Opera being one of those hardest hit. Dozens of the City Opera's members and two administrators had died by then. In addition, Mr. Keene's longtime companion, Thomas Forsythe, was dying of AIDS at the time.

Although Mr. Keene's treatment at the Betty Ford Center was not entirely successful, he eventually surmounted his drinking problem with treatments at an outpatient clinic in Manhattan. The City Opera saw him through this period, renewing his contract to 1997. But over his objections, it named an executive director, Mark Weinstein, to take over some of Mr. Keene's administrative responsibilities. "The company is more important than I am," Mr. Keene told *The New York Times* in November 1993. "I owe my career to it. I would never do anything to make it suffer, and I don't want to leave it."

Mr. Keene's innovations at the City Opera extended well beyond repertory. Last year the company abandoned its summer season, which extended into the fall, in favor of a more conventional fall and spring format, a change intended to attract the more serious operagoers needed to support the more serious repertory. Even in the standard repertory, he cleaned up many directorial excesses. He also reduced the number of productions, performances, and cast changes each season and tightened up performance and rehearsal schedules to allow for better stage preparation and a greater ability to accommodate singer cancellations. "A lot of the changes that I'm proudest of are totally invisible," he said.

In his twenty-six-year association with the City Opera, Mr. Keene conducted numerous world, American, and New York premieres. He recorded Philip Glass's *Satyagraha* with the company for CBS Masterworks, now Sony. And his other recordings include John Corigliano's soundtrack score for Ken Russell's film *Altered States*, on RCA.

He also carried his efforts into the literary sphere. He wrote about opera; prepared performing translations, including that of *Kinkakuji* from the original German; and wrote librettos. Most recently, he was collaborating with the composer Charles Wuorinen on *Celia, a Slave*.

Mr. Keene recently restated his intention to stay on as general director of the City Opera until 2000. Also remaining active as a symphonic conductor with leading American orchestras, he said he hoped to devote more time to that pursuit after the year 2000, and ideally to become the music director of a major orchestra. Instead, he was destined to be forever identified with his first love, opera, and the company with which he worked for more than half his life.

Mr. Keene is survived by his wife, Sara; two sons, Anthony and Nicholas, and a stepdaughter, Gigi Teeley, all of Manhattan; his mother, Yvonne San Jule, of Berkeley, California; a brother, Philip, of Redondo, California; two sisters, Elodie, of Van Nuys, California, and Tamsen Calhoun, of Martinez, California, and his companion, Michael Brandow, of Manhattan.

October 9, 1995

OPERA AS AN ACT OF FAITH

BERNARD HOLLAND, the chief music critic of The New York Times, *added this assessment:*

Christopher Keene took a lot of the New York City Opera with him when he died. Anyone who wanted to know what was right about this company, and why a lot of what it did didn't work, had only to follow him around for a while. Mr. Keene had a way of staking his opera house on ventures that never had much chance of succeeding in the first place, but ones that had to be tried just the same. The cards dealt him when he took over the job of general director in 1989 were for the most part losing ones, but how cheerfully and gracefully he bluffed and sometimes won.

His epitaph is already written on the current performance calendar, in the titles of works like *Mathis der Maler* and *Kinkakuji*. The first is known for Hindemith's music, but how many avid operagoers had ever seen the opera itself? The second is twenty years old, and not many people know much about it at all. Indeed, the most famous thing about *Kinkakuji* is not its Japanese composer (Toshiro Mayuzumi) or its German librettist (Claus Henneberg) but their literary source, the great writer Yukio Mishima. The public did not clamor for these pieces, and I doubt that City Opera board members pounded their fists in enthusiastic insistence that they be done.

As to *Kinkakuji*, we shall have to see, but no right-minded music lover will complain about the substance of Hindemith's opera or its right to be acknowledged. And despite the less than brilliant production Mr. Keene's forces were able to muster, no one can deny that New York received a gift others in this city were unwilling or unable to give it. The stage was too small, the production somewhat cheesy. The chorus did not sing well, nor was the orchestra terribly brilliant. Plagued by illness, the cast sang valiantly. It took a lot of faith to get through this *Mathis der Maler*, but a lot of us are glad we had enough.

Frail and shorn yet filled with high humor, Mr. Keene conducted the opening night of *Mathis*. Not very well, I'm afraid. One of the cards dealt him was a pit orchestra of intractable mediocrity; and despite all his energy and musical intelligence, he never quite had the conductorial skill to make it play much better than it always had. One accepted Mr. Keene's conducting for much the same reason audiences struggle through John Crosby's Strauss performances at the Santa Fe Opera and Plácido Domingo's on-the-job training exercises in the pit at the Metropolitan Opera. All three men have given largely of themselves to the institutions in question. Let them conduct, we have thought to ourselves, and bless them.

What Mr. Keene inherited at the City Opera was a company set down in the wrong place and pulled in different directions by conflicting mandates. The New York State Theater has neither the shape nor the facilities for opera, and it is disastrously situated only a few feet from the Met, which dwarfs it in every conceivable way. The fair-minded can fight back the comparisons, but geography makes it difficult to avoid them. How happy this company would be in more modest surroundings, a mile or so away, in a theater that reflected its limited resources and its occasional flights of fancy.

One of the City Opera's traditional duties has been to provide tidy, affordable versions of the standard repertory. In the years before Mr. Keene's accession, Verdi, Puccini, and Bizet had come to look shabby indeed, but he began a systematic sprucing up: a series of new productions of old favorites that have largely been successful. The policy of casting young American singers has continued, but so unfriendly is the New York State Theater to developing voices that many singers have been advised to avoid a space so large and unforgiving.

Adventure has been the other side of this company and one that Mr. Keene leapt into enthusiastically. A lot of the new operas were bad (*Marilyn, Harvey Milk*), but at least we were given a sense of expectancy and a chance to hope. Although *Carmen* is nice, it is hard to feel much expectancy when it is on the bill. But these new operas freed us, for a moment at least, from the masterpiece syndrome, the rather addled modern expectation of genius every time out. How many operagoers in 1840 awaited eternal verities, or even competence, with every premiere? Operas came and went much as musicals do now on Broadway.

The City Opera is a company in precarious straits, and whom it can find and persuade to be the new Christopher Keene may influence its fate to a high degree. What a job awaits the newest happy warrior: finding a program so plausible that generous benefactors on the board of directors will be moved to deepen their pockets once again; continuing the refurbishment of familiar repertory; summoning the requisite imagination and guts to strike out boldly even when failure threatens.

This company may never be able to move to a new home despite its recent dreams of doing so. Lincoln Center needs its presence and its audiences, and the pressures to stay must be strong. The cost of resettling a company with such a shaky future would be dauntingly risky in any case. A lot of deep thinking will be going on during the next months. Christopher Keene has just left us, but one can already hear the cry from the southern end of Lincoln Center: "Where are you when we need you?"

October 15, 1995

The Lad Who Lunched

JERRY ZIPKIN

By Enid Nemy

Jerry Zipkin, a celebrated fixture on the international social scene for almost half a century, died at his home in Manhattan. He was eighty. The cause was lung cancer, said Harold Daitch, his lawyer.

Mr. Zipkin, an heir to a Manhattan real-estate fortune who until his death lived in a Park Avenue building that was built by his father, was often referred to as "a man about everywhere." He was a colorful presence at glamorous balls, parties, and private dinners in this country and in Europe. He also was a favorite escort of fashionable women whose husbands were too busy or too bored to accompany them to social events. It is believed that the term "walker," first used by *Women's Wear Daily*, was coined to describe him.

Mr. Zipkin traveled widely with many female friends, and lunched with one or more on most days of the week, usually at Le Cirque or Mortimer's. He was a longtime friend, escort, and confidant of Nancy Reagan and a member of the Reagans' intimate coterie during their years in the White House, when he commuted to Washington about once a week. He was with the Reagans the night Ronald Reagan was elected President, and he was on the phone almost daily with Mrs. Reagan, exchanging news and gossip.

"He was the best friend you could ever have," Mrs. Reagan said. "I can't remember when and how I met him, but it must have been about forty-five years ago. It seems that Jerry has always been part of my life." President Reagan, she said, "didn't see as much of him as I did, but he was very fond of him."

Mr. Zipkin, known for his sharp wit, was a confidant to many women, listening to their concerns and offering advice. He had no hesitation in criticizing their clothes or coifs; his comments, often barbed, whether taken seriously or ignored, were rarely resented. "You knew he meant it lovingly," said Nan Kempner, the New York social figure, a friend for more than forty years. She added that he could be a devoted friend and the nicest person in the world, "if he liked you."

Sirio Maccioni, the owner of Le Cirque, said: "He was nice to me at the very beginning when I was still at the Colony. He was very loyal." He added, "He could complain, but he also wrote the nicest letters."

Jerome Robert Zipkin was born in Manhattan, the son of Annette and David Zipkin. He graduated from the Hun School of Princeton, New Jersey, and studied art and archeology for two years at Princeton University.

Although he was known principally as a social moth, he worked for years as his father's assistant, and after his father's death he looked after the family real-estate interests, which were later sold.

His ability to respect confidences was legendary. The designer Bill Blass, a longtime friend, said it was one reason for his extraordinary popularity with women. Mr. Zipkin once said: "A woman cannot have a best woman friend. A best woman friend will do her in."

His friends admitted that he could be sharp and even rude. Once, at a luncheon, a waiter asked if he could do anything for him. "You can remove the lady on my right," he said.

His caustic remarks were often directed at waiters, clerks, and taxi drivers. One woman kept a cache of ten- and twenty-dollar bills handy when he was her escort to a restaurant. The money was to placate the staff. Sometimes, his remarks were meant as humor, but they could be misunderstood. Once, on the way to a dinner party, he argued with a taxi driver and, the story went, left the door of the cab open when he got out. The driver, infuriated, also got out, and knocked him to the ground. Mr. Zipkin said that his ribs were broken, but he didn't miss the dinner party.

Mr. Zipkin's eccentricities were usually excused with, "That's Jerry." He made his displeasure more than clear if his seat at a fashion show or a gala wasn't to his liking. He frequently plucked two flowers from centerpieces at restaurants, one for his companion and the other for his lapel.

He was known, too, for taking an extra gift when party favors were given at charity events and public-relations functions. But his own gifts to friends were frequent and often lavish.

In his last years, his immediate family consisted only of a sister, Eleanor Cervantes of Madrid, but he had several godchildren in the United States and Europe, whom he visited regularly.

In the weeks before his death, he organized items in his apartment that he wished to leave to friends. He had each gift wrapped and labeled and wrote a message to accompany it. Some gifts were sent before his death: a small Rodin sculpture of a hand to a friend whose hands he admired, a set of wineglasses to a woman who had admired them.

"Nobody ever gave him credit for being as bright as he was," Mrs. Reagan said. "His friendship wasn't just on the frivolous side. He had much more to him than that."

June 9, 1995

The "Granny" of Alabama

ONNIE LEE LOGAN

By Robert McG. Thomas, Jr.

Onnie Lee Logan, the Alabama midwife who used what she called her God-given motherwit to deliver hundreds of babies before her 1989 autobiography made her a favorite in feminist circles, died at the Mobile Infirmary in Mobile, Alabama. By her own reckoning she was about eighty-five. When she was born "somewhere about 1910," she once noted, midwives in rural Alabama weren't overly scrupulous about filing birth records for the grandchildren of slaves.

Mrs. Logan, the fourteenth of sixteen children, was born on a farm in Marengo County, outside Sweet Water, about 120 miles north of Mobile. On the surface, her life was little different from those of other black women of her era in southern Alabama. As a child she picked cotton, sewed, and ironed to make money for her family. And for all her infectious optimism and perpetual good cheer, even as a "granny," as midwives were known in the South, Mrs. Logan, the daughter and granddaughter of midwives, was hardly unique.

In 1910, about half of the births in the United States were assisted by midwives, and the percentage was far higher in the rural south. Even so, their clients were generally so poor that even Mrs. Logan, who delivered virtually every child born in the predominantly black Mobile suburb of Prichard from 1931 to 1984, had to supplement her income by working as a maid.

What ultimately set Mrs. Logan apart was not her work, but her compelling sense that hers was a story that had to be told. Or, as she put it, "I just got so much experience in here that I just want to explode."

Although she was barely literate, Mrs. Logan said she was so determined to tell it she would be prepared to "scratch it out" herself. That proved unnecessary when a family she worked for introduced her to Katherine Clark, a young Harvard graduate who came to Mobile in 1984 to teach English at the University of South Alabama and who went on to be a professor of English at the University of New Orleans.

"As soon as I met her, I knew there was a book in her," Professor Clark said, recalling that she had taped one hundred hours of Mrs. Logan's recollections before editing them into what became *Motherwit: An Alabama Midwife's Story* (1989). The book, still in print as a paperback, was widely praised both for its vivid accounts of Mrs. Logan's life told in her distinctive vernacular and for her unflinchingly optimistic spirit in the face of pervasive adversity.

Motherwit made Mrs. Logan something of a folk hero, and in 1993 she was represented along with Simone de Beauvoir, Anne Frank, Maya Angelou, Lillian Hellman, Joan Didion, and other luminaries in *The Norton Book of Women's Lives*.

Although lay midwives were outlawed by the state of Alabama in 1976, Mrs. Logan had attained such stature in Mobile that she was allowed to continue her practice under a permit from local authorities until 1984, when she received an abrupt notice telling her there was no longer a need for her services. Mrs. Logan, who had delivered babies for almost two decades before receiving a state license in 1949, retired from her profession, but refused to abandon her calling. Despite all the advances in medical services to the poor, she knew that midwives were too often not the alternative to hospitals, but to husbands. "They're not going to stop me from doing the gift that God give me to do," she said. "I don't be going there on no license. I be going there as a friend to help that husband deliver his baby."

Mrs. Logan, who was married three times, is survived by her husband, Roosevelt Logan; a son, Johnnine Watkins of Moss Point, Mississippi; a sister, Louise Blackman of Pensacola, Florida; six grandchildren, and nine great-grandchildren.

July 13, 1995

"Very Quiet and Very Tough"

DEKE SLAYTON

By John Noble Wilford

Donald K. Slayton, one of the original seven American astronauts and an influential manager in the space agency, died at his home in league City, Texas, near the Johnson Space Center in suburban Houston. He was sixty-nine. The cause of death was brain cancer, said Howard Benedict, executive director of the Mercury Seven Foundation.

Of the first astronauts, Mr. Slayton, known to everyone as Deke, made the least immediate impression on a public that for a time could not read or hear or see enough of these newly minted space celebrities. In part this was because a heart problem kept him out of space for years. But he was also naturally laconic and presented a stern-faced image in public to mask his impatience with just about anything that did not involve flying.

In truth, other astronauts and space officials say, Mr. Slayton probably exerted a greater influence on the American space program over a longer period than any other single astronaut. For years, as chief of flight operations at the Johnson Space Center, he directed astronaut training and selected the crews for nearly all missions, including the Apollo flights to the Moon. Christopher C. Kraft, Jr., a former director of the Johnson center, said that Mr. Slayton "had the qualities you really wanted in the American astronaut of his time: He was a superb flyer, a good engineer, and was cognizant of the importance of his position to the country, what he had to do and how he had to do it."

At the time of his death, Mr. Slayton was director of Space Services Inc., a pioneering company in the business of launching small satellites.

He was a founder of the company when he retired from the National Aeronautics and Space Administration in 1982.

Donald Kent Slayton was born March 1, 1924, in Sparta, Wisconsin; he was one of seven children and grew up on the family's dairy farm. Upon graduation from high school in 1942, he entered the air force and flew fifty-six combat missions over Europe as a B-25 pilot and seven missions over Japan.

After World War II, he earned a bachelor's degree in aeronautical engineering at the University of Minnesota and went to work at the Boeing Aircraft Corporation. With the outbreak of war in Korea in 1951, he was recalled to duty as a fighter pilot. Eventually, he advanced to one of the choice roles in aviation, that of an experimental test pilot at Edwards Air Force Base in California. That was the finishing school for many future astronauts.

Stunned by the Soviet Union's launching of the first artificial Earth satellite, *Sputnik 1,* in October 1957, the United States rushed to establish its own space program. Personifying this much-ballyhooed effort were the seven young military aviators selected in April 1959 to be the first astronauts. They were called the Mercury Seven for the tiny one-person capsules they would begin flying in another two years, and they were immediately hailed as heroes. No one was more uncomfortable with the sudden celebrity than Mr. Slayton, who looked upon it as something to be tolerated. "I just learned to cope with it," he said years later.

Mr. Slayton was assigned to fly the second Mercury mission in orbit. Alan B. Shepard, Jr. and Virgil I. Grissom had each made test flights in 1961, and the next February John H. Glenn, Jr., had become the first American to orbit Earth. Then came the most bitter disappointment of Mr. Slayton's career.

Two months before his scheduled flight, doctors grounded Mr. Slayton because of an abnormal heartbeat caused by atrial fibrillation. His place on the flight in May 1962 was taken by Scott Carpenter. The two other Mercury astronauts, Walter M. Schirra, Jr., and L. Gordon Cooper, Jr., would get their flights, too, concluding the project the next May. Of the original seven, only Mr. Slayton never got a Mercury flight.

But he contributed significantly to the space program in a number of managerial positions, mainly directing astronaut training and selecting the crews for the subsequent Gemini and Apollo missions. Astronauts described him as "one hell of a leader, very quiet and very tough," said Mr. Benedict, a former Associated Press space reporter who is now director of the Mercury Seven Foundation, which raises money for science scholarships. Mr. Slayton was vice president of the foundation.

Mr. Slayton tried everything to cure his heart problem, including dieting, exercising more, quitting smoking, giving up coffee, and reducing alcohol consumption. Then, in 1971, the heart problem went away just as mysteriously as it had appeared, in time for Mr. Slayton to qualify for the last available seat on the last Apollo mission. With two other Americans, Mr. Slayton flew the Apollo in July 1975 to a docking with a Soviet Soyuz spacecraft. The joint mission symbolized a passing thaw in American-Soviet relations.

Mr. Slayton returned to managerial duties with the space agency, directing early tests of the space shuttles. Perhaps it was age and the satisfaction of having had his flight in space, but Mr. Slayton seemed to shed his stone-faced reserve. Asked before one shuttle mission what the astronauts would be doing between then and the launching, a question that used to elicit a sober listing of flight plans to be studied and so forth, Mr. Slayton replied, "I think they'll be goofing off." But when asked what might happen if one of the two solid-fuel boosters failed shortly after liftoff, he reverted to fatalism. "It'll be a bad day," he said.

After retiring from NASA to go to work for Space Services, the first privately financed American space enterprise, he directed the Houston-based company's first launching of a dummy spacecraft in September 1982. He became the company's president later that year.

Five of the original seven astronauts survive. Gus Grissom died in January 1967 when fire erupted in an Apollo spacecraft during a test on the launching pad. Mr. Glenn is a Democratic Senator from Ohio; Mr. Shepard, a Houston business executive; Mr. Schirra, an aerospace consultant in Rancho Santa Fe, California; Mr. Carpenter, an author and aerospace consultant in Vail, Colorado, and Mr. Cooper, chief executive of Galaxy Group Inc., a company in Van Nuys, California, that refurbishes airplanes.

Mr. Slayton was married in 1955 to Marjorie Lunney. They were divorced in 1983, and she has since died. He is survived by his second wife, the former Bobbie Osborn, whom he married in 1983; a son, Kent, of Houston; two sisters, Marie Madsen and Beverly Schlenz, both of Madison, Wisconsin; two brothers, Dick, of Los Gatos, California, and Elwood, of Marshall, Wisconsin, and two grandchildren.

June 14, 1993

The Mitten Lady

HELEN BUNCE

By Robert McG. Thomas, Jr.

Helen Bunce, who knitted so many mittens she didn't know what to do unless she was knitting more mittens, died at a nursing home in Watertown, New York, where she was known as the Mitten Lady. She was eighty-six and had been knitting mittens until a few days before her death.

Mrs. Bunce had been a legend in Watertown and in international church circles for decades, although until December only a few people knew she was the Mitten Lady whose anonymous handmade donations to an annual church clothing drive had spread her fame far and wide.

Since 1948, when the third-grade Sunday school class at the Emmanuel Congregational Church in Watertown established a special Christmas tree to collect clothing for poor children, Mrs. Bunce spent every otherwise spare moment knitting away. "She could knit in her sleep," her daughter, Helen McDonald, said, estimating that her mother had knit at least four thousand pairs of mittens over the last forty-seven years, and probably a lot more. "She didn't keep records in the early years," Mrs. McDonald added, "but some years she did more than two hundred."

For all the mittens she turned out, her sobriquet, the Mitten Lady, didn't tell the whole story. Mrs. Bunce, who knew that little heads as well as hands needed protection against the cold, knitted a matching cap for every pair of mittens and also turned out scarves. The sets, which included a handwritten tag saying "God Loves You, and So Do I," were distributed to various churches and charities in Watertown and through Church World Service, the Protestant relief agency, to poor children across the nation and abroad.

As word of Mrs. Bunce's work spread, people across the country began sending her yarn in care of the church, and she kept a scrapbook of thank-you notes from children she had helped and photographs showing some of them wearing her handiwork. Like the donated packages of yarn, the notes, addressed simply to the Mitten Lady, were delivered to the church and then passed on to her.

Mrs. Bunce, who lived in Watertown most of her life, carried her knitting wherever she went, clicking away whenever she could. Her mittens, which always included two contrasting colors in striking designs, came in three sizes, with the colors becoming darker as the sizes increased.

Although she suffered from osteoporosis so painful that she found it difficult to sit in a wheelchair in her last months, Mrs. Bunce, who had taught herself to knit lying down after entering the nursing home, insisted on being taken to the church in December to make her usual surreptitious donation of her year's production.

This time her cover was blown. She was introduced to the congregation as the Mitten Lady, and the woman who had once explained that she labored anonymously because the purpose of her work was to help poor children and not to have people say, "Oh, that's wonderful," had to endure a five-minute ovation.

Then she went back to the nursing home and continued her knitting. Mrs. Bunce, who always made it a point to start a new pair of mittens or a cap as soon as one was completed (on the assumption, she once explained, that God would not let anything happen to her as long as she had unfinished work), apparently knew the end was near. When she died, her daughter said, her needles were empty.

Mrs. Bunce's husband of sixty-seven years, Karl, died three days later. In addition to her daughter, of Alexandria Bay, New York, she is survived by two sons, Roy, of Strasbourg, France, and Jack, of Watertown; eleven grandchildren, and ten great-grandchildren.

March 4, 1996

Shaper of the City's Skyline

IRWIN S. CHANIN

By Paul Goldberger

The death of the builder and architect Irwin S. Chanin did not have any immediate impact on the shape of the city—Mr. Chanin was, after all, ninety-six years old, and had not put up a new building in years, even though he did manage the remarkable feat of going to his office almost daily until a couple of months before he died. But the end of his life was an event of great significance nonetheless, for he was the last of the men who built the extraordinary skyline of New York in the 1920s and 1930s—and now that he is gone, so, too, is any direct link between us and that remarkable period. The great towers of the twenties and thirties have become the models to which we look, and Irwin Chanin built many of the best of them.

The Century and the Majestic apartments that have come to epitomize Central Park West and the Chanin Building at Forty-second Street and Lexington Avenue were his triumphs, streamlined Art Moderne buildings that summed up the energetic, confident spirit of the Jazz Age in New York. The Majestic, between Seventy-first and Seventy-second streets, and the yellow-brick Century, between Sixty-second and Sixty-third streets, were the products of a builder who believed not only in the future of New York, but also in the idea of modernity, and he saw his mission as trying to persuade an upper-middle-class tenancy that it was possible to have futuristic zest and bourgeois respectability at the same time.

More than any other buildings in New York, the Majestic, completed in 1931, and the Century, finished in 1932, each with twin thirty-story towers, were designed and marketed as celebrations of skyscraper living. Their strong verticality called to mind the great commercial towers of that period, and their signature corner solariums, with windows wrapping entirely around column-free corners, emphasized light, air, and views in a way that gave further drama to the idea of living high in the sky.

Not for Irwin Chanin, then, the idea of making a high-rise apartment building feel like a Renaissance palace, as his rival Emery Roth tried to do in the San Remo, another twin-towered building farther up Central Park West at Seventy-fourth Street, which is quite similar to the Majestic and the Century in its basic shape, but garbed in classical detail instead. All three buildings were stage sets of a sort, but for very different plays: The builders of the San Remo were selling conservative luxury, while Mr. Chanin was selling the idea of a new skyscraper lifestyle.

It took some risk, and some hype that calls to mind the brash statements of many latter-day developers. Mr. Chanin talked frequently about the importance of light and air in Manhattan living and tried to emphasize the latest technology in his apartments; at the time the Majestic opened in 1931 he gave an interview in which he predicted that the future of Manhattan lay in immense, two-thousand-foot-high "super-buildings, erected over acres of ground and capable of housing twenty-five thousand to thirty thousand people." Most of the rest of the city would be open space, Mr. Chanin predicted, and he said he expected that by 1981 the city's zoning laws would have been repealed, since "they would have outlived their function." He concluded: "The basic purpose of these laws is to ensure sunlight and fresh air . . . Fifty years hence science and engineering will supply fresh air and sunshine more dependably and more efficiently than machinery."

There is a certain science-fiction terror to the vast buildings Mr. Chanin envisioned, which would hardly have been as humane as he imagined; almost everyone has learned by now that immense structures do not guarantee a civilized city. But it is important not to dismiss Irwin Chanin's dream as the thoughts of a kind of proto–Donald Trump, for it is not really about bigness for its own sake.

Irwin Chanin, unlike most developers of his time or our own, really did think about the future of the city, and his desire to meld technology with an improved way of life was genuine. He saw himself not only as a provider of a commodity—housing—but also as a man of his time, whose products reflected the best thinking of the age and brought it to the marketplace.

There is a great difference between dreaming of the liberating possibilities of larger and larger apartment towers in 1931, at the dawn of high-rise living, and advocating immense projects now, when the idea of the huge tower sitting alone in open space has been generally discredited by bitter experience. (Mr. Chanin's social conscience eventually brought him to the realization that more and more huge towers were not the answer: In the late 1970s he even went so far as to lend his name to the opposition to a large apartment project on Broadway near Lincoln Center.)

Mr. Chanin was born in Brooklyn on October 29, 1891. He studied architecture and engineering at Cooper Union—whose architecture school was renamed in his honor in 1981—and he was listed as the architect of record for most of his buildings with the exception of the handsome, fifty-six-story Chanin Building, once midtown Manhattan's largest, on which he collaborated with the firm of Sloan & Robertson. In truth, he worked closely with the architect Jacques Delamarre on his staff, who gave buildings like the Century and the Majestic much of their Art Deco–like flair, and with the sculptor Rene Chambellan, who contributed to the design of the Majestic's brick façade.

But the basic design directions were Mr. Chanin's own; forty years before the Atlanta architect John Portman became famous for trying to merge the roles of architect and developer, he was doing the same thing, and he is worth remembering for that as much as for his actual buildings.

Beyond the Century and the Majestic—Mr. Chanin lived to see them become official city landmarks—his finest accomplishment was the Chanin Building itself, finished in 1929, a proud Art Deco building with a base of terra-cotta ornament and a lobby of remarkably intricate detail. Its overall form showed the influence of one of the most innovative and important unbuilt skyscrapers in American history, Eliel Saarinen's distinguished second-place entry in *The Chicago Tribune* competition of 1922. Consistent with Mr. Chanin's commitment to new ideas, his office building originally contained an elaborate auditorium on an upper floor and a bus depot built into the ground floor. (Both eventually gave way to additional commercial space, as did the upper section of the lobby.)

Mr. Chanin also built the Lincoln Hotel on Eighth Avenue at Forty-fourth Street (now the Mitford Plaza), the Beacon Theater (now also a landmark) on Broadway at Seventy-fourth Street, and the Green Acres shopping center and suburban development in Valley Stream, Long Island.

Mr. Chanin was the president and founder of the Chanin family enterprises. The Chanin Construction Company, begun in 1919, was under the direction of Irwin and his brother, Henry, an accountant who looked after business while Irwin supervised construction. Henry Chanin died in 1973. Two other brothers, Sam and Aaron, played smaller roles in the company.

The Chanins first made a name for themselves on Broadway by building six elegant legitimate theaters: the 46th Street, the Biltmore, the Mansfield (now the Brooks Atkinson), the Theater Masque (now the Golden), the Royale, and the Majestic. They also built New York's ultimate movie palace, the Roxy.

When they built the 46th Street Theater in 1925, the Chanins abolished the institution of the gallery, with its separate entrance and stairway, where the lower-priced seats were confined. Irwin Chanin explained: "We made a sign when we started that theater: 'Everybody goes in the same door. Whether you've got a nickel or a five-dollar bill, go right inside. No climbing stairs. You're part of the audience—whether you have a million dollars or you borrow money."

Mr. Chanin was responsible too for one building that is perhaps best forgotten—his last project, finished in the late 1960s. It is the boxy white office tower at 1411 Broadway, at Thirty-ninth Street, the site of the old Metropolitan Opera House. This is as conventional and uninspired a building as there is in Manhattan, and it is a sadly banal ending to a remarkable career. But it surely embodies the dullness of most commercial architecture of the 1960s, and thus it leaves us with a tantalizing question: Was Irwin Chanin merely exhausted by the time the 1960s rolled around, or were his splendid buildings of the 1920s and 1930s fundamentally just reflections of their time, as his final building is a reflection of its era?

March 20, 1988

Ma Perkins's Ma

ANNE HUMMERT

By Robert McG. Thomas, Jr.

Faithful followers of soap operas have learned over the years that after a brief and bitter first marriage a young single mother can find love, marriage, and singular professional success with a much older man, but now the question is: Can a career woman who sacrificed her leisure to keep a nation of enthralled housewives glued to their radios for the better part of two decades survive a heart-wrenching regimen of producing as many as ninety cliff-hanging episodes a week to live a full, rich, and long life?

No need to stay tuned or wait for a toothpaste commercial. It can now be revealed that when she died in bed in her Fifth Avenue apartment, Anne Hummert, the woman widely credited with creating the radio soap opera and spinning out many of the classics of the 1930s and 1940s, was a ninety-one-year-old multimillionaire who had maintained a vigorous life almost to the end.

At a time when televised soap operas have become a postfeminist cultural sideshow, it is hard to imagine the era when *Stella Dallas, Helen Trent, Ma Perkins,* and *Lorenzo Jones* were more than household names, and when virtually every woman in America knew that Mary Noble was the *Backstage Wife* and were familiar with every detail of the anguished but inspiring lives of *John's Other Wife* and *Young Widow Brown.* It is even harder to imagine that all of these plus more than a dozen others were the creations of a diminutive dynamo from Baltimore and the man she married seven years after taking a job as his assistant at a Chicago advertising agency.

By the time she met E. Frank Hummert in 1927, the former Anne

Schumacher had lived something of a soap opera herself. A brilliant student who graduated magna cum laude from Goucher College at age twenty in 1925, she had begun her career as a college correspondent for *The Sun*, then worked as a *Sun* reporter before going to Paris in 1926. She became a reporter for the precursor of *The International Herald Tribune* her first day in the city, but within a year she had married and divorced a fellow reporter, John Ashenhurst, and was back in the United States with an infant son.

Settling in Chicago, she failed to get a newspaper job but became an assistant to Mr. Hummert, a former St. Louis newspaperman who had become a renowned copywriter and a partner in the Chicago agency Blackett, Sample & Hummert. He was some two decades older than she and he had never met a woman quite like his captivating twenty-two-year-old assistant with the tinkling voice, who was such a fount of ideas and organized efficiency that she became a vice president just two years later.

She, on the other hand, had already been married to one newspaperman, thank you, and was in no hurry to marry another. The couple didn't marry until 1934, when they began what friends recall as one of the great love matches, which lasted until Mr. Hummert's death in 1966.

At a time when commercial programming in the infant medium concentrated on working people who returned home to sit in front of their radios at night, advertisers were dimly aware that the housewives who stayed home all day were the nation's primary purchasing agents. But these women were considered too busy to pay more than cursory attention to the family radio.

The Hummerts didn't argue with the theory of the distracted housewife. They simply seized her attention and changed the pattern of her life. After *Just Plain Bill* hit the daytime airwaves in 1933, housewives arranged their work so they would never miss an episode of the small-town barber who married above himself. Although a short-lived 1930 program, *Painted Lives* by Irna Phillips, is regarded as the first radio soap opera, it was *Just Plain Bill*, which began at night in 1932, that created the cultural juggernaut that would eventually be nicknamed for the product that often sponsored it.

Within months the show had spawned many copycats, few as successful as those turned out by the Hummerts themselves, who had as many as eighteen separate fifteen-minute serials running at a time for a total of ninety episodes a week, each ending with an unresolved crisis that was heightened for the Friday episode.

The couple, who formed their own company, Hummert Productions, and moved to New York in the mid-1930s, eventually farmed out the writing after they had dreamed up the original idea and mapped out the initial story line. But they were deeply involved in every aspect of each production, from casting to script editing.

Mrs. Hummert, who had a photographic memory, was renowned in the industry for her ability to remember each intricate twist of every one of their creations.

It was a reflection of the grip the Hummerts had on their audience that their programs generated more than five million letters a year, and it was a measure of their commercial success that by 1939 Hummert programs accounted for more than half the advertising revenues generated by daytime radio.

The Hummerts were also well rewarded. At a time when the average doctor made less than five thousand dollars a year and the average lawyer half that, they were each making one hundred thousand dollars a year from their enterprise, which included several evening musical programs, like *Waltz Time*, and mysteries, including the haunting *Mr. Keen, Tracer of Lost Persons*.

When television began to displace radio, the couple simply retired and enjoyed a well-traveled life of leisure. After her husband's death, Mrs. Hummert gave up their Park Avenue triplex and cut down a bit on her travels, but she continued her active life, which until a few months before her death included daily three-mile walks.

Mrs. Hummert, whose son died several years ago, is survived by two granddaughters, Pamela Pigoni of Hinckley, Illinois, and Anne Jeskey of Park Ridge, Illinois, and two great-grandchildren.

July 21, 1996

LOVE BEGINS AT THIRTY-FIVE

ANNE HUMMERT *and her husband, Frank, created forty-odd shows between 1933 and 1960 that dominated daytime radio programming. With convoluted plot twists, melodramatic dialogue, and Friday cliffhangers, these shows laid down the formula for soap operas to come. A classic Hummert radio serial,* The Romance of Helen Trent, *began in 1933 and lasted for twenty-seven years, ending in 1960 after 7,222 chapters. According to John Dunning's 1976 book* Tune in Yesterday, *the soap opera, served up in daily fifteen-minute doses of Good versus Evil, began with a "plunking banjo... the soft humming of 'Juanita'... and the voice of Fielden Farringon:*

"Time now for The Romance of Helen Trent... *the real-life drama of Helen Trent, who—when life mocks her, breaks her hopes, dashes her against the rocks of despair—fights back bravely, successfully, to prove what so many women long to prove in their own lives; that because a woman is thirty-five and more, romance in life need not be over; that the romance of youth can extend into middle life, and even beyond..."*

As the humming faded, Helen would face another crisis in her intense love for the devilishly handsome and brilliant lawyer Gil Whitney. Here is one scene suggesting their famously complicated courtship:

HELEN: It's about Gil Whitney, Jeff... Betty Mallory called to say she had word he was staying in Marble Hill.

JEFF: Is this Mallory woman married to Gil or isn't she?

HELEN: She must be, Jeff.

JEFF: Then, why should she tell you about Gil, when you're the woman he was about to marry just when Betty and her child arrived on the scene?

HELEN: I know it must sound strange, and even illogical, but the fact of the matter is that I've been trying to help Betty get started in Hollywood.

JEFF: You asked me for the names of the best talent agents in Hollywood so you can give a helping hand to the woman who broke up your life?

HELEN: Oh, it isn't Betty Mallory's fault, you know that, Jeff. She knew Gil Whitney eight years ago during the war, when he was called Hugh Packard while he did confidential government work.

JEFF: The point is that he used his government alias to marry this girl and to live with her and have a child. And then he ran out and never so much as sent her a penny postcard after he left!

HELEN: Gil has explained all that, Jeff. He's admitted that the whole thing is probably true. But he didn't remember anything about that time. He'd been hurt, Jeff. His memory was impaired!

JEFF: Now you're calling all over the country to find the guy. Can't you get it through your head that he's not the man you took him for?

HELEN: Perhaps I can get it through my head, Jeff, but my heart won't accept that answer...I must find him, Jeff. I can't let Gil throw away his whole life. I've got to let him know that I believe in him, that I'm ready to stand by him—no matter how long it takes.

December 29, 1996
THE NEW YORK TIMES MAGAZINE

Football's Best-Kept Secret

HERB McCRACKEN

By Tom Friend

Things to bring to a football huddle: A play. A breath mint. A low voice. A quarterback.

The huddle was invented seventy-one years ago by a paranoid coach, and, remarkably, it is still the sport's most sacred place. Without this mini–board meeting, the game of football would be without its defining attribute: the secret.

Scandal led to the huddle's inception. In 1924, Herb McCracken, the coach of the Lafayette College football team, discovered that his hand signals had been scouted and decoded by Penn, his upcoming opponent. On game day, McCracken countered by ordering his players to gather en masse, several yards behind the line of scrimmage, and talk over the plays in a whisper. It immediately became ritual.

While he was coaching at Lafayette, Mr. McCracken also helped Maurice R. Robinson start up the Scholastic publishing company, where McCracken would spend sixty-three years. But he told family members he was most proud of giving birth to the huddle.

And quarterbacks are glad he did. "If you had something to say, you could say it in there," says Phil Simms, the former New York Giants quarterback. "You had immunity as a quarterback. What a great invention."

Talking back to the quarterback is usually, but not always, against huddle law. "Hank Stram sent in a running play once," recalls the former Kansas City Chiefs quarterback Len Dawson, "and a lineman said, 'Better change it 'cause it won't work.' And I'd listen to my linemen. Unless, of course, I was mad at my running back and wanted to get him killed."

Coaches, barred from the huddle, may insist on controlling its ambiance. In the 1970s, Coach Red Miller of the Denver Broncos ordered his players to hold hands in the huddle. Stram, meanwhile, actually tried reconfiguring the huddle, instructing Dawson to stand with his back to the defense and talk to his players "in the open." There was a good reason for it, too. "Bad breath," Dawson says. "I'm serious. Our tight end, Freddy Arbanas, claimed our fullback never brushed his teeth."

Practically every quarterback's favorite huddle moment is designing a play in the dirt. "Oh man. The infield at Yankee Stadium was great for that," says the former Washington Redskins quarterback Sonny Jurgensen.

But, alas, Herb McCracken is gone—he died at the age of ninety-five in Boynton Beach, Florida—and now it is almost impossible to find a good patch of dirt to draw on.

"I feel cheated," said Phil Simms. "I had to play on Astroturf."

December 31, 1995

THE NEW YORK TIMES MAGAZINE

Saloonkeeper with a Soul

Barney Josephson

By John S. Wilson

Barney Josephson, who brought down racial barriers as the owner of the legendary Cafe Society and who brought recognition to Billie Holiday, Teddy Wilson, Alberta Hunter, and other jazz singers and musicians during nearly half a century of showmanship, died of gastrointestinal bleeding at St. Vincent's Hospital in Greenwich Village. He was eighty-six.

When Mr. Josephson opened Cafe Society in a basement room at 2 Sheridan Square in Greenwich Village in December 1938, he changed a longstanding custom in American nightclubs. "I wanted a club where blacks and whites worked together behind the footlights and sat together out front," he once said. "There wasn't, so far as I know, a place like it in New York or in the whole country."

Although from the earliest days of jazz, black musicians played for white audiences, few nightclubs permitted blacks and whites to mix in the audience. Even the famous Cotton Club in Harlem, where Duke Ellington, Lena Horne, and Cab Calloway made their names, was a segregated place, admitting only an occasional black celebrity to sit at an obscure table. In 1938, Mr. Josephson's Cafe Society was the first nightclub in a white neighborhood to welcome customers of all races.

For the next decade, Cafe Society and Cafe Society Uptown, which he opened two years later on East Fifty-eighth Street, were consistent incubators of talent, producing a long list of singers, comedians, jazz musicians, and dancers who came to prominence there. They included Billie Holiday, who sang in Cafe Society's opening show in 1938 and remained there for nine months; Lena Horne, Sarah Vaughan, Nellie Lutcher, Rose Murphy, the Golden Gate Quartet, Sister Rosetta Tharpe,

Hazel Scott, Josh White, and Susan Reed. The boogie-woogie pianists Albert Ammons, Meade Lux Lewis, and Pete Johnson, along with Big Joe Turner, the blues singer, were in Cafe Society's first show and remained for four years, stimulating the boogie-woogie fad that swept the country.

Jack Gilford, who had been a stooge for Milton Berle, was the comedian and master of ceremonies in that opening show. He stayed for two years and was followed by Zero Mostel, making his professional debut; Imogene Coca, Jimmy Savo, and Carol Channing, among other comedians.

Pearl Primus and the Krafft Sisters danced at the two cafés, and such jazz musicians as Mary Lou Williams, Art Tatum, Teddy Wilson, Red Allen, Joe Sullivan, Edmond Hall, and Eddie Heywood played there.

Mr. Josephson was in his mid-thirties and had had no experience in the nightclub or entertainment fields when he opened his Greenwich Village club. He had worked in shoe stores in Atlantic City and Trenton, where he was born in 1902, the youngest of six children, two years after his parents emigrated from Latvia. His father, a cobbler, died shortly after his birth. His mother, a seamstress, worked for a ladies' tailor. Two of his brothers, Leon and Louis, became lawyers.

When Mr. Josephson graduated from Trenton High School, his oldest brother, David, put him to work in his shoe store. After the store went bankrupt during the Depression, Mr. Josephson got a job in another shoe store in Atlantic City, earning forty dollars a week as a buyer, window trimmer, and orthopedic fitter. "I knew it all," he said years later. "I still think I know more about shoes than I do about the café business."

He soon tired of Atlantic City and shoes. In the mid-1930s, he moved to New York with $7.80 in his pocket and a vague notion about opening a nightclub.

During a vacation in Europe he had become fascinated by the political cabarets of Prague and Berlin. He had also become a jazz fan as a result of trips to Harlem to hear Duke Ellington's band at the Cotton Club when he visited New York as a shoe buyer. "One thing that bugged me about the Cotton Club was that blacks were limited to the back one third of the club, behind columns and partitions," he once recalled. "It infuriated me that even in their own ghetto they had to take this. Of course, in any club below Harlem that had black entertainment, such as the Kit Kat Club, a black couldn't even get in."

Mr. Josephson, a trim, soft-spoken man, also was offended by "the mugs—the gangster-looking people with policies of clipping and padding checks," who, it appeared to him, ran most nightclubs. "Why can't the nightclub business be legitimate, like shoes?" he asked.

In the fall of 1938, after seeing a political cabaret put on by the Theater Arts Committee, he decided to try his hand at a "legitimate" nightclub. With $6,000, borrowed from two friends of his brother Leon, he rented the basement of 2 Sheridan Square for $200 a month and had the bare walls covered with murals by prominent Greenwich Village artists—Adolph Dehn, William Gropper, Sam Berman, Abe Birnbaum, Syd Hoff, John Groth, Ad Reinhardt, and Anton Refregier. "I told them I was going to open a political cabaret with jazz—a satire on the upper classes," Mr. Josephson later recalled. " 'You guys paint anything you want,' I said. I told them I'd pay them each $125 and a due bill for another $125 so they could come in and eat and drink any time."

His music adviser and talent scout was John Hammond, who discovered Billie Holiday, helped develop the Benny Goodman and Count Basie bands, and who brought a great number of jazz musicians and singers to the attention of the American public.

Cafe Society ("The wrong place for the right people" was its slogan) seemed to be an immediate success. The name was meant to parody the Stork Club and El Morocco and other uptown clubs that would not admit blacks. But although it was filled virtually every night, primarily with Villagers, Mr. Josephson lost money in his first year. He began to feel it had been a mistake to open in Greenwich Village.

"I should have opened where the money was," he reflected. "So I decided to open a place uptown, get that going and then close the Village place." But when he found the premises on East Fifty-eighth Street for his uptown branch, his press agent—a former Trenton schoolmate named Ivan Black—sent out a press release saying, with traditional hyperbole, that Cafe Society had been such a success in Greenwich Village that it was opening an uptown branch. This brought people from midtown and uptown flocking to the Village to find out what was going on. Suddenly, the Cafe Society in the Village *was* a success, and when Cafe Society

Uptown opened in October 1940, it was making money within three months.

All through the war years, the two clubs were consistently successful. That they were integrated, that Billie Holiday could sing an anti-lynching song like "Strange Fruit" there, was regarded as a basic element in their success. The song was written by Lewis Allan, the pen name of Abel Meeropol, a friend of Mr. Josephson's who had also written "The House I Live In."* Mr. Josephson persuaded Miss Holiday to sing "Strange Fruit" and it became one of the songs most associated with her.

In 1947, Mr. Josephson's brother Leon, an avowed Communist, was subpoenaed by the House Committee on Un-American Activities, found guilty of contempt when he refused to answer any questions, and sentenced to ten months in prison. As Leon's brother, Barney Josephson was attacked by such columnists as Dorothy Kilgallen, Lee Mortimer, Westbrook Pegler, and Walter Winchell. Within three weeks of these guilt-by-association assaults, business at the two clubs dropped 45 percent. Mr. Josephson hung on for a year, but after losing ninety thousand dollars, he sold both clubs.

He soon opened a small restaurant, the Cookery, offering hamburgers and omelets. It blossomed into a chain of four. "Part of the reason I started the Cookeries," he said, "was that I could be unknown, anonymous." But by November 1969, he had trimmed his chain down to a single Cookery, at University Place and Eighth Street in the Village. After almost two decades away from the nightclub business, he found he was getting an urge to hear the sound of music in his restaurant again.

Mary Lou Williams, the jazz pianist who had played at Cafe Society, was looking then for a place to perform after a long period of inactivity. She asked Mr. Josephson if he would put a piano in the Cookery, and he agreed, starting an entertainment policy.

Many of those who once performed at Cafe Society appeared at the Cookery, including Nellie Lutcher, Eddie Heywood, Teddy Wilson,

---

*Abel Meeropol, who composed "Strange Fruit" and the lyrics for "The House I Live In" under the pen name of Lewis Allan, and his wife adopted the two young sons of Julius and Ethel Rosenberg in 1957, four years after the Rosenbergs were executed for passing atomic secrets to the Soviet Union. He died in 1986 at the age of eighty-six.

Sammy Price, Susan Reed, Ellis Larkins, and Helen Humes. But the performer who brought the greatest success to the Cookery was Alberta Hunter, the singer whom Mr. Josephson brought to his Eighth Street club at the age of eighty-two in 1977 and who was a regular until her death nearly seven years later.

The Cookery itself, plagued by high costs and changing musical styles, was forced to halt its entertainment policy in 1984.

Mr. Josephson is survived by his fourth wife, Terry Trilling Josephson; two sons, Edward and Louis, and a stepdaughter, Kathe Trilling.

September 30, 1988

The Lady and the Tiger

JOSEPHINE PATTERSON ALBRIGHT

By Lawrence Van Gelder

Josephine Patterson Albright, who flew the mail, shot tigers in India, covered Chicago crime in journalism's colorful "Front Page" era, ran an Illinois dairy and pig farm, bred horses in Wyoming, wrote a column about her family, and helped establish a foundation for journalists, died at her home in Woodstock, Vermont. She was eighty-two. A daughter, Alice Arlen of Manhattan, said the death was caused by complications after a stroke.

Mrs. Albright was a member of one of the most prominent families in American journalism. Her father, Joseph Medill Patterson, founded *The Daily News* in New York and was co-editor and co-publisher of *The Chicago Tribune*. Her aunt, Eleanor Medill Patterson, published *The Washington Times-Herald*, and her older sister, Alicia Patterson, founded, published, and edited *Newsday*.

Like Alicia, who was seven years her senior, Josephine was told by her father that journalism was not for women. Both proved him wrong.

When Josephine earned her spurs in Chicago in the early 1930s, interviewing killers like George (Baby Face) Nelson and covering murders and the criminal courts, she worked not for her father's newspaper but for a rival paper, *The Chicago Daily News*, whose staff members served as models for the characters in the classic Ben Hecht–Charles MacArthur comedy *The Front Page*.

In *Ladies of the Press* (1936), Ishbel Ross wrote, "She sailed along successfully under her own steam, in spite of the professional handicap of being born into a noted newspaper family."

Josephine Patterson was born in Libertyville, Illinois, on December

2, 1913, and educated at the Foxcroft School in Middleburg, Virginia. Although her father disapproved of women in journalism, he did approve of women as pilots, and she got her pilot's license at the age of sixteen. Before her eighteenth birthday, she was the youngest pilot flying the mail route between Chicago and St. Louis.

But Josephine's career as a commercial mail pilot lasted only a few months. At eighteen, in the midst of her debutante party, she decided to fly with Alicia to India to hunt tigers. Without telling their mother, the two young women hopscotched their way across the world, dancing every night.

When they arrived in India, Josephine, who was later to become an ardent animal-rights activist and naturalist, quickly bagged a tiger. Alicia, who was supposed to shoot the tiger, was angry. She told her sister to stay out of the next hunt. So Josephine went on the next hunt carrying only a book. She was sitting in a tree reading when a leopard bounded up behind her. Josephine threw the book and hit the leopard in the nose. Alicia finished it off.

In 1936, Josephine married Jay Frederick Reeve, a Chicago lawyer she met while covering the courts. At that time she operated a dairy and pig farm that became the Hawthorne-Melody Dairy, a major Illinois enterprise.

In the mid-1940s, after a divorce, she moved to Dubois, Wyoming, bought a stallion from an Indian reservation, and began raising horses.

In 1946, in Red Lodge, Montana, she married Ivan Albright, an artist of the Chicago school who was known for his realistic paintings. The couple traveled extensively, and Mrs. Albright's travels fostered her enthusiasm for geography. Near the end of her life, she sponsored a statewide geography bee that was held in every Vermont school district.

In 1949, Mrs. Albright returned to journalism for three years as the author of a weekly *Newsday* column, "Life With Junior," which chronicled her foibles and successes in rearing her four children.

In 1963, she and her husband moved to Woodstock, where she obtained a bachelor of arts degree from Goddard College in Plainfield, Vermont.

Mr. Albright, whose centennial is to be observed next year with retrospectives at the Art Institute of Chicago and the Metropolitan Museum of Art in New York, died in 1983.

After Alicia Patterson died in 1963, Mrs. Albright helped establish and became a major benefactor of the Alicia Patterson Foundation, which awards fellowships to print journalists and photographers.

Mrs. Albright was also a supporter of the Pentangle Theater in Woodstock, the River City Arts and White River Opera House in White River Junction, Vermont; the Hood Museum in Hanover, New Hampshire, and the Art Institute of Chicago. Dartmouth College named her a Lathrop Fellow in honor of her support for its arts collection.

Besides her daughter Alice, Mrs. Albright is survived by another daughter, Dinah Albright Rojek of South Woodstock, Vermont; two sons, Joseph Medill Patterson Albright of Moscow and Adam Medill Albright of Richmond, Massachusetts; ten grandchildren, and two great-grandchildren.

January 18, 1996

The "Jewish James Madison"

ALBERT P. BLAUSTEIN

By Richard Perez-Pena

Albert P. Blaustein, a law professor who dedicated nearly three decades of his life to drafting constitutions for nations in transition, died at Duke University Hospital in Durham, North Carolina, after suffering a heart attack. He was seventy-two.

A fervent believer that a constitution could help a nation define its legal, political, and moral identity, Mr. Blaustein wrote the constitutions now in use in Liberia and Fiji, contributed large parts of the constitutions of Zimbabwe, Bangladesh, and Peru, and had a hand in the drafting of about forty others, including those of Nicaragua, Romania, and post-Soviet Russia.

From his home in Cherry Hill, New Jersey, Mr. Blaustein, who taught at the Rutgers University School of Law in Camden, was frequently summoned by dissident groups as disparate as the Inkatha Freedom Party in South Africa and a coalition of lawyers in Nepal to help them stake out their positions in drafting new constitutions. Those calls became frequent in recent years, as areas of the world, from Central America to Eastern Europe, underwent wrenching change.

"A constitution is more than a structure and framework for government," Mr. Blaustein once said. "It is in many senses a nation's frontispiece. It should be used as a rallying point for the people's ideals and aspirations, as well as a message to the outside world as to what the country stands for."

Mr. Blaustein would try to interject Western liberal notions into the constitutions he drafted; in the 1970s he tried, unsuccessfully, to persuade the leaders of the new majority-rule government of Zimbabwe to grant equal rights to women. But he acknowledged that for a constitution to work, it must reflect a country's culture and history. "We cannot put constitutions together like prefabricated henhouses," he said in a 1983 interview.

Mr. Blaustein's contributions to nation building began in 1966, when, at the request of the United States government, he traveled to South Vietnam to advise that country in drafting a constitution. By that time, he had established a formidable reputation as a legal scholar and the author and editor of many books. *Desegregation and the Law* (1957), of which he was co-author with Clarence Clyde Ferguson, Jr., was a critical and commercial success. His other works include *The American Lawyer: A Summary of the Survey of the Legal Profession* (1954), which he wrote with Charles O. Porter. He also was co-editor, with Gisbert Flanz, of a seventeen-volume series, *Constitutions of the Countries of the World*.

"Three quarters of the world's constitutions have been written since 1965, many of them with American assistance," said Professor Blaustein in a 1990 interview, after having made more than eighty trips overseas to consult with foreign governments and constitutional scholars.

"This is my life," Professor Blaustein said. "My son calls me a Jewish James Madison."

The professor's usual fee for such constitutional consulting work was two hundred dollars an hour, or one thousand, five hundred dollars a day. When he arrived in a country, Professor Blaustein said, "I ask them what they want, what values and heritage they want to see reflected in the document, and then I make suggestions, drawing on my knowledge of different constitutions from all over the world."

Born on October 12, 1921, in Brooklyn, Mr. Blaustein graduated from Boys High School at age sixteen. He graduated from the University of Michigan at nineteen and became a reporter for *The Chicago Tribune*. He served in the army during World War II and again in the Korean War, attaining the rank of major. Between the wars, he went to law school at Columbia University and practiced law in Manhattan at his father's firm. He taught at New York Law School in the mid-1950s and at Rutgers from 1955 until his retirement in 1992.

He is survived by his wife, the former Phyllis Migden; a daughter, Dana Litke of Northfield, New Jersey; two sons, Mark Blaustein of Fort

Lee, New Jersey, and Eric Blaustein of Cary, North Carolina; a sister, Marjory Simon of Purchase, New York, and four grandchildren.

August 23, 1994

ON MAKING A CONSTITUTION

ALBERT B. BLAUSTEIN, "who collected constitutions the way some other people collect stamps," once shared some thoughts with LINDA GREENHOUSE of The New York Times *about a lifetime of constitution watching and writing.*

Q: What makes a good constitution good?

A: Virtually every successful constitution is a constitution of compromise. It aims at achieving equilibrium. Remember, a constitution is more than a structure and framework for government. It is in many senses a nation's frontispiece. It should be used as a rallying point for the people's ideals and aspirations, as well as a message to the outside world as to what the country stands for.

Q: But isn't there a problem of form over substance? Some of the most totalitarian countries in the world have nice-looking constitutions.

A: Fair enough, but without constitutions, those countries might be even worse. The constitutional process is worth trying.

Q: Is a constitution that's good for one country necessarily good for another?

A: No. All constitutions have to be autochthonous. That's a key word meaning "arising from the self." It must spring from the soil. It must be the constitution to represent the needs of these people. We cannot put constitutions together like prefabricated henhouses.

For example, it may be all right for the U.S. Constitution to say no slavery is allowed. But you have a problem in parts of Africa and Asia where you have a responsibility in a certain community to build a road. Each community is obliged to build a part of the road, but they have no money to go out and hire a road builder, so everyone is required to get out on Sunday and chop rocks and build a part of the road. Under our Thirteenth Amendment, that could well be construed as slavery.

We talk glibly about one man, one vote. But the majority of the population of Fiji are settlers from India. What about all the Fijians? You have a dual voting system, so that it's guaranteed that the Fijians will win elections. Otherwise, the Indians would just open the door and invite all the other Indians to come in, and they'd swamp the country.

Q: Is there such a thing as an objectively bad constitution?

A: You might say that some of the British colonial constitutions are bad because they try to take care of everything. A constitution can't work if it tries to spell everything out. Here's a beauty. The Yugoslav constitution guarantees the human right of family planning. The Chilean constitution guarantees the right of the unborn. I just think this is an area the government ought to stay out of. The constitution doesn't have to go into everything. As soon as you go into too much detail, you open up a hornet's nest. On the other hand, some of the French-style constitutions in Africa fail because they don't say enough. They say, "We ascribe to the principles of the UN." Well, what does that mean?

Q: Do you have a personal list of all-time favorite constitutions?

A: Oh, there are some wonderful constitutions. The Mexican constitution of 1917, such a far-reaching constitution on the role of the clergy, on the government ownership of land, on the social values. A tremendously influential constitution. And the Irish constitution of 1937 has a lot of good ideas. The new Spanish and Portuguese constitutions are favorites. There's a lot of thinking in the Indian constitution. It can't be ignored. The Nigerian constitution of 1979 is worth looking at too.

Q: If you were hired to draft a new constitution for the United States, what changes would you make?

A: No one drawing up a constitution for America today would fail to include a right of privacy. I would also include the right to leave and to return. We have these rights now, but they're not set forth in the Constitution.

The American method of selecting the President of the United States if nobody has a majority is not very good, you know, throwing it to the House of Representatives. I would adopt the French style and have another election the following week. Also, I wouldn't have elections on the first Tuesday after the first Monday. I'd have them on a Sunday.

I would want to clarify the relative difference between individual rights and group rights. There's a famous Supreme Court case in which John Marshall leaned across to the lawyer and said: "But aren't all group rights individual rights?" Well, they're not, but this was a melting-pot country concerned with individual rights. Today we have to worry about the rights of groups, about the Spanish-speaking people. We've ignored the Indian people.

Q: If you had a chance to get the framers in a room, say for five minutes, and ask them to clear up some of the enduring mysteries, what would your questions be?

A: I'd like to know what they meant by the free exercise and establishment clauses. That's one thing that obviously needs clarification. Then I would ask them if they meant to have the provisions of the first eight amendments apply to the states. And then, of course, judicial review, the scope of the judicial power.

Q: Do you think the framers meant judicial review to play such an important role?

A. I have no idea, but I would say no, I don't think they ever envisioned such power in the judiciary.

Q: Could the framers possibly have envisioned the sort of unproductive stalemate that exists today between the executive and legislative branches?

A: Probably not. They tried to come up with a compromise, on the basis of everything they knew, between the absolute executive and the absolute parliament. The French writers of the time thought in terms of an absolute parliament, because they had a king, who was much worse by the way than the English king. But then there was a question that if you had an assembly, you had a rabble, and you had to protect against the rabble. I know that war powers is the question of the day, but you didn't think then about the U.S., this little dinky country over in a corner of the world, going out with police actions, peacekeeping missions. That wasn't part of the concept. But the point is, the constitutions must meet changing needs, and we meet it judicially.

Q: How closely do you think our system today approximates the vision of the framers?

A: I think they would be very proud of how we turned out, I really do. I think our Constitution has met the test of time. When Mr. Nixon left power, the only person with a gun was a policeman directing traffic.

September 14, 1983

Anguish as a Comic Art

JACK WESTON

By Robert McG. Thomas, Jr.

Jack Weston, the chubby, bejowled actor who elevated anguish to a comic art in a forty-year career on television, in the movies, and on Broadway, died at Lenox Hill Hospital in Manhattan. He was seventy-one and had had lymphoma for six years, his wife said.

In a career in which he appeared in hundreds of television productions, two dozen movies, and another two dozen Broadway plays, Mr. Weston became such a recognizable figure and played so many distinctive roles with such élan that no one doubted him when he bragged—or complained—that he never got a part from an agent. He didn't have to. Mr. Weston was a master at bumping into the right people at the right time. At restaurants, parties, or on the street he was forever running into producers, directors, and playwrights whose eyes would inevitably light up as they told him to be sure to call them the very next day.

Mr. Weston, a shy man who never trusted his own luck, would just as inevitably dismiss the overture as routine social shtick and not make the call. Sure enough, the producers would call him and Mr. Weston would be hired for yet another role that would stick in some other producer's mind the next time Mr. Weston bumped into him.

That, more or less, is how Woody Allen came to hire Mr. Weston for his acclaimed stage role as a sleazy personal manager in *The Floating Lightbulb*, which led to a Tony nomination for Mr. Weston in 1981. And that is how he got his even more acclaimed role in *The Four Seasons*, the 1981 movie with Alan Alda, Carol Burnett, and Rita Moreno that led to a spinoff television series starring Mr. Weston in 1984.

He had appeared in his share of Broadway hits, including *California*

Suite and *The Ritz* in 1976, but for Mr. Weston, who had survived for years on comic shtick, the role of a cantankerous dentist with depth marked a transition point in his career. From then on he would take only roles with substance, including parts in Shakespeare's *Measure for Measure* and Paddy Chayevsky's *The Tenth Man*, at Lincoln Center in 1989.

Like many of the characters he played, Mr. Weston was the quintessential New Yorker, which is to say he was born in Cleveland and lived in Los Angeles for eighteen years, hating every minute of it when he wasn't actually in front of the camera. "Every afternoon at three something hits this town," he said during an interview in Los Angeles in 1984. "It's called flash boredom. If you're an actor and not working and you don't play tennis or golf, you can go stark, raving mad. I know. I lived here for eighteen years."

Mr. Weston, who said he hated Cleveland too—until he spent two years as an army machine gunner in Italy in World War II—got his first break at birth. His father, a shoemaker, was a surprisingly understanding man. When one of his son's teachers told him that Jack, a failing student and the class clown, had an aptitude for acting, rather than being aghast, his father actually enrolled him in classes at the Cleveland Playhouse, a storied nurturing ground for young talent, including Paul Newman.

After his army service, Mr. Weston came to New York to study at the American Theater Wing along with such future stars as Lee Marvin, Rod Steiger, and Jack Klugman. Although he did his share of menial work, including a job as an elevator operator that he got because he was the first applicant who fit the suit, Mr. Weston found ready work in the theater, including a part in *South Pacific*, and even more on television, where he became a regular during the fabled golden age of the 1950s.

His Hollywood years began on a whim in the spring of 1958 when he and his first wife, Marjorie Redmond, abruptly quit their parts in the Broadway hit *Bells Are Ringing*, and struck out for Los Angeles in a vintage Volkswagen, fully expecting to return to New York in the fall. Then the car broke down and the couple were stranded for what turned out to be an eighteen-year stay as Mr. Weston appeared almost constantly on television and his wife did even better: a ten-year stint as the Cool Whip lady, a commercial gig, Mr. Weston once noted, that required her to work five days a year and paid her six figures.

In much of his early work, Mr. Weston was the villain, most memorably as one of the men who terrorize Audrey Hepburn in the 1967 cult classic *Wait Until Dark*, but movies like *Cactus Flower* and *Please Don't Eat the Daisies* led him to comedy.

His standing as a character actor took some of the edge off the fact that people were forever recognizing Mr. Weston and never knowing his name.

Mr. Weston was only slightly exaggerating when he claimed that he was everything about his role in *The Four Seasons* except a dentist. "I'm a hypochondriac," he said. "I'm paranoid. I'm a nervous wreck. Why are those people talking about me?" Perhaps because they had seen him in any number of roles they will never forget.

Mr. Weston, who was divorced from Miss Redmond, is survived by his wife, Laurie Gilkes; a stepdaughter, Amy Gilkes of Manhattan, and a brother, Sam, of Los Angeles.

May 5, 1996

The Eye of Harlem

AUSTIN HANSEN

By Lawrence Van Gelder

Austin Hansen, who chronicled life in Harlem in thousands of photographs over six decades, died at the Veterans Affairs Medical Center in Manhattan. Mr. Hansen, who lived in Harlem, was eighty-five.

Through his lens, Mr. Hansen, who began taking pictures as a twelve-year-old in the Virgin Islands, captured a vast spectrum of activity in the community he joined in 1928. Among his images were enraptured young couples, David N. Dinkins's wedding, and the street-corner grief when Franklin D. Roosevelt died in 1945. Here was Lena Horne being interviewed in the Hotel Theresa, and there was a man walking a picket line, carrying a sign that read: DO NOT RIDE THESE BUSES UNTIL YOU SEE NEGRO DRIVERS.

The photographs Mr. Hansen took were also the story of his life. "And it hasn't all been beautiful," he said one day in 1994. "Some has been sad, the way they treated black people in those days. And I have been part of the suffering."

Mr. Hansen made his last public appearance a few days ago at the opening of an exhibition of works by twenty-one African-American photographers at the Adam Clayton Powell Jr. State Office Building in Harlem. The senior artist in the show, Mr. Hansen was the featured speaker before an audience of five hundred, many of whom sought him out before and after his remarks to ask for his autograph. Later that night, he suffered a stroke.

At the time of his death, "Hansen's Harlem," an exhibition distilled from the fifty thousand images he donated to the Schomburg Center for Research in Black Culture, was touring the world.

Mr. Hansen was born in 1910 in St. Thomas. When he was twelve, he started to take pictures with an Eastman Hawkeye camera made of cardboard and imitation leather. He never forgot the first photograph that made him money. "Hansen, take my picture," said a friend who had a new car.

"And he gave me twenty cents," Mr. Hansen recalled. "My mother couldn't come by two cents, we were having it so hard. We were able to get ten loaves of bread."

Eventually, a naval officer, F. A. Dibling, hired Mr. Hansen as a photographer, and when Mr. Hansen left St. Thomas for New York in 1928, he carried with him a reference from his employer.

But the reference did Mr. Hansen little good when he reached the city. "Everywhere I went, they said, 'We're not hiring colored,'" he remembered. "So I went and got a job washing dishes, running the elevator, and doing all the menial things blacks were doing at that time."

Sometimes, he played drums in gigs around town. And always, he kept his camera nearby. One night at the Essex Hotel, he saw a young black woman perform. "She was singing for Mrs. Roosevelt," he said. "A black girl! I figured it was news. And I took the picture."

He sold it to *The Amsterdam News* for two dollars, and for the next six decades, his portraits and news photographs captured the ordinary and extraordinary in Harlem. Eventually, he opened a studio on West 135th Street, where he worked for forty-seven years, with time out for a hitch as a navy photographer during World War II and a job as a darkroom technician for the Office of War Information.

But most of his career was spent making portraits and free-lancing for newspapers like *The Amsterdam News* and *The Pittsburgh Courier*. He took photographs for Malcolm X and for Adam Clayton Powell, Sr., and Jr. He recorded historical images of Emperor Haile Selassie of Ethiopia, Marcus Garvey, the Rev. Dr. Martin Luther King, Jr., Langston Hughes, Mary McLeod Bethune, and Marian Anderson.

For more than forty years, Mr. Hansen was the official photographer for the Abyssinian Baptist Church, and for more than twenty years Mr. Hansen and his brother, Aubrey, who died before him, documented events at the Cathedral of St. John the Divine. For the last five years, Mr. Hansen was the artist in residence at the Photographic Center of Harlem, a nonprofit school that teaches photography to children, young adults, and the elderly.

Mr. Hansen is survived by his wife of fifty-three years, Lillian; a daughter, Joyce Hansen of Manhattan; two sons, Austin Hansen, Jr., of Pomona, New York., and Arnold Hansen of Syracuse; a sister, Cynthia Marcee of Alexandria, Virginia; seven grandchildren, and two great-grandchildren.

January 25, 1996

The First Gray Panther

MAGGIE KUHN

By Robert McG. Thomas, Jr.

Maggie Kuhn, who called herself a little old woman and celebrated her forced retirement in 1970 by founding the Gray Panthers, died at the home she shared in Philadelphia with a like-minded coterie. She was eighty-nine. "She died peacefully in her sleep," said her personal assistant, Sue Leary, who could not say which of Miss Kuhn's many ailments, from arthritis to osteoporosis, had caused her death.

For all Miss Kuhn's ailments, none had slowed her down. She spent the last twenty-five years leading people young and old in the fight against age discrimination and other forms of what she saw as social injustice and stereotypical thinking and just two weeks ago she had joined striking transit workers on their picket line.

Even so, there was some evidence that Miss Kuhn knew that the end was coming. Although she had made it her goal to live until her ninetieth birthday in August, she had allowed her friends and admirers to celebrate it on April 1. And in a recent issue of the Gray Panthers' publication, *The Network,* she had lectured the organization's forty thousand members in thirty-two states on the need to prepare for the twenty-first century.

It was hardly the first time Miss Kuhn had been ahead of her time.

It was in 1970 that Miss Kuhn, who had worked twenty-five years for the United Presbyterian Church in New York, commuting daily from her home in Philadelphia, reached the mandatory retirement age of sixty-five and was forced to leave her job. "They gave me a sewing machine," she once recalled, "but I never opened it. I was too busy."

Within months of her retirement, she joined several friends in

founding an organization quickly dubbed the Gray Panthers, a name derived from the radical Black Panthers.

Despite the name and the initial emphasis on championing the elderly, as conceived by Miss Kuhn the organization knew no age boundaries. Its credo described it simply as an advocate for "fundamental social
change that would eliminate injustice, discrimination, and oppression in
our present society." For example, in addition to seeking a ban on mandatory retirement, which was eventually enacted into law, the group called
for "publicly owned and democratically controlled" utilities.

No one who knew Miss Kuhn was surprised that in last year's
health-care debate her organization championed what was widely seen as
the most radical of the various proposals: health insurance paid totally by
the government, a position that had been on the Gray Panthers' official
agenda since 1977.

A tiny woman who wore her hair in a prim bun that gave her the
look of an ideal candidate to be helped across the street by a Boy Scout,
Miss Kuhn, who detested the term "senior citizen," made no apologies
for her looks or her age. "I'm an old woman," she told *The New York Times*
in 1972. "I have gray hair, many wrinkles, and arthritis in both hands.
And I celebrate my freedom from bureaucratic restraints that once
held me."

Miss Kuhn, whose opposition to the war in Vietnam made her a
hero to many young protesters, had a disarming argument in recruiting
younger people to her cause: "Every one of us is growing old."

Known as an inspirational speaker, Miss Kuhn was just as persuasive
in private conversation, combining honey with the hammer. "Forceful, yet
gracious" is the way Miss Leary put it.

Miss Kuhn was a champion of social causes long before the Gray
Panthers.

As she noted in her 1991 autobiography, *No Stone Unturned*, she was
conceived in Memphis, where her father, a traveling district manager for
Dunn & Bradstreet, was working at the time. But her mother, refusing to
deliver a child into a racist society, insisted on returning from Tennessee
to her home in Buffalo to give birth.

As a student at Flora Stone Mather College of Case Western Reserve University in Cleveland, Miss Kuhn helped organize a college chap-

ter of the League of Women Voters. And in a succession of jobs as a manager of social programs for the Young Women's Christian Association in Cleveland, Philadelphia, and Boston and in similar work with the Presbyterian Church in New York, Miss Kuhn took what were then unconventional positions on issues like peace and social justice.

Miss Kuhn, who could also be somewhat unconventional in her private life, attributed the fact that she had never married to "sheer luck."

According to her book, she had many love affairs, including one in her seventies with a student in his twenties. Miss Kuhn did not identify him, but Christina Long, who helped her with the book, said the man, now in his forties, was at the recent birthday gala. "He seemed very proud of the romance," she said.

Miss Kuhn leaves no immediate survivors.

April 23, 1995

Lonesome Pioneer

Bill Monroe

By Jon Pareles

Bill Monroe, who helped lay the foundation of country music as the universally recognized father of bluegrass, died in a nursing home in Springfield, Tennessee. He was eighty-four. He had suffered a stroke earlier this year, said his booking agent, Tony Conway.

Mr. Monroe, who played the mandolin and sang in a high, lonesome tenor, created one of the most durable idioms in American music. Bluegrass, named after his band, the Blue Grass Boys, was a fusion of American music: gospel harmonies and Celtic fiddling, blues and folk songs, Tin Pan Alley pop and jazz-tinged improvisations. The Blue Grass Boys sang, in keening high harmony, about backwoods memories and stoic faith; they played brilliantly filigreed tunes as if they were jamming on a back porch, trading melodies among fiddle, banjo, and Mr. Monroe's steely mandolin. By bringing together rural nostalgia and modern virtuosity, Mr. Monroe evoked an American Eden, pristine yet cosmopolitan.

He perfected his music in the late 1940s and stubbornly maintained it, and he lived to see his revolutionary fusion become the bedrock of a tradition that survives among enthusiasts around the world. He was also an indefatigable traveling musician, and a taskmaster who challenged his sidemen with difficult keys and tempos. Every musician now playing bluegrass has drawn on Mr. Monroe's repertory, his vocal style, and his ideas of how a string band should work together. And his influence echoes down not just through country music but from Elvis Presley (who recorded Mr. Monroe's "Blue Moon of Kentucky" on his first single disc) to bluegrass-rooted rock bands like the Grateful Dead and the Eagles.

"I never wrote a tune in my life," Mr. Monroe once said. "All that music's in the air around you all the time. I was just the first one to reach up and pull it out."

William Smith Monroe grew up on a farm in Rosine, Kentucky, thirty miles north of Bowling Green. He was the youngest of eight children, and shy because one eye was crossed. Both his mother and an uncle, Pendleton Vandiver (later memorialized in Mr. Monroe's tune "Uncle Pen"), were fiddlers, and the young Bill Monroe sometimes accompanied his uncle on guitar. But his older brothers monopolized the family's fiddle and guitar, leaving the nine-year-old Bill to play the mandolin. His mother died when he was ten, and his father six years later. "It was a hard life, to come up with no money," he said. "You'd sing a lot of sad songs."

Mr. Monroe followed his brothers to the Chicago suburb of Whiting, Indiana, and worked through the Depression at an oil refinery. He began performing with two of his brothers, and in 1934 he started playing music full-time in a duo with his brother Charlie on guitar. The Monroe Brothers made their first recordings in 1936, but split up after two contentious years.

Mr. Monroe put together the Blue Grass Boys in 1939, and the band soon joined the *Grand Ole Opry* radio broadcasts. They performed everything from hymns to fiddle tunes to comedy, and toured thousands of miles between Saturday-night broadcasts. He described his audience as "people who get up in the morning and make a lot of biscuits."

Sidemen came and went during World War II. In 1942, the group took the lineup of the classic bluegrass quintet—mandolin, fiddle, guitar, bass, and banjo—although it also briefly used accordion and harmonica. Lester Flatt, a guitarist who had worked with Charlie Monroe, joined the group in 1945, followed by the innovative banjoist Earl Scruggs in 1946. With Chubby Wise on fiddle and Howard Watts on bass, that lineup of the Blue Grass Boys defined bluegrass music.

"Bluegrass is competition," Mr. Monroe once said, "with each man trying to play the best he can, be on his toes."

Mr. Flatt and Mr. Scruggs left in 1948, tired of working for sixty dollars a week. But Mr. Monroe continued to recruit extraordinary musicians, among them Don Reno and Bill Keith on banjo; Mac Wiseman, Del McCoury, and Peter Rowan on guitar and vocals; and Vassar Clements, Byron Berline, Richard Greene, Buddy Spicher, and Kenny

Baker on fiddle. During the 1950s and afterward, he sometimes expanded the group with two or three fiddles in harmony.

His traditionalism brought him a new audience among urban folk-music fans in the 1960s, and in 1967 he started the annual bluegrass festival in Bean Blossom, Indiana. While bluegrass became harder to find on the radio, pushed aside by more modern country music and by rock-and-roll, it spread among do-it-yourself musicians, who now support more than five hundred annual bluegrass festivals.

Mr. Monroe was named to the Country Music Hall of Fame in 1970. It was the first of many awards, including a National Heritage Fellowship Award in 1982, the first Grammy Award for the Best Blue-grass Recording in 1989, and a Lifetime Achievement Award from the National Academy of Recording Arts and Sciences in 1993. He was acknowledged as a patriarch by performers such as Ricky Skaggs, who collaborated with him on the Grammy-winning tune "Wheel Hoss"; he also continued to tour indefatigably, despite health problems.

In 1985, someone broke into his home and smashed the 1923 Gibson F-5 mandolin he had been playing for four decades; technicians at Gibson Guitars spent three months reassembling it with microscopes and tweezers. In 1994, bad investments led Mr. Monroe to sell the 288-acre homestead in Goodlettsville, Tennessee, where he had lived for forty years; the company that owns the *Grand Ole Opry* bought it and agreed to let him stay there. That year, MCA Records released a four-CD collection, *The Music of Bill Monroe: From 1936 to 1994*, produced by the Country Music Foundation, a tribute to Mr. Monroe's virtuosity and perseverance.

"If I'd have changed," Mr. Monroe said in Rachel Liebling's documentary *High Lonesome: The Story of Bluegrass Music*, "the people wouldn't have liked that at all."

He is survived by a son, James, and a grandson.

September 10, 1996

Good Sad

NICHOLAS DAWIDOFF, *the author of* In the Country of Country: People and Places in American Music, *attended* BILL MONROE'S *eighty-third birthday party and wrote this remembrance.*

The invitation said this:

> *Come Help Me Celebrate*
> *My 83rd Birthday in a Powerful Pickin' & Picnicin' Way!*
> *6:00 PM 'Til the Cows Come Home!*
> *Monroe Farm, Goodlettsville, Tennessee.*
> *Bring Your Instrument and Covered Dish.*

Once when I asked Bill Monroe about his music, he said, "It's for everybody," and on September 13, 1994, some of everybody came to Monroe Farm. There were record producers, farmers, fiddlers, mechanics, neighbors, neighbors' children, men named Hoss, colonels down from Mr. Monroe's home state of Kentucky, and Porter Wagoner too, and they had all cooked up their country best. The security guard at the Ryman Auditorium, where Mr. Monroe performed for thirty-one of his fifty-seven years on *The Grand Ole Opry*, had made ham and sweet potato biscuits. Emmylou Harris brought a moist lemon poppyseed cake baked by her mother. One hapless soul shambled in with a dish full of Kentucky Fried Chicken, but even that was fortunate; everyone else seemed to have brought beans. Bill Monroe was, as he would put it, powerful fond of beans.

Bob Dylan once described Mr. Monroe's music by saying, "That's what America's all about." Mr. Monroe certainly dressed the part. He sat in a rocking chair under an elm tree, wearing a white Stetson, a rhinestone American flag pin on his lapel, and an American flag tie. Beside him sat Earl Scruggs, Mr. Monroe's old banjo player, old friend, old enemy, and, apparently, old friend again. The sight of the two provoked much discussion among the party guests. After Mr. Scruggs quit Mr. Monroe's band, the Blue Grass Boys, in 1948, Mr. Monroe refused to say a word to him for more than twenty years. Now they looked thoroughly congenial. Was Mr. Monroe mellowing? Most people thought it was too early for Mr. Monroe to be mellowing. After all, he was only eighty-three.

Some time passed, Mr. Monroe took up his mandolin, and the pickin' portion of the picnic began on his front porch. Mr. Monroe grew up learning to play music on porches in Rosine, Kentucky, with his fiddle-playing Uncle Pendleton Vandiver—"Uncle Pen" in Mr. Monroe's song—and so he was in entirely familiar circumstances. He ripped through "Raw Hide" at astonishing speed and sang "Rabbit in a Log," which is a meditation, of sorts, on how to capture a wild hare when you have no hunting dog. He yodeled high during "Mule Skinner Blues" before Emmylou Harris shared "Kentucky Waltz" with him. Ms. Harris is a soprano, but Mr. Monroe's keening tenor soared right up with her. Mr. Monroe always wanted women to know that he could sing as high as they could, just as he liked to assure men that his handshake was firmer than theirs.

Mr. Monroe's conversation was usually as silent as the pines of old Kentucky, but at his party, he paused to thank everyone for coming: "I want y'all to pull for me and I'll keep pulling for you." Then he struck up "Blue Grass Breakdown," whereupon an old woman sprang to her feet and danced a brief, impromptu jig.

Mr. Monroe always thought of bluegrass as dance music. That's why in addition to borrowing from traditional string-band music and gospel hymns, his sound was heavily informed by the syncopated blues licks he learned from a black freight hauler and guitar player named Arnold Schultz whom Mr. Monroe met at a dance near Rosine. Mr. Monroe also liked jazz, and he melded it all into a sophisticated acoustic-band music that featured complex rhythm structures and instrumental precision. Rather than simply featuring his mandolin, Mr. Monroe wrote music that assigned each string a place in an exotic musical dialogue. "Bill used the old music, but he invented bluegrass with it," says Jean Ritchie, the Kentucky folk singer. "In that day it was punk, it was hip-hop. He took the old music and he made it new."

For Mr. Monroe, the air was full of songs, and as his band car, the

Blue Grass Special, sped from gig to gig, he willed his new ones into generations of sleep-deprived fiddlers and banjo players. Still, when show time came, no group played as fast as Mr. Monroe's, something he ensured by hurrying across the stage to shove anybody who slowed the music. "He grew up in a mean period, the Depression," says Mr. Monroe's fellow singing Kentuckian, Don Everly of the Everly Brothers. "He had to be tough. You were raised that way. You go somewhere and people treat you like a hillbilly if you're from Kentucky."

If the man shouldered his way through life, many of his song lyrics are delicate, often wistful and full of pathos. "It's played from my heart to your heart and it will touch you," Mr. Monroe said once, and according to millions of other people, it certainly did. "His music brings back my younger days," says Frances Johnson Harvey of Rosine. "Sometimes I wish I could be back in those days. But, you know, there's a good sad and a bad sad. Bill Monroe's music is good sad."

Out on the porch Mr. Monroe was still playing.

December 29, 1996
THE NEW YORK TIMES MAGAZINE

Not a Household Name but a Household Presence

BROOKS STEVENS

By John Holusha

Brooks Stevens, an industrial designer whose works ranged from corporate logos and clothes dryers to the Oscar Mayer Weinermobile, died in Milwaukee at eighty-three. The cause was heart failure, said his son William.

Mr. Stevens was a founder of the industrial-design business in the 1930s, along with men like Raymond Loewy, who designed the Coca-Cola logo, and John Vassos, who modernized the exterior appearance of radios. But unlike them, he resisted the temptation to move to New York, keeping his business, Brooks Stevens Design Associates, in the Milwaukee area.

In later years he recalled how difficult it was to persuade companies to pay him to redesign their products during the hard times of the Depression. "I had to fight my way in to talk to anybody in the thirties," he said. "I had to not only justify myself, but justify my profession." But gradually he convinced manufacturers to engage his services, often with memorable results. The front fender design he did for the 1949 Harley-Davidson Hydraglide motorcycle is still used by the company in its Heritage Classic series of motorcycles.

"He did everything from cigarette lighters to pavement rippers," said Gary Wolfe, curator of the Brooks Stevens Gallery of Industrial Design at the Milwaukee Institute of Art and Design. "His specialty was to make products more user-friendly. He was best at understanding how products were meant to function and modifying them so the customer could use them more easily." Mr. Stevens worked for a total of 585 different clients, designing lawn mowers for Briggs & Stratton and Lawn-Boy, outboard motors for Evinrude, and the civilian Jeepster after World War II. He designed the corporate logo for Miller beer and persuaded the company to use clear bottles, rather than the traditional brown ones, to go with its advertising slogan "the champagne of bottled beer."

Automobiles were a favorite of Mr. Stevens, who both designed and collected them. He designed the two-seat sports car called Excalibur for the ailing Kaiser-Frazier company in 1964, and later formed a company to produce cars bearing that name that had styling vaguely reminiscent of a 1930s Mercedes-Benz. Although they looked exotic, they were thoroughly conventional under the skin and drew mixed reviews. He also designed the last prototypes for Studebaker, including a station wagon with a sliding roof to permit hauling tall objects. The cars were never produced, but the prototypes wound up in the Brooks Stevens Car Museum in Mequon, Wisconsin, along with the seventy-five antique cars he had collected. In 1958, he designed the Weinermobile, with a giant hot dog replica on the top, for the Oscar Mayer Company.

Mr. Stevens was born in Milwaukee in 1911 and attended local schools. He contracted polio as a boy and was encouraged by his father to develop his talent for drawing. He attended Cornell University from 1929 to 1933, studying architecture, but he returned to Milwaukee without graduating because the Depression had put a stop to most building. At the suggestion of his father, who was a vice president of the Cutler-Hammer Company, a producer of industrial equipment in Milwaukee, he opened an office in 1934 as a design consultant. One of his first projects was to design a line of electrical controls for Cutler-Hammer and a corporate logo for the company.

In 1944, along with Raymond Loewy and eight other men, he helped form the Industrial Designers Society of America, which today has thousands of members. Mr. Stevens turned the design company over to his son Kipp in 1979, but continued to speak and teach.

In addition to Kipp and William, Mr. Stevens is survived by his wife, Alice; a son, David; a daughter, Sandra A. Stevens, and five grandchildren.

January 7, 1995

HE PUT A SPIN ON DESIGN

A few years before he died, a feisty BROOKS STEVENS *played host to* ISABEL WILK-
ERSON *of* The New York Times *in his home in Milwaukee.*

The year was 1936, when television and fax machines and remote-
control compact disc players were science fiction, and a Wisconsin
manufacturer was puzzling over an easier and quicker way to dry clothes.
The idea was a crude, heated box with a rotary drum that could spin
clothes dry. Brooks Stevens, a rising industrial designer before the world
knew it needed one, told the manufacturer there was just one glaring
problem.

"You can't sell this thing," Mr. Stevens said. "This is a sheet metal
box. People won't even know what it is. Who's going to pay $375 for what
looks like a storage cabinet? Put a glass window on the door, get some boxer
shorts flying around in there, put it in the stores, and it'll take off."

"That," Mr. Stevens said, "was the beginning of the clothes dryer."

It was also one of the more ubiquitous of the thousands of innovations spawned by the prolific Mr. Stevens, a founding father of industrial design whose name may not be a household word, but whose
imprimatur is surely felt in every American household. From steam irons
and vacuum cleaners to motorcycles and power lawn mowers, Mr. Stevens
has made life easier for entire generations by turning clunky, function-
over-form contraptions into practical and appealing timesavers that everyone on the block wanted after the Joneses got one.

He is one of the last of a generation of product-design pioneers
whose creations paved the way for the everyday gadgetry that people now
take for granted, like the steam irons that keep people from having to
sprinkle their clothes with water or the cookware with knobs that do not
burn. "He was responsible for not just designing so many things but
designing so many things that had not existed before," said Robert
Schwartz, executive director of the Industrial Designers Society of America. "The body of work he accomplished in his lifetime is staggering to

the imagination of any designer currently in practice. There is a whole list of firsts, firsts, firsts, firsts."

Mr. Stevens is the man who designed the snowmobile, the outboard motor, the mass-marketed Jeep, the Lawn-Boy power lawn mower, the 1950 Harley-Davidson motorcycle, the Hiawatha luxury train, the Oscar Mayer Weinermobile, cars for automakers from Alfa Romeo to Volkswagen, and the first wide-mouth peanut butter jar that allowed people to get to the bottom of the container.

"We're dealing with ancient history here," Mr. Stevens said. "It's archaic by now, but that was the beginning."

His innovations ranged from the whimsical—like a speedboat that was also a helicopter—to the quietly revolutionary. He was one of the first to use color in appliances, first out of boredom with black and white and later out of disgust with what he calls "that rash of avocado green business in the fifties."

Many consider him the Frank Lloyd Wright of industrial design, not surprising since both men were born and raised in Wisconsin and did perhaps their most important work in the Midwest. Now the Milwaukee Institute of Art and Design is building a design center dedicated to the study and preservation of his work.

He got his start in the Depression and helped shape the golden age of industrial design. Many staples of modern-day life were just being thought of, and, in New York, men like Raymond Loewy, and John Vassos, who designed the first radio that did not look like a tombstone, were modernizing consumer products.

Mr. Stevens dropped his studies in architecture at Cornell because of the Depression, and returned to Milwaukee in 1933 to open a studio to redesign machinery. But he had a hard time persuading cash-strapped companies to pay him to reinvent their wheels. In time, he won over manufacturers. "He increased sales and made a lot of manufacturers very happy," said Willie G. Davidson, a vice president of Harley-Davidson and grandson of a company founder.

By the mid-1930s, the country's few industrial designers began publicly calling themselves that and declaring their work "the wedding of art to industry." "What it meant was that product design had to be something more than pure function," Mr. Stevens said. "The argument from an engineer would be, 'If it sawed the wood, that's good enough.' But we say that if it was a good-looking chain saw it would be much more palatable."

Skeptics remain who consider his work trickery and packaging and style over substance. He dismissed such talk and argued that, with the clothes dryer, for instance, his design sold the product. "We made it an understood household appliance by giving life to the thing," he said. "We gave it its appearance, which is what gives it its ability to be used."

To help explain what all this design business was about, some say he coined the phrase "planned obsolescence." "It is the desire to own something a little newer, a little better, a little sooner than is necessary," Mr. Stevens said. Indeed, customers have come to depend on exterior changes—new color, new trim, new size—to tell them that one product is different from the rest. "You can't see function," Mr. Stevens said. "How can you look at a vacuum cleaner and know it works better? The point of purchase, or eye appeal or buy appeal, has to be in the product itself."

Among the most stubborn naysayers were the engineers whose work Mr. Stevens improved upon. He once ran into trouble with the chief engineer of Allis-Chalmers over a jazzed-up design for the Milwaukee company's farm tractors. "What man worries about how a tractor looks?" the engineer told him. "If it plows the field, that's enough." In the end, Mr. Stevens's curvaceous tractors with the teardrop fenders became so popular that farmers even took to driving them to church.

His most enduring contribution, however, may be the everyday fixtures on countertops and in garages, reliable after all these years. "My father-in-law has one of those original 1959 Lawn-Boy lawn mowers," Mr. Schwartz said, "and every weekend it starts on the first pull."

July 11, 1991

Outcast Poet

MIGUEL PINERO

By Mel Gussow

In 1972 I visited the Ossining Correctional Facility (Sing Sing) in order to write about theater in prisons. While I was there, the inmates presented an anthology of their own short plays, monologues, and poems. Twelve of the twenty pieces were written by—and some of them were performed by—one inmate, Miguel Pinero.

It was immediately evident that he had a striking, raw talent, as he demonstrated in a poem he entitled "Gospel." In it, he brought God down to earth, announcing, "In the beginning God created the ghettos and slums/ And God saw this was good/ So God said let there be more." By the seventh day, his God was so tired he "called in sick" and collected overtime. This and other pieces by Mr. Pinero were marked by a bitter humor and a lilting kind of street poetry.

After the show, I spoke with the author. Mr. Pinero was born in Puerto Rico and grew up on the Lower East Side. He said that he had started stealing when he was eight in order to provide food for his seven brothers and sisters, and that he had spent seven of his twenty-five years in prison. Sentenced most recently on a charge of second-degree robbery, he had written poetry in his cell and kept his artistic interest to himself. Then he joined Clay Stevenson's prison workshop where he was encouraged by, among others, Marvin Felix Camillo, an actor and director with the workshop. Mr. Pinero said that when he was released, he planned to go into the theater rather than back on the street.

After reading my subsequent article, Arthur Bartow, director of the Theater at the Riverside Church, contacted Mr. Pinero in prison and asked him if he were writing a full-length play. This began a cycle of events that led, after the inmate's release, to the Riverside production of his play, *Short Eyes*, directed by Mr. Camillo. Wrenched from the author's own experience, *Short Eyes*, a harrowing slice of prison life, was like a message from a combat zone.

In my initial review, I commented on Mr. Pinero's originality and suggested that we would be anticipating and witnessing his work for many years to come. The prediction proved only partly correct. The playwright died of cirrhosis of the liver a few days ago at the age of forty-one.

In 1974, *Short Eyes* went from Riverside to the Public Theater to the Vivian Beaumont Theater in Lincoln Center, deservedly won the New York Drama Critics Circle prize as best American play of the year, and was subsequently made into a film. The success of the play transformed the playwright's life. He became famous while never losing his air of notoriety. Miguel—or Mikey as he was known to his friends—seemed to cherish his role as an outcast, playing it in real life as well as in movies and on television. As an actor, he appeared on such shows as *Miami Vice*, often cast as a drug addict or pusher.

Even as he continued to win acclaim for his plays and his performances, he still had trouble with the law. I was in court the day that a judge dropped a charge against him for using obscene language to a subway attendant. The judge suggested that if he were abusive he should apologize because, as an artist, "other avenues of expression" were open to him, and added, "We're proud of you. You're a talented man."

Outside the courthouse, the Transit Authority officer who had made the arrest shook his hand and praised *Short Eyes*—one of many favorable reviews he was to receive in his lifetime. In a further twist of irony, while Robert Young was directing the film of *Short Eyes* on location in the Tombs, the playwright was being indicted in that same building on charges of grand larceny and possession of heroin.

As Mr. Pinero increasingly became a public personality, he seemed to divert his energies further away from playwriting, spending much of his time helping younger writers. He was one of the founders of the so-called Nuyorican movement, a group of Puerto Rican New York poets, and he edited an anthology of their work called *Nuyorican Poetry*.

But periodically he returned to the theater. Though none of his other plays measured up to *Short Eyes*, several demonstrated the vibrancy of his talent. *Eulogy for a Small-Time Thief, The Sun Always Shines for the Cool, A Midnight Moon at the Greasy Spoon.* His titles as well as his plays were redolent with authenticity. The most provocative was *Midnight Moon*, which treated the author's favorite subject, the underclass, with a lingering sense of hopefulness.

His life and work were celebrated in a memorial at the Public Theater, with relatives and fellow actors and writers paying homage. Joseph Papp, who presented *Short Eyes* at two of his theaters, said that Mr. Pinero was a man of a thousand faces—and before he died, he was wearing his writing face. He was working on a new play called *Every Form of Refuge Has Its Price.* The producer added that Mr. Pinero's effect on other playwrights was not to be underestimated.

Short Eyes was a breakthrough, not only in personal terms, but also as a harbinger of the art that is coming from the Hispanic-American community. In that sense, it served a purpose not unlike that of John Osborne's *Look Back in Anger*, challenging theatrical tradition and preconceptions. *Short Eyes* opened the door to urban reality, and among those who entered was Reinaldo Povod, the author of *Cuba and His Teddy Bear*, and one of a number of emerging young artists who studied with Mr. Pinero.

The playwright never made a secret about his own problems. As he freely confessed in a poem, "A thief, a junkie I've been / committed every known sin."

But that poem also demonstrated a lingering idealism. It began:

Just once before I die
I want to climb up on a tenement sky
to dream my lungs out till
I cry
then scatter my ashes out thru
the lower East Side

Sadly, Mr. Pinero's death came soon after the death of Marvin Felix Camillo. If Mikey was, by his own admission, "bad" (in the Michael

Jackson sense), Pancho Camillo was good, even saintly, a man whose theater group, The Family, is an invaluable resource as a human reclamation project. As playwright and as director, each man went his individual way. The partnership that produced *Short Eyes* was dissolved. But each remained active within the community and both were devoted to former inmates and potential offenders who found that, through theater, they could make a creative contribution to society.

Thinking about Mikey, I remember the enthusiasm with which he greeted my review of *Short Eyes*. It was the first indication that his voice was reaching the outside world, that his message was being received. He telephoned me and vowed an oath of eternal friendship. With the authority of someone who had grown up on the streets, he added that if I ever needed protection, he would see that it was provided. More compassionate words were never said to a critic.

Miguel Pinero's death cuts short what could have been—what should have been—a remarkable career.

July 3, 1988

MARVIN FELIX CAMILLO

Earlier in 1988, MEL GUSSOW, a New York Times drama critic, remembered MARVIN FELIX CAMILLO, another Hispanic-American man of the theater whose life was cut short.

Mr. Camillo, who was born in Newark, began to teach theater workshops at the Bedford Hills state prison in New York in 1972. A professional company evolved from his workshops; its members taught and performed in prisons, drug rehabilitation centers, homes for unwed mothers, and in conventional theaters too. The company under Mr. Camillo's direction was called The Family and it served as a training ground as well as a road to rehabilitation for many former inmates and former addicts. Most of the company's members were blacks and Hispanic people from inner-city areas, like Mr. Camillo himself, whose mother was black and whose father, a boxer, was Mexican.

Mr. Gussow said of him:

In a profession filled with competitiveness, Marvin Felix Camillo was a man of scrupulous decency and goodwill. As the founder of The Family and as a theater director, Pancho, as he was known, never placed personal ambition ahead of his altruistic goal. He dedicated his life to a double-edged purpose—to bring theater into prisons and to encourage former inmates to benefit from the theatrical process.

He discovered Miguel Pinero performing and writing in prison and later directed Mr. Pinero's prize-winning play *Short Eyes* in productions at the Riverside Church, the Public Theater, and Lincoln Center. Then, heartened by the response and seeing the need to expand opportunities for those coming out of prison, he created The Family, providing a home and a stage for former offenders. Through his efforts, the mission of his company spread from the United States to other countries, including France, which now has its own Family.

Pancho Camillo was an inspirer, and when he died January 16 at the age of fifty-one, in France after injuries in an automobile accident, he left a legacy that others will have to live up to. At a memorial service at the Public Theater, Colleen Dewhurst, who was instrumental in organizing The Family, said he was "one of the greatest life forces," Joseph Papp called him "a saint" and the poet Miguel Algarin spoke for all of Mr. Camillo's countless friends and admirers when he said, "Pancho viva!"

January 30, 1988

REINALDO POVOD

After the deaths of Marvin Felix Camillo and Miguel Pinero, much was expected of another young Hispanic-American man of the theater, REINALDO POVOD. But death was to come in threes.

By William Grimes

Reinaldo Povod, the author of the plays *Cuba and His Teddy Bear* and *La Puta Vida Trilogy*, died. He was thirty-four and lived in Brooklyn. The cause was tuberculosis, said Richard Barbour, a friend and colleague.

Mr. Povod (pronounced puh-VAHD) quickly achieved prominence when his first full-length play, *Cuba and His Teddy Bear*, was produced by Joseph Papp in 1986 at the Public Theater and then on Broadway, with Robert De Niro in the role of Joseph Cuba, a Cuban drug dealer, and Ralph Macchio in the role of his sensitive son, Teddy. Although Frank Rich, in *The New York Times*, called the play "messy, wildly overlong and sometimes soppily autobiographical," he judged it a promising start. "Mr. Povod has an ear, a heart and a sense of humor," he wrote.

Mr. Povod grew up on the Lower East Side, the son of a Puerto Rican mother and a Cuban father of Russian descent. At seventeen he was discovered by Bill Hart, the literary manager of the Public Theater, who attended his play *Cries and Shouts* at the Nuyorican Poets Cafe, where Mr. Povod was a protégé of Miguel Pinero. Mr. Hart brought Mr. Povod to the attention of Joe Papp, who invited him to become a resident playwright at the Public.

Mr. Povod's second work there, *La Puta Vida Trilogy* (*This Bitch of a Life*) was presented in 1987. Like *Cuba*, the three one-act plays presented a grim picture of life on the Lower East Side.

At the time of his death, Mr. Povod was at work on a play, *Super Fishbowl Sunday*, with Mr. Barbour.

He is survived by his father, Reinaldo, of Manhattan, and a brother, Edward, of the Bronx.

August 2, 1994

The Thinking Man's Nathan Detroit

HOWARD HIGMAN

By Robert McG. Thomas, Jr.

Howard Higman, the agile-minded academic impresario whose annual World Affairs Conferences at the University of Colorado attracted a dazzling and diverse array of fun-loving intellectuals, died at Boulder Community Hospital. He was eighty.

Officially, Mr. Higman was a sociology professor, but that was merely an academic cover for his role as the thinking man's Nathan Detroit, the founder and proprietor of the oldest established permanent freewheeling gabfest in academia, a week-long extravaganza of discussion and debate that was once compared to a cross between a think tank and a fraternity party.

Whatever it was, it lasted forty-seven years.

Lured by the chance to meet and debate articulate, quick-witted specialists from different backgrounds and disciplines, the conference's participants over the years included such diverse personalities as Eleanor Roosevelt, Henry A. Kissinger, Abba Eban, Henry Steele Commager, Buckminster Fuller, Marshall McLuhan, Brian Wilson of the Beach Boys, Arthur Miller, Ted Turner, Ralph Nader and Roger Ebert, a perennially popular panelist who proved he could hold his own with the reigning resident wits when he inverted Veblen to sum up the weeklong conference as "the leisure of the theory class."

Mr. Higman, the son of a miner turned contractor, was born in a hospital on the University of Colorado campus and grew up, as he once acknowledged, wanting to know everything. A brilliant man known both for the breadth and depth of his knowledge, he apparently majored in art as a Colorado undergraduate and then switched to sociology in its grad-

uate school only because "everything there is to know" was not a recognized discipline.

Although Mr. Higman served on various government committees
over the years and spent four years directing a Vista training program,
his abiding passion was the conference, which he started as a young
instructor in part to offer students at Colorado, known at the time as a
party school, an alternative to skiing—thinking.

The conference, which began with a single speaker in 1948, was
originally designed as a one-shot tribute to the United Nations, but it
proved so popular that the university asked Mr. Higman to make it an
annual event. It attracted major attention in 1953, the height of Senator
Joseph McCarthy's anti-Communist crusade, when Mr. Higman stacked
the panels with speakers who turned the conference into a continuous
attack on the senator's tactics.

A measure of the conference's popularity was that the 125 invited
participants not only received no stipends for spending a week serving
on one panel discussion after another, but also had to pay their way to
Boulder. There, at least, room, board, and local transportation were provided. The panelists bunked with local families and were driven around
town by Colorado students who also served as waiters, bartenders, and
awed acolytes.

Like an astute hostess who makes it a point to seat the duchess next
to the dustman, Mr. Higman, who once arranged a debate between Tim-
othy Leary and G. Gordon Liddy, was a master at orchestrating creative
tensions. Among other things, he required participants to take part in at
least one discussion on a topic they knew nothing about. And to ensure
that his panelists would talk about what they knew and not what they
had boned up on, he made it a point not to disclose the list of topics
or panel assignments until after the participants had gathered in Boulder.

The subjects of the two hundred overlapping panel discussions could
be profound ("Third World Development—Women as a Force of
Change") or prophylactic ("The Resurgent Condom"). Such a rich smor-
gasbord attracted thirty thousand townspeople and Colorado students
each year. Even so, the university suspended the conference earlier this
year, saying it had gotten out of touch with its student interests.

A chief attraction of the conference was Mr. Higman himself, a man of such enormous intellectual range that he taught himself architecture and gardening because he could not afford to hire skilled professionals, and, for the same reason, made himself into an accomplished French chef. For all his brilliance, though, Mr. Higman could also be something of an absent-minded professor. During a stay with a friend in Washington, for example, he once cooked an elaborate meal for thirty guests, but forgot to invite anybody, leaving his host, John Midgley, to eat beef Wellington for three weeks.

Known as everything from dictatorial to lovable, Mr. Higman could sometimes be impatient with the world, especially when it failed to keep up with his own inventive mind. Unwilling to wait for the development of portable telephones, for example, he had seventeen telephones installed in his house so one would always be handy.

He is survived by his wife, Marion, and three daughters, Anne and Elizabeth of Boulder, Colorado, and Alice Reich of Denver, Colorado.

December 1, 1995

Justice the Hard Way

BURNITA S. MATTHEWS

By Linda Greenhouse

Burnita Shelton Matthews, the first woman to serve as a federal district judge, died in Washington, D.C., at the age of ninety-three after a stroke.

Judge Matthews was named to the Federal District Court for the District of Columbia by President Truman in 1949. At the time of her nomination, she was a familiar figure in Washington as a lawyer for the National Woman's Party and an active campaigner for women's rights. Judge Matthews presided over a number of major trials, including the 1957 bribery trial of James R. Hoffa, then vice president of the teamsters union, at which he was acquitted.

She recalled in an interview several years ago that her friendship with a number of senators had blunted opposition to the notion of a woman on the federal bench. When her nomination was being considered, one of the judges on the district court, T. Alan Goldsborough, said publicly that while "Mrs. Matthews would be a good judge," there was "just one thing wrong: she's a woman."

While Judge Goldsborough told her some years later that his opposition had been mistaken, she received an icy welcome from her fellow judges, who agreed among themselves to assign her all the "long motions," the most technical and least rewarding part of the court's docket.

Judge Matthews never retired from the court. In 1968 she took senior status, permitting her to reduce her workload on the district court while also hearing occasional cases in other federal courts in Washington. She sat on the United States Court of Appeals for the District of Columbia and on the United States Court of Customs and Patent Appeals. She continued hearing district court cases until five years ago.

Judge Matthews retained a strong sense of her own role as a pioneer, and never wavered in her commitment to expanding opportunities for women. In a 1985 interview in the *Third Branch*, a newsletter published by the federal court system, she said she had always chosen women to be her law clerks. "The reason I always had women," she said, "was because so often when a woman makes good at something they always say that some man did it. So I just thought it would be better to have women. I wanted to show my confidence in women."

Burnita Shelton decided as a young girl that she wanted to be a lawyer, although professional opportunities in the law were extremely limited for women. She was born December 28, 1894, in Copiah County, Mississippi, where her father owned a plantation and served as clerk of the local chancery court. She often accompanied him to court. But while the family sent her brother to law school, she was sent to the Conservatory of Music in Cincinnati, where she studied voice and piano.

She was teaching piano when the United States entered World War I. Hoping to find a government job that would enable her to go to law school at night, she moved to Washington, passed a Civil Service examination, and took a job with the Veterans Administration. She went to night school at National University Law School, which later became part of George Washington University.

After her graduation in 1919, Mrs. Matthews, then married to a lawyer, Percy A. Matthews, applied to the Veterans Administration for a job as a lawyer. When the agency told her that it would never hire a woman in the legal department, she opened her own law office.

There were other stumbling blocks as well. The local bar association refused to accept her application for membership, returning the check she had sent for membership dues. Judge Matthews included that check among the papers she donated to what is now the Burnita Shelton Matthews Collection at the Arthur and Elizabeth Schlesinger Library on the History of Women in America at Radcliffe College.

Her activities on behalf of women's rights began in law school. In 1919, she was among several dozen women who regularly picketed the White House on Sundays on behalf of women's suffrage. "You could carry a banner," she recalled in the 1985 interview, "but if you spoke, you were arrested for speaking without a permit. So when they asked me why I was there, I didn't answer."

After women got the vote in 1920, she shifted the focus of her activities. She became the lawyer for the National Woman's Party, which was trying to persuade state legislatures to lift legal barriers to women. Mrs. Matthews researched state laws and drafted proposed bills. The National Woman's party owned the property across the street from the Capitol where the Supreme Court's building is now located. In the 1920s, when Chief Justice William Howard Taft proposed acquiring the land for the Court, she went to the Chief Justice's home to try to persuade him to look elsewhere. Her efforts failed, but she represented the party in the condemnation proceedings and won a generous settlement for it.

In the 1940s she also taught at the Washington College of Law, now part of American University. In 1949, President Truman named her to one of twenty new district judgeships that Congress had created to relieve a backlog in district court dockets. Among her rulings was one upholding the right of Black Muslims in the local prison to conduct religious services.

In a 1955 case, she refused to order the State Department to issue a passport to the singer Paul Robeson, who was accused of being a member of the Communist party and of supporting various pro-Communist activities. Mr. Robeson's passport was withheld from 1950 to 1958 and was restored to him when, in a similar case, the Supreme Court ruled the State Department's action unconstitutional.

On the Court of Appeals, Judge Matthews ruled that the Social Security Administration could not cut off disability benefits without a hearing.

In 1984, President Reagan commended her for her "diligence, distinguished efforts, and pioneering spirit."

Her husband died in 1969. They had no children. Judge Matthews is survived by four sisters-in-law and eleven nieces and nephews. She will be buried in the family cemetery in Copiah County, Mississippi.

April 28, 1988

Uncle Seven

BENNY ONG

By Robert D. McFadden

Benny Ong, a Manchurian-born immigrant who rose through underworld struggles in New York to become what law-enforcement officials called the leader of the most powerful organized-crime group in Chinatown over the last twenty years, died at New York Downtown Hospital. He was eighty-seven years old.

The cause of death was not disclosed, but Mr. Ong's family, who had kept a vigil at his bedside in his last days, had said in an interview earlier in the week that he entered the hospital suffering from prostate cancer and pneumonia. In keeping with the secrecy that surrounded much of his life, Mr. Ong, whose real name was Kai Sui Ong, had apparently been hospitalized under a pseudonym.

But Richard Eng, executive secretary of the Hip Sing Association, confirmed that the man long known as the Godfather of Chinatown had died, and he said three days of public ceremonies marking the occasion would be held in Chinatown. Mr. Eng denied that Hip Sing or Mr. Ong were involved in criminal activities, and referred to Mr. Ong as "a very nice old man."

From the pushcart days of the Roaring Twenties through the era of cellular phones and global networks, Mr. Ong was a familiar figure on Pell Street in Chinatown, where he lived and operated, walking about with a cane, consulting associates in the tangled, narrow byways, and sipping tea or playing pai gaw poker with friends.

Mr. Ong, also known as Uncle Seven because he was the seventh child in his family, had the formal title of Adviser in Chief for Life of the Hip Sing Association, the largest of the tongs that have dominated life for a century in the teeming Chinatown district in lower Manhattan, where three hundred thousand people live in forty blocks of shops, factories, restaurants, tenements, and housing projects.

Organized like traditional secret societies in China, tongs are business and neighborhood associations, many with tens of thousands of members and with chapters in cities across the country and abroad. They provide merchants and immigrants with credit unions, social outlets, job markets, and other legitimate services. But law-enforcement officials say the Hip Sing—whose New York headquarters are on Pell Street—and a few other major tong groups have provided cover for wide-ranging, behind-the-scenes criminal activities, from extortion and theft to gambling, smuggling, drugs, prostitution, and murder, using international contacts and employing notorious street gangs to carry out many of their activities.

Mr. Ong has repeatedly been identified by the New York Police Department and federal government investigators as a Hip Sing organized crime leader. A U.S. Senate subcommittee report in 1992 described him as the "so-called Godfather of Chinatown" and leader of the Hip Sing tong, which had used members of the Flying Dragons street gang as its enforcers. While others held executive titles, real power was exercised by Mr. Ong in his advisory role, the report said. "Now in his eighties, Ong has long been associated with organized crime in Chinatown," it continued. "Mr. Ong invoked the Fifth Amendment and refused to answer questions during a staff deposition."

An organizational chart in the report included three tongs in Chinatown besides the 140-year-old Hip Sing—the On Leong Association, which reportedly uses the Ghost Shadows gang; the Tung On Association, reportedly using the Tung On Boys; and the Fukien American Association, reportedly employing a gang known as Fuk Ching.

According to *Chinatown: A Portrait of a Closed Society*, a 1992 book by Gwen Kinkead, Mr. Ong was born in Harbin, China, in 1907 and, following an older brother, arrived in New York in 1923, when he was sixteen. He first worked in a Chinatown laundry and took other menial jobs, and like thousands of young immigrants he soon joined the Hip Sing tong. Inducted by an elaborate ritual that included solemn vows and chanted oaths, swearing blood brotherhood to avenge wrongs to fellow members and to die before cooperating with the police, he made himself available to provide protection or revenge and to fight rival gangs, and by degrees joined Hip Sing's criminal activities and began his rise through the hierarchy, the book says.

Mr. Ong was convicted of second-degree murder in 1935 and went to prison for seventeen years; the origins of the case are obscure, but experts said the word in Chinatown for many years was that he had allowed himself to be framed and imprisoned to protect someone higher in the organization. After emerging from prison in 1952, Mr. Ong resumed his activities in Hip Sing, by then under the presidency of his brother, Sam, and became the organization's leader after his brother's death in 1974, according to Ms. Kinkead.

He went to jail once more in 1977–1978 after a conviction for bribery. "In conversations recorded by investigators, he boasted that he was the payoff man in Chinatown and had numerous friends among district attorneys, police inspectors, and chiefs of detectives," Ms. Kinkead said.

In recent years, as Mr. Ong's health deteriorated, his power is believed to have eroded somewhat; in any case, his death was regarded in his community as the end of an era. Since Mr. Ong was technically a mere adviser to Hip Sing, it will not be necessary to select a replacement leader at the organization's next annual convention in Chinatown, officials note.

August 8, 1994

The Man Who Loved Children

From Douglas Martin in Chinatown after news of Benny Ong's death became known:

People gathered in little groups in coffee shops and in front of the Hip Sing Credit Union and some discussed the old days in Chinatown when residents were almost entirely men who sent their earnings back to their families in China. One person mentioned that Benny Ong's toughness was evident in the fact that everybody was afraid to date his daughter. Another told of the time a man just released from prison threw himself at his feet, begging for mercy for an affront committed before he was incarcerated.

One friend recalled how Mr. Ong, who walked Pell Street with a cane and always had lunch at the same restaurant, tried to give the appearance of never having learned English. Those who knew him well were sure he followed conversations perfectly. He loved children, acquaintances said. His generosity in giving to day-care centers and language schools was remembered more than once.

August 8, 1994

Flowers, Joss Sticks, and Boiled Chicken

From John Kifner:

Benny Ong, Uncle Seven, Adviser in Chief for Life of the Hip Sing tong, the Godfather of Chinatown, lay in state at the Wah Wing Sang Funeral Home the other day, surrounded by enough flowers to cover much of lower Manhattan. Floral wreaths from businessmen, families, and the myriad associations of Chinatown's social network—family organizations like the important Lee family, the Engs, associations from villages and regions in Canton province, home of the original settlers—lined the walls and were stacked up on the floor. Funeral banners hung in long narrow strips, proclaiming Mr. Ong's many qualities, notably from officials of the Nationalist government in Taiwan.

"High Virtue, Great Expectations" read the characters flanking one side of the entrance, where bulky men in tight black suits greeted mourners for the eighty-seven-year old tong leader. The sign on the other side said: "Your success is reflected in the Chinese Community in New York."

Across Mulberry Street, the police, the Drug Enforcement Administration, the FBI and other law-enforcement operatives photographed the mourners from surveillance trucks and observation posts. On a high terrace of the new federal courthouse a long-lensed camera on a tripod recorded the scene.

For decades, Benny Ong and the Hip Sing—and the rival On Leong tong—dominated the shadowy life of Chinatown, a world almost totally isolated from the larger American society, impenetrable to low faan, the universal term for outsiders, meaning "barbarian." But Benny Ong's world—traditional Chinatown, the tight, inward-looking, circumscribed few blocks of homogeneous Cantonese mores, strictly, often harshly, ordered—is, in many ways, being buried along with him.

It was a world created not just by Chinese culture, but American racism. Poor farmers were recruited from Canton in the mid-nineteenth century for the mines and railroads in the West. But by the 1870s, scapegoated for economic depression, pitted against white workers and union organizers, the Chinese were being lynched and murdered. The Chinese Exclusion Act of 1882, barring importation of Chinese laborers, shaped the future; Chinese could not become citizens until 1943.

Some fled the violence to Mott and Pell streets in the 1890s. The Chinese formed an institution called a tong ("meeting hall"), drawing on the tradition and romance of secret Triad societies of the late seventeenth century that challenged invading Manchu rulers. It was a self-help organization, like those of other immigrant groups, but it also provided protection against the larger, hostile society, a means of settling disputes, since no law applied. Tongs, too, ran the high-stakes gambling dens and houses of prostitution that served an almost entirely bachelor society. By loophole and subterfuge, Chinatown grew as men came to climb the Golden Mountain.

Benny Ong arrived in 1923, worked in a laundry at sixteen, and soon took the ritual oath of the Hip Sing. He was a soldier in the Tong Wars raging into the 1930s, where the weapon of choice led to the term "hatchet man" and the crook in Doyer Street became the "bloody angle." In 1935 he was jailed for seventeen years for second-degree murder (taking the fall, it was said, for a higher-up) and in 1974 he became tong boss. He did another year in 1977. Oft-cited in government reports on organized crime, he was said to have spent his final years quietly playing mah-jongg.

The vast, sometimes contradictory changes sweeping the Chinese community stem from the 1965 Immigration Act opening the door to Asians. Chinatown has leapt Canal Street, displacing all but a few carefully preserved restaurant blocks of Little Italy—once a similar closed enclave, where men of mysterious income sipped espresso in unmarked social clubs—and spread to new Chinatowns in Flushing, Queens, and Sunset Park, Brooklyn. The new families are no longer all Cantonese, and the tongs do not rule the outlying areas.

Chinese crime is not ending. Chinese organizations are supplanting the Mafia in heroin. Gangs extort merchants. Fujianese smuggle immigrants, enforcing the thirty-thousand-dollar debt by kidnapping and torture.

But change is inevitable. Joss sticks burned in the funeral home and the old gangster's favorite dish, boiled chicken, was there to sustain him on his trip to the afterworld, along with the bribes that would get him past the devils along the way.

He really couldn't speak about Chinatown, Benny Ong's stepson said politely. He himself worked for IBM.

August 21, 1994

CHINATOWN'S FAREWELL

From SETH FAISON:

With the red flag of a Chinese secret society draped over his body, and a favorite gray fedora laid next to his head, Benny Ong took his last trip through Chinatown yesterday. A parade of more than 120 black limousines extended like a long exclamation mark on his role as the godfather of New York City's most enduring ethnic neighborhood.

The normally noisy, teeming sidewalks slowed to a near silence as residents paused to stare at Mr. Ong's beflowered funeral procession snaking through Chinatown's tiny streets, stopping outside his home on Pell Street, at his tong's headquarters a few doors away, and again at the restaurant where he held court at lunchtime each day.

Just as in Chinese legend, where the heavens weep at the passing of a notable earthling, rain began to fall just moments before Mr. Ong's bronze coffin was carried out on the shoulders of ten men. A brass band called Red Mike's Italian Feast—apparently a holdover from the days when Italians still ran the funeral homes on Mulberry Street—played an old dirge as Mr. Ong's family followed: his adopted son, Eugene, carrying a thick stick of incense; Mr. Ong's second wife, Ong Sinn Ching-yee; five grandchildren; and his only daughter, Yuen-yuk Ong, who, as the lone family member who was visibly distraught, wailed ceaselessly.

August 20, 1994

Simplicity Himself

James J. Shapiro

By Robert McG. Thomas, Jr.

James J. Shapiro, who helped revolutionize the home-sewing industry as a founder and president of the Simplicity Pattern Company, died at his home at the Carlyle Hotel in Manhattan. He was eighty-five. The cause of death was cancer, said his younger brother, Robert M. Shapiro.

Mr. Shapiro, who was born in Borisov, Byelorussia, in 1909 and brought to the United States as a toddler, was a teenager in 1927 when his father, Joseph M. Shapiro, a magazine ad salesman, had an idea that would transform their lives.

At the time, producing dress patterns for the home-sewing market was the exclusive province of McCall's and other women's magazines, including one long-forgotten publication that the elder Mr. Shapiro worked for in New York. When the magazine failed, the father, recognizing the strong appeal of its pattern offerings, decided to form an independent pattern company with his elder son as his partner.

Given the entrenched competition of the women's magazines, the idea was daring, but as implemented by the Shapiros, it had an irresistible appeal. For the first time, women interested in making their own clothes did not have to buy a magazine, then send off for a pattern that might cost as much as twenty-five cents. Instead, they could riffle through an open-top box on the counter of a local store, slap down a dime for a pattern and, as often as not, buy the required fabric in the same store.

As a result, Simplicity, which started off using a single designer and relying on commercial printers, soon dominated the home-sewing market. At its peak in the 1970s, the company, which went public in the 1930s, had four thousand employees, its own paper mill and printing operations, factories in several countries, an extensive catalogue business, twenty thousand retail outlets in the United States alone, and a flourishing sideline supplying patterns to fashion magazines. It also sold more than 150 million patterns a year, accounting for more than half the international home-sewing market. It was, in effect, the world's largest dress manufacturer, one whose vast home-based work force actually paid the company for the privilege of turning its patterns into finished garments.

James Shapiro was given much of the credit for the success. "He was a marketing genius," Sidney Greenman, a former Simplicity director and general counsel, said, noting that it had been Mr. Shapiro who conceived the idea of enlisting chain stores as outlets and who then signed up Woolworth's, a major coup in the 1930s.

He also created a full-scale education department, which supplied high school home economics departments with equipment so millions of teenage girls could learn to sew using Simplicity patterns.

"We were the first to introduce color," Robert Shapiro said. "We were the first to use photography, the first to go to four colors, the first to do a lot of things."

Robert Shapiro acknowledged that his brother had been an appropriately demanding executive in a business in which perfection must be standard (women buying patterns cannot try on a dress before buying), but he denied a widespread report that his brother had fired him as company president. "I retired," he said, citing failing eyesight.

After selling most of his stock in the company, James Shapiro himself retired in 1976, which turned out to be the peak year for the industry. It has shrunk considerably as women have flooded into the work force.

In addition to his brother, Mr. Shapiro is survived by a daughter, Paula Lund of Jupiter, Florida; two grandchildren, and five great-grandchildren.

June 3, 1995

She Saw Through Us

MARTHA ENTENMANN

MARTHA ENTENMANN *was the matriarch of the family that turned a small bakery on Long Island into America's largest and best-known baked goods company.*

She was a saleswoman in 1925 when she married her boss, William Entenmann, Jr., whose father founded the bakery in Brooklyn in 1898. For the next fifty years she took a major role in the company, keeping the books, managing the office after her husband's death in 1951, and sharing managerial decisions with her three sons. When Entenmann's went public in 1976, it was her picture on the company's stock certificates.

By the time she died at the age of eighty-nine, in September, 1996, the family-owned company she helped to build into an empire had been sold several times over, the last time to CPC International as part of an $865 million deal. WENDY WASSERSTEIN, the playwright, remembered her and the slice of America she represented.

The see-through cake box was invented by Martha Entenmann in the same way that Jennie Grossinger built a Catskills resort and Julia Waldbaum created the supermarket bearing her family's name. Of course, I'm exaggerating slightly. But if you're looking for female role models in the fifties, the story of Martha Schneider and her rise from bakery salesgirl to czarina of all the metropolitan strudels was one any girl with a little talent would envy.

Martha married her boss, William Entenmann, when she was nineteen, then expanded their bread-and-rolls trade into a thriving Long Island home-delivery business. After her husband's death, Mrs. Entenmann and her sons realized they could make their cake and sell it too. Quality baked goods at the time came in white paper boxes tied up with red strings. Any child or mouse had to gnaw a small hole in the side to get a preview of the best part of dinner. But an Entenmann pie or chocolate doughnut arrived in that see-through box with a proud blue Entenmann banner. Just that hint of homemade heaven caused those Entenmann baked goods to jump off the shelves in supermarkets from Long Island to Miami.

When parents came to visit their children at summer camp, they brought Entenmann's cookies. When college students pulled an all-nighter, they had Entenmann's doughnuts. When families sat shiva for the dearly departed, they served Entenmann's crumb cake. Entenmann's meant quality goods. Ann Page, Sara Lee, and Betty Crocker had their talents, but Entenmann's, even from the supermarket, was family.

For fifty years, until her retirement fifteen years ago, Mrs. Entenmann took an active role in the family company. This is important to know: Mrs. Entenmann cannot be blamed for the current fascination with "fat-free" baked goods. One wonders if Frank Sinatra would have been quite so obsessed with Entenmann's crumb cake—for years he had them shipped to his home in Palm Springs—if there was absolutely nothing to feel guilty about. Memories of coffee cakes and bundts have much more to do with comfort and pleasure than with abstinence. I like to think Mrs. Entenmann knew that.

Long before there were luncheon panels and seminar weekends devoted to female role models juggling career and domesticity, Mrs. Entenmann helped to run a baking empire and raised a family that extended to nine great-grandchildren. Only someone with that kind of patience, loyalty, and initiative could invent the see-through bakery box top. Martha knew what it took to make it through the night.

December 29, 1996

THE NEW YORK TIMES MAGAZINE

He Didn't Need Scenery

BERNARD B. JACOBS

By Mel Gussow

Bernard B. Jacobs, the president of the mighty Shubert Organization for twenty-four years and one of the most powerful men in the American theater, died at St. Francis Hospital in Roslyn, Long Island. He was eighty and had homes in Manhattan and on Shelter Island. The cause was complications after heart surgery, said Gerald Schoenfeld, chairman of the Shubert Organization.

As joint heads of the Shubert enterprises, the largest and most important theater owner in the country, Mr. Jacobs and Mr. Schoenfeld controlled a formidable cultural and real-estate empire that has had considerable bearing on the American theater and the civic health of New York City. The empire owns and operates sixteen Broadway theaters plus half of the Music Box Theater (with the estate of Irving Berlin), in addition to theaters in Philadelphia, Washington, Boston, and Los Angeles, and other real-estate property.

For more than two decades, everything that transpired on Broadway was heavily influenced by the taste and judgment of the two men, who from adjacent offices in Shubert Alley managed to forge their own inimitable means of sharing their special power. Acting as producers as well as theater owners, Mr. Jacobs and his partner have had more to say than anyone else about what shows opened on Broadway—from *A Chorus Line* to *Cats* to *The Life and Adventures of Nicholas Nickleby* to the Pulitzer Prize–winning *Glengarry Glen Ross* and *The Heidi Chronicles*. At the same time, they also determined what shows closed in their theaters, and when. Although there are other competitive theater owners, none approaches the extensive range of theaters and the sweeping authority of the Shuberts.

With Mr. Jacobs's death, the seventy-one-year-old Mr. Schoenfeld continues as the head of both the theater organization and of the Shubert Foundation. "We lost not only an esteemed colleague," Mr. Schoenfeld said, "but also somebody we believe made a major contribution to this company and the American theater during his forty years in the Shubert Organization."

A somber man, sparing and blunt with his words, Mr. Jacobs very much coveted his privacy. He rarely granted interviews, and his name seldom appears in books about the theater. But behind the scenes, he exercised untold influence. Around Broadway, he and Mr. Schoenfeld were collectively known as "the Shuberts," although they were unrelated to the three Shubert brothers who founded the theater empire early in the twentieth century. Indeed, they rose to the top of the organization largely through chance. And although they stepped into the theater world knowing little about it, the two men are universally credited with taking a faltering theater concern and transforming it into a modern and financially potent enterprise. Some have suggested that they saved commercial theater in New York.

As enduring as the longest-running Broadway hit, Mr. Jacobs and Mr. Schoenfeld perfected the art of perpetuating control. Who their successors would be has been a persistent subject of speculation in the theater world. Neither ever indicated any inclination to retire, nor did they reveal a succession plan. In an interview some years ago, Mr. Jacobs said: "Of all the things in the world I think the least about, it's what happens after you die. Dead is dead."

Mr. Schoenfeld and Mr. Jacobs enjoyed equivalent status within the company, and they shared responsibilities as they saw fit. "It's always been that some deals I make and some deals Gerry makes," Mr. Jacobs said. "There are times when I get sick and tired of dealing with a person and Gerry will take him over. And vice versa. You can get sick of a person fast in this business." In 1994, Mr. Schoenfeld said, "We've had disagreements, but if either one felt so strongly about something and the other didn't, the other would defer." Mr. Jacobs responded, "We've learned to put up with each other's foibles."

Temperamentally as well as professionally, the two men were a study in contrasts, with Mr. Schoenfeld the outside man and Mr. Jacobs the inside man. On opening nights, Mr. Schoenfeld would stand in the aisle before the curtain went up, smiling and embracing the people who had come to his theater, while Mr. Jacobs was more likely to be found in his seat, quietly contemplating the show and its prospects. With his sad, dark-rimmed eyes, Mr. Jacobs had the look of a basset hound, but a basset hound who could tell any potential master to take a walk.

Although Mr. Jacobs often kept his emotions buttoned up, he could be a man of enthusiasm. But he did not let that enthusiasm carry him away into a financial mistake. He was most persuasive in business dealing, a demon in contract negotiations. Sam Cohn, the theatrical agent, said that negotiating with Mr. Jacobs was like "the worst migraine you've ever had in your life." Mr. Jacobs never hesitated to speak what was on his mind. His reply to Mr. Cohn's comment was "I don't like Sam."

In terms of theater as well as people, in the classic Broadway sense, he always knew what he liked, and he had the clout to express his taste and judgment in the Broadway arena. Though some criticized him for being too commercial in his taste, Mr. Jacobs had an innate theatrical savviness, and more than many of his peers, he had a healthy respect for creativity.

Perhaps above all, he liked *A Chorus Line,* and he and Michael Bennett, the creator and director of that landmark musical, played the roles in life of father and surrogate son. Helen diFiglia, Mr. Bennett's mother, said: "Bernie Jacobs was the father Michael never had. Michael treated him that way, and he treated Michael like a son."

Many people were important to the life of *A Chorus Line,* beginning with Mr. Bennett and including Joseph Papp and Bernard Gersten, who produced the musical at the New York Shakespeare Festival Public Theater. Mr. Jacobs, who encouraged the show's move to the Shubert Theater on Broadway, saw both the artistic value and the phenomenal commercial potential. Before *A Chorus Line* opened at the Public Theater, when there was some disagreement about the show's future, Mr. Jacobs told Mr. Bennett that he did not think "dynamite or hell could blow this show out because it was such an overwhelming hit." As in many other cases, he proved to be prescient. The show ran at the Shubert Theater for fifteen years.

Despite occasional differences about individual projects, he and Mr.

Bennett remained close throughout the director's life, and in his home in Manhattan and on Shelter Island, he kept memorabilia of Mr. Bennett and the musical that made him famous. Mr. Bennett died in 1987 at the age of forty-four.

The plays and musicals that Mr. Jacobs and Mr. Schoenfeld jointly produced represent a broad cross-section of the American and English theater. Among them are *Nicholas Nickleby*, Stephen Sondheim's *Sunday in the Park with George* and *Passion*, *The Gin Game*, *Amadeus*, *Jerome Robbins's Broadway*, and *Indiscretions*. In the 1996 season, the Shuberts are producing David Hare's *Skylight*. Naturally, there were major failures, too, like the musical *Chess*, but for the Shuberts, those tended to be forgotten.

Despite his immense influence, Mr. Jacobs resolutely avoided the spotlight. "Bernie was the most unpretentious man I ever met—and this in a field in which names mean everything," said Dasha Epstein, a Broadway producer and a close friend of Mr. Jacobs and his wife, Betty. "He was a man who didn't need scenery."

In private, he was known for his sharpness. The producer Albert Poland said he recalled hearing him on the telephone with Baron de Rothschild, saying angrily: "I can't give you tickets. I'm in the business of selling tickets." Then he hung up and explained that the Baron wanted him to donate all the tickets to a performance of *Cats* for a benefit. "What is he?" said Mr. Jacobs, "Just a man with a "de" in front of his name."

Mr. Jacobs was born in Manhattan in 1916. His father ran a woolen waste business, in which he assembled scraps of material from clothing businesses and resold them. Mr. Jacobs graduated from De Witt Clinton High School, New York University, and Columbia University Law School. After serving in the army in the South Pacific in World War II, he practiced law with his brother, dealing mainly with jewelry companies.

Since the turn of the century, the Shubert brothers—Sam, Lee, and J. J.—had been a dominant force in the American theater. By 1914, their empire of 350 theaters stretched from New York to California. In 1950, the federal government brought an antitrust suit against the organization, and in 1956, the Shuberts were forced to sell part of their holdings and to relinquish their role in theatrical booking.

In 1957, Mr. Schoenfeld became the company's primary lawyer. The next year, J. J. Shubert suggested that Mr. Schoenfeld hire another lawyer to help him, and Mr. Schoenfeld brought in Mr. Jacobs, a high school friend of Mr. Schoenfeld's older brother. Mr. Jacobs had first met Gerald Schoenfeld when he was eight, during one of his visits to his house to play cards.

Mr. Jacobs reported for work at the Shubert offices on St. Patrick's Day, 1958. As a welcoming gesture, J.J. Shubert made clear to Mr. Schoenfeld that he would be held accountable for anything that Mr. Jacobs did wrong.

After J.J. Shubert died in 1963, his will turned over the bulk of his estate, including the theaters, to the Shubert Foundation, which until then had been a small and little-known arm of the theater company. During an unruly power struggle among irreconcilable directors, Mr. Jacobs and Mr. Schoenfeld managed to move to the top of the integrated enterprise in 1972.

It was not an auspicious time for the company or for Broadway, and neither man began with any theater background. As new theatrical entrepreneurs and real-estate owners, they began investing money in plays and acting as producers. By 1974, Mr. Jacobs felt that the Shubert empire was back on track. "Last year was terrible," he said. "Two years ago was disasterville. Qualitatively and quantitatively, this season is the best in years." That season in Shubert houses included *Equus, Pippin, Grease,* and *Sherlock Holmes.* The next year, there was *A Chorus Line,* which put the operation on solid footing.

For years controversy followed Mr. Jacobs and Mr. Schoenfeld. In 1974, State Attorney General Louis J. Lefkowitz filed civil charges against Mr. Jacobs and Mr. Schoenfeld, as well as the executors of J.J. Shubert's estate, saying there had been "grossly excessive" claims. The charges were withdrawn in return for a reduction in the claims. Further scandal enveloped the Shuberts when Irving Goldman, who shared power with Mr. Jacobs and Mr. Schoenfeld, was indicted three times in the 1970s on various corruption charges though he was never prosecuted.

Both Mr. Jacobs and Mr. Schoenfeld benefited greatly from a highly unusual and little-known tax ruling in 1979 that gave the Shubert Foundation an exemption to federal tax laws that declare that private charities generally can not own a controlling stake in a profit-making business. Without the ruling, the foundation would have had to divest itself of the theaters, and there is no telling where Mr. Jacobs and Mr. Schoenfeld would have ended up. By keeping the empire intact, Mr. Jacobs and Mr. Schoenfeld continued as heads of both the foundation and the theater organization. Under the tax ruling, the organization's profits are taxed at the normal corporate rate, but what remains after taxes can flow to the foundation and be invested to produce tax-free income for the foundation.

To a great extent, the two lawyers succeeded in giving the company a different image, partly through the success of the shows in their houses, but also through the increased activity of the Shubert Foundation. The foundation, whose value is estimated at more than $149 million, provides support to nonprofit theaters and dance companies. Mr. Jacobs also introduced computerized methods of ticket sales, linking his box offices to Ticketron outlets in other cities.

Mr. Jacobs was vice president of the League of American Theaters and Producers and an adjunct professor of theater at Columbia University's School of the Arts. In 1992, he was awarded the Actors' Fund Medal, and in 1995 Columbia Law School presented him with a Distinguished Achievement Award.

Although he may have seemed like a pessimist, Mr. Jacobs was actually more of a realist, who could be buoyed by his anticipation of the next show, the next season. But in 1986, he suddenly woke up one morning and didn't know where he was or who was President of the United States. He was told he had transient global amnesia. Apparently the condition vanished, but in recent years rumors persisted that he was not well. A month before his death, however, he was in London scouting the theater.

In addition to his wife, he is survived by a daughter, Sally Jacobs Baker of Manhattan; a son, Steven, of Oyster Bay; a sister, Edith Kaufman, of Manhattan, and three grandchildren.

August 28, 1996

The Princess Honeychile

HONEYCHILE WILDER

By Robert McG. Thomas, Jr.

Honeychile Wilder is dead, and if the "21" Club is not in actual mourning, it's because the venerable former speakeasy on West Fifty-second Street was closed for vacation when word got around that one of its most memorable former patrons had died at Memorial Sloan-Kettering Cancer Center.

Her original name was Patricia Wilder, and at her death at the age of seventy-six, she was officially known as Princess Alexander Hohenlohe. But from the moment she hit town in the 1930s and took New York by storm, the woman from Georgia who called everybody "honeychile" was never called anything but that herself. Even after she married a German prince and became a celebrated international hostess, she was known as Princess Honeychile.

By her own account, within a day of her arrival in New York in 1934 she had been hired as a show girl and was appearing with Bob Hope at the Palace Theater. The gig led to a lifelong friendship, a number of appearances on Bob Hope's radio show, some forgettable movie roles, a series of unforgettable encounters at New York nightclubs, and eventually to a series of celebrated liaisons, including a dalliance with King Farouk.

"She was a character," said her friend, Susie Schneider, who reported that the Princess, a longtime resident of Marbella, Spain, had died of lymphoma.

She may not have been the actual prototype of Truman Capote's Holly Golightly, his *Breakfast at Tiffany's* heroine, as some said. If not, it was probably because Mr. Capote was only sixteen years old in 1941 when Miss Wilder was charging New York nightlife with her special brand of electricity.

There was hardly a night the slender dark-haired beauty with the affecting Southern drawl couldn't be found at the Colony or the Monte Carlo for dinner, followed by stops at the Stork Club, the Cafe Pierre, and El Morocco. She had lunch at "21" so often that the bartender there created a Honeychile drink in her honor (a whiskey sour made with honey rather than sugar). In those halcyon days, Condé Nast sent his limousine to take her to black-tie dinners at his town house, George Gershwin asked her to sit next to him at the piano while he was composing "Porgy and Bess," and she went barhopping with Walter Winchell and his pal J. Edgar Hoover.

She had a well-chronicled affinity for millionaires, one that would probably have raised fewer eyebrows if their wives had been more understanding. One who apparently was not was Beverly Paterno, whose husband was the heir to a real-estate fortune, calculated at $63 million in 1941 dollars. What was said between the two women at the Cafe Pierre on the night of February 22, 1941, was not recorded, but Honeychile's riposte made headlines the next day: She peppered her rival with a flurry of rights and lefts, then doused her with a pitcher of water.

Honeychile wondered what all the fuss was about. After all, by her own claim, she had done much the same thing to the date of her former beau Alfred Bloomingdale at another nightclub a few years earlier.

Although she said she had attended a finishing school in Charlottesville, Virginia, there was some evidence that she hadn't been all that finished. As she once told an interviewer, "Everybody was my friend, but I wasn't in love with nobody."

That apparently changed when she met Prince Alexander. After her husband's death in 1984, the Princess, who lived in a small house in Marbella (where a wealthy Hohenlohe cousin owns the Marbella Club), spent much of her time visiting rich friends around the world.

She is survived by a brother, Henry Wilder, of Macon, Georgia.

August 20, 1995

Philanthropic Loner

GEORGE T. DELACORTE

By Marilyn Berger

George T. Delacorte, the founder of Dell Publishing and a philanthropist who gave millions to embellish New York City with fountains, statues, theaters, and schools that bear his name, died at his home in Manhattan. He was ninety-seven years old and also lived in North Palm Beach, Florida, and Sharon, Connecticut. A son, Albert, said Mr. Delacorte had not been ill and apparently died in his sleep of natural causes.

Mr. Delacorte made his fortune publishing everything from penny-a-word mysteries and romances to comic books and the novels of best-selling authors. But his name became chiseled into the consciousness of New Yorkers as the man who gave them the Delacorte Clock, the Delacorte Fountain, the Delacorte Amphitheater in Central Park and, at Columbia University, the Delacorte Professorship in the Humanities and the Delacorte Center for Magazine Journalism.

His most popular contribution may be the enchanting Alice in Wonderland statue that he placed in what he called "the finest spot in Central Park" in 1959. The statue, just north of the Conservatory Pond, was given as a memorial to his first wife, Margarita, because, it was said, she used to read *Alice's Adventures in Wonderland* to their six children. "I don't know," he said. "It's a good story. It just seemed a nice thing to have in the park. On Sunday mornings I watch the kids climbing over it, under it. It's a regular parade."

Not far away to the south is the Delacorte Clock at the Children's Zoo, a whimsical carousel with a dancing bear, an elephant playing a concertina, a kangaroo with a horn, and other animal figures that perform every half hour to the music of a glockenspiel. "I like whimsical things,"

Mr. Delacorte said. He went all the way to Italy to find the right sculptor—Andrea Spadini—for his clock. "When he sculpted a bear, it looked like a bear," he said approvingly. "When he sculpted a dog, it looked like a dog."

To the west is the Delacorte Amphitheater, home to Shakespeare in the Park. A mobile Delacorte Theater makes it possible to take Shakespeare to other parks around the city. At Columbus Circle and at Bowling Green and at City Hall are Delacorte fountains.

In 1975 he gave seven hundred and fifty thousand dollars to Columbia, his alma mater, to establish the Delacorte Professorship in the Humanities. In 1982 Columbia awarded him an honorary doctorate after he had contributed the ornamental iron gates that formed the entry to the university and had paid for the planting of cherry trees, shrubs, and ivy ground cover on the campus. Three years later, Mr. Delacorte, by then in his nineties, gave Columbia two million two hundred and fifty thousand dollars to create the George T. Delacorte Center for Magazine Journalism. He then pledged an additional two million dollars to establish a chair in his name.

But of all his contributions, his own favorite remained the Delacorte geyser at the tip of Roosevelt Island. He and his wife called it "Delacorte's Folly." In 1969, Mr. Delacorte conceived the idea that New York should have a geyser equal to the Jet d'Eau in Lake Geneva, Switzerland.

His geyser, at four hundred feet, was to be the highest fountain in the world, but many New Yorkers were outraged that, when built, the three-hundred-and-fifty-thousand-dollar jet spewed polluted East River water into the air. He was forced to chlorinate the fountain, but the chlorination withered trees that Sutton Place residents had placed on the island to improve their view. Mr. Delacorte was more annoyed than moved by the complaints. He said his geyser was there before the trees. In an editorial when the fountain was installed, *The New York Times*, citing the city's crucial needs and noting that the money might have been put to better use instead of being thrown "literally down the drain," called him "the Wrong Way Corrigan of New York philanthropy."*

---

*Beset by mechanical problems and unloved by New Yorkers, the geyser is no more. It was turned off in 1986. In wet years it looked "like a sewer outfall," said the city's

In his nineties, when he was asked whether he had given any thought to using the three hundred and fifty thousand dollars to help the poor, he said, "People are poor because they're dumb or because they're lazy. If you feed them you just keep them in the same strata."

Mr. Delacorte was a philanthropic loner who did not like to serve on the boards of museums or schools or hospitals. "I hate hospitals," he said. Instead, he gave money where and when he liked to and for whatever struck his fancy. Only once did he join with others. That was in 1964, when he helped create a group called Make New York Beautiful Inc. to "promote interest and aid in the donation of permanent improvements to the City of New York for its cultural advancement and beautification." With the straightforwardness that characterized his public comments, he said, "We want guys who are going to kick off, and want to do something for the city before they do, to give maybe a hundred thousand or five hundred thousand dollars."

George Thomas Delacorte, Jr., was born in New York City on June 20, 1893. He attended Boys High and went to Harvard before switching to Columbia, where he graduated in 1913. By that time he was married and brought his first son to his graduation ceremony. Afterward, determined not to be a lawyer as his father was, Mr. Delacorte went to work for a small publishing company.

He was dismissed, but the company paid him ten thousand dollars he had been promised in his contract, enough to found his own company, Dell Publishing. It was 1921 and the beginnings were small—two employees and one title, *I Confess*. Soon, he was turning out dozens of pulp magazines with penny-a-word stories: *Cupid's Diary, Screen Stories,* and *Inside Detective.*

A satirical magazine, *Ballyhoo,* became a huge success. But there was a gimmick. *Ballyhoo* came wrapped in a new invention called cellophane and carried the slogan: "Read a fresh magazine." By the fourth issue, more than two million copies had been sold.

Park Commissioner Henry J. Stern. In drought years city officials expressed concern the geyser might be regarded as a symbol of conspicuous consumption—even though the water, most of which fell back into the East River, was unlikely to be consumed by anybody.

Soon Mr. Delacorte was on his way to building his fortune, sup-plemented by millions that he earned through an investment in Ballantine Beer just as Prohibition was ending.

His pulp magazines were soon joined by comic books featuring Woody Woodpecker and Bugs Bunny and the Walt Disney characters, from Mickey Mouse to Pluto. Dell was selling three hundred million comic books a year, with Walt Disney comics alone sometimes accounting for three million copies in a single month.

Long before women were given responsible positions in business, Mr. Delacorte hired Helen Meyer, still in her twenties, who was to be-come a major force at Dell and in American publishing. When he was ninety-two, Mr. Delacorte still remembered why. "I'm a great believer in hiring women," he said. "If you have a capable man and your competitors know about it they'll start propositioning him. Women are more loyal. Women of course have their shortcomings . . . They leave to have babies."

Mrs. Meyer recalled that on the day her daughter was born a tele-gram arrived from her boss—who was the first to admit that he liked to see his name on monuments and fountains. "If you don't name her after me," he wired, "you can't have your job back." The baby was called Adele. She said her second baby was a boy and Mr. Delacorte wanted him to be called Cort. She named him Robert.

After World War II, Dell became one of the major American pub-lishers of paperback books. In 1963, Dell formed Delacorte Press prin-cipally to assure itself a continuing supply of material for the paperback division. Among the authors who came to Delacorte to be published first in hard-cover editions and later in Dell paperbacks were Kurt Vonnegut, James Clavell, Irwin Shaw, James Jones, Danielle Steel, Belva Plain, and Robert B. Parker.

Although Mr. Delacorte nominally retired in 1976 when Dell was sold to Doubleday & Company for $35 million in cash, he continued to walk to an office he kept in midtown during the months that he and his second wife, the former Valerie Hoecker, spent in New York.

He met the second Mrs. Delacorte in 1959 at a party in his home three years after his first wife died. A widow, and once considered the most beautiful woman in Hungary, she arrived at the party with the Maharaja of Jaipur and his wife. When Mr. Delacorte introduced himself, he led her out into the gallery where he started showing her pictures of his eighteen grandchildren. "A very sexy approach," she recalled. Mr. Delacorte said, "She fell in love with my grandchildren so she married me."

In 1985, he sold their apartment on Fifth Avenue—"We had twenty-four rooms and all of them were occupied"—and moved a few blocks down the avenue to a six-room pied-à-terre, which they used when they were not in their oceanfront home in Florida or at their Connecticut estate. The New York apartment was filled with paintings he had collected over the years, including a Rubens, a Canaletto, a Corot, and several from the school of Rembrandt.

Mr. Delacorte always said he liked to see something tangible for his money, especially if it would have his name on it. He said the inspiration for his sort of philanthrophy was the Pulitzer Fountain in front of the Plaza Hotel, which he passed each day when he walked to work. He had been enchanted by fountains since childhood, when he first visited the great fountains of Europe. Mr. Delacorte said he briefly considered making improvements to the fountain that was donated by the late Joseph Pulitzer and that had long given forth with more of a dribble than a gush. "But it still would have been the Pulitzer Fountain," he concluded with an impish smile. "So, being selfish, I let it go." He built his own fountain instead, at Bowling Green, in lower Manhattan.

Mr. Delacorte was never reluctant to write a check when it came to Central Park. Thomas Hoving, the city's Parks Commissioner in 1966 and 1967, remembered a scheme he had devised to relieve Mr. Delacorte of some of his money. He set up tables at the Bethesda Fountain, and knowing that Mr. Delacorte always came that way as he walked to work, got some photographers to hide in the bushes to await his arrival. On schedule, Mr. Delacorte walked by, saw Mr. Hoving, and asked what was going on. Mr. Hoving replied that he was trying to set up a restaurant but needed fifty thousand dollars. On cue the two photographers popped out of the bushes to ask Mr. Delacorte what he was doing there. Without missing a beat, Mr. Delacorte replied, "I have decided to sponsor this wonderful thing in the park."

When Mr. Hoving confessed that he had set him up, Mr. Delacorte told him, "Next time just pick up the phone and ask me." The Bethesda

Terrace restaurant was a success for a while but closed after a few years, and the city decided to restore the terrace to its original design.

When the twenty-five-hundred-seat amphitheater in the park was about to be abandoned for lack of funds, Mr. Delacorte came through with an unsolicited gift of one hundred fifty thousand dollars for its completion and added another fifty thousand dollars later. In 1964 he gave thirty-five thousand dollars for a mobile stage for the Shakespeare theater and in 1970 gave another thirty thousand dollars to the Shakespeare Festival.

During his last years Mr. Delacorte continued to take long walks in Central Park, even after a mugging in December 1985, when one attacker grabbed him and another held a knife to Mrs. Delacorte, taking her new mink coat.

Mr. Delacorte was an avid storyteller in his later years. One day, however, when he was in the middle of an anecdote he lost his train of thought. "You know," he said, "at ninety-two the memory is the first thing to go." He paused for a moment and said, "Well, to tell you the truth, the first thing that goes is sex. Then your memory goes. But the memory of sex never goes."

He remained tanned and trim throughout his life—"I weigh 139 pounds, same as I did in college," he said. He stopped playing tennis when he was ninety-one but continued to play golf. Had he ever been seriously ill? "I caught a cold once," he said.

In addition to his wife and his son Albert, Mr. Delacorte is survived by another son, Malcolm, of Cornwall, New York; three daughters, Consuelo Carson of McLean, Virginia, Marianne Holland of Cos Cob, Connecticut, and Margarita of Manhattan; a sister, Letty Osserman, and a brother, Eugene, both of New York; eighteen grandchildren, and nineteen great-grandchildren.

May 5, 1991

A Woman of the Century

RACHEL NEUFELD

By Robert D. McFadden

On Saturday night, at the Brooklyn intersection she crossed on her way home every evening after twilight, Rachel Neufeld went down under the right front wheel of a city bus and was crushed to death. She was seventy years old, and a woman unknown in a city where fame and riches are the ordinary measure of a life.

The details of the accident at Avenue J and Bay Parkway in Midwood were hazy and under investigation, the police and the Transit Authority said, though the driver was on probation for reasons that were unclear yesterday, so no one was able to say precisely how or why Mrs. Neufeld had been killed.

But after her funeral at a Jewish chapel in Borough Park yesterday, as her family sat shiva at her apartment at 1134 East Second Street, two blocks from the accident scene, her sister, Anna Klein, choked back tears and said some of the things that needed to be said about a small graceful woman of the twentieth century.

She was an intelligent, courageous woman, Mrs. Klein said, and had come halfway around the world since the 1920s from their village in Czechoslovakia. It was a journey that had taken her to the Nazi death camp at Auschwitz, where she lost everyone but her sister; to Bremerhaven, where she made German bombs in a cavern while Allied bombs shook the earth; to a Saxony woods, where she ate grass and leaves and waited for liberation; to postwar transit camps in Budapest and Vienna; to Jerusalem, and finally to New York.

She had survived the Holocaust, married, given birth to a daughter and a son. She had worked at job after job—sweatshops, day care centers, kitchens, and offices—to send her children to college, to see them settled, one as a school principal and the other as a banker. And she had somehow retained her faith and an appreciation for the world at her fingertips.

"We walked together on Ocean Parkway—it was Shabbat," Mrs. Klein said of her last day with her sister. "It was cloudy. I like this kind of day. But she said, 'Oh, what a lot of lovely flowers.' I am very cynical about flowers. None of them are related to me. She was angry with me. 'You don't have a sense of beauty,' she said. She enjoyed every leaf, every blade of grass.

"And now," she added, the accents of her East European childhood still husky in her throat, "I am devastated. I don't know where to put myself, or how I will get up in the morning."

She was born Rachel Zhwartz on February 3, 1925, in what was then known as Sevlus, a town of fourteen thousand—including four thousand Jews—in southwest Czechoslovakia. She had an older sister, Gabriella, who had been born in 1922. Her younger sister, Anna, was born in 1926. Their family had been in the wine business for many years and the three sisters lived in a big house on the main street with their mother, Ilona, and father, Martin, who was secretary to the Jewish community.

Mrs. Klein remembered the day the Nazis arrived: March 19, 1944.

"There was no time to hide," she said. "They came in with their tanks. There was no time. They had guns and we were taken away. They took all the Jews in town and put us into a ghetto in the poorest part of town. We had nothing but the clothes on our backs. We were in a room with thirty-two people packed on the floor, and we were kept there for two months until May.

"Then they took us to Auschwitz—in a railroad train, in cattle cars. It was horrible: It was the three of us and our parents and, by then, my sister Gabriella had a baby thirteen months old."

When they arrived at the infamous arch, *"Arbeit Macht Frei"* (Work Makes You Free), Rachel and Anna were separated from the other members of the family. "We, the two of us, were sent to the shaving of the hair, and then to the barracks," Mrs. Klein said. "We never saw our family again."

She remembered the torments in the barracks—the terrible conditions, the forced labor, and the waiting; the only consolation was that the sisters, Anna and Rachel, were together. "We were waiting for our turn," she said, "but our time didn't come. They demanded labor and we were chosen."

In August, in an extraordinary reprieve apparently made possible by the Nazis' need for slave labor in the production of war matériel, Mrs. Klein said she and Rachel were sent to northern Germany, to a cavernous underground plant near Bremerhaven, where they helped construct bombs for the Luftwaffe. She told of terrifying days and nights working on bombs while the earth shook from explosions as Allied bombers roared overhead. "But we were together," she said. "Rachel and I kept together like two fallen birds."

Through autumn, winter, and into the spring of 1945, the Allied bombing grew heavier. Then April arrived. "Two days before the end, there were 40 percent casualties," she said. "The Germans took us out then from where we worked. They wanted us as security when the liberators came. But it never worked out. They got scared and ran. We were left in the middle of the woods. We ate grass and finally the British came and took us out."

After the war, they wanted to go to Israel, but found themselves in the limbo of a transit camp in Budapest, where they stayed for four years and where both were married—Rachel in 1946 to Zev Neufeld, a Hungarian twenty years her senior, who had lost his first wife and a daughter at Auschwitz; and Anna in 1948 to Samuel Klein. The two couples were inseparable and in 1949 they went to live in the newly independent State of Israel, settling in Jerusalem.

Mrs. Neufeld's first child, Chaya, was born that year, and her son, Shimshon, was born in 1955, Mrs. Klein said. A decade later, she said, they all agreed to move to America, but there were immigration quotas and it could not be done quickly or easily. "Sam and I came first in 1959 through a transit camp in Vienna," she said. "We were on the quota. Rachel and her family came in 1960. We arranged it through a friend who vouched for them. There were immigration restrictions, and these friends had property and a business and said they would not be a burden on the state."

Mr. Neufeld did "manual work, hard work, anything he could find" and later became a bookkeeper and a rabbi who sometimes helped supervise the production of kosher food, she said. Meanwhile, her sister, too, went to work to help raise the family, laboring in what she called sweatshops and taking jobs in day care, cooking, and office work.

"She always worked," Mrs. Klein said. "They saved and saved to raise their children and send them to college." Chaya and Shimshon both attended Brooklyn College, and Chaya went to graduate school at Hofstra University, receiving two master's degrees. Shimshon became a foreign exchange broker for Chemical Bank and lives in Brooklyn with his wife, Olivia Gross-Neufeld, a lawyer, and their two children, she said. Chaya became the principal of an elementary school in New Jersey. She lives in Morganville, New Jersey, with her husband, Thomas Friedman, a writer and professor of English who commutes to Syracuse University, and their two children.

"She was so proud of her children," Mrs. Klein said of her sister. "Children—if everybody would be like them, it would be a good world."

Mrs. Neufeld stopped working five years ago, when she was sixty-five, but never gave up her daily twenty-minute walks to the home of her sister at 1233 East Ninth Street. After Mrs. Klein's husband died two years ago, her sister's love and quiet courage were crucial, she said. They often strolled in the neighborhood in the late afternoon or early evening, talking quietly in the dusk. "She could look into my heart," Mrs. Klein said. She recalled her sister as small, five feet two inches tall, with dark brown eyes and a good sense of humor, an intelligence and wit that a hard, tragic life had not trampled.

The police said the accident occurred at 9:30 at night as Mrs. Neufeld was crossing Avenue J from north to south. They said a city bus driven by James Greene, twenty-eight, struck and killed her instantly as it turned south onto Bay Parkway. While the incident was under investigation, the police called it an apparent accident.

"After all we had been through, we held on to each other for dear life," Mrs. Klein said. "I come from a family—my father, mother, Gabriella, Marta her baby—they all died the most awful violent deaths. I am the only survivor of that family. The tragedy is indescribable. And I don't know why, but I can't cry."

April 10, 1995

The Junkie Muse

HERBERT HUNCKE

By Robert McG. Thomas, Jr.

Herbert Huncke, the charismatic street hustler, petty thief, and drug addict who enthralled and inspired a galaxy of acclaimed writers and gave the Beat Generation its very name, died at Beth Israel Hospital. He was eighty-one. The cause was congestive heart failure, said Jerry Poynton, his friend and literary executor.

Mr. Huncke (whose name rhymes with "junkie") had lived long enough to become a writer himself and a hero to a new generation of adoring artists and writers, not to mention a reproach to a right-thinking, clean-living establishment that had long predicted his imminent demise.

In an age when it was hip to be hip, Mr. Huncke was the proto-typical hipster, the man who gave William S. Burroughs his first fix, who introduced Jack Kerouac to the term "beat," and who guided them, as well as Allen Ginsberg and John Clellon Holmes, through the nether world of Times Square in the 1940s. They in turn honored him by making him an icon of his times. He became a major character (Herman) in Mr. Burroughs's first book, *Junkie* (1962). He was Ancke in Mr. Holmes's 1952 novel, *Go*. He appears in innumerable Ginsberg poems, including "Howl" (1956)—with its reference to his "shoes full of blood on the snowbank docks waiting for a door in the East River to open a room of steamheat and opium."

And if it was the fast-talking, fast-driving Neal Cassady who became Mr. Kerouac's chief literary obsession, as the irrepressible Dean Moriarty in Mr. Kerouac's 1957 breakthrough classic, *On the Road*, Mr. Huncke (who was Elmo Hassel in *On the Road*) was there first. As Junkey, he was the dominant character in the urban half of Mr. Kerouac's first book, *The*

Town and the City, and made later appearances as Huck in *Visions of Cody* and *Book of Dreams.*

All this for a teenage runaway who said he was using drugs as early as twelve, selling sex by the time he was sixteen, stealing virtually anything he could get his hands on throughout his life, and never once apologizing for a moment of it. "I always followed the road of least resistance," he said in a 1992 interview. "I just continued to do what I wanted. I didn't weigh or balance things. I started out this way and I never really changed."

Actually, he didn't quite start out that way. Born into a middle-class family in Greenfield, Massachusetts, on January 9, 1915, he moved with his family to Detroit when he was four and two years later to Chicago, where his father ran his own machine-parts distributing company. By his own accounts he seems to have had an uneventful early childhood, but his parents divorced, and by the time he was in his early teens he was on the street, acquiring a lifelong passion for drugs and discovering the joys—and lucrative possibilities—of sex with men. He was also beginning a life of crime, first as a runner for the Capone gang and later as a burglar and thief.

Hitting the road early, he served for a time with the Civilian Conservation Corps during the Depression. He traveled around the country until 1939, when he arrived in Manhattan and found a psychic home in Times Square. Making his base of operations the Angle bar at Forty-second Street and Eighth Avenue, he sold drugs at times and himself at others, not always with notable success. Mr. Huncke once confided to a friend that he had not been a successful hustler: "I was always falling in love."

It was in 1945 that an elegantly dressed man in a Chesterfield coat knocked on the door of an apartment where Mr. Huncke was living. The visitor, who was in search of Mr. Huncke's roommate in the hope of selling him a sawed-off shotgun, was Mr. Burroughs. Mr. Huncke would recount that he took one look and told his roommate to get rid of him. "He's the FBI," he said.

Mr. Burroughs proved anything but, and within days Mr. Huncke had introduced him to heroin and sealed a lifelong friendship that included a 1947 visit to a marijuana farm Mr. Burroughs had started in Texas. It was through Mr. Burroughs that Mr. Huncke soon met Mr.

Ginsberg, then a Columbia University undergraduate, and Mr. Kerouac, a recent Columbia dropout who became so enchanted with Mr. Huncke's repeated use of the carny term "beat," meaning tired and beaten down, that he later used it as his famous label for the Beat Generation. (Mr. Kerouac later clouded things by suggesting it was derived from "beatific.")

An aspiring, Columbia-centered literary crowd was soon learning at Mr. Huncke's feet. Among other things, he introduced them to the sex researcher Alfred Kinsey, who after meeting Mr. Huncke at the Angle had interviewed him about his colorful sex life and hired him to recruit other subjects. Though it seemed strange to some people that such a wide array of literary figures found Mr. Huncke so enchanting, he was always more than he seemed. For all his disreputable pursuits, he had elegant, refined manners and a searing honesty. He was also uncommonly well read for someone who had never been to high school, and such a natural and affecting storyteller that he could keep a table of admirers enthralled until the wee hours.

He also had a code of honor. Yes, he might steal from his pals if he needed a fix, but he did not inform on them, something he proved on a number of occasions when the police sought his help in developing charges against his celebrity friends.

Mr. Huncke, who spent a total of eleven years in prison, including almost all of the 1950s, was unrepentant, a man whose acceptance of crime as his fate bolstered his friends' views that he was a victim of a rigid, unfeeling society.

If his friends saw him as fodder for their literary work, Mr. Huncke, as he later claimed, saw them as marks. There is, perhaps, a certain paradox in Mr. Huncke's use of his literary friends as his own literary fodder. Mr. Huncke himself began writing in the 1940s, locking himself in a stall in the men's room in the subway. He described it as the only place he could work in peace, scribbling away in his notebooks.

Taking the Kerouac idea of writing nearly automatic prose even further than Mr. Kerouac did, Mr. Huncke turned out a series of memoirs that have been praised for their unaffected style. Those who heard him regale listeners say his books read as if he were telling a spontaneous anecdote around a table at the Angle. *Huncke's Journal* (1965) was followed by *Elsie John and Joey Martinez* (1979), *The Evening Sun Turned Crimson* (1980), and *Guilty of Everything* (1990). *The Herbert Huncke Reader* will be published in 1997.

The books and Mr. Huncke's role in a brash new literary movement made him known to a younger generation, and he had several successful lecture tours in recent years. His books did not make much money, but they didn't need to. Friends contributed willingly to the upkeep of Mr. Huncke, who seemed proud that he had no talent for regular work.

It was a reflection of his continued standing among self-styled counterculturists that one of his most generous benefactors was a man who had never met him: Jerry Garcia of the Grateful Dead, who is said to have helped with his rent at Manhattan's Chelsea Hotel, where Mr. Huncke lived the last several years.

Mr. Huncke, whose longtime companion, Louis Cartwright, was killed in 1994, is survived by his half brother, Dr. Brian Huncke of Chicago.

August 9, 1996

Can-Do Do-Gooder

ELAINE WHITELAW

By Molly O'Neill

Elaine Whitelaw, the grande dame of the March of Dimes who for half a century hatched fashion shows, society dinners, and a myriad of other strategies to raise hundreds of millions of dollars to rid the world of polio, died at a hospice in Manhattan. She was seventy-seven. She died of cancer, said her daughter, Patricia Snyderman of San Francisco.

In 1943, when President Franklin D. Roosevelt tapped her to join the national women's committee of the March of Dimes, the charity that he founded to fight the deadly disease, Miss Whitelaw recognized the philanthropic potential of middle-income Americans. By creating a network of volunteers and programs for children and mothers, she made them the backbone of the March of Dimes, one of the country's most successful volunteer efforts to conquer a disease, in this case one that crippled and killed children.

A dozen years after it began, the March of Dimes was not only triumphant in its war against polio, but it also was able to use the network Miss Whitelaw created to continue financing the fight against a variety of birth defects.

"She was the general of a volunteer army," said Beverly Sills, the opera singer and national chairwoman of the March of Dimes and a longtime friend of Miss Whitelaw's.

As a fixture on the national charity ball scene, Miss Whitelaw embodied can-do do-gooding. Both colleagues and those she tapped relentlessly for contributions said she practiced what she preached. They described her as demanding, innovative, boundlessly energetic, and fiercely determined. Miss Sills recalled: "When she approached me about becoming involved with the March of Dimes she said, 'Other charities want to put your name on their stationery. I want your time, your energy, and your money.' She was irresistible."

The general of the volunteer army against polio was a tall, regal woman with a shock of white hair and a swath of Joan Crawford–red lipstick who would sweep into hotel ballrooms, a cyclone of Fracas perfume in her wake. Wherever she went, cab drivers, short-order cooks, politicians, beauty queens, the Junior League, and gentlemen half her age stood at attention before her. "Her natural elegance just bowled people over," said Ms. Sills, who traveled about twenty-five thousand miles a year with Miss Whitelaw for the charity.

Her voice bowled them over, too. "Where are the goddamn name cards for the guests?" she would bellow at a clutch of New York socialites setting up for the annual March of Dimes Gourmet Gala. "Where the hell are the seating assignments?" The same woman who fretted about stepping outside without wearing gloves sounded like a cement truck. And for the past half century, hers was the voice of America's most successful charity.

Rosamond Elaine Whitelaw was born on November 21, 1914, the oldest child of Louis Whitelaw, a wealthy diamond merchant of fiercely liberal politics, and Dora Whitelaw, his meticulous and stylish wife. Along with two younger brothers, Seymour and Jordan, Miss Whitelaw grew up in a rambling apartment on the Upper West Side of Manhattan where daily life resembled a novel by Edith Wharton. The family's social conscience was shaped by Thorstein Veblen, and dinner conversation ranged from analysis of the latest work of Robert Sherwood or Eugene O'Neill to debates over the affluent society's obligation to the rest of the world.

Her grooming began early, in a New York City where front doors were left unlocked and children walked alone to public schools. When she was eleven, Miss Whitelaw was one of two little girls chosen to present flowers to Queen Marie of Romania at the dedication of the Joan of Arc monument on Riverside Drive. "We were beside ourselves, darling, to be this close to such elegance," she recalled in an interview a year before she died. "My God! Well, up pulls the silver-gray limousine, out slide the perfect gray suede shoes." Pausing, she pulled on her cigarette, waved it like a conductor summoning a crashing finale, and exhaled. "She was chewing gum! It was appalling."

In the next ten years Miss Whitelaw's definition of appalling expanded. She entered Smith College in 1930, the same year as Julia Child did. "Half the girls didn't come back after Christmas," she said. "By Christmas vacation there were a hundred thousand homeless men living along the river between Seventy-second Street and Grant's Tomb. I remember their campfires at night."

She also remembered the shocking chartreuse Vionnet gown that she wore to the theater, the satin slippers, the string of pearls. "In those days you dressed for theater, darling," she said. "Oh, it was marvelous. Helen Hayes! John Barrymore! Everybody went dancing at the Rainbow Room or on the roof of the Biltmore. Everybody rode the subway home, or your beau walked you home through the park."

When she graduated from Smith College, where she had studied American history and art, "There was no question that I was going to work," she said. "But of course I wasn't going to work at some perfume counter and take a job from someone who needed it."

After a brief stint as a script reader, an early marriage that ended in divorce, and the birth of her daughter, Patricia, she volunteered to raise money for the Loyalist side in the Spanish Civil War. She moved on to volunteer for the National War Fund.

Over the next fifty years, in both the professional and philanthropic spheres, the name Elaine Whitelaw would become synonymous with charity fund-raising. In the late 1930s she was a smartly dressed young woman with bobbed red hair embarking on a lifelong dance between society and its entitlements and the New Society and its responsibility. In large part, her success was based on a shrewd appraisal of her cause and a keen sense of the era. The Spanish Civil War, for instance: "You had consommé, roast beef, and some kind of dramatic bombe, and always speakers like André Malraux and Vincent Sheean; those were the idols." In World War II, as a volunteer for the National War Fund: "You'd get Madame Chiang Kai-shek or Mrs. Roosevelt. You'd have a modest dinner dance at the Park Lane. Everything was less indulgent, darling. Why, even our skirts were slender and short to save fabric."

"Oh, those were wonderful years. There was a sense that we had to win that war," she said. "And the city! The servicemen could get into Radio City for twenty-five cents. The landlord in my building—I lived on the same block as Greta Garbo, dear—didn't raise the rent on any family whose husband or father was enlisted. Now that was a city!"

Women ate chicken à la king at fund-raisers. The menu followed her: "Rubber chicken, darling, always undercooked or overcooked. I've been eating that meal in ballrooms for forty-seven years." The immediacy of the charity shaped her approach. "People could give five dollars for a carton of cigarettes or five thousand dollars for a field ambulance," she said. "Fund-raising was not abstract; it was very specific."

So were the dimes that Miss Whitelaw asked children to donate to the March of Dimes, and the donation baskets that she had distributed in movie theaters across the country, after she joined the March of Dimes in 1943.

In addition to the creation of the network of volunteers who sought donations, Miss Whitelaw also used her prodigious organizational abilities to help orchestrate the field tests of the Salk polio vaccine. "Her influence was all pervasive," said Dr. Jonas Salk, the developer of the vaccine and later the founder of the Salk Institute in San Diego, California.

Along with Eleanor Lambert, she organized a fashion show to benefit the March of Dimes that *Time* magazine called "the event of the year." In 1976, she began "Gourmet Galas," dinners prepared in various cities by local celebrities and judged by culinary experts. Today, there are forty different galas across the United States.

After retiring from the March of Dimes in 1991, Miss Whitelaw volunteered as a regional director of the Enterprise Foundation, a national organization involved in housing the poor. Increasingly concerned with homelessness, drug use, and AIDS, she spent nights riding a Planned Parenthood van and counseling women who lived or worked on the streets in the Bronx. "The only way we're going to get them in for treatment is to feed them," she told a reporter at the time. "They don't know they might be sick. They know they're hungry, their children are hungry." Within days, she had cooking equipment and food donations, and, in her Adolfo suits and Ferragamo shoes, she helped serve hot meals from midnight to dawn.

One of the young women she fed, a runaway, took words from Miss Whitelaw's vocabulary to describe her. "She's a great dame," she said.

Miss Whitelaw's second husband, Otto Brodnitz, an economist and stockbroker, died in the mid-1970s. She is survived by her daughter; her brother, Seymour Whitelaw of San Francisco, and two grandchildren.

December 17, 1992

Instinctive Healer

ALEXANDER G. SHULMAN

By Lawrence Van Gelder

Alexander G. Shulman, a physician who instinctively plunged his hand into cold water when he accidentally seared it with boiling grease one day in the 1950s and thereby altered medicine's approach to the emergency treatment of burns, died at his home in Los Angeles. He was eighty-one. The cause was cancer, his wife, Constance Stone-Shulman, said.

Before his retirement about a year ago, Dr. Shulman, whose specialty was surgery, was director of the Lichtenstein Hernia Institute of Los Angeles, an organization devoted to research, teaching, and treatment related to abdominal wall hernias. In addition to maintaining a private practice, Dr. Shulman was also for many years the chief of surgery at Midway Hospital in Los Angeles. A frequent contributor to medical journals, he was known as a champion of the use of the blood-thinning drug heparin to ward off heart attacks and as an advocate of rapid return to work for hernia patients who underwent the institute's innovative treatment using tension-free mesh.

But he was perhaps best known for his direct, effective approach to first aid for burns, which were usually treated with an application of butter or grease. In the *Journal of the American Medical Association* of August 27, 1960, Dr. Shulman told how personal experience taught him the efficacy of cold water. About eight years earlier, he wrote, he burned a hand when he accidentally spilled boiling grease. "In the ensuing agonizing few minutes it seemed logical to plunge the hand into a tub of cold water," he wrote. "The immediate relief of pain was so impressive that I kept the hand immersed in water for about one hour, since its momentary removal caused the return of the original intense pain. After about one hour, it was possible to remove the hand without pain. From that moment on there was virtually no pain, and the burn seemed to heal more rapidly than was expected."

Dr. Shulman continued: "A few weeks later, a three-year-old child who had grasped the hot water pipes leading to a shower room was brought in screaming with fright and intense pain of her hands. When the hands were immersed in cold water, the child immediately displayed complete relief and refused to remove her hands until some time later. Once she was able to remove her hands without pain, the skin did not blister and no further treatment was necessary.

"These two initial cases demonstrate what has been known to the ancients but seems to have been ignored by physicians and laymen alike."

After the initial cases, Dr. Shulman wrote, he treated 150 patients with burns of less than 20 percent of the body using ice water or ice-cold moist towels, and found the treatment effective not only for burns of thermal origin, but also for chemical and electrical burns. Dr. Shulman noted that he had been reluctant to experiment formally by withholding treatment of a portion of the burn area. But, he wrote, a fortuitous error occurred in which a small area of abdomen was overlooked in the treatment of a man whose face, arms, and torso had been splattered with steam. All the areas treated with ice water healed within a day, he wrote. But, he said, "The abdominal patch blistered, remained painful, crusted over, and required two weeks for complete healing."

He concluded: "Immersion of burns in ice-water baths, or the application of ice-cold moist towels to burned areas is recommended as first-aid emergency management for burns involving less than 20 percent of the body surface."

Mr. Shulman, known as Alex, was born on June 22, 1915, in Toronto. He received his medical degree from the University of Toronto in 1939 and was a resident, first in pathology and then in surgery, at Cedars Sinai Medical Center in Los Angeles.

During World War II, he served as a neurosurgeon with the rank of captain in the Army Medical Corps.

In addition to his wife, Dr. Shulman is survived by a daughter, Stefanie Le Plastrier, and a son, Lawrence, both of Los Angeles; a brother, Milton, of London, and five grandchildren.

July 12, 1996

At Home on a Horse

ALICE GREENOUGH ORR

By Robert McG. Thomas, Jr.

Alice Greenough Orr, who broke horses as a youngster on a Montana ranch, delivered mail through snowdrifts on horseback as a teenager, and later reigned for two decades as the rodeo queen of the bronc riders, died at her home in Tucson, Arizona. She was ninety-three and a member of both the Cowboy and the Cowgirl Halls of Fame.

In a career that took her from the wilds of Montana to Madison Square Garden and the capitals of Europe, Mrs. Orr was always at home on a horse. If it was bucking, so much the better. When she was a child growing up on a ranch near Red Lodge, Montana, her father regularly gave her wild horses, knowing that by the time they got tired of trying to dislodge his tenacious daughter, they would be tame enough for regular people to ride. In time, her skill led to four world saddle bronc championships and made her a star attraction on rodeo tours in the United States, Australia, and Europe.

Although bronc riding was her specialty, she and her little sister, Marge Henderson, excelled at virtually every rodeo event from trick riding to bull riding. Together with their brothers Bill and Turk, they became known as the Riding Greenoughs. Like Turk, a legendary bronc rider who also died this year at the age of eighty-nine, Mrs. Orr also did occasional stunt work for the movies.

Her skill brought her considerable attention. On one European tour in the 1930s she had tea with the Queen of England, and, without benefit of sword, rode fighting bulls into Spanish arenas before dismounting and leaving them to the matadors.

Mrs. Orr, who once said she had been "born liberated," dropped out of school to take over a thirty-five-mile rural mail route at the age of fourteen. She kept the route for three winters and two summers and had her heart set on a career as a forest ranger until the return of servicemen from World War I closed off such employment opportunities for women.

After the failure of her marriage to Ray Cahill, a marriage that produced two children, she was working in a rooming house in 1929 when she saw an advertisement for bronc riders for a wild west show, the precursor of modern rodeos. She and her sister answered the advertisement and were hired on the spot.

Early competitors were sometimes shortchanged by tour operators, at least until 1936, when Mrs. Orr and others formed what is now known as the Professional Rodeo Cowboys Association.

In the 1940s she and her second husband, Joe Orr, operated their own rodeos, with Mrs. Orr providing exhibitions of saddle bronc riding, a specialty that rodeo experts say requires so much more skill and finesse than bareback riding that it no longer exists as a competitive event on the women's rodeo circuit.

Mrs. Orr retired from rodeos in 1954, but continued to accept occasional movie assignments until she was eighty. She climbed into the saddle for the last time in 1992 when she rode in a parade in Red Lodge, where few of those who lined the route could remember the time when it was a girl on horseback who delivered the mail.

In addition to her sister, also of Tucson, she is survived by a son, Jay Cahill of Grandview, Missouri; eleven grandchildren; twelve great-grandchildren, and two great-great-grandchildren.

August 24, 1995

The Harder He Fell

TOMMY COLLINS

By Gerald Eskenazi

Tommy Collins, a popular fighter of the 1950s who was once beaten so savagely that his defeat sparked a national outcry to reform boxing, died in Boston. He was sixty-seven years old.

Although he was only 123 pounds, Collins packed a powerful punch that let him knock out 70 percent of his opponents. He also faced four world champions in thirteen months, and early in his career fought twenty-six times in a year. He was the only opponent to knock down the featherweight champion Sandy Saddler, in a 1952 fight he lost in six rounds.

But Collins, who never won a title, became a national figure in 1953 when he was battered to the canvas ten times by the lightweight champion, Jimmy Carter, in a bout at Boston Garden. The referee, Tommy Rawson, did not end the fight, and the punishment continued until one of Collins's cornermen leaped into the ring to stop it in the fourth round.

The fight, which attracted more than twelve thousand fans and was one of the biggest events in Boston's boxing history, was televised nationally and created widespread controversy, including calls for reform in the sport by Congress. The savagery of the beating helped to create the three-knockdown rule almost universally in effect now; when a fighter is knocked down three times, the bout is ended.

The boxing writer for *The New York Times*, Joseph C. Nichols, was so appalled by the beating that he started his account of the fight: "In one of the most reprehensible mismatches in modern ring history..." Later, Rawson, explaining why he had kept counting over the fallen fighter until Collins's corner stopped the fight, said, "I thought it my duty" to let the fight continue because it was a championship.

Rawson was cleared of negligence by a Massachusetts commission, and Collins himself absolved the referee of any wrongdoing. But the bout, which was quickly dubbed the "Boston Massacre," prompted switchboards to light up at newspapers across the United States as viewers protested the brutality of the match. Joseph W. Martin, Jr., the Republican Speaker of the House, said he supported a federal investigation into the safety of the sport.

Tommy Collins, who was considered Boston's most popular fighter since John L. Sullivan, was his usual cheerful self after getting out of the hospital the next day. "I feel fine," he said. "Haven't got an ache in my body. Don't I look okay?"

Collins continued his career for the next eighteen months, but he was never again as dominant as he had been earlier in his career. He made two attempts at retirement before finally hanging up the gloves at the age of twenty-five. He had posted a 60–12 won-lost record that included forty-three knockouts. Among the fighters he defeated was the former featherweight champion Willie Pep. In a photo published around the world, Collins sat in the ring and wept after knocking out Pep, thinking he had severely hurt the legendary but aging fighter after catching him with a vicious left hook.

Collins is survived by his wife, May MacAllister Collins; two sons, two brothers, and three sisters.

June 6, 1996

The King of Checkers

MARION TINSLEY

By Robert McG. Thomas, Jr.

Marion Tinsley, the perennial world checkers champion who was widely regarded as the game's best player ever, died in Humble, Texas, five years after he ran out of worthy human opponents and began winning his last titles by beating ever more powerful computers. He was sixty-eight and lived in Conyers, Georgia. The cause was cancer, relatives said. He was visiting his twin sister, Mary Clark, in Humble when he died.

Mr. Tinsley, a retired Florida State University mathematics professor who had lost only nine checkers games since first winning the world championship in 1955, abandoned his title last August at the world championship final in Boston sponsored by the American Checkers Federation and the British Draughts Federation. Illness forced him to withdraw from the championship match after playing six games against an enhanced version of the Chinook computer program that he had beaten in three previous title matches.

Although Chinook eventually won the 1994 title by beating a stand-in, the victory was a hollow one for the program's developer, Jonathan Schaeffer, a Canadian computer scientist. "Tinsley was the Mount Everest we wanted to scale," Mr. Schaeffer said, noting that the latest Chinook, which has a repertory of 250 billion moves and can make 3 million calculations a minute, was 5 times as powerful as the version Mr. Tinsley defeated in 1992.

Before his forced withdrawal, Mr. Tinsley provided evidence that the souped-up Chinook still needed more soup. He had fought the computer to six straight draws.

Mr. Tinsley once attributed his awesome mental development to a childhood belief that his parents favored his twin.

A mediocre checkers player as a child, he began his ascent at the age of fourteen when he stumbled on a book on checkers while researching a math problem at the Ohio State University library.

A fierce competitor who acknowledged that he hated to lose more than he loved to win, Mr. Tinsley developed a virtual obsession for a game whose appeal never ceased to captivate him. "Checkers can get quite a hold on you," he once said. "Its beauty is just overwhelming—the mathematics, the elegance, the precision. It's capable of wrapping you all up."

A Christian who worked for years making an outline of the Old Testament from the New Testament perspective, Mr. Tinsley scoffed at repeated suggestions that his mastery of the Chinook computer proved that his intelligence was somehow otherworldly. "I'm human," he said. "It's just that I have a better programmer than Chinook. God gave me a logical mind."

Mr. Tinsley was a native of Ironton, Ohio. In addition to his sister, he is survived by two brothers, Ed, of Sarasota, Florida, and Joe, of Thornville, Ohio.

April 8, 1995

Hoochie-Koochie Man

WILLIE DIXON

By Jon Pareles

Willie Dixon, who wrote blues standards and produced many classic blues albums, died of heart failure at St. Joseph Medical Center in Burbank, California. He was seventy-six years old and lived in Southern California.

As a songwriter, producer, arranger, and bassist, Mr. Dixon was a towering figure in the creation of Chicago blues, which was in turn a cornerstone of rock-and-roll. His songs were performed by leading blues figures, including Muddy Waters and Howlin' Wolf, and picked up by rock bands including the Rolling Stones, Cream, and the Doors. The lusty imagery, laconic humor, and hints of mysterious ritual in his best songs made them sound like age-old folk poems.

Mr. Dixon was born in Vicksburg, Mississippi, in 1915. By the early 1930s, he was writing songs and selling them to a local country band. He also joined a gospel group, the Jubilee Singers. In 1936, he moved to Chicago to become a boxer. He won the Illinois State Golden Gloves heavyweight championship (novice division) in 1937, but a disagreement with his manager soon ended that career.

He returned to music, singing and playing bass with Leonard (Baby Doo) Caston, and made his first records for the Bluebird label as a member of the Five Breezes in 1940. In 1941, he refused induction into the army. "I didn't feel I had to go because of the conditions that existed among my people," he said later. After a year in and out of jail, Mr. Dixon formed the Four Jumps of Jive, who recorded for Mercury.

In 1945, Mr. Dixon and Mr. Caston formed the Big Three Trio, a rhythm-and-blues vocal group that had a hit with "Wee Wee Baby,

You Sure Look Good to Me" in 1946. Playing a one-stringed bass with a tin-can resonator, Mr. Dixon also backed up Tampa Red, Memphis Minnie, and other blues musicians at recording sessions. He started playing studio sessions for Chess Records in 1948, and after the Big Three Trio dissolved in 1951 he started working for Chess full-time.

Mr. Dixon recorded for Chess as a singer but was far more successful as a songwriter, beginning with his first major blues hit, Muddy Waters's 1954 "Hoochie Koochie Man," with its stop-time riff. At Chess and, from 1957 to 1959, at Cobra Records, he provided songs and guidance for Little Walter, Lowell Fulson, Buddy Guy, Otis Rush, Magic Sam, and, most important, Howlin' Wolf, for whom he wrote "Back Door Man," "Wang Dang Doodle," "Spoonful," "Little Red Rooster," "You Can't Judge a Book by Its Cover," and other blues classics. In his wryly witty lyrics, Mr. Dixon artfully combined Southern folk wisdom with urban street slang.

At Chess, he also played bass behind Chuck Berry and Bo Diddley and worked with gospel singers and vocal groups. Mr. Dixon took hard Chicago blues to Europe as the bandleader for the traveling American Folk Blues festival from 1962 to 1964. There his songs inspired the Yardbirds and the Rolling Stones.

As the Chess label shifted away from blues, Mr. Dixon turned to performing, leading a band called the Chicago All-Stars. He wasn't a deep, brooding blues vocalist, but he projected an irresistible sense of fun and he continued to write lyrics that connected with his listeners. He recorded for the Columbia, Ovation, Pausa, and Capitol labels; he also wrote a song for the soundtrack of Martin Scorsese's film *The Color of Money* and produced Bo Diddley's remake of "Who Do You Love" in the movie *La Bamba*.

Although he had sold the copyrights to many of his songs during the 1950s, he gradually won some of them back. He founded the Blues Heaven Foundation, a nonprofit organization that helps older blues performers and gives scholarships to young musicians.

He is survived by his wife, Marie, and several children.

January 30, 1992

REIMAGINING THE BLUES

In a "Pop View" column, the critic PETER WATROUS *told why Willie Dixon made the blues worth listening to again.*

One of the worst myths Americans have about African-American art is that it comes directly from the soul, unmediated by intellect—that the artistic expressions of black culture appear without the need for study or refinement.

The idea that the blues reflected nothing but raw emotion was perpetrated by journalists, usually white, who were looking for the noble savage in their black blues musicians, as well as by the musicians themselves, who knew what role they were being asked to play. The notion, like the music itself, has become part of the rock-and-roll aesthetic, where expressionism and extremism have been valued over craft and refinement.

Willie Dixon was an arranger, producer, and the writer of such blues classics as "Hoochie Koochie Man" and "Wang Dang Doodle." His career shows how fraudulent the high value placed on the primitive can be. Mr. Dixon, the architect of the Chicago blues sound, knew exactly what he wanted and how to get it. He was the man that in good measure turned the rural impulses of a group of musicians from Mississippi— Muddy Waters, Little Walter, Howlin' Wolf, Otis Rush—into the urban and varied music that found a new audience and became an influence on future generations.

Willie Dixon was someone who, within the limited options open to black men in the first half of the century, chose to work with the blues even though he had the resources to go into more musically sophisticated rhythm-and-blues or even jazz.

He was open-minded and knowledgeable, and he realized that the music that worked in Mississippi couldn't work in cities. So along with the Chess brothers (the owners of Chess Records) and other blues musicians, he rewrote the music in the 1950s and 1960s, giving it wit and novelty, adding rhythms taken from Latin music, touches of jazz and pop, and new harmonies. He changed the lyrics around, sometimes emphasizing older themes and slang to play on the sentiments of the city's rural immigrants.

He arranged each song to make it distinct. To wander through a collection of his tunes is to hear the wondrous variety that Mr. Dixon helped bring to the simple three-chord blues form. Using savage or stately riffs, smooth horns or rhythmic stop-time figures, he made the blues new and worth listening to again. And he never forgot that the blacks who had been drawn to cities by the promise of work and a better life still had a taste for the rural flavors they had left behind.

Mr. Dixon changed the sound of twentieth-century popular music without having any stake in stardom. He wasn't much of a stage person-ality, he had no significant hits as a performer, and only late in life did he become anything like an icon to the white fans who had taken over as the main audience for the blues. His most famous group was the Big Three Trio, started soon after World War II, which mixed novelty and jump and blues and came up with a minor hit in "Wee Wee Baby, You Sure Look Good to Me," in 1946. His own releases for Chess—the label that, under his direction, recorded Muddy Waters, Howlin' Wolf, Little Walter, Lowell Fulson, and others—went nowhere. He released his first solo album, *Willie's Blues,* in 1959.

But a list of his songs shows how clearly he recognized the nuances required of a popular song. He wrote, for Muddy Waters, "I Just Want to Make Love to You," "I'm Ready," and "I Love the Life I Live, I Live the Life I Love"; for Howlin' Wolf, "Evil," "Back Door Man," "Spoon-ful," "Built for Comfort," "Little Red Rooster," and "Three Hundred Pounds of Joy," among others. For Little Walter he composed "My Babe," and "Mellow Down Easy"; for Otis Rush, tunes like "I Can't Quit You Baby." "Pretty Thing" and "You Can't Judge a Book by Its Cover" were written for Bo Diddley.

Not only were many of the songs hits within the blues market, but they also supplanted the standards that had been generated by more rural blues. And when English rock groups like Led Zeppelin, the Rolling Stones, the Yardbirds, and Cream adopted some of Mr. Dixon's material, his songwriting became acknowledged internationally.

Aware of the vernacular, unafraid to reimagine the down-home, Mr. Dixon synthesized all sorts of experiences into a new form. His music was restricted by the desire to reach a wide market, to make something people might remember, something that could stand out in the onslaught of the fresh images and language that modern life brought with it. A lot of people were trying to do the same thing; Mr. Dixon succeeded better than anyone else.

February 9, 1992

Chicago Says Good-bye

Don Terry described how Chicago said its farewell to Willie Dixon.

This city of Southerners in the North borrowed a page from the New Orleans book of mourning to say good-bye to one of its natural resources, the legendary bluesman Willie Dixon, who died last week.

It was the page that said celebrate. Celebrate a wonderful life. Celebrate with music and song. And that is exactly what Chicago did today, with the city's first New Orleans–style funeral procession in memory.

Mr. Dixon's coffin was carried through the weary streets of the South Side in a horse-drawn, Civil War–era hearse. It was followed by strutting, horn-blowing, gray-haired blues musicians, a high-stepping high school marching band, and a great lake of umbrellas bobbing up and down to the beat in the chilly morning breeze.

Hundreds of fans, black and white, from across this segregated city marched along as residents of the neighborhood waved from their porches and held up posters of Mr. Dixon's smiling, gentle face.

Rita Wallace displayed a homemade sign that said it all: CHICAGO LOVES WILLIE DIXON. BYE-BYE.

"I've never seen a send-off like this for any musician in Chicago," said Cicero Blake, a blues singer and one of dozens of musicians who came out to pay their respects to the man they called "the Blues."

Koko Taylor, a legend in her own right, said Mr. Dixon was not only a gifted songwriter "but he also had the best song titles I ever heard." He had written her trademark tune, "Wang Dang Doodle." "He kept the blues alive so far as keeping people supplied with songs," she said. "There will never be another Willie Dixon."

The procession stretched for three blocks and stopped several times as Mr. Dixon's comrades and spiritual offspring played his music in the streets of the neighborhood where the Chicago blues sound was born.

As she watched the chestnut-colored horse pull the hearse down a tree-lined avenue, Andrea Denham, an administrator at the University of Chicago, said she had taken the day off and made her husband do the same "so we could be part of history."

Before the procession began, Elizabeth Gates, a retired postal worker, decorated her porch and fence along the funeral route with black and blue paper. "The blue represents the blues," she said. "I'm so proud of him as a black man. He wrote different songs about our inside feelings. He told the world how we feel."

Like so many Chicagoans, Mr. Dixon was born in the Jim Crow South and migrated to Chicago in the 1930s to seek his fortune. He died in Southern California, where he had moved in 1982 for health reasons. Since his death he has also been honored by Congress, Los Angeles, and Vicksburg, Mississippi, where he was born.

The novelty of the procession was clear by the first uncertain steps of Alvin (Twine Time) Cash, the grand marshal. His early strut was a little stiff, but he quickly got the hang of it and proudly led the band down the block to the tune of "Just a Closer Walk with Thee."

February 6, 1992

Benevolent Tinker

ALEX MANOOGIAN

By Lawrence Van Gelder

Alex Manoogian, the Armenian immigrant responsible for making the single-handled faucet a ubiquitous fixture in modern bathrooms and kitchens throughout the United States and around the world, died at St. John Hospital in Detroit. Mr. Manoogian, who lived in Grosse Pointe Farms, Michigan, was ninety-five.

Thanks to his realization of the promise of the ball valve joint patented by three inventors, Mr. Manoogian, who came to the United States from Turkey as a teenager in 1920, amassed a fortune. He proceeded to dispense it by donating millions of dollars to religious, educational, charitable, and cultural institutions and hospitals—many of them serving the Armenian community—in scores of countries in North and South America, Europe, the Middle East, and Australia.

Mr. Manoogian, who founded a small but successful machine shop in Detroit called the Masco Screw Products Company, specializing in automobile parts, was approached in 1952 by the inventors of the ball valve joint, which was capable of making hot and cold water run from a single tap. They were looking for someone to develop a faucet based on the valve at a time when there were virtually no single-handled faucets on the market.

"It appealed to me," Mr. Manoogian said later. "I said, 'Why wouldn't people want to do something with one hand instead of with two?'" He signed an agreement with the inventors, and he put his shop to work. Two years later he had a faucet whose handle could be turned left or right for hot or cold water and be pushed or pulled to control the volume. And the faucet was dripless, having no washers to wear out.

Although Mr. Manoogian was intrigued by manufacturing the single-handled faucet, his interest in selling it was minimal. But when plumbing companies told him there was no market for such a fixture, Mr. Manoogian felt he had no choice but to market it himself. In 1995, the Masco Corporation, based in the Detroit suburb of Taylor, realized sales of $3 billion from home furnishing and building products, including plumbing and brass goods, kitchen cabinets, appliances, spas and locks manufactured in one hundred factories in fifteen countries. The faucets, marketed under such names as Delta, Peerless, and Sherle Wagner, are made in single- and double-handled models that range in price from about forty dollars for a relatively simple chrome fixture for do-it-yourselfers to thousands of dollars for top-of-the-line models made from precious metals. The faucets account for $698 million, or 23 percent of the company's total sales, and the company says its products hold 38 percent of the domestic market for faucets.

Stock in Masco, which barely survived the Depression, was first sold to the public in 1936 for a dollar a share. A year later it was listed for sale on the Detroit Stock Exchange, and Masco shares began trading on the New York Stock Exchange in 1969. Masco officials calculate that a $10,000 investment in the stock in 1958 would be worth $25 million in 1996.

Mr. Manoogian, a somewhat shy Old World figure who spoke in lightly accented English, was widely regarded as one of the most prominent persons of Armenian descent in the world. For thirty-six years he was the international president of the Armenian General Benevolent Union, a worldwide educational, cultural, and humanitarian organization. In 1970, he was elected life president, and in 1989, honorary life president.

In such countries as Argentina, Australia, Canada, Iran, Israel, the Netherlands, and the United States, institutions created or assisted by Mr. Manoogian's generosity were named for him, his wife, the former Marie Tatian, who died in 1992 after sixty-one years of marriage, or his parents, Tacvor and Tacoohie Manoogian.

Mr. Manoogian donated the home he had once lived in to the city of Detroit, which uses it as the official residence of its mayor.

In 1990 he received the Ellis Island Medal of Honor, a special award to outstanding Americans, and last year the Republic of Armenia awarded him its National Hero Medal and declared him an Armenian citizen, the first individual outside the country to be so honored.

Mr. Manoogian was born in 1901 in Smyrna (now Izmir), Turkey. In the years 1915 to 1923 an Armenian community of more than one million people was reduced to negligible numbers. Hundreds of thousands of Armenian men, women, and children were slaughtered or driven into the desert to fend for themselves. Mr. Manoogian was one of the many Armenians who fled the country. He left in 1920 for the United States, where he was later joined by his parents, two brothers, and two sisters. Mr. Manoogian settled first in Bridgeport, Connecticut, where he worked in a factory and taught Armenian in evening courses for adults. In 1924 he moved to Detroit, where, as a skilled machinist, he founded Masco Screw Products in 1929.

He is survived by a son, Richard A. Manoogian of Grosse Pointe, Michigan, now chairman and chief executive of Masco; a daughter, Louise Simone of Manhattan, who succeeded her father as president of the Armenian General Benevolent Union; six grandchildren, and two great-grandchildren.

July 13, 1996

Sitting Cross-Legged on a K'ang

DAVID KIDD

By Robert McG. Thomas, Jr.

David Kidd, an American expatriate who became so imbued with traditional Chinese and Japanese art and culture that by the end of his career
he was teaching Japanese traditions to the Japanese, died in Honolulu.
He was sixty-nine and had homes there and in Kyoto, Japan, where he
was the founding director of the Oomoto School of Traditional Japanese
Arts. His friends said the cause of his death was cancer.

Maybe it was something about growing up in Corbin, Kentucky,
where his father operated a coal mine, or the experience of coming of
age in Detroit after his father became an automotive executive, but as
soon as Mr. Kidd heard Stravinsky's *Le Sacre du printemps* as a teenager, he
knew he was not quite of the American world.

Although he was never able to explain his original fascination with
China, Mr. Kidd, who may only have wanted to get as far away from
home as possible, seemed to know that time was running short. Rushing
to Peking as a nineteen-year-old University of Michigan exchange student
in 1946, he spent the next four years teaching English at suburban col-
leges, developing a lifelong fascination with ancient Chinese art and serving as an eyewitness to the end of an era.

Through an unlikely marriage to Aimee Yu, the daughter of a former
chief justice of the Supreme Court of China, he moved into her aristocratic
family's 101-room mansion, a labyrinth of courtyards and corridors packed
with ancient treasures and housing two-dozen Yu relatives, who served the
new son-in-law as guides to the ways of a dying regime.

As a participant in old China's last great Chinese wedding celebration, as a mourner at its last great funeral, of his wife's father, and as

perhaps the only American in Tiananmen Square for the formal Communist takeover, Mr. Kidd was more than an awed observer. His insightful inside account of the last days of the ancient regime was published as *All the Emperor's Horses* in 1960 and revised and reissued as a paperback retitled *Peking Story* in 1988.

When heavy taxes and constant harassment by the new rulers finally forced the Yu family to sell its mansion to the Communist authorities, Mr. Kidd took his wife to the United States in 1950. But the couple were eventually divorced and went their separate ways, she to pursue a career as a physicist in California, he to immerse himself in Asian art circles in New York. Scrambling, as he later told it, to stay a page ahead of his students, he taught at the old Asia Institute until 1956, when he succumbed to the pull of the Orient once again.

With the old China gone and the new China off limits to Americans, Mr. Kidd made Japan his base for the rest of his life, but with the thaw in Sino-American relations he made a poignant trip back to Beijing in 1981. He set out to find the Yu mansion, but, as he described in his book, it was gone: "Soldiers with bayonets stood guard beside a gate I had never seen before, while within, where the courtyards and gardens should have been, rose a forbidding, multistoried brick building—a branch office of the secret police, the driver said, warning me not to get out of the car."

He also found some members of the Yu family, living in poverty. "There was a sadness about my in-laws and their self-effacing behavior that I had never seen before, as if the New China had beaten them down and kept them down so long that they had forgotten who they had been," he wrote. Nevertheless, after he had invited them to dinner at the Beijing Hotel, they returned his hospitality, presenting him with two cloisonné vases for which they had spent a large sum of money. "They were reminding me that they were still the Yu family, people of culture to whom the old ways still mattered. . . . I accepted the vases with gratitude and a sudden lightening of the heart," Mr. Kidd wrote.

After moving to Japan in 1956 and settling in a three-hundred-year-old mansion in Ashiya, he taught at Kobe and Osaka universities and spent his spare time turning his house into a veritable museum of Chinese and Japanese art and antiques. With the help of a student, Yasuyoshi

Morimoto, who became first his driver and then his partner in art and in life, he found bargains galore, partly because in their rush to build an industrial society, Japanese collectors were scorning their own treasures and those that had been sent back as plunder from China.

When his landlord decided to raze the property to make way for a modern development, Mr. Kidd, who received permission to dismantle the house, moved to Kyoto, where he opened a school to teach the tea ceremony, calligraphy, and other traditional arts, initially to foreigners and eventually to Japanese who had lost the thread of their own culture in the rush toward Westernization. In the school's sponsor, the Oomoto Shinto sect, Mr. Kidd found a kindred spirit. Its motto is "Art is the mother of religion."

In Kyoto, Mr. Kidd, who had been arranging seminars for years, was soon a prime attraction for individual travelers interested in ancient art and even a regular stop on tours arranged for wealthy members by the Museum of Modern Art. As a tourist attraction, Mr. Kidd did not disappoint. To sit on a cushion before his throne, listening to his erudite patter, and seeing him sitting cross-legged on his k'ang, a divided wooden sofa, rustling his silken gown as he gestured extravagantly with his inevitable cigarette, was to be in the presence of a presence.

When a wealthy visitor offered him some exorbitant price for one of his treasures, Mr. Kidd, whose friends say would have swooned at the crass suggestion that he was, ahem, a d-e-a-l-e-r, would gasp that he could not bear to live without that particular piece. Nevertheless, in some mysterious process that would help finance his lifestyle and other acquisitions, the object would find its way into some American museum or private collection.

Mr. Kidd, whose major disappointment was that his friend David Bowie had not gotten around to portraying him in a movie of his days as a blond, wavy-haired dandy in Peking, was consoled during the last year of his life by news that a Kyoto society had agreed to reassemble his old Ashiya house as a museum.

Mr. Morimoto is his only survivor.

November 27, 1996

He Didn't Sell Plastic

WALTER HOVING

Walter Hoving, the sometimes imperious, always self-confident head of Tiffany & Company from 1955 to 1980, died yesterday at Newport Hospital in Rhode Island. He was ninety-one.

Mr. Hoving resolutely maintained Tiffany's standards, which included no diamond rings for men, no silver plate, and no charge accounts for customers found being rude to the salespeople. These of course were also his own standards, and they paid off. His firmness in matters of taste took Tiffany's from $7 million worth of business in 1955 to $100 million for the Fifth Avenue store and its five branches in 1980, when he stepped down as chairman.

Perhaps the most often repeated story about Mr. Hoving involves President John F. Kennedy's request in 1962 for thirty-two Lucite calendar mementos to be presented to close aides who had worked with him on the Cuban missile crisis. Mr. Hoving's precise words in reply differ from version to version, but his meaning was clear: "We don't sell plastic."

In the end, Tiffany's got the order, anyway—to make the mementos in silver.

The only exception to the "no silver plate" rule during Mr. Hoving's tenure at Tiffany's—small pins with the message "Try God"—illuminated another facet of Mr. Hoving's character: his certainty that he was guided by God during his entire career.

His conviction of the correctness of his taste allowed him to give great freedom to designers, both those who created jewelry, like Jean Schlumberger, Angela Cummings, and Elsa Peretti, and those like Gene Moore, who designed Tiffany's eye-catching windows. "Design what you think is beautiful," he told them, "and don't worry about selling it. That's our job."

No item was too small to escape his notice. No cellophane tape, he decreed, was to be used in gift-wrapping boxes with that special Tiffany robin's egg blue paper, and there were to be no knots securing the white bows.

A tall and distinguished-looking man, always impeccably tailored, Mr. Hoving was not hesitant about expressing his tastes outside the store. He won the battle against a plan to put a café in a corner of Central Park, but he lost the fight against making Fifth Avenue traffic one-way.

A man of conservative political bent, he expressed his opinions in various ways. In one year's annual report, he commented on the taxes paid by the store, saying, "It is our hope, but not our expectation, that these sums will be spent with due diligence and a modicum of wisdom."

He used Tiffany advertisements as a soapbox, too. Some of them he wrote as little essays with titles like "Is Profit a Dirty Word?" In another he assailed the First National City Bank for its "loud and vulgar Christmas tree" and urged the bank to practice "good aesthetics." In yet another he attacked as unconscionable the hoarding of silver, an unmistakable reference to the Hunt empire's efforts to corner the silver market in 1980.

"Every store must have a point of view," Mr. Hoving said in a 1973 interview. "Generally it doesn't."

Tiffany's did. "We don't claim to have the best taste in America," he said. "But we do say it is our taste." The concept of "aesthetic excitement" was supremely important to him, and he was able to make it sell. "Give the customer what Tiffany likes, because what it likes, the public ought to like" was his motto. His skill was in somehow making the public want to like it, and pay for it.

Tiffany & Company was a publicly owned company until it was acquired in 1979 by Avon Products. Mr. Hoving's resignation the following year was one of a series of management changes stemming from the Avon takeover. In 1984, Tiffany & Company was bought by private investors, and in 1987 it again became publicly owned. Its stock is listed on the New York Stock Exchange.

Mr. Hoving was born in Stockholm on December 2, 1897, the son of a surgeon and an opera singer. He was brought to the United States with his parents in 1903 and attended the Barnard School and De Witt Clinton High School in New York City. He received a bachelor's degree from Brown University in 1920.

In 1924, after working at various jobs, Mr. Hoving found his field: merchandising. He went to work for R. H. Macy & Company in its training program and was an immediate success. By the age of thirty, he was a vice president. He also underwent his own training program to polish his knowledge of the arts. For four years, he took courses at the Metropolitan Museum of Art in subjects like painting, textile design, old silver, and furniture.

When he went to Montgomery Ward & Company as vice president in charge of sales in 1932, he set up a bureau of design to overhaul Ward's catalogue. He left the mail-order house in 1936 to go to Lord & Taylor, where he was president until 1946.

Mr. Hoving continued to stress the great importance of design, reportedly asking job seekers to choose between well and badly designed objects and hiring them or rejecting them on the basis of their taste.

In 1946 he founded the Hoving Corporation, whose properties came to include Bonwit Teller, the department store, until he sold it in 1960. In 1955 he bought control of Tiffany's, which at the time seemed to many to be on the brink of going out of business. He started his regime by getting rid of everything in the store that did not meet his standards, holding a giant sale—the first in the store's history—of everything from silver matchbook covers for $6.75 to a diamond and emerald brooch marked down to $29,700.

Under his guidance, the faltering store reacquired its cachet and a new popularity—Tiffany's salesclerks were under orders to treat everyone, even the most obvious browser, as a potential customer—until by Christmas 1980 its aisles were jammed with shoppers.

Mr. Hoving's writings included the book *Tiffany's Table Manners for Teen-Agers.*

His 1924 marriage to Mary Osgood Field ended in divorce in 1936. He married his second wife, Pauline Vandervoort Rogers, in 1937. She died in 1976. He is survived by his third wife, the former singer and actress Jane Pickens Langley, whom he married in 1977; a son and a daughter by his first marriage, Thomas Hoving—who is a former New York City Parks Commissioner and a former director of the Metropolitan Museum of Art—and Petrea Hoving Durand, both of Manhattan, and four grandchildren.

November 28, 1989

Gamblin' Rose

ROSE HAMBURGER

By Robert McG. Thomas, Jr.

Rose Hamburger, who spent half a century as a real-estate agent before eagerly coming out of a reluctant five-year-retirement to start a new career—as a racing handicapper for *The New York Post*—died at St. Vincent's Hospital. She was 105. Her daughter Nancy Sureck said the cause was pneumonia.

As a handicapper, Mrs. Hamburger, whose daily selections appeared with her photograph under a headline identifying her as Gamblin' Rose, brought a certain perspective to her work. A longtime resident of Baltimore who spent a good deal of time at the nearby Pimlico Race Course, she attended every Preakness Stakes from 1915 to 1988 and may have been the last person alive to have seen all eleven Triple Crown winners triumph in a Triple Crown race, from Sir Barton in 1919 to Affirmed in 1978.

The daughter of a department store executive, Mrs. Hamburger, whose maiden name was Rosenbaum, was born in Manhattan on December 29, 1890. A precocious student, she majored in mathematics and music at Normal College, the precursor of Hunter College. When she graduated in 1910, Mrs. Hamburger, who was to become Hunter's oldest living graduate, was only nineteen years old.

Too young to obtain a teacher's license, she joined her father and uncle on a long trip to Germany, where she had an experience that would change her life. She not only was taken to her first horse race, she also stumbled on an instinctive betting system. "I saw this adorable jockey in a little green silk shirt," she explained, recalling that she bet the equivalent of five dollars on the jockey's mount and came away with twenty-five dollars in winnings. "I was hooked," she said.

Indeed, after her father was transferred to Baltimore in 1915, she began haunting Pimlico, becoming such a familiar and cherished figure that by the time of the 1920 Preakness she watched Man 'o War win from the owner's box.

After her marriage in 1925 to Mark Hamburger, a member of the prominent clothing store family, she continued her interest in racing, but had to cut down a bit in 1938 when, at age forty-seven, she became the first woman in Baltimore licensed to sell real estate. Mrs. Hamburger, who had an infectious personality that charmed both buyers and sellers, operated her own business, selling homes with enthusiasm for thirty-seven years and becoming a well-known figure in Baltimore.

Not that Mrs. Hamburger ignored the race track. As she later explained, she managed her schedule so that she could make almost daily visits to Pimlico.

With her two daughters grown and living in New York, Mrs. Hamburger, by then a widow, was persuaded to move to Manhattan in 1975, but not to give up her career or her hobby. At the age of eighty-five she got a job as a rental agent for a Manhattan building and transferred her racing interest to Belmont and Aqueduct.

Mrs. Hamburger, who loved her work almost as much as horse racing, was finally persuaded to retire at the age of 100. This allowed her to concentrate full-time on racing. A letter she wrote to *The Daily Racing Form* led to a wave of publicity about the 100-year-old horseplayer. She became even more famous when Aqueduct held a race in her honor on her 102d birthday.

Widowed since 1955, Mrs. Hamburger never remarried but contented herself with flirtations, in her later years evincing a special interest in younger men, perhaps because in her later years that was virtually all there were. At a party at Aqueduct on her 102d birthday in 1992, a guest she introduced as "my gentleman friend" admitted that he had not seen Man o' War win the Preakness in 1920. "I wasn't even born," he said.

The fact that she began work for *The Post* on her 105th birthday and that she later appeared on *Late Night with David Letterman* and other television programs and gave many newspaper interviews might suggest she was employed more for her promotional value than for her expertise.

To be sure, her editors graciously refrained from keeping tabs on the record of her daily picks, but Mrs. Hamburger, who took her work so seriously she would be plunged into despair during an inevitable slump, had her share of winners. Indeed, the woman who began her betting life taking a flutter on an adorable German jockey in 1910 ended her career with a flourish. Her last daily selection before she became ill ten days ago came home a winner at Saratoga.

In addition to her daughter, Nancy, of Manhattan, she is survived by another daughter, Caryl Goldsmith of Manhattan, and three granddaughters.

August 8, 1996

Just When the World Was Listening

WILLIAM VICKREY

By Janny Scott

For fifty years, William Vickrey was the ultimate absentminded professor, a brilliant eccentric using abstract economic theory to find solutions to everyday problems. When he won the Nobel Memorial Prize in Economic Science on Tuesday, five days ago, he seemed finally to have a platform from which to make his ideas widely known. Television crews descended. His telephone rang incessantly. Admirers offered to set up meetings with people with the power to put his proposals to work. The world appeared once and for all to be ready to listen. And then, as suddenly as it had happened, it was over.

Professor Vickrey, who was eighty-two, was found slumped behind the wheel of his car on the Hutchinson River Parkway in Harrison, New York, on Thursday, just before midnight. He died, apparently of cardiac arrest, while driving to a conference in Cambridge, Massachusetts, after a whirlwind three days of nonstop attention.

Just hours earlier, sitting in the tiny office at Columbia University where he still went to work every day, encircled by the encroaching paper undergrowth of a well-lived academic life, Professor Vickrey had been asked how it felt to be getting a hearing after so many years. "It feels swell," he sighed. "Ahhhh, at last."

A man described by colleagues as so idiosyncratic and uninterested in material comfort that he barely knew how much he was paid, Professor Vickrey said that he cared far less about his half of the $1.12 million prize from the Bank of Sweden that he shared with James A. Mirrlees of Cambridge University than about what he called "the bully pulpit" it offered for his ideas. For he had devoted much of his energy over sixty years at Columbia to what he described as carrying economic theory to "its ultimate logical conclusions," fashioning unorthodox solutions for such maddening problems as traffic congestion, crowded subways, and bewildering taxes.

He is also credited by other economists with having revolutionized the way they think about auctions, and with having done seminal work in many areas of public economics—taxation, pricing in public utilities, and urban transportation.

"He never drew attention to himself, he never cared where he published," said Ronald Findlay, the chairman of the economics department at Columbia and friend of twenty-seven years. "He was interested in propagating the ideas, not in getting credit for them."

Born in Victoria, British Columbia, on June 21, 1914, the eldest son of a Canadian mother and American father, Professor Vickrey grew up in New York City and its suburbs. His father was executive secretary of Near East Relief, a nonprofit organization devoted to helping orphans from the Armenian holocaust earlier in the century. That experience marked him permanently, as did coming of age during the Depression. "I was raised with the Armenian orphans on the breakfast table," he recently said. He said he had come to feel that any dollar he spent was a dollar not spent to help the orphans.

During World War II, he did civilian public service as a conscientious objector. As a result of that experience, he became a Quaker. Asked about his political views, he said: "Well, I have voted for Norman Thomas, if you want to know." He said he intended to vote for Ralph Nader for President.

Professor Vickrey graduated from high school in Scarsdale at sixteen and was sent to prep school for a year before enrolling at Yale. He majored in mathematics, figuring he knew enough of it already that he would have time for electrical engineering, sociology, and his other interests. It was on a weekend trip home to Scarsdale from New Haven by train that one of his most provocative ideas took root. Noticing how many seats were empty, he thought: What a waste. He figured that his fellow students would enjoy a trip to New York in off-peak hours if the railroad would drop the price to fill the seats.

Out of that, he said this week, emerged many years later some of his proposals for so-called congestion pricing. If the price of traveling from place to place varied by time of day, toll-booth tie-ups would vanish, subways would run pleasantly full, and people would waste less time.

In 1959, for example, Professor Vickrey suggested that one way to control traffic in congested cities would be to equip every vehicle with a transponder, then monitor when and how often each vehicle entered and left the congested area and bill the owners for the so-called social cost of their trips. The fees would be highest during rush hour and diminish gradually at other times. Professor Vickrey went on to make similar proposals to dissipate congestion at bridges and tunnels and to relieve subway and bus overcrowding. He suggested that parking meter fees should vary by time of day and congestion level—and even by the number of meters available that moment.

He had little luck, however, getting his ideas enacted. As he told it, he was given a hearing in 1959 before the chairman of a congressional committee investigating what were called Washington metropolitan problems. He found that his transponder idea was politely ignored: "There was generally a discreet silence."

But he published a paper on the subject and the idea turned up in the 1960s in a paper on road pricing put out by a commission in England. He was invited to England and given an audience with the minister of transport. "I got on TV beside a trained dog act," he recalled.

Since that time, though, Singapore has instituted a similar system. Something like it came close to fruition in Hong Kong, Professor Vickrey said. But at home, he suggested congestion pricing for Hudson River crossings to the Port Authority of New York and New Jersey in the 1970s and was again ignored.

He suggested a new fare structure for the New York City subways in the early 1950s and also had no success. He spent two summers in Japan drawing up a plan for income tax reform that, he said, was rejected. He counted as "a minor victory" his role in 1947 in a new inheritance tax law for Puerto Rico.

But much of his other work heavily influenced other economists. In particular, a paper he wrote in 1961 exploring the theory of auctions and devising a new approach that became the cornerstone of much subsequent work in that field. "It got people thinking about the different ways in which you can design an auction," Professor Findlay said. "In the modern theory of auctions, on which a large number of very brilliant economists around the world are working, they all acknowledge the seminal influence of Vickrey 1961."

Though that work helped win him the Nobel Prize, Professor Vickrey described it on Thursday with characteristic self-deprecation as "one of my digressions into abstract economics. At best, it's of minor significance in terms of human welfare."

Professor Vickrey first arrived at Columbia University as a graduate student in the mid-1930s. To save money, he was living at home. He would ride the train to the station at Park Avenue and 125th Street, then roller-skate across town, a practice he kept up until the late 1940s. At Columbia, he was admired but seen as truly eccentric.

When he took a sabbatical at the Institute for Advanced Study in California in the late 1960s, he received an award he proudly displayed years later known as "The Rip Van Winkle award." "For deep, uninterrupted concentration while attending seminars," the handmade certificate stated. Asked about his qualifications, he said: "Not only there but elsewhere, I have a reputation, not undeserved, for sitting with my eyes closed and possibly even dozing off."

What was more remarkable was that Professor Vickrey would suddenly stir and deliver "the most cogent comment or blockbuster question of the whole discussion," as James Tobin, the economist and Nobel laureate, described it while introducing Professor Vickrey at an award ceremony in 1992.

Though Professor Vickrey retired from teaching and became an emeritus professor in 1982, he remained what one administrator called an "omnipresence" on the Columbia campus, publishing books and papers and slipping quietly into seminars and brown-bag lunches on every imaginable subject.

Over the years, he found himself bounced into progressively smaller offices until he ended three years ago on the eighth floor of a building on Amsterdam Avenue and 118th Street in a shoe box of an office that he cheerfully described as "the world's biggest mess." There were file cabinets topped with cardboard boxes piled as high as the ceiling, files spilled across the floor, prehistoric coffee cups, articles of clothing, broken eyeglasses, tins of evaporated skim milk, a half-dozen oversized but empty soda bottles, and walls of sloping books. In the middle, in a space clear enough to allow his desk chair to roll six inches in any direction, Professor Vickrey would settle in daily, a large man with an expanding middle and wispy white hair, in a rumpled suit, its pockets stuffed with pens and occasionally papers.

Jagdish Bhagwati, a professor of economics and friend who occupies the office two doors down, described Professor Vickrey as "a man of shining honesty" and a kind of innocence, a person who took problems like unemployment deeply to heart.

In recent years, Professor Vickrey had become consumed with trying to fight what he called "the mania for budget balancing," arguing to anyone who would listen that every $10 billion budget deficit cut would mean $10 billion less consumer purchasing power and thus less production and higher unemployment.

He was an inveterate writer of letters to the editor; he said many never got published. But the sudden attention after the Nobel Prize had left him hopeful that an article, "Fifteen Fatal Fallacies of Financial Fundamentalism," which he had sent to *The New York Times Magazine*, would see the light of day.

But for the time being, the Nobel Prize had happily robbed him of free time. From the moment the call from Stockholm woke him up at home in Hastings-on-Hudson on Tuesday at 6:30 A.M., his telephone had not stopped ringing with requests from people suddenly interested to hear what he had to say. There had been a press conference at Columbia at 11:00 A.M. at which he was mobbed by reporters, then several hours of interviews back to back, then a champagne reception in the economics department, then radio interviews and television appearances and requests for more constantly piling up.

By Thursday afternoon, he was back in his office returning reporters' calls, enthusiastically elaborating on whatever anybody wanted to know. He said there was even a move afoot by someone he could not remember to arrange a meeting between him and city transit officials.

He was planning, he said, to leave for Cambridge sometime before 11:00 P.M. About 11:45 P.M., the Westchester County Police received a call from a driver on the Hutchinson River Parkway reporting a car stopped in the right, northbound lane. When the police arrived, the man behind the wheel, Professor Vickrey, was not breathing. He was pronounced dead at St. Agnes Hospital at 12:43 A.M., said Detective William Rehm of the Westchester County Police.

Dr. Louis Roh, a deputy medical examiner for the county, said in an interview yesterday that an autopsy found that Professor Vickrey had suffered from a mildly enlarged heart. He appeared to have died of sudden cardiac death brought on by an arrhythmia, or irregular heartbeat, Dr. Roh said.

Whether the experiences of the previous three days might have triggered the problem is unclear. But Dr. Myron Weisfeldt, chairman of the department of medicine at Columbia Presbyterian Medical Center and a past president of the American Heart Association, said research strongly suggests that stress can precipitate sudden cardiac death.

Shortly after dawn, Professor Findlay received a call from Professor Vickrey's wife, Cecile, who is his only surviving family member. "It was, of course, absolutely devastating," he said, all the more so because just three days earlier, almost to the hour, he had called the Vickreys to congratulate them on the prize.

"It was going to provide him a new platform for his ideas," said Jonathan R. Cole, provost and dean of the faculties at Columbia. "And many of those ideas still bear real consideration and would have had a new life. They would have been part of a new drama. The denouement came too soon."

October 12, 1996

Giving Well Is the Best Revenge

ELIZABETH BOTTOMLEY NOYCE

By Robert McG. Thomas, Jr.

Elizabeth Bottomley Noyce, a microchip millionaire's scorned first wife who showed as much imagination and verve in deploying her half of his Silicon Valley fortune as he had in making it, died at her seaside home in Bremen, Maine. She was sixty-five and had been the state's premier philanthropist and most innovative investor for two decades. Her lawyer, Owen Wells, noting that Mrs. Noyce had long suffered from emphysema, said the cause was a heart attack.

The daughter of a blue-collar worker from Auburn, Massachusetts, who had to hold two jobs to support his family in the Depression, Elizabeth Bottomley was majoring in English at Tufts University in the early 1950s and dreaming of becoming a writer when she signed on as costume director of a summer theatrical production and caught the eye of one of the cast members, a graduate student at the Massachusetts Institute of Technology named Robert N. Noyce. The couple were married in 1953, and Mrs. Noyce, who had dreamed of writing novels and short stories, became the most dutiful of corporate wives, bearing four children and following her husband from job to job, including a somewhat reluctant move to California for a woman who never felt comfortable away from her beloved New England. "We were under the distinct impression that we would try it for a year and if I didn't like it we wouldn't stay," she recalled years later, suggesting that her husband had forgotten the bargain. "We stayed nineteen years."

By then the life of the blue-collar worker's daughter had changed considerably, largely because her husband had become a co-inventor of the microchip, which laid the foundation for the vast personal computer industry, and had helped found three of the industry's leading companies, including the giant Intel Corporation.

Her life changed even more in 1975 when Mr. Noyce left her to marry an Intel executive. Although bitter over the circumstances of the breakup of her marriage, Mrs. Noyce, whose ex-husband died in 1990, managed to console herself somewhat in the divorce. Under California's community property laws she claimed half his Intel stock and all his other assets, including full title to their fifty-acre Maine estate, where Mrs. Noyce had been spending summers.

How much she received from the divorce could not be determined, and a spokesman for Intel, which has a market capitalization of $86 billion, could not say how much stock she owned at the time of her death. Mr. Wells, her lawyer, said, however, that after all her charitable donations, her estate was worth $100 million to $1 billion.

Putting her husband and California behind her, Mrs. Noyce did not so much move to Maine as adopt the state. In a whirlwind of philanthropy that began almost as soon as she settled into her house on Muscongus Bay and continued the rest of her life, she systematically gave away some $75 million, primarily to Maine charities.

Oh, there would be the occasional out-of-state donation—a million to Tufts here, a half million to Harvard there—but for the most part, Mrs. Noyce, whose donations covered the gamut of public causes, including education, medicine, the arts, and the environment, concentrated her giving in Maine, responding to virtually any cause, charity, or public institution in the state that needed money. Among other things, she built a golf course for the town of Bremen, and gave lavishly to the Portland Museum of Art, the Maine Maritime Museum, and the University of Maine. When the Cumberland County Civic Center was so pressed for cash that it was looking for a corporate sponsor that would give it money in exchange for the right to give the center its name, Mrs. Noyce came through with a $1.3 million donation that allowed the center to retain its identity.

But for all the acclaim Mrs. Noyce received for her direct philanthropy, including the $15 million in endowments for charitable trusts that make independent grants to Maine charities, Mrs. Noyce gained even more applause when she began pioneering what she called "catalytic philanthropy," investments designed to bolster the state's economy. In 1991, for example, when out-of-state financial institutions were picking off Maine's banks one by one and it appeared that Maine businesses and other borrowers would soon be at the mercy of distant lenders, Mrs. Noyce blithely created a brand-new bank, the Maine Bank and Trust Company, with an initial $7.7 million investment that eventually grew to some $14 million. What made such "philanthropy" especially appealing became apparent when the bank prospered. Mr. Wells, who advised Mrs. Noyce on her investments, estimated that the bank was now worth at least twice what she paid for it.

During a lull in Maine's construction industry, Mrs. Noyce built five homes to provide jobs for construction workers, and when Maine's leading bakery was threatened with a takeover by a company that intended to move it out of state, Mrs. Noyce came to the rescue, buying the bakery and saving its twelve hundred jobs.

A short time before her death, Mrs. Noyce had turned her attention to Portland's deteriorating downtown, going on a buying spree in which she acquired about 10 percent of the city's office and retail space. The rehabilitation effort attracted L.L. Bean and other tenants.

Although her efforts won wide praise, there were some rumblings that Mrs. Noyce was becoming too big a factor in the Portland economy. As a result she had recently announced that she had no further designs on downtown property.

For all her fortune, Mrs. Noyce lived fairly simply, shunning the usual trappings of wealth and even driving her own car, most recently a Cadillac, to be sure, but only, she told her friends, because after a wreck in her smaller Oldsmobile, she felt more secure in a larger car. Although she was always appropriately dressed, Mrs. Noyce had no interest in fashion and even less in travel, preferring to stay in Maine rather than visit the world's resorts.

Not that she was above the occasional indulgence. When she found that the steep driveway to her house became dangerously slick with wintertime ice, she built a more accessible winter home a thousand feet away.

Her only real material weakness stemmed from her love of the water, but it was a tribute to her reputation for innovative "catalytic philanthropy," that when she indulged her passion by commissioning a multimillion-dollar sixty-foot yacht a few years ago, the acquisition was not viewed in Maine as an example of conspicuous consumption. Instead, the purchase was trumpeted in the Maine press as a rescue of Maine's boat-building industry. In recent months Mrs. Noyce had apparently developed renewed concern about the state's beleaguered boat builders; she commissioned a ninety-foot yacht.

Mrs. Noyce is survived by a son, William, of Hollis, New Hampshire; three daughters, Pendred, of Weston, Massachusetts, Priscilla, of Kenya, and Margaret, of Montana; two brothers, Frank Bottomley of Ohio and Bruce Bottomley of New Hampshire; a sister, Frances Broomhead of Rhode Island, and thirteen grandchildren.

September 20, 1996

Save the Cheesecake

HARRY ROSEN

By Eric Asimov

Harry Rosen, who founded Junior's Restaurant, the Brooklyn institution renowned for cheesecake so rich and creamy it makes tough men swoon, died at his home in Fort Lauderdale. He was ninety-two. The cause was bladder cancer, said a son, Marvin Rosen.

For almost forty-six years, Junior's has anchored the intersection in downtown Brooklyn of Fulton Street, DeKalb Avenue, and the Flatbush Avenue extension. The lively, brassy restaurant with orange booths that can seat nearly four hundred diners has been a magnet for politicians who come to make deals, journalists who come to meet politicians, and moviegoers who come for refreshment. But above all, everyone comes for the cheesecake.

"It was perfect, it was the platonic cheesecake, as smooth as alabaster," said Michael Stern, who with his wife, Jane, writes about American regional foods. "If you think of great cheesecake, you think of New York cheesecake, and when you wanted great cheesecake in New York, you went to Junior's."

When Mr. Rosen opened Junior's on November 4, 1950, it quickly became the place to go before seeing a movie and a stage show at one of the downtown palaces like the Albee, the Fox, and the Strand. After a Dodgers game, people would travel to Junior's on the Flatbush Avenue trolley. Later, it became a hangout for Brooklyn politicians. "Guys like Meade Esposito would go in there and make judges in the back room," the writer Pete Hamill said.

Even today, Junior's is an obligatory stop on the campaign trail. Bill Clinton ate cheesecake there while campaigning for President in 1992, while Mayor Rudolph W. Giuliani, District Attorney Charles J. Hynes of Brooklyn, and the Rev. Al Sharpton are among those noshers who believe flashbulbs are just another kind of icing on the cheesecake.

Mr. Rosen was born in 1904 on the Lower East Side of Manhattan. At thirteen, he dropped out of school to work as a soda jerk. Before long, he opened his own sandwich shop in Manhattan, the Enduro, named after the equipment company that provided him with stainless steel. Eventually, he owned five Enduro sandwich shops, four in Manhattan and one in Brooklyn, on the site of Junior's. In the 1930s, Mr. Rosen sold his Manhattan branches to concentrate on the Brooklyn Enduro. "It was a large bar with entertainment and a steakhouse," Marvin Rosen recalled. But after World War II, he said, his father decided he had to change with the times. He closed the Enduro, and after a year of renovation, Junior's was born.

Mr. Rosen ran Junior's with his two sons, Marvin and Walter, a family arrangement that inspired the restaurant's name. "Working with him was not a picnic," Marvin Rosen said. "He was a tough, demanding man. He was a perfectionist."

He brought this perfectionist attitude to the creation of Junior's cheesecake, which he devised with the restaurant's head baker, Eigel Petersen. As Marvin Rosen remembers it, his father brought to Brooklyn cheesecakes he had tasted all over the country. "My father was the type of man who, when he saw a product, would buy it and bring it back, even from Oshkosh, to examine it," he said.

While Junior's is a full-service restaurant, offering corned beef, steaks, and seafood carried by its fast-talking waiters, cheesecake gradually became its signature dish. And though Junior's is generally thought to be a product of earlier, more Runyonesque times, it was not until 1973, when Junior's won a cheesecake contest held by *New York* magazine, that its claim to the world's cheesecake throne was finally made, Marvin Rosen said.

Since then, Junior's has drawn a steady stream of tourists to Brooklyn for a taste, but these pilgrimages were interrupted in 1981 by a fire that left the restaurant a scarred ruin. Shouts of "Save the cheesecake" rose from the crowd anxiously watching the firefighters. It took almost a year to repair, but, like an irrepressible soufflé, Junior's rose again, reopening in 1982.

Mr. Rosen retired in the mid-1970s, ceding control of the restaurant to his sons. Marvin and Walter Rosen now are turning the restaurant over to a third generation, Walter's sons, Kevin and Alan, who have added a mail-order cheesecake business.

In addition to his two sons and two grandsons, Mr. Rosen is survived by his wife of sixty-seven years, Ruth; a sister, Marcia, of Boca Raton, Florida; seven other grandchildren, and six great-grandchildren.

Recipe of a Lifetime: Junior's Cheesecake

¼ cup graham cracker crumbs
¾ cup plus 2 tablespoons sugar
3 tablespoons sifted cornstarch
30 ounces (3¾ large packages)
    cream cheese, softened

I large egg
½ cup heavy (whipping) cream
¾ teaspoon vanilla extract

1. Preheat the oven to 350 degrees. Generously butter the bottom and sides of an 8-inch springform pan. Lightly coat the bottom of the pan with the graham cracker crumbs and refrigerate the pan.

2. In a large bowl, combine the sugar and the cornstarch. Beat in the cream cheese. Beat in the egg. Slowly drizzle in the heavy cream, beating constantly. Add the vanilla and stir well.

3. Pour the mixture into the prepared pan. Bake until top is golden, 40 to 45 minutes. Cool in the pan on a wire rack for 3 hours.

Yield: 8 to 10 servings

October 11, 1996

The Littlest Aviator

JESSICA DUBROFF

By Sam Howe Verhovek

Cheyenne, Wyoming, April 11—A seven-year-old California girl on a quest to become the youngest cross-country pilot was killed today when her single-engine plane crashed shortly after takeoff in thunder and driving sleet. Her father and a flight instructor were also killed.

The brown-haired, four-feet two-inch Jessica Dubroff had flown out of Half Moon Bay, California, yesterday (Wednesday morning), and executed a flawless landing in high winds that evening in Cheyenne. But this morning her plane, bound for the next stopover in Indiana and ultimately for Cape Cod, Massachussets, crashed just moments after it lifted off in Wyoming.

Although Jessica was clearly at the controls as the four-seat Cessna 177B took off, the authorities could not say whether or not the veteran flight instructor, Joe Reid, fifty-two, had taken command of the craft in the final moments before, eyewitnesses said, it plunged, almost straight down, and hit a residential street nose first. All three people aboard were dead at the scene.

"I was shocked to see an airplane taking off in these weather conditions—my wipers on high speed could barely keep up," said Mel Montoya, a clerk at a Sam's Club store, who was stopped in his car at an intersection near the airport. "The plane was struggling and dipping."

Mourners converged on the crash site, where the police had quickly placed a heavy tarpaulin over the wreckage, leaving flowers, stuffed animals, and written scraps of Bible verse. "God's newest little angel" read one note.

Jessica was breaking no aviation rules when she flew. The plane had dual sets of controls, meaning that the flight instructor was legally considered in charge and had the ability to take control instantly, though the plans called for Mr. Reid to take over only in an emergency. But within hours of the crash, federal authorities announced that they would reexamine existing regulations on underage pilots.

Even before the crash, the exploits of the spunky, freckle-faced Jessica with her "Women Fly" baseball cap commanded news coverage from coast to coast. After landing in Cheyenne late Wednesday in a Cessna outfitted with a booster seat so she could see out the window and extensions on the pedals so her legs could reach them, Jessica quickly captivated people in Cheyenne at a news conference at the airport. "It's been a long day," she said then. "I can't wait until the next day. I can't wait to sleep. I had two hours of sleep last night."

Her father, Lloyd, said: "She really does love to fly. This started off as a father-daughter adventure and it's gotten wonderfully out of hand."

Barely twelve hours later Jessica was dead. Her mother, Lisa Blair Hathaway, said she had heard no word of problems as the three began to take off. Ms. Hathaway had spoken via cellular telephone to Jessica moments before the takeoff here. "Do you hear the rain?" Jessica had asked her excitedly. "Do you hear the rain?"

"I beg people to let children fly if they want to fly," a teary-eyed Ms. Hathaway told the Associated Press before flying from Boston to Wyoming to claim her daughter's body. She had flown ahead to Massachusetts to await the arrival of Jessica and her ex-husband. "Clearly I would want all my children to die in a state of joy. I mean, what more could I ask for? I would prefer it was not at age seven but, God, she went with her joy and her passion, and her life was in her hands," Ms. Hathaway said.

The Mayor of Cheyenne, Leo Pando, broke down at a news conference this morning, saying that Jessica had reminded him of his own daughter, who had died in a flood eleven years ago at the age of sixteen. "I cared deeply for this little girl," he said. "She had a refreshing optimism that is plainly lacking in today's world." The Mayor said Jessica had told him she had drawn up the flight plans herself, picking Cheyenne as the first stop after calculating how far a tank of gas would take her from her home in California.

But for all of Jessica's moxie and precocious intelligence, many people here and around the country wondered why she had been allowed to pilot a plane at such a young age.

Still, some aviation experts insisted the question was less why she was at the pilot's seat—after all, she had flown for months before without incident and several other young children have accomplished aviation feats—than why the plane took off at all, in a thunderstorm and near-freezing conditions. The distance record she was trying to set, from the Pacific Ocean to the Atlantic and back again, did not hinge in any way on making good time.

"I don't think we should look at it from the view of whether a seven-year-old should be encouraged to fly airplanes," said David Boone, an Atlanta lawyer who is a specialist in aviation issues and a pilot of twenty-four years. "I do think we should look at it from the view of the judgment made to take off in a small, one-motor private airplane, in light of what I understand was a thunderstorm. Thunderstorms have all of Mother Nature's flying troubles in a bundle. Updrafts and down-drafts and turbulence, potential for icing, hail, all in one local area. And any of those things can upset an airplane."

Jessica, who was a fan of biographies of the aviator Amelia Earhart, had arranged to visit her grandparents in Massachusetts and Florida and to stop over on her return trip in Washington, D.C., where she had even hoped to entice President Clinton to fly with her aboard the Cessna. "To visit you at the White House would be wonderful and clearly to pilot an airplane that you would be in would bring me an even greater joy," the girl wrote in a hand-written letter quoted in *The San Jose Mercury News*. The article said her plea to the President had drawn no response.

Jessica, born at home in a birthing tub, lived with her mother and her two siblings—Joshua, nine, and Jasmine, three,—in Pescadero, about forty miles south of San Francisco. The children were educated at home and also taught things like how to build furniture and repair houses. Their father, Lloyd, lived with his second wife in San Mateo, also in the Bay Area.

Mr. Dubroff said that he had thought of the idea of the cross-country flight after being inspired by a similar odyssey by a little girl a few years ago. He said he had asked Jessica and she loved the idea.

The *Guinness Book of World Records* once kept official records in the "youngest pilot" category but stopped doing so a few years ago because it did not want to encourage unsafe flights, a spokesman said. A similar decision was made by the National Aeronautic Association, which keeps American aviation records. But the unofficial record was set in 1991 by Daniel Shanklin of San Antonio, Texas, then seven, who flew from San Diego to Kill Devil Hills, North Carolina. Jessica was less than a month younger than Daniel was at the time of his flight.

The Cheyenne police chief, John Powell, said that whoever was piloting the plane had evidently made an attempt to avoid hitting houses even as the plane plunged to the ground. Several witnesses also said the plane never appeared to have got higher than a few hundred feet. There was some speculation that Mr. Reid may have been reluctant to take the controls for fear of technically negating Jessica's accomplishment. But Jessica suggested that he may have done so on the first leg of the journey. "Over the Sierra it was just perfect, until we got over to the Rockies and they were bumpy, kind of bumpy," she told radio station KGO in San Francisco on Wednesday.

A solo pilot of a plane must be at least sixteen years old. But a person of any age may fly next to a licensed pilot, who may let that person take control if he or she feels it is safe to do so.

Jessica carried a wallet with an ace of spades in it for luck while she flew. In an interview with *The Times* of London she had said she could not wait until she turned sixteen and could fly solo.

"I just love to fly," said Jessica. "I'm going to fly 'til I die."

April 12, 1996

"SHE WILL SOAR WITH THE ANGELS"

MICHAEL J. YBARRA went to JESSICA DUBROFF's hometown of Pescadero on the day she was killed and talked to the people who remembered her.

The small buzzing dot in the sky over the gentle green hills of Pescadero, California, circled around and around the farm until Kelly McKnight realized that it was his seven-year-old pony-riding pupil practicing flying a Cessna. "We said, 'That's Jess,' and waved," Mr. McKnight recalled.

Jessica Dubroff was a smiling young girl that everyone waved at and few knew terribly well, a child whose mother took her to this small town and yet kept her apart by imbuing her with a New Age philosophy that disdained toys and games in favor of making furniture and other pursuits far from the ken of most young children.

The mother, Lisa Hathaway, forty-one, gave birth to Jessica at home in a tub of warm water to ease her entry into the world and taught her three children at home—a fact that local school officials discovered only recently, since Ms. Hathaway had not filed the proper papers for home schooling when the family moved here about a year ago. Whether they handled power tools or the controls of an airplane, Ms. Hathaway believed that her children should strive for fulfillment in anything that interested them. "She allowed those kids to go for their dreams," said Alexis Glattly, who works at Duarte's, a family restaurant in this town of four hundred people, halfway between San Francisco and Santa Cruz.

Those dreams turned to ashes when Jessica, her father, Lloyd Dubroff, fifty-seven, and her flight instructor, Joe Reid, fifty-two, were killed on the second day of Jessica's quest to become the youngest pilot to fly across the country. Mr. Reid's Cessna, in which Jessica had logged about forty hours of flight time over the last five months, crashed in bad weather shortly after takeoff in Cheyenne, Wyoming.

The accident has moved critics to say Jessica's parents might have pushed her beyond her years, and might have been tempted by the publicity that the venture attracted. But those who knew Jessica said her parents believed that they were encouraging their children to realize dreams and aspirations—whether through music lessons, daily pony rides, or twice-a-week flights in single-engine planes that could reach 160 miles an hour. "Whatever they wanted, their mother supported them," said a neighbor, Patty Sarabia. "She believed they could do anything."

Ms. Hathaway has told reporters that she did not believe in letting her children use negative words like "scared," "fear," and "sadness." "Children are fearless," Ms. Hathaway told *The San Jose Mercury News*. "That's their natural state until adults ingrain fear in them."

In Pescadero, Jessica had plenty of nature to explore. The town, which was established in 1856 by Portuguese and Italian farmers, sits in a verdant valley two miles from the coast and about twenty-five miles of winding country roads away from suburban San Mateo County, where Mr. Dubroff, a corporate consultant, lived with his new wife. The pace here is quiet, with little activity evident except for laborers tending to artichokes and strawberries on family farms. The grocery store closes at 7:00 P.M., and a gift shop opens its doors only Friday through Sunday. Ms. Hathaway, who lived with Jessica and her other children—Joshua, nine, and Jasmine, three—had rented a white two-story house at the beginning of North Street, the main thoroughfare in the small residential area. Recently, they moved across the street to a small tan house, with a stream running through the woods behind it.

Jessica, described as mature and well-spoken beyond her age, played with her siblings in the street, helped neighbors tend their gardens, or rode her bicycle down the lonely country road to Mr. McKnight's farm, where she learned to ride and took a pony into the hills almost every day in exchange for taking care of the animals.

Mr. McKnight said Jessica seemed to want to fly cross-country as soon as she started taking flying lessons, five months before her death. She appears to have become interested in aviation when her parents sent her up in a plane for her sixth birthday and the pilot let her take the controls. "The kid just carried enthusiasm with her everywhere," he said. "She was never pushed into anything."

And neighbors did not begrudge the family its unorthodox way of life, even when Ms. Hathaway spurned the local produce for organic vegetables sold fourteen miles up the coast in Half Moon Bay or avoided most of the fare at Duarte's except for the four servings of French fries that were the normal order for the family heading home after a flying lesson. "We're very eclectic around here," said Ms. Glattly at the restaurant. "That's why we live out here, because no one else can stand us."

Pescadero is the kind of place where the large flag at the post office near the single flashing red traffic signal at the town's crossroads comes down to half-staff when a local person dies, and does not come up again until after the funeral.

On Thursday, the flag went down for Jessica, flowers piled up at its base and one of the little girl's neighbors added a note: "Jessica—She will soar with the Angels."

Another patron in the bar at Duarte's, who gave his name only as Charlie, said, "I know a lot of people fifty years old who never lived as much as that little girl."

April 13, 1996

MAKING SENSE OF JESSICA'S DEATH

A New York Times *editorial took this view:*

The death of seven-year-old Jessica Dubroff has obsessed America. There were few park bench conversations, lunchroom discussions, or even telephone calls yesterday that did not include an exchange of opinions about the little girl who crashed her plane while trying to become the youngest cross-country pilot ever.

In retrospect, the whole idea was lunatic. Leaving aside the question of whether small children should be allowed to operate planes, it is obvious that they should not be maneuvering tiny craft over mountains, flying for long periods that would tempt any adult to lose concentration, or taking off in high winds and heavy rain.

Jessica's father, who underwrote the fifteen-thousand-dollar cross-country flight and described it as a bonding experience with his daughter, died in the crash, along with her flying instructor, who was the official pilot. Her mother, Lisa Hathaway, has continued to insist that the flight—and even the decision to take off in bad weather—was a good idea. "I did everything so this child could have freedom in choice, and have what America stands for," she said.

Ms. Hathaway's insistence that adults could best serve her seven-year-old by encouraging her to take enormous chances has already opened her up to widespread criticism. But outrage from the public and the media, which until yesterday had applauded the guts and charm of baby pilots like Jessica, may include a smattering of sour guilt.

America's attitude toward children and risk is wildly contradictory. Parents are increasingly obsessive about safety. *The Times* reported this week, for instance, that monkey bars are becoming an endangered species in parks because they are regarded as too dangerous. "I put safety before imagination," said a former president of a Manhattan playground association. Yet the same country that now debates whether grocery shopping carts should be required to have children's seat belts seemed comfortable to cheer on a fifty-five-pound girl piloting a plane across the Rocky Mountains.

The spectacle of ten-, nine-, and eight-year-olds flying planes across country has been occurring for nearly a decade even though the *Guinness Book of World Records* wisely stopped keeping tabs on the youngest pilots in order to forestall just the kind of tragedy that occurred this week. Now members of Congress are mulling legislation to prohibit children from flying. Stricter rules are clearly in order.

Balancing the dangers and rewards of childhood risk-taking is a subtle challenge. Piloting a plane with proper supervision in good weather is probably no more dangerous than horseback riding, or riding a bicycle in traffic. We celebrate the image of Huckleberry Finn floating free on the Mississippi, but drag our heels when our own children request Rollerblades.

The most troubling part of Jessica's death is the suspicion that her flight was not spontaneous childish adventurousness but an idea promoted by the adults around her. This was a lapse of parental responsibility.

Whether or not she was directly pushed into trying to become the youngest cross-country flier, those close to Jessica failed in their duty to protect her from her innocent sense of invulnerability.

April 13, 1996

THE DREAM MACHINE

A column by MAUREEN DOWD *maintained the following:*

It's a familiar story. The Dream becomes a Nightmare. Television logos shifted seamlessly from the Jessica Dubroff Adventure to the Jessica Dubroff Tragedy. Newspaper headlines went from a little girl with a big dream to the death of a little girl and her big dream.

We learn early on, in this business, how to gussy up macabre curiosity as public service. Ted Koppel interviewed a child psychologist on the issue of parental pressure. Forrest Sawyer asked David Hinson of the FAA about his review of regulations on kids' manipulating airplane controls. "Age is not an issue here," he replied.

Larry King asked nine-year-old aviator Killian Moss about whether Jessica's accident made him fearful of flying. "Um," Killian replied, "it just made me stop and think, like, no more flying through bad weather."

The solemn concern about nutty juvenile stunts comes too late. Before the trip, everyone treated a dangerous gimmick as cute. Jessica was hyped as a fifty-five-pound Amelia Earhart, in her brown leather jacket and "Women Fly" cap, with a red booster seat to help her see over the instrument panel and three-inch aluminum extensions on the rudder pedals.

"You are actually going to take off, fly the plane the whole way, and do all the landings as well?" Forrest Sawyer asked on ABC.

"Yes," she said.

She and her father told reporters it was his idea to have his daughter fly sixty-nine hundred miles in eight days. "Out of the blue," he said, "it occurred to me that Jessica could do this."

Why didn't we all just get up and begin screaming THIS IS CRAZY!!!

At seven, you should be taking your first trip around the block on your bike. You should not be expected to have the maturity to tell your immature father and miscalculating flight instructor that the weather looks too icky to take off. Especially when your father is in a rush to arrive in Massachusetts and make NBC's *Today* show.

No, we should never have treated the lovely little girl trying to break a silly record as a heroine. And, though it may be hard to draw the line in a society where people will say and do anything to get on TV, we never should have rewarded Lloyd Dubroff for using his daughter to quench his own thirst for celebrity. This was an inhuman interest story.

It's heartbreaking to watch the tape made just before the fatal Cheyenne takeoff, as Jessica tries to answer a TV reporter's chirpy questions, even as she distractedly looks back at her small plane being pelted by hail and sleet.

People gripe about too much regulation. But there's no minimum age to learn to fly? A child may be called a passenger and there may be a flight instructor with dual controls, but so what? And there's no rule that small planes can't take off in hail and wind shear?

The *Guinness Book of World Records*, not wanting to encourage pushy parents, no longer recognizes the "youngest pilot" category. But who needs *Guinness* when you've got the networks falling all over themselves?

It is creepy to see the film of Jessica in the cockpit, which her father shot from the back seat with a camera provided by ABC News.

Lloyd Dubroff: "What would you do, Jess, if the engine quit right now?"

Jessica: "I don't know."

A video camera was found in the wreckage.

After the crash, FAA officials sounded disturbingly like NRA and cigarette lobbyists: Any controls would be bad. Young customers are good. This is a free country. "There was ridiculous exploitation of her by the media and her family," said one FAA official, speaking privately. "But we shouldn't have a reaction to that, so that nobody below the age of fifteen will ever be able to feel the joy of flight."

The aftermath was surreal. Befitting the age of Oprah, when Jessica's mother was comforted by a pilot who saw the crash and knew that Jessica died too quickly to suffer, the entire exchange was done on camera.

Lisa Blair Hathaway, the mother and "spiritual healer" who raised Jessica in New Age freedom, said her daughter had died "in a state of joy": "She had the room to be, she had the room to choose, she had the room to have her life."

Perhaps too much room? Ms. Hathaway urged the FAA to let children fly.

Surely, Jessica is flying. Only angels have wings.

April 14, 1996

THE DEMON SUCCESS

This is what RUSSELL BAKER *had to say in his column:*

The death last week of Jessica Dubroff, the seven-year-old flier, produced a spate of un-American criticism of parents who push their children too hard too soon. This outburst resulted not from a sudden public onset of good sense, but only because of the melodramatic way Jessica died. After the fatal crash it suddenly became obvious, even to parents who are maniacal about driving their children to succeed, that Jessica's situation had been surreal all along. Until she crashed, our perceptions were not so keen.

A little girl out to break a bizarre record by becoming the youngest human ever to fly across the continent was treated as a cute and blessedly light news feature with which to offset the hard stuff about graves in Bosnia and political raids on the Constitution.

If anybody in press, television, or pulpit thought before Jessica's death that there was something unhealthy about what Father and Mother were up to with their seven-year-old, I missed it.

Precisely because it was so nutty, it was easy after the fact to blame her parents. How many parents are leaning on seven-year-olds to set new aviation records?

And yet, what could be more American than loving parents leaning on their children to grow up and set the world on fire? Those parents who would kill to have their toddlers admitted to New York's most celebrated private schools—are they really so superior to Jessica's with their silly ambition for their daughter to excel?

And what is the point of preparing those kiddies to join the set-the-world-on-fire crowd? It is to get them admitted to Harvard, Yale, Princeton, and other such temples of learning, whence they will go forth and actually, in many cases, set the world on fire.

I mean no disrespect for good education, but many a child would be happier for having been spared parental insistence on acquiring it. Many a child who might have made an excellent cobbler or police sergeant or vegetable manager at a supermarket is instead forced into high-toned work at which he acquires an elegant title, a corner office, and magnificent psychiatrist's bills.

I speak, of course, of those grown-up kiddies—and they must be legion—who agree to excel at something in which they are not much interested, because their parents will feel good about having begot such a famous daughter or son.

This is not to denigrate every Harvard grad who winds up as a grandee of Washington, or Wall Street, or the courtroom. Many find it easy to accommodate their parents' egos and would not do anything else. Many not only enjoy their careers immensely, but also enjoy sitting around with the old folks, flashing their cuff links and dropping White House names just to let the old folks see what a swell job they did at parenthood.

Our society does not abuse these parents for having forced their children from the cradle to work at becoming big shots. To the contrary, parents are judged commendable for having leaned on their progeny to make something of themselves.

Parents who make their children's lives hell in order to make the parents proud of themselves are a commonplace of American life. "Theater mothers" push six-year-olds to become Broadway stars. Tennis-crazed parents push them toward stardom at Wimbledon. Fathers far gone in dreams of basking in the glory which a World Series winner would bring the family often turn Little League baseball into a nightmare for sons. Football-oriented fathers who dream of huge, brutal running-back sons have been known to pump up high school boys with growth hormones.

Which is even more bizarre, if you ask me, than letting your seven-year-old reach for fame by flying airplanes around the continent in pursuit of nonsensical aviation records.

It is hard for children to save their own identities from hard-driving parents determined to make their children be what the parents want them to be. After an event as macabre as the death of Jessica Dubroff it is easy to see and to deplore the parental impulse to force children to do their utmost to get to the top. And yet, what could be more American? The parent who lets the children go their own way is a parent who is a disgrace to American parenthood.

April 20, 1996

JUST A LITTLE GIRL IN A BOOSTER SEAT

An essay by ANNA QUINDLEN, *a novelist and a former columnist for* The New York Times, *took this view:*

She delivered newspapers on her bicycle, helped neighbors pull weeds, and sent half her allowance each month to a relief group for children. Other kids liked to be around Jessica Dubroff because, as one family friend said, she was "so loving and happy." Jessica Dubroff was, by all accounts, a joyful child, just over four feet tall, just under eight years old, until the moment when, in a tangled twisted sarcophagus of metal that had once been a single-engine Cessna, she became a symbol of the American zest for blame and recrimination.

"Women Fly," said the baseball cap she wore. But, of course, Jessica Dubroff was not a woman when she set out to become the youngest person to pilot a plane across America, just a little girl who needed a booster seat to see out the windshield. And almost as soon as the plane had gone, nose down, into the asphalt of a residential street in Cheyenne, Wyoming, she had ceased in the collective American mind to be even that. Instead, the spot where the plane had crashed, killing Jessica, her father, and her flight instructor, became the intersection of second-guessing, social commentary, and scathing criticism.

Even before the California-to-Cape Cod journey began, Jessica had become the media flavor of the month, questioned and photographed by a constant coterie of reporters. After the crash came uglier questions: Had the enormous amount of press attention fueled a quest that seemed first quixotic, then simply mad? And would the two men who were flying with Jessica have decided to take off in a thunderstorm, the plane pummeled by driving sleet and winds, had they not felt that the whole world was watching?

But press criticism paled in the face of the pillorying of Jessica's parents, particularly her mother, who as she buried her child was being buried herself under a barrage of blame. Lisa Blair Hathaway made an easy target. She became famous for saying her daughter had died "in a state of joy," when all most of us could imagine was the look the little girl might have had on her face as the ground came rushing up, a final destination that her mother, who refused to let her three children use negative words, seemed never to have let her imagine. How cheap and easy it became to mock Jessica's mother in her bereavement, to write condescendingly of the New Age proscriptions, the vegetarianism and the underwater births, the children who played with tools instead of toys and were not permitted to go to school.

Jessica Dubroff's death set off a national debate about an America that has forgotten the meaning of childhood. But lost in all the public discussion about what it means to be a kid was the kid herself. In a time when we find our children too often ill-mannered and unengaged, she was by all accounts polite, personable, and intensely interested in the world around her. She liked to read about Amelia Earhart, to stop on her bike on a country road to look at snails and insects, to slip an extra scoop of grain to one of the older horses at the stable where she learned to ride. Commentators and callers to talk-radio savaged Jessica's mother in the days after the crash. But somehow she had produced a lovely little girl.

That was an inconvenient bit of cognitive dissonance in a story about which so many found it simple to be judgmental. In hindsight, which is always twenty-twenty and which sometimes seems to be the only way we in America care to look at anything, there was a macabre resonance to Jessica's words about her flight. "I just love to fly," she said. "I'm going to fly 'til I die." But divest the sentence of its horrible aftermath and what is left is excitement, and passion, and youth, irrepressible youth, which always believes "'til I die" is forever away. The little girl died in a plane crash, but part of her, the memories of the way she was in life, were snuffed out as well by the reflexive, almost gleeful way in which we turned her from a child into merely a collection of issues.

December 29, 1996
THE NEW YORK TIMES MAGAZINE

The Long Good-bye

FLORENCE HOSCH

By Dudley Clendinen

My cousin Florence Hosch finally died the Wednesday before Christmas, about a thousand days after she had wished to. Her Christmas card, mailed from the nursing home in Dunedin, Florida, came the following Tuesday. Florence herself didn't arrive for almost a month, but I knew she was en route.

After three years of hospitals, nursing homes, doctors, social workers, lawyers, accountants, and real-estate agents, the last employee of the last enterprise in charge of her long and exhausting death telephoned to say that it was over. "Hi, this is American Burial and Cremation calling, just to let you know that the remains for Florence Hosch are being sent out today," the woman said.

Like so many others, Florence had been delayed by the snowstorm, as she had been delayed in dying—like so many others—by the System. Delayed against her principles. Against her wishes, oral and written. She was, in harboring the wish to die when life seemed over, ahead of her time.

Nursing homes are full of people like Florence, trapped in transit between retirement and death. They are the parents, the aunts and uncles of my generation—the boomers—and their number is going to grow and grow, because they are being cared for by a system that considers it irresponsible to let them die.

When Florence succumbed to lack of oxygen and increased morphine, she was almost ninety-three. She had had ninety good years and three wretched ones, the wretchedness relieved mainly by drugs, by the calls and visits of those who loved her, by her intermittent plotting of how to leave us all behind, and, mainly, by her own splendid spirit.

Intellectual, well-educated, passionate about life, Florence and her husband, Louie, were liberal to a fault. He was a United Nations official. She was a professor of social work at the University of Illinois and later a consultant in the fields of social welfare and public health in New York, Rome, Panama, and, after they retired, in Clearwater, Florida. They had no children, and in the ten years after Louie died the question of what made life worthwhile seemed increasingly a part of Florence's consciousness and conversation; it was as if this afternoon or tomorrow morning she might decide that the glass was more empty than full, and reach for her pills. But the highly developed sense of responsibility that made her see life as hers to keep or leave also made her see it as hers to fill. So she kept on with her friends and family, her books and magazines, her boards and commissions and her hot-line volunteer work, taking desperate, nighttime calls from pregnant young women when she was past ninety.

She was devoutly atheistic and rational to a fault. She didn't think her life belonged to God or to anyone else. She thought it belonged to her. "You know, you can make a new life," she said to me when Louie died. "But I'm eighty-three. I'm too old to make a new life. I have to live the one I have, or decide not to."

She wanted to leave gifts to the organizations she believed in and to the people she loved, and to leave their house and savings, as she and Louie had agreed, to her beloved sister-in-law and nephew in California. That was her plan, and she was perfectly prepared to put it in motion. She kept the pills in her bedside table drawer against the day when she decided that life had gone on too long. Her family knew it, her doctor and lawyer knew it, everyone knew it.

But she waited too long. One month she was a handsome, independent woman of ninety, and the next, felled by a lung infection, she was breathless, bedridden, hospitalized.

She went home, then back to the hospital. Home. Hospital. Home. Her medical care at home, first with nurse's aides and eventually with registered nurses around the clock, went from seventy-five hundred to fifteen thousand dollars a month. She had been diagnosed with end-stage respiratory disease and was released to die in her own house under hospice care. If she had had her way, that would have taken about two hours. Back in her own bed again, with her bedside table and her pills, she called for a bourbon and water and swallowed as many as she could before she conked out. But she woke the next day to find herself still alive. "I botched it," she said.

Bedridden, tethered to an oxygen machine, trapped in a house staffed with witnesses, in a state whose laws could make a felon of anyone who tried to help her die, Florence pushed herself for months to recover the strength to walk again. She had gotten as far as the kitchen, where the nurses had moved her sleeping pills, when part of her spine, hollowed by osteoporosis, collapsed. She gave up and decided to wait for pneumonia.

When I saw her last, on Thanksgiving weekend, her money had run out, her house and car and furniture had been sold to pay for her care, she no longer had the breath to do anything but breathe, and she was lying, panting, in her bed at the nursing home, four months past a bout of pneumonia that should have killed her. The nursing staff had given her antibiotics, and she had survived.

Her appearance was the perfect statement of her condition. Her complaint was that her mind stayed strong while her body declined, so that she was a horrified, captive, lucid witness to her own decay. Her wasted body lay under the sheet like a stick, like the stem of a rose, and at its head, lying on the pillow, glowing with spirit and intelligence, was Florence. She was all cheekbones, eyes, eyebrows, and teeth.

In the bed next to her was a woman of 105 who lay perfectly still, her arms folded across her stomach, her white hair sprayed out across the pillow. Her mouth was open. "Help me," she kept saying. "Someone please help me." Her eyes were closed. Twice in the last year, the nurse told me later, she had gotten pneumonia. Twice, the nursing home had given her antibiotics. Twice the pneumonia had lost its grip. She did not seem happy about it.

I told Florence I didn't think she would have much longer now. "Oh?" she said, eyes brightening, eyebrows arching. "Do I have that phos-phorescent glow?"

I said I thought so. We went on to talk about death, about family, and about my aunts Carolyn Smith and Bessie Clendinen in a nursing home across Tampa Bay. Florence always wanted to know how they were. They were terrible: deaf, crippled, incontinent. But they had also lost their minds years ago—Bessie's brain starved for oxygen from hardening of the arteries, Carolyn's withered by Alzheimer's. "They're the lucky ones," Florence said, and smiled. She died three weeks later.

Florence is in her burnished metal box in the bookshelf in the study now, behind the rosy clay bust of her that Louie made some years ago. Carolyn and Bessie are still in the Tampa nursing home. Carolyn is eighty-seven. Bessie is ninety. I am responsible for them. Like Florence, they had each signed a living will and power of attorney. "I do not fear death as much as I fear the indignity of deterioration, dependence, and hopeless pain," the will says. "If there is no reasonable expectation of my recovery from physical or mental disability, I wish to be allowed to die and not be kept alive by artificial means or heroic measures."

Bessie and Carolyn had a different reason from Florence for not wanting to linger. They were old-fashioned Southern Christian women. They believed that drinking, dancing, divorce, abortion, and homosexuality were sins and that when they died they would go to heaven. Twice, pneumonia almost got Carolyn there. But each time, the Bay to Bay Nursing Center shipped her to the hospital, which, for fifteen thousand dollars, pumped her full of oxygen and antibiotics, cured her and shipped her back. Medicaid paid.

Before penicillin, most old people died from pneumonia. Now, giving antibiotics has become routine. "I'm not going to let her lie there and die," the head nurse said when I protested. We have been at war ever since. I wrote them all a letter: no emergency room, no intravenous anything without my approval. I have not said no antibiotics, period. Maybe I should.

I last saw my aunts on Thanksgiving morning. Bessie, looking through her one eye—the other shattered when another patient pushed her and her head hit the tiled hall floor—didn't know me, and with Carolyn I did a stupid thing. I sat down, took one of her crippled hands in mine, and as she smiled at me in her glazed, gentle way, wished her a happy Thanksgiving. For a short, awful moment, her eyes lit with awareness, and she began to cry. Then, mercifully, the dementia closed in again, and her vacant look returned.

Carolyn and Bessie had always looked forward to heaven. Now they wouldn't know the difference if they got there. But if they still had their minds, they'd know where they are now. Florence did. "This is really hell," she said.

February 5, 1996

Forever Sixteen

TERAYA STARNES

By David Gonzalez

When the echo of gunshots dies down and the smoke fades, Benjamin Robinson goes to work. He hauls a gurney from his hearse and wheels it through the Kings County morgue to the refrigerator where the lifeless, blood-streaked body of Teraya Starnes, forever sixteen, waits for the final trip home to Bedford-Stuyvesant.

Mr. Robinson, the director of the Merritt Green Memorial Chapels, has made this grim journey countless times before, and although he has the steely demeanor of the former police officer that he is, it still rattles him when his passengers are children. His job is to prepare their bodies for viewing and burial and gently attend to the living. With the proliferation of guns and unfocused anger on the streets, Mr. Robinson said he and the others at chapels find themselves arranging the funerals of at least one child each week. "They're not all bad kids, and they're not all from bad families," he said. "Most of the time they usually know each other. It's rough. Really rough."

Mr. Robinson, who grew up in Savannah, Georgia, remembers when a child's violent death was rare and when children viewed it with fear and respect. Not anymore. "Death now is only worth twenty-five cents," he said. "That's what a bullet costs. Today, they don't talk about fighting, they talk about killing you. Next thing you know, it's bang bang."

Teraya, her mother said, was a student at the Brooklyn College Academy with dreams of becoming a psychologist. Her mother, Merit Burvick, said Teraya accompanied two girl friends to the house of one friend's grandmother, and they got into an argument with a boy who lived in the same building. She said the boy—to whom Teraya had spoken only once before—was annoyed by the way Teraya looked at him and pulled out a gun.

"He put the gun to her head and said, 'I will kill you,'" Ms. Burvick said, relying on what her daughter's friends had told her.

"'No, you won't,'" she said Teraya had replied.

"And he did. Right there. On a dare, you can take somebody's life."

Hours later, the police arrested Damon Smith, seventeen years old, and when Teraya died the next day, they charged him with second-degree murder and criminal possession of a deadly weapon. Lt. Eugene T. Albright, commander of Brooklyn's 73d Precinct, called the arrest "an easy apprehension." The gun has not been found.

Last Wednesday, before Teraya's body arrived, gospel music played softly in the background of Charles Toomer's office at the funeral parlor at 415 Gates Avenue, which he and Mr. Robinson bought in 1985. Today's young people are "weaker and wiser," he said, quoting a biblical passage about the apocalypse. They may know all the latest styles and desire the latest gadgets, but they are weak in their regard for God and sometimes each other, he said.

Teraya was the daughter of Mr. Toomer's cousin. Like her, many of the teenagers he buries have died by gunshot. According to the latest police body count, seventy New Yorkers sixteen years and under were shot to death in the first ten months of 1991.

"It's sick," said Mr. Toomer, wondering what would drive a teenager to snuff out another's life. "They seem to have no hope in life and a lot don't have a goal." He never imagined he would bury so many children. In fact, he has lost count. "I guess we did so many," he said quietly.

Willie Saunders, a stocky clear-eyed young man who is an assistant at the funeral home, walked out of the preparation room after looking at Teraya's recently arrived corpse. He leaned against the wood-paneled walls outside the office. "I'm sick and tired of seeing these young people inside these funeral homes," said Mr. Saunders, who is twenty-three. He was referring not only to the dead, but also to some of their friends, who mourn one day only to forget the next. "They come in and view their friend or brother, and they'll be out there the next day doing the same thing," he said. "On a corner out there, shooting at people."

Just hours before the viewing, Bernard Couch dabbed the final touches of makeup onto Teraya's face, concealing the bullet hole in her cheek. "It's kind of spooky," said Mr. Couch, twenty-five, who is training to be a mortician. "Because when we get them in here and they're close to your age, the same thing could happen to you. I don't even go out so much."

The sight of a child's body still shakes Desalee Neptune, another trainee, who often gives the bodies their final hairstyles. Sometimes, Ms. Neptune, the mother of two teenage sons, halts her work and calls home. "I always thought you died when you got old," she said. But she remembered something her grandmother told her when she attended the funeral of a child—"They have caskets in all sizes."

Earlier that morning, Robert Kearney dropped by from his job at the Kings County morgue and chatted for a while. The previous week, he had handled the bodies of two boys who were shot and killed at Thomas Jefferson High School. "It's nothing new; it's routine," he said. "There was hoopla because it was in the school. If it was out in the street, you never would have known about it."

When Mr. Couch finished applying the makeup, Mr. Robinson entered the chapel and looked at Teraya, neatly dressed in purple, her favorite color, and wearing dainty white lace gloves. "She looks like my little granddaughter," he said.

It was children's hour inside the funeral chapel that afternoon, as Teraya's classmates filed in after school. Until she had recently transferred to Brooklyn College Academy, she had been a student at Brooklyn Tech. With their backpacks, baggy pants, and oversized jackets, the teenagers approached hesitantly, some hugging each other and crying softly as they neared the coffin. One boy walked to the coffin, turned on his heel, and walked out muttering, "It's not Teraya. It's not Teraya," as if the words were an incantation.

"This child you see lying there had great potential," said Ms. Burvick with a nod to the coffin. "She was bright. She was in the talented and gifted in junior high school."

She recalled how her daughter, the future psychologist—one of five children she raised alone after her husband died six years ago, on the same date Teraya was shot—used to come home after school and quiz her about her dreams, offering instant analyses. "She always said, 'Mommy, you're going to be my first patient and you're going to have to pay me,'" Ms. Burvick recalled.

Teraya did not have a boyfriend and did not hang out on street corners, said Ms. Burvick, adding that her daughter observed an 8:00 P.M. curfew on school nights and one at 10:00 P.M. on the weekends.

The day before she was shot, she and her mother had discussed the shootings at Thomas Jefferson. "I saw the pain those parents went through, and I felt so bad for them," Ms. Burvick said. "Not knowing two days later I would go through the same thing."

Teraya's death was not the first for many of the teenagers at the funeral home. As they sat on the metal folding chairs in the chapel, they talked among themselves about the cruel calculus that governs street life in some neighborhoods. "Putting metal detectors in schools won't make a difference," said one girl. "They'll wait to kill you. They'll come up after school and shoot you."

"It's easier to get a gun than to get into college," said another girl. "You just got to mind your business and get a high school diploma."

With tidy, rounded strokes, a few youths entered their names in the visitors' book set upon a podium at the rear of the chapel. One boy, holding back tears, picked up the pen but put it down without signing, then walked away.

"I just can't take this anymore," moaned a girl as a friend stroked her back.

"You can't run from it," said another. "Where are you going to run?"

Two women entered the chapel, a toddler scrambling behind them. He peered up at the coffin, then turned to his mother. "How did she die?" he asked. The room was silent, save for the sounds of quiet tears.

Some of the teenagers returned the next day for final services, and many of them tried in vain not to cry as a children's choir sang, "Make way for love/Don't stand in the way of love."

The coffin was opened for one last time after the service, and the 150 mourners approached for their final good-byes. Khalia Blackwell, a classmate of Teraya's who wore a purple blouse that matched the dead girl's dress, bent over her friend's body. She planted a gentle kiss on Teraya's cheek. She collapsed and was eased out of the chapel by a teenage boy who finally let his emotions sweep him away.

"I can't deal with this anymore," he said as tears streamed down his cheeks. "It shouldn't have happened. Why?"

March 10, 1992

Life Is Long

MARY ELECTA BIDWELL & MARY THOMPSON

By Gail Collins

Mary Electa Bidwell (1881–1996) was supposed to be listed as the *Guinness Book of World Records*'s oldest living American, but she died shortly before the publication's deadline.

Mary Thompson (1876–1996), who was slightly older, couldn't qualify for the *Guinness* title, either—as the daughter of ex-slaves she had no birth certificate—but in 1992 she did receive the ultimate American tribute to longevity, a mention by Willard Scott on the *Today* show.

Being the oldest living American is a kind of negative celebrity. You're famous for *not* doing something. By the time you get the title, your most productive days are long gone, along with everybody who remembers them. Even those who know you best tend to be short on colorful anecdotes. "She always had a warm smile," said the administrator of the Florida nursing home where Mary Thompson died on August 3, 1996 at 120.

There are certain conventions to telling the oldest-living-American story. We feel compelled to note that Mary Bidwell, who died two weeks shy of her 115th birthday in 1996, had a weakness for coffee; Mary Thompson's favorite vice was a bit of chocolate every now and then. It is always necessary to report who was President when the titleholder was born: (Ulysses S. Grant for Mrs. Thompson; James Garfield for Mrs. Bidwell) and to plumb for secrets of long life. "Tend to your own business," Mrs. Thompson advised. Mrs. Bidwell endorsed doing everything in moderation.

Inevitably, both had outlived most of their loved ones. Mrs. Bidwell's husband died at ninety-three in 1975; their only son had been dead since 1945. Mrs. Thompson outlived two husbands and several children.

Yet this year's oldest-livings seem to have had spunk that peeped through the formulaic summaries. Shortly before she died, Mrs. Bidwell was asked by a visiting relative if she was tired of sitting so long. "Not particularly," she retorted. "I can't stand up anyway."

It is unclear how much pleasure oldest-living Americans take in their titles. "She would complain quite often when they'd have a party," said William Bidwell, Mary Electa's grandson. "She'd say, 'I don't know what all the fuss is about.'" But Mrs. Thompson, who was something of a party animal, took a different view. "I seen more fuss than this," she said somewhat critically during her 115th birthday celebration in 1991.

Mrs. Thompson. who lived most of her life in Florida and worked as a hotel cook, woodcutter, housekeeper, fruit-stand owner, and horse-and-buggy driver, did yardwork until she was 105 and always kept her pistol in her bra for protection. Mrs. Bidwell, who lived in Connecticut, worked before her marriage, earning six dollars a week as a teacher in a one-room schoolhouse heated by a wood-burning stove that she had to stoke.

Late in life, she became hard of hearing, a problem that she said "put a damper" on her attempts to develop a social life when she moved to a nursing home. But her grandson said she had a strict reading regimen in which she devoted the daytime to history and the evenings to fiction— mainly Victorian literature. Mrs. Thompson couldn't see well enough to read, but she liked singing; the nurse said she kept time by using her wheelchair as a bongo drum.

In the great oldest-living tradition, both women reported that they never smoked or drank. Mrs. Bidwell added that her father had not allowed her to dance. "He thought I might get in trouble, as my Aunt Jenny did," she explained. Unfortunately, the story of exactly what happened to Aunt Jenny was lost with Mrs. Bidwell's passing.

December 29, 1996
THE NEW YORK TIMES MAGAZINE

A LEASE ON LIFE

The *Guinness Book of World Records* at this writing lists the oldest authenticated living person as Jeanne Calment of Arles, France, who celebrated her 122d birthday on February 21, 1997.

Among Mme. Calment's distinctions is that she is the last person on earth who can claim to have seen Vincent van Gogh. The painter was "very ugly, ungracious, impolite, and not well," she remembered. "One day, my future husband wanted to introduce him to me. He glanced at me unpleasantly, as if to say 'not worth bothering with.' That was enough for me."

That was 107 years ago, when van Gogh was living in Arles.

In 1965, a forty-seven-year-old lawyer named André-François Raffray bet that he would outlive Mme. Calment, who was then ninety. He agreed to pay her about five hundred dollars a month for the right to move into her splendid apartment on the second floor of a classic old building in the center of Arles when she died.

Buying apartments this way is common in France, where the transaction is called *en viager* ("for life"). If all goes according to the actuarial tables, it can be a good deal for both parties: The elderly apartment owner gets to enjoy a monthly income from the buyer, who gets a real-estate bargain—provided the owner dies in reasonable time. Upon the owner's death, the buyer inherits the apartment, regardless of how much was paid.

M. Raffray did not get a bargain.

He died at Christmas, 1995, at the age of seventy-seven, having laid out the equivalent of one hundred and eighty-four thousand dollars, more than twice the market value of an apartment he never got to live in. On the day he died, Jeanne Calment dined on foie gras, duck thighs, cheese, and chocolate cake at the nursing home she was living in while her prized apartment stood vacant.

Moreover, M. Raffray's widow was legally obligated to keep sending that monthly check. If Mme. Calment outlives her too, then the Raffray children and grandchildren will have to pay.

"In life, one sometimes makes bad deals," Mme. Calment said on her 120th birthday.

As Craig R. Whitney observed on Mme. Calment's 120th birthday, "When she was born, Victor Hugo was still alive, and Marcel Proust was just a boy. Alexander Graham Bell had yet to invent the telephone. The automobile, the airplane, electric power all lay in the future." Anxious to protect the "Doyenne of Humanity" from exploitation, doctors for her 122d birthday scaled back the partying of recent years. On her 121st birthday, for example, there was a huge fête with Camargue horses and a music company released a compact disc, *Mistress of Time*, on which she talked while funk-rap, techno, and dance music played in the background.

It was difficult to know what she thought of the low-keyed approach. "I had to wait 110 years to become famous," she said more than a decade ago. "I intend to enjoy it as long as possible."

The Unwanted

By William E. Geist

"Lovely day to be on the water," Brendan Herity, captain of the little red ferryboat, said in his Irish brogue. Pleasure craft scooted this way and that around the ferry as she churned across a half-mile stretch of the glistening Long Island Sound carrying her cargo of dead bodies. Captain Herity pilots the unclaimed dead in the city across the waters from a dock on City Island to Hart Island, where they are buried by a detail of jail inmates in Potter's Field.

A plain old gray truck marked "Department of Hospitals, City of New York" is on board, its cargo being four deceased adults in thirty-seven-dollar pine boxes with their names scrawled in crayon on the sides, and twenty-three one-foot-long pine boxes containing the bodies of newborns and fetuses. There were no amputated limbs today, which are also buried in Potter's Field, named after the burial field for strangers in the Bible.

"Light load," said Captain Herity, who worked for many years on the Staten Island Ferry, but likes it up here, away from the living public, which is more prone to complaining and to aggravating crew members.

"I don't mind it anymore," John Gerace, who has driven the hospital truck fourteen years, said. "But a lot of people won't do it. There is an odor of death, which gets in your clothes and gets in your system, and you can't shake it. There is a sadness, too. The loads are bigger after a cold spell, when people freeze on the streets."

Some of the fifty-three inmates who live on Hart Island met the ferry, loading the boxes—marked "Baby Girl Patel," "Baby Boy Keating,"

"Baby Newborn Male," and "Lenore Davidson"—onto a front-end loader that bumped along a narrow dusty road to the burial site.

There have been 750,000 burials in Potter's Field, which occupies half the 130-acre island, since 1845. In 1986, there were 3,116. "After thirty or forty years," said Capt. Eugene Ruppert, who oversees the site for the Correction Department, "we reuse the areas. The bodies are not embalmed. Nature takes over."

Inmates were taken on the ferry for burial work until six years ago, when an encampment was established on the island. "It's a privilege," one inmate said. "There are no bars. You're outside." There are no guns either. There have been no escapes. The inmates have a vegetable garden and egg-laying hens. There is a chain-link fence around the encampment, but, paradoxically, it is to keep out vandals who ravaged buildings before the inmates arrived.

The buildings date from fifty or one hundred years, from when the island was used as a prison for several thousand inmates, an institution for cholera victims, an insane asylum for women, a drug-rehabilitation center, and a Nike missile site. The structures now amount to a ghost town, with windows broken out and weeds shooting up through floors and streets. The inmates live in mobile units.

Current plans are to increase the number of inmates on the island to four hundred, a move City Island residents are protesting at rallies and in court, saying they do not want the added traffic and danger.

"Our mission out here," Captain Ruppert said, "is to clear and maintain the area. Weeds grow like jungle here. We also want to restore an aura of dignity and respect. I'm not a statesman. But I just kind of feel like we owe these people some respect. They die in rooms, on the streets, and no one claims their bodies. We try to show respect and dignity. Maybe it's more than was shown to them in life."

Other than the foot-tall concrete block plot markers, the only monuments on the island are a ten-foot cross of wood and rocks erected by Captain Ruppert, a crumbling monument put up by inmates in 1948, and a conventional burial stone purchased by a man who once operated the backhoe that dug the graves.

This day, the front-end loader stopped, and suddenly, there it was.

The chilling sight of two rows of exposed coffins stacked three deep in the eight-foot-deep, fifty-foot-long, twenty-foot-wide working trench.

"It's a rewarding, satisfying job," Jerome DiSisto, a Correction officer supervising the detail, said. "You feel you're doing something for these people."

"Some of the Correction officers and inmates can't do it," Captain Ruppert said. "They are transferred or put on landscaping."

David Applig, one of the inmates pulling on rubber gloves, said he liked the work. "It's physical," he said. "You can go crazy sitting in jail."

The adult pine boxes were handed down and placed with the others, Clarence Dare laid to rest for all time on top of Charles Copper and Charles Copper atop a man buried the day before, Eddie Blue.

"You always think someone should at least say something," one inmate said. "You wonder who they were," said a second. "And why no one cared," said a third.

"Ought to worry about these poor folk when they're alive," said a muscular man, vigorously shoveling dirt. "Not now. Not now."

August 8, 1987